D0225394

WITHDRAWN FROM
MACALESTER COLLEGE
LIBRARY

SURVIVING THE SWASTIKA

SURVIVING
THE
SWASTIKA

Scientific Research in Nazi Germany

KRISTIE MACRAKIS

New York   Oxford
OXFORD UNIVERSITY PRESS
1993

Oxford University Press

Oxford   New York   Toronto
Delhi   Bombay   Calcutta   Madras   Karachi
Kuala Lumpur   Singapore   Hong Kong   Tokyo
Nairobi   Dar es Salaam   Cape Town
Melbourne   Auckland   Madrid

and associated companies in
Berlin   Ibadan

Copyright © 1993 by Oxford University Press, Inc.

Published by Oxford University Press, Inc.,
200 Madison Avenue, New York, New York 10016

Oxford is a registered trademark of Oxford University Press

All rights reserved. No part of this publication may be reproduced,
stored in a retrieval system, or transmitted, in any form or by any means,
electronic, mechanical, photocopying, recording, or otherwise,
without the prior permission of Oxford University Press.

Library of Congress Cataloging-in-Publication Data
Macrakis, Kristie.
Surviving the swastika : scientific research
in Nazi Germany / Kristie Macrakis.
p. cm.   Includes bibliographical references and index.
ISBN 0-19-507010-0
1. Research—Germany—History.
2. Kaiser Wilhelm-Gesellschaft zur Förderung der Wissenschaften—History.
3. Science and state—Germany—History.
4. Germany—Politics and government—1933–1945.
I. Title.   Q180.G4M3   1993
506'.043'09043—dc20   93-19919

Figures 1–11, 13–16, 18, and 19 reproduced by courtesy of
the Archives of the Max Planck Society.
Figures 12 and 17 reproduced by permission
of the Ulstein Bilderdienst, Berlin.

1 3 5 7 9 8 6 4 2

Printed in the United States of America
on acid-free paper

To My Parents

Acknowledgments

It is a pleasure to acknowledge the help, support, and encouragement of a number of people and institutions. Since this is a revised version of my Harvard University dissertation I am grateful to my mentors there, especially Everett Mendelsohn who followed the whole development of the project from its inception to the first complete manuscript, answered my letters from Germany, listened to my initial ideas and read the manuscript. Charles Maier was also very supportive of the project. I. Bernard Cohen showed me the way when I was a novice in the history of science. I am most grateful to Michael Kater, jazz musician and prolific historian, who not only supported my endeavors in German history, but also carefully read and commented on the manuscript, providing stimulus for its transformation into a book.

I have fond memories of the two years I spent in then divided Germany absorbing the culture and history and gathering material for this study. This stay would not have been possible without the generous support of several fellowships. The Social Science Research Council (SSRC) funded my one and a half years in the Federal Republic of Germany and West Berlin. My six months in the German Democratic Republic would have been impossible without a fellowship from the International Research and Exchanges Board (IREX). Not only did they provide material support but they were also helpful in securing access to various archives and for facilitating bureaucratic problems (after the wall fell in 1989 these barriers also vanished). More important, both these fellowships allowed me to immerse myself in the society and culture of both Germanies, to improve my German vastly, and to experience East and West during an interesting time. During my stay in Germany, the American Institute of Physics (AIP) gave me a grant-in-aid to interview scientists in Germany and England. Two of these interviews—with Carl-Friedrich von Weizsäcker and Ernst Telschow/Adolf Butenandt—

have been transcribed and deposited in the AIP's Niels Bohr library for all scholars to use. On my return to America, write-up support was provided by the SSRC, the German Academic Exchange Service (DAAD), and the National Science Foundation (NSF) (Grant SES 8701055). I am particularly grateful to the American Association of University Women (AAUW) for a writing fellowship for the year I completed most of the manuscript.

Material support is obviously important in order to carry out a book project, but without the help and interest of a number of archivists, friends, and colleagues, the book would have not only been less successful but less pleasurable. My greatest thanks go to Silva Sandow, a staff member of the archive for the Max Planck Society in Berlin-Dahlem where I spent many happy months poring over documents in Otto Warburg's library, the present-day reading room of the archive. From the day I arrived in Berlin to the end of the project she selflessly assisted me in my research, and became a friend during the process. I am also grateful to the director Eckart Henning, to Marion Kazemi, Klaus Schulz, Dagmar Klenke, and Andreas K. Walther. It would be impossible to list all the individuals at the numerous other archives I visited in the course of my research, but I am grateful to all the personnel at the archives listed at the end of the book.

A number of scientists and administrators from the Kaiser Wilhelm Society and its institutes were gracious enough to grant interviews with me. I was delighted to be received in their homes and to enjoy their warm hospitality. Not only did they share their memories with me, but their tea, dinner, and wine. I would especially like to thank Adolf Butenandt for helping to arrange and take part in an interview with Ernst Telschow, general director of the Kaiser Wilhelm/Max Planck Society from 1937–1960, who just died in 1988 at the age of ninety-eight. Butenandt also agreed to talk to me independently at a later date. Carl-Friedrich von Weizsäcker took time out from a busy schedule for a stimulating discussion late one afternoon and evening. Warmest thanks also to Karl Wirtz, Karl Zimmer, Georg Melchers, Gerhard Borrmann, Georg Menzer, Erika Bollmann, Hermann Blaschko, and Dietrich Schmidt-Ott.

Writing a book on science in National Socialist Germany is no longer an isolated task. One of the nice things about research is entering into a world of historical actors and scholars grappling with a controversial and often ambiguous past and participating in the dialogue. I met numerous historians in the archives, discussed with them either formally at conferences or in letters, or informally over coffee. Although Alan Beyerchen sat on the sidelines after his pioneering work on physicists under Hitler, his work has influenced all of ours. I am also appreciative of the friendship of several colleagues in Germany. In West Berlin I was fortunate to meet Michael Hubenstorf and Gerhard Baader at the Institut für Geschichte der Medizin of the Freie Universität. They made my stay in West Berlin particularly pleasant, interesting, and fruitful. Herbert Mehrtens and Burghard Weiss also contributed to a friendly intellectual atmosphere.

A number of friends and colleagues in the German Democratic Republic made my stay particularly comfortable and successful. Günter Wendel generously shared his knowledge of the Kaiser Wilhelm Society and helped me gain access to some archives. I am grateful to Reinhard Siegmund-Schultze, Horst Kant, and Dieter Hoffmann for their warm hospitality during my half year in East Berlin and the German Democratic Republic.

Several historians either read chapters or provided material for the book: Roger Stuewer and Michael Neufeld commented on chapter eight; Chandos Brown on an early version of chapter four. David Irving and Mark Walker provided some material for chapter eight. During the final stages, my research assistant Ralph Bauer ably helped me clean up the final manuscript. Vince Brannigan inspired the title of the book.

Helen Rayburn and Andrew Miller were wonderfully sympathetic friends during the writing stage while Nathan Stoltzfus, Scott Eddie, and Michael Daumer shared some of the time in Germany and America. During the final stage Werner J. Dannhauser warmly supported the book and talked me into handing it in to the publisher. I am grateful to Nancy Lane, senior editor at Oxford University Press, for signing me on and tempering my inexperience with pragmatic realism. Carole Schwager did a professional and careful copy-editing job. Thanks also to my parents and to my grandmother for their understanding during the long project. Best of thanks to Ernst Rummeny who prodded me to write when other activities seemed more interesting.

Contents

Abbreviations

AIP	American Institute of Physics
APS	American Philosophical Society
AVA	Aerodynamische Versuchsanstalt
BA	Bundesarchiv, Koblenz
BDC	Berlin Document Center
DFG	Deutsche Forschungsgemeinschaft
FRG	Federal Republic of Germany
GDR	German Democratic Republic
GStA	Geheimes Staatsarchiv
HWA	Heereswaffenamt
IfZ	Institut für Zeitgeschichte
KWG	Kaiser Wilhelm Society
KWI	Kaiser Wilhelm Institut
LC	Library of Congress
MPG	Max Planck Society
MPGA	Archiv zur Geschichte der Max-Planck-Gesellschaft
NA	National Archives
NGW	Notgemeinschaft der deutschen Wissenschaft
NSBO	Nationalsozialistische Betriebszellen Organisation
NSDB	Nationalsozialistischer Deutscher Dozentenbund
NSDAP	Nationalsozialistische Deutsche Arbeiterpartei
NSLB	Nationalsozialistischer Lehrerbund
MPI	Max Planck Institut
OMGUS	Office of the Military Government, US
PTR	Physikalisch-Technische-Reichsanstalt
REM	Reichsministerium für Wissenschaft (Reichserziehungsministerium)
RF	Rockefeller Archives
RFR	Reichsforschungsrat
RMdI	Reichsministerium des Innern
StPKB	Staatsbibliothek Preußischer Kulturbesitz
Uk	Unabkömmlich

SURVIVING THE SWASTIKA

Introduction

This is a book about the ways in which Germany's most prestigious scientific research organization—the Kaiser Wilhelm Society (KWG; the present-day Max Planck Society)—functioned and survived in National Socialist Germany. It examines the Society's response to National Socialist policies and traces the development and transformation of its structure and scientific research during the Third Reich. Unlike some other scientific, cultural, or educational institutions, it was not created as, or transformed into, a "Nazi" organization. The Society was an umbrella organization which founded and maintained about thirty research institutes by the 1930s, primarily in the natural sciences. The institutes of the Society were at the forefront of scientific advance during the first half of the twentieth century, and the Society can boast at least twenty-one Nobel Prize winners as members; three of the Nobel Prizes were awarded during the late thirties and forties.

While I was writing this study, I was frequently asked what my book was about. Once questioners placed the topic under the general theme of "science in Nazi Germany," they assumed it was about Nazi doctors, the holocaust, or the decline and destruction of science under the Nazis. It is these kinds of assumptions and misconceptions that I hope to correct here. This was a much richer and more complex period of time than the public, intellectuals, and many historians have come to believe. The book is not about the Nazis. It is about a normal scientific research organization, its leaders and its scientists, and the way in which they attempted to carry out their activities during the Third Reich. I hope to correct the prevalent view that all of science during this period was ideologically injected like *Deutsche*

Physik (German physics), *Deutsche Mathematik* (German mathematics), or eugenics, or that Germany was a scientific wasteland. Although there was a real loss of scientific talent with the expulsion and exodus of Jewish scientists, much high-quality science existed at the Society. The subject of ideologically molded science is, of course, taken into account, but I hope to contribute to a more nuanced image of the fate and transformation of science and its organization. A more differentiated approach to the analysis of the role, function, and fate of scientific research in National Socialist Germany can lead to a deeper understanding of the way in which extreme political movements affect the scientific community and the structure and priorities of scientific research.

By shifting focus away from the extremes to the gray zone in between, much can be learned about the behavior of scientific leaders in times of political stress, about the subtle influences of the social order on scientific research, about degrees of complicity and accommodation in a totalitarian regime, and about survival mechanisms. A scientific institution displays the full panoply of the modern scientific enterprise from the level of its historical and social context, to general structural and administrative influences, to the scientific work of individual scientists. A study of a scientific institution in a totalitarian system can therefore illuminate the multifaceted interaction between science and society. This book examines the interaction of the Society with National Socialist culture in its various manifestations. National Socialism intensified and accelerated the science–society interface while simultaneously making aspects of the inherent interaction more visible. Many of the ways in which the social order influences science in turbulent times are present in dormant forms in science organizations, science policy, and the practice of scientific research in normal times, or in a democracy.

The layer-cake cross section of a scientific institution in historical context can therefore also begin to answer a host of new questions about science under National Socialism. Can a prestigious institution resist or insulate itself against those cultural values and social structures in an authoritarian society traditionally seen as hostile to, or destructive of, science? What kind of mediating role does an institution play between scientists, on the one hand, and the reigning political regime, on the other? To what extent did National Socialist goals and ideals filter down to the scientists, and how were they implemented, if they succeeded? What role did party membership play in appointments to newly vacant positions as Jews and communists were expelled? To what extent was the Society transformed in National Socialist Germany, and to what extent did it maintain its traditions and autonomy? Were changes a result of social policies or a result of policies specifically designed for the scientific world?

The developments at the Society were not always typical of other institutions, or of science and technology in general, nor can generalizations always be made within the Society itself. For example, although in some respects the pattern of development at the universities was similar, many differences existed in the degree of the political influence and the political measures applied. There is also differentiation within the Society; not only did scientists and leaders respond to and accommodate the regime in different ways, but there was variation in the ideological importance of the scientific disciplines. The Society had a special character within German scientific and educational organizations which shaped its interactions with the regime and its various power blocks. It enjoyed more prestige and had a higher concentration of more visible and internationally recognized scientists and leaders than other institutions. This special role and function within Germany's scientific landscape was recognized by National Socialist leaders and the scientific community.

Historical research on totalitarianism and on the character and nature of the Third Reich has begun to change the conventional image of Nazi Germany as a monolithic well-oiled machine under the control of one leader. Instead, historians have drawn our attention to the contradictory and paradoxical nature of life in the Third Reich, and to the chaotic and inefficient system consisting of competing organizations engaged in a struggle to expand influence and power at one anothers' expense. More recent work has persuasively characterized the regime as "polycratic" rather than monocratic. Peter Hüttenberger, for example, identifies competing power blocks among the National Socialist German Worker's Party (NSDAP) and its organizations, the civil service, the army, and big industry and traces the development of their interaction between 1933 and 1945.[1]

The Society found niches in these cracks in the system and maneuvered itself among the competing agencies. As a result, it could continue much of its science "as usual." It interacted with the four major power centers while having a different relationship with each one. For example, during the early years its relationship with the ministerial bureaucracies was strained as the Civil Service Law dismissing Jewish scientists was applied, but by the war, it reestablished a more positive, if not complex, contact as the ministries supported the scientific research of the Society. The industrial power block, on the other hand, proved the most useful and helpful alliance throughout the Third Reich. It intervened on behalf of those Jewish scientists in the early years while, by the war, with an industrialist at the helm, it helped the Society function and survive. As a result, the Society thrived both institutionally and in its scientific research; its research budget doubled within the first six years of the Third Reich, reaching unparalleled heights during the war. In many respects the Society and its institutes survived the nazification process more intact than the universities and other scientific organizations. In part, it was the inherent nature and character of the institution, separate from the educational realm, which insulated it. As a semiprivate research organization founded to advance basic research it differed from the universities in Germany, which were entirely state-supported, and from industrial and governmental laboratories, which tended to do applied research.

Another persuasive and powerful paradigm in the sociology of science has been the thesis that science flourishes only in societies of a particular kind. Formulated in its fullest form in the mid-thirties, with the rise of

National Socialism, by the sociologists of science Bernard Barber and Robert Merton (who both expanded Talcott Parsons's thesis), it pointed to liberal democracy as the most conducive form of government for the development of science. The free world of liberal democracy was pitted against the dark evils of authoritarian regimes. The cultural values of rationality, utilitarianism, individualism, and progress were parts of a model Barber developed in which science flourished in a democracy, while Merton argued that four sets of institutional imperatives—universalism, communism, disinterestedness, and organized skepticism—were part of an ethos of science necessary for its survival. Some of the sociological argument is still valid today, but many of the historical (then contemporary) examples selected about the anti-intellectualism of the National Socialists and the pronouncements of early theorists on science, for example, are less applicable to the period following 1938, when Merton's seminal work was written. In fact, at the end of his 1952 chapter on science in liberal and authoritarian societies, Barber admits that quality science did exist in Nazi Germany and asks the question: "If German science was not utterly destroyed by the Nazis, but only seriously weakened, how long does it take to 'kill' science?" The passage of time and new historical research thus changed his initial theoretical question.[2]

Despite the validity of many of Barber's and Merton's conclusions, more recent historical research has begun to enlarge our picture of what actually took place, in its various phases, in the scientific world during National Socialist Germany. But aside from its intrinsic value, their work began the tradition of scholarship which focused on the corruption of liberal values and the decline and destruction of science under the Nazis.[3] This is an important aspect of the topic of science under National Socialism, but other areas need to be explored, including the way in which pockets of scientists and scientific research survived and thrived under National Socialism. This book seeks to sort out the various historical, social, institutional, and personal factors which allowed variation to exist in the quality of science, and to document the survival of certain kinds of science at a high level in National Socialist Germany.

The development of the Society during the Third Reich and its relationship with National Socialist culture was a dynamic, not a static, process. These changes and phases need to be kept in mind when examining the degree to which the new political and social order affected the scientific community at the Society and the extent to which the Society, or its scientists, contributed to National Socialist policies. During the early years, for example, with Max Planck at the helm, the Society maintained much of its autonomy. But simultaneously, the greatest change occurred in the composition of the personnel at the Society through what the National Socialist state did *to* the scientists and their response. But by the time of World War II, the Society had become more integrated into National Socialist society and therefore questions of complicity become the focus of attention. Adaptation and survival were part of these dynamic developments.

The structure and organization of the book is as follows. Part I traces the origins and the founding of the Kaiser Wilhelm Society in Wilhelmine Germany through the Weimar years. The Society's character, structure, and relation to the state were formed and developed during these periods preceding the Third Reich. During its formative years the Society invented and established traditions that formed its role and function within Germany's scientific landscape; some of these traditions were challenged during the Third Reich while others protected and ensured the Society's survival.

Part II traces the development of the Kaiser Wilhelm Society and its institutes in the dramatically altered sociopolitical and economic context of National Socialist Germany. To what extent did National Socialist policies threaten the autonomy of the Society? How did the Society respond to the measures? Was there resistance or accommodation and acquiescence? To what extent did social measures become an unspoken policy for science? These are the questions addressed in Chapter 3 as the Kaiser Wilhelm Society faced the first couple of years after the seizure of power. Chapter 4 breaks away from the chronological narrative in order to place the Society in the broader context of a polycratic science policy where some centers of power emphasized education over research in the early years, while others attempted to integrate the Society into a reorientation of science policy. As the National Socialists became aware of the utility of science late in the war, they began to establish new science organizations for the development of war research. Little use was made of the Kaiser Wilhelm institutes. Chapter 5 returns to the chronological narrative in 1936 as major changes occurred in the leadership of the Society with Max Planck's retirement and as concomitant changes occurred in society with the passing of the Four Year Plan and the preparations for war. Up until this point we examined the Society and its institutes and their interaction with the state as a whole. In Chapter 6 the level of analysis shifts from the macroscopic to the microscopic scale, and I turn to the actual scientific research done at the institutes and focus on the survival of the life sciences in Berlin. This example illustrates that the scientific research of the Society was differentially affected by National Socialist policies. On one end of the spectrum there was the little-known phenomenon of the flourishing of basic research in biology in Berlin, and on the other end of the spectrum there was the institutionalization of eugenics, or race hygiene, at the Kaiser Wilhelm Institute for Anthropology, Human Heredity, and Eugenics, with clues of links to National Socialist eugenic policies.

Chapters 7 and 8 are devoted to the war years. In Chapter 7 the narrative returns to the macroscopic level of analysis as we watch the Society take a deeper step into the National Socialist state. To what extent were changes in the structure and practice of science the result of National Socialist ideology, and to what extent were the developments part of a war research mentality which could take place in any country, whether a democracy or a dictatorship? Even during the war the Society could preserve much of its autonomy and was not controlled by state or party organizations, yet the war took its toll. Many of the scientists continued basic research at the institutes but some took on war contracts, while others were involved in founding new institutes influenced by an ideological matrix of living space, blood and soil, and a new order of German science. Chapter 8 focuses on one major example of perhaps the most important project undertaken at the Kaiser Wilhelm institutes during the World War II—the nuclear power project. This project in the physical sciences illustrates the interaction among scientists, the military, and the government; unlike other studies, this overview places the research program in its institutional context. Our story ends with a brief discussion of the fate of the Kaiser Wilhelm Society in the early postwar years as it emerged after the occupation of Germany by allied troops. The question of Nazi party membership and denazification is discussed. Many of the themes about self-government versus the control of the state, about the nature of the Society's activities during the war, about the loss of scientific talent, and the Society's posture toward a changing sociopolitical context emerge again as it faced the second interference with its autonomy [the first being *Gleichschaltung* (coordination)] during the denazification, democratization, and division of post–World War II Germany.

I

BEGINNINGS

1

Origins

It was a typical rainy and gray fall day in Berlin-Dahlem as Kaiser Wilhelm II took part in the official opening of the Kaiser Wilhelm Institutes for Chemistry and for Physical Chemistry on 23 October 1912. Clad in a cape, exhibiting his usual enthusiastic stride and characteristic walrus moustache, he marched down the shiny wet street as curious schoolboys looked on. He was ceremoniously followed by Adolf von Harnack, the president of the Society, who donned a top hat and raincoat, and Emil Fischer, the Nobel prize–winning chemist. But what did the Emperor of Wilhelmine Germany have to do with the actual origins and founding of the Kaiser Wilhelm Society (KWG), a scientific research organization dedicated to the "advancement of science"? Who were the other dignified gentlemen, and how were they involved in the creation of this richly endowed complex of research institutes?[1]

With the hegemony of German science at the turn of the twentieth century it seems incongruous that serious discussion began in Wilhelmine Germany on the creation of independent research institutes. Also puzzling is the argument used that Germany was falling behind in its lead over other nations, and that as a consequence a new organization of science was needed. But *fin de siècle* Germany began to face some structural flaws in the organization of its scientific activity as the now perhaps outmoded university-based research institutes had to cope with the emergence of specialized, cost-intensive, large-scale scientific research.

As with many new enterprises, false starts, plans, and preparations preceded the official act of inauguration by many years. Whereas these are common occurrences in the founding of new scientific institutions in general, the Kaiser Wilhelm Society exhibits certain features unique to its context of Wilhelmine Germany.[2] The notion of an independent research institute was hardly novel internationally, but it was a new organizational form for Germany. One thinks immediately of the Pasteur Institute, the Rockefeller Medical Institute, and the Nobel institutes. Despite the organizers' attempt to break from Prussian traditions in establishing institutions of learning, the Society ended up shaped by the state while adopting and incorporating some of the features of science organization in America. A new feature for Germany in this new enterprise was also the heavy participation of industrialists in a period when they were beginning to become more influential.

From a 1909 blueprint essay by Adolf von Harnack—the eminent theologian and future president of the Society—it would appear that the idea for the creation of this new scientific research organization came from his pen. Yet this was hardly the case; agitation came from different quarters. The most important stimuli came from a group of chemists interested in creating a research association and the Prussian Ministry of Education (Kultusministerium).[3] Discussions about the creation of research institutes at the Prussian Ministry began during the last two decades of the nineteenth century with the powerful and influential Minister Friedrich Althoff, who was responsible for university affairs.[4] The idea for the creation of scientific research institutes was initiated by Althoff when he was preparing his plans for the plush Berlin suburb of Dahlem, where new institutes were to be created in a colony, or a "German Oxford," to accommodate the expansion of the University of Berlin. The land—the "Royal domain in Dahlem" —would be divided and used for state and scientific goals, with the blessings of the Emperor, who became interested in the project after Althoff's death.[5]

In these early plans for a scientific community in Dahlem most of the institutes to be created were conceived of as *university* institutes representing fields not yet institutionalized. Within this community, however, Althoff also urged the founding of "new pure state research institutes" because they would be a fundamental requirement for further scientific progress. This kind of institute was necessary, he argued, because not all scientists are talented in both research and teaching. Furthermore, it would give outstanding scholars an opportunity to pursue their interests in institutes modeled after the Nobel institutes where there were no teaching duties.[6]

There is no doubt that the Prussian Ministry played a central role in the founding of the Society, but it cannot be forgotten that Althoff's actions were informed by the scientists with whom he associated and that complaints by scientists about the failure of the university to accommodate the new needs of science were funneled to him. Emil Fischer, the Nobel prize–winning chemist and one of the few scientists directly involved in creating the Kaiser Wilhelm Society, was an adviser to Adolf von Harnack as he wrote his 1909 essay to the Emperor on the creation of this new form of science organization. Fischer's importance cannot be underestimated, and it is no wonder that he was dubbed Harnack's "powerful man behind-the-scene."[7]

In order to be aware of the scientists' wishes, Althoff often asked them to prepare memoranda on the needs of their disciplines. Two examples illustrate the protracted efforts leading to the founding of the Kaiser Wilhelm Society: the memoranda of the physicist Philipp Lenard and of Otto Jaeckel, a palaeontologist. Jaeckel seems to have turned to Althoff with his ideas on the creation of a biological research institute that would be independent of teaching as early as 1904. By 1909 he had written a memorandum in which he suggested a big institute for biontological research.[8] In the proposal he argued that Germany's hegemony in science was threatened by the increase in teaching load and the decline in financial support. In a strong nationalistic tone, he suggested the founding of scientific institutes on the American model so that "our nation" can find "glory" in the international competition.[9]

Althoff had solicited a memorandum from Lenard soon after the experimental physicist had won the Nobel Prize in 1905 for his work on cathode rays. Lenard outlined plans for a "German Institute for Physical Research" and described the advancement of physics as a state need, referring to the historical development of the Royal Institution of England as being a good model; he also included detailed plans for such an institute.[10] Lenard's ideas were soon forgotten and he was not directly involved in the later founding of the Kaiser Wilhelm Institute for Physics, although his advice to Althoff may have been useful in an indirect way.[11] Lenard, an antisemite and one of the leading proponents of *Deutsche Physik,* did not forget his early involvement in 1933. After the National Socialists' seizure of power he wrote to the Minister of the Interior attacking the Society, which he claimed had been founded with "Jewish sponsors," one of whom—Leopold Koppel—had stipulated that Fritz Haber, a Jew, be appointed director of the institute.[12]

In the context of this book, which focuses on the National Socialist period, the role of the Prussian Ministry of Education and its relationship to the Kaiser Wilhelm Society is of central importance. During the Wilhelmine period, the state played an important role in science policy, and the Ministry worked closely with scientists from the university and the Academy of Science. Steven Turner has demonstrated the importance and influence of the state on university appointments in the first half of the nineteenth century, whereby the ideal of the professorate was transformed from an emphasis on teaching to one of research and publication.[13] This Prussian tradition of state intervention continued in different forms through the period of the Third Reich, although, as the Kaiser Wilhelm Society became more established as an independent, semiprivate research organization, the ministries usually approved the choices for scientific members or directors of institutes made by the scientists on a pro forma basis. Despite the growing independence of the Society in a monarchy or democracy (the Weimar period), the rise of a totalitarian state in the thirties threatened to decrease its autonomy.

Discussions also began around 1900 among the chemists Emil Fischer, Walther Nernst, and Wilhelm Ostwald, and representatives of the chemical industry who wished to create a Reich Chemical Association (Chemische Reichsanstalt), modeled on the Physical-Technical Reich Institution (Physikalisch-Technische Reichsanstalt),[14] in order to carry out non-university research supported by the Reich government and industrialists. Rapidly occurring developments in pure chemistry and physical chemistry led to the perception that in order to attract scientists who would otherwise be hired by industry, it was necessary to create research institutes free of administrative and teaching duties. The scientists and industrialists again presented their plans to the government with an emphasis on international competitiveness. A recurrent fear in the founding period discussions is that German science would be overtaken by institutions abroad. For example, Fischer, Nernst, and F. Oppenheim wrote to Theodor von Bethmann-Hollweg at the Reich Ministry of the Interior that "German chemistry had been frequently surpassed by countries abroad" and that if Germany wanted to maintain its national standard of living, it should not lose its leading position in chemistry. Despite concrete plans and the actual creation of an association in 1908—the Reich Chemical Association Club (Verein Chemische Reichsanstalt)—and despite the interest and support of industry, this project was never realized because the Reich government declined its support. As a result, the chemists decided to join the Society in 1910 in order to found a chemical institute with new facilities.[15] Emil Fischer had been highly influential in the plans for a Reich Chemical Association, and some of his ideas were incorporated into the planning and execution of the Kaiser Wilhelm Institute for Chemistry and the Institute for Coal Research.

Germany's Scientific Hegemony Threatened

By 1909 the early plans of the Prussian Education Ministry and those of the Reich Chemical Association had not been realized. On the one hand, the Chemical Association found no state support; and on the other, the ministries of finance and agriculture rejected the plan for reasons that are not entirely clear. With the upcoming centenary of the University of Berlin, however, the Emperor, who never missed an opportunity to present himself as a great friend and supporter of science and technology, asked Harnack to prepare a detailed sketch on new ways to organize science. The anniversary served to call the attention of the government to the project. At first Harnack declined the invitation to write an essay because he thought he was not qualified. Instead Hugo Andreas Krüß composed a piece entitled "The Kaiser Wilhelm Foundation for Scientific Research (Scientific Research Institutes)." Krüß was a physicist by training and after proving himself a capable organizer at a St. Louis exhibit on physics he was appointed an assistant at the Prussian Educational Ministry in 1907. He quickly rose in the ranks and by 1922 was a ministerial director. In 1925 he became head of the Prussian State Library but continued to maintain close connection with the Society through the period of the Third Reich as a senator.[16] Harnack solicited the help of three scientists over the summer—Emil Fischer, August von Wassermann, and Max Rubner—who could advise him on scientific matters. Now he was prepared to write his seminal blueprint.

The official founding of the Kaiser Wilhelm Society on 11 January 1911 had been preceded by many years of planning and conceptualization for a new research center for science; and the idea of creating pure research institutes was in the air. Adolf von Harnack's essay on the state of German science, its problems, and possible remedies, presented to the Emperor on 21 November 1909, offers a synthesis, if not a brilliant account, of the weaknesses of German science at the turn of the century. This fourteen-page historical document was a blueprint for the Society and is illuminating in its analysis of the needs of German science. It became effective in attracting attention from industrialists and potential members because of its eloquent prose and appeal to national sentiments with the argument that German science was behind that of other nations. There is no doubt that this programmatic organizational document was written to persuade, but it also contains many insights on the state of German science at the beginning of the twentieth century. Harnack begins his piece with Wilhelm von Humboldt's call one hundred years before for the unity of research and teaching as well as of the need for "independent research institutes" to complement scientific activity at the universities and academies. Harnack uses Humboldt's ideas to legitimate and justify his enterprise by appealing to the past and by referring to a preeminent science organizer who inaugurated the era of cultural supremacy for German science.

Harnack's argument unfolds in the next six sections of the essay. He describes the present state of German science and then turns to achievements abroad in order to show that German science is behind. Finally, he suggests a way to organize these new institutes, to carry through the plans, and to find support from the state and industry in order to create a private institution. Harnack plays on the nationalistic emotions of his prospective donors and the Emperor: Military strength and science *(Wehrkraft und Wissenschaft)* are the two strong pillars of Germany's greatness, he proclaims, but German science has fallen behind other countries in some important areas of research. Therefore, he argues, a "national-political" danger exists in Germany because its lead in science is threatened. He astutely points out that the creation of research institutes has not kept pace with the great developments in science. In other words, Germany's institutions were lagging in the world of modern science. There are whole disciplines, he continues, that can no longer be accommodated by resources at universities, because they require "big machines and instruments."[17]

In contrast to Germany, other scientifically advanced countries *(Kulturnationen)* recognized the changing times and recently made enormous contributions for the support of scientific research institutes. Harnack bolsters his argument by a review of the scientific achievements in various fields abroad. Especially impressive and threatening to him are the developments in America with the recent advances in the biomedical sciences and the creation of the Carnegie Institution and the Rockefeller Medical Institute. It is in this way that German science is behind, and a solution to the problem is to create research institutes. Under the influence of Emil Fischer's advice, he delineates the disciplines to be housed in the various institutes, beginning with chemistry; he then stresses the need and importance in Germany for the creation of biological institutes.[18]

Organizationally he sets forth the ideal, which was later carried out in the Kaiser Wilhelm institutes, whereby the research direction is determined by the director of the institute. Furthermore, the institutes ought not to be overspecialized. He is also careful to emphasize that these institutes will be "supporting" institutes for the university in order to sidestep the issue of a new competitive enterprise, which in many respects it later became. Despite the fact that these new research institutes were to institutionalize areas not represented at the university, there was, and is to this day, a tension between the Kaiser Wilhelm/Max Planck Society and the universities. Having made clear the need for these scientific research institutes, Harnack then turns to the means required for support of this enterprise.

By the turn of the century most educational or research institutions, chiefly the universities, were state-supported in Germany (as was the case in most European countries). By contrast, in the United States private foundations began to predominate as a source of financial support. The American developments had already become a model, and Harnack wished to find ways to graft the American tradition of private initiative onto the Prussian tradition of state support. Harnack's compromise was a combination of state and private support. This graft, however, did not take hold and was criticized early on. This process of "Americanization" found its critics among the social democrats and liberals. Especially noteworthy is an article in the *New York Staatszeitung* titled "One Approach May Not Do in All Cases" (27 April 1910). Minister August von Trott zu Solz appealed to the German money aristocracy in the Prussian house of parliament to give to scientific research as the "rich Americans do." The anonymous author of the article wrote: "It will alienate everyone who only considers for a moment: what appears to be obvious and natural for America, would be a bit abnormal for Germany's totally different social and political conditions." Germany would have to create the same sort of preconditions for such an idea, the author argued, and it is questionable whether Germany would find these changed circumstances pleasant because Germany is used to being looked after by the government, which acts like a "concerned father." In America, where the state universities are not good, the Americans need a Rockefeller; in Germany, where the universities are state-supported, there is no need for the American "money, money, money."[19]

The fundamental argument of Harnack's essay was congruent with the national-political justification to found the Society: In Germany scientific research was undertaken primarily at universities and academies, but no independent research institutes existed. With more specialized and cost-intensive research there was a growing need to create them. Moreover, in other countries, and especially in America, research institutes had prolifer-ated at an ever-growing rate for more than a decade. As Reich Minister Theodor Lewald interpreted it, the claim for "scientific hegemony" was just as important for Germany, and consequently a state necessity, as was the army.[20] Therefore, founding institutes modeled on the American example was an urgent duty for German science and culture, and he considered Germany prosperous enough to undertake the project. There is also evidence for the importance and influence of American science organiza-tion in the Krüß memorandum written about a half-year before Harnack's. The first title of the report, and the name of the organization to be founded, was the "Kaiser Wilhelm-Foundation"—it had initially been conceived of as a foundation like those existing in America.

Within two weeks after receiving it the Emperor read Harnack's piece "word for word" and gave it his "liveliest, unrestrained applause."[21] Soon after the dissemination of the Harnack essay, organizational preparations began. First, it had to be decided what the Society would be named in order to characterize its goals and function. Krüß first dubbed it the "Kaiser Wilhelm Foundation (Institute) for Scientific Research." Harnack, in his essay, refers to a "Royal Prussian Society for the Advancement of Science." The name would reflect not only the character of the organization but also its sponsor and what it meant as a German scientific organization. Harnack initially used the term "Royal Prussian" because of his authorship of the definitive four-volume work on the "Royal Prussian Academy of Science." He conceived the new enterprise as a "Prussian" creation in the sense that the Prussian Ministry was heavily involved as well as Berlin scientists; it would be located in Berlin, the world city of science. But would not such a name offend the chemists from southern Germany or other states who were interested in the aborted Reich Chemical Association project, and who might be expected to contribute to the new project? These were the thoughts of Theodor von Bethmann-Hollweg when he wrote to the Emperor discuss-ing the project. He suggested the Society be called the "Kaiser's Society for the Advancement of Science" because then other states could take part.[22] In a May 1910 meeting at the Automobile Club, Harnack discussed this issue with some governmental officials. The name he proposed, "Royal Prussian," seemed too narrow because the first institute of the Society was to advance some of the Reich Chemical Association plans. Also, many scientists and industrialists from south Germany belonged to it and would prefer the name "Kaiser-Wilhelm-Institute." The idea was to select a name without consti-tutional or territorial meaning: The Kaiser Wilhelm Society would be as short and pregnant in meaning as the "Royal Society" in England.[23] Inescapably, however, it conjures up images of a saber-rattling emperor at the helm of an imperialistic state.

Whatever the name—"Kaiser Wilhelm" or "Royal Prussian"—the Society was shaped by the Prussian Ministry of Education and had the approval and blessings of the Emperor. We already examined the role of the Ministry of Education in the founding period, but the Prussian state's influence was certain to be built into the Society when Prussia agreed to donate the land (in Dahlem) and to fund the director positions; both contributions had dire consequences with the rise of a totalitarian regime. There were two classes of membership in the Society: paying members and senators, including a large number of industrialists. In an early meeting it was decided that the senators would be named by the Emperor and would be asked to contribute 300,000 marks or 50,000 marks on a yearly basis. The paying members were expected to contribute 30,000 marks or 5,000 marks on a yearly basis. Donors were also initially sought who could contribute at least one million marks to help establish the Society. The Emperor would bestow his grace on these people by awarding them a special insignia or decoration *(Abzeichen)* and other honorific privileges.[24]

Support for the enterprise was sought from bankers and industrialists, who, as a group, had become the German financial equivalent of American foundations. Soon after the meeting at the Automobile Club, ten invitations to join the Society were sent out to the various industrialists along with a shortened version of Harnack's essay outlining the plans for the new Society. Of these invited executives from industrial and banking circles, those who would play important roles in the Society later as members or senators included Eduard Arnold, the banker Ludwig Delbrück, Dr. Henry Theodor von Böttinger, Ludwig Max Goldberger, the banker Leopold Koppel, Dr. Gustav Krupp von Bohlen und Halbach, Dr. Franz von Mendelssohn, Dr. Walther Rathenau, and Dr. Eduard Simon.[25] By the fall of 1910 a capital of 6 million marks had been gathered. After the centenary celebration at the University of Berlin in October 1910, Fischer wrote to Harnack expressing the "great joy" he and his fellow researchers felt about the announcement of the founding of the Kaiser Wilhelm Foundation for Scientific Research. He also thanked Harnack on behalf of the scientists for his "conception" of, and "happy support" for, the plan. Because of his hope that the "Royal founding" would give science a "new, strong impulse," he was also ready to support the Society with 20,000 marks—a sum he had collected for the Reich Chemical Association.[26]

Foundations

By the beginning of the twentieth century no great foundations existed in Germany. Stimulated by the rise of philanthropists such as Andrew Carnegie and James Smithson in America, some industrial magnates began to organize foundations similar to those that emerged in the first two decades of the twentieth century in America. The extent to which these accumulators of capital implemented their own interests by creating foundations for specific purposes remains a controversial issue.

Leopold Koppel, the Berlin banker, and Gustav Krupp von Bohlen und Halbach, the Ruhr industrialist, were to become important figures in the founding of the Kaiser Wilhelm Society. Both donated large sums for the institutes of physical chemistry and biology, respectively, and the former became a senator while the latter became vice president of the Society. Koppel had already established a foundation as early as 1905 for the "Advancement of Intellectual Exchange between Germany and Other Countries" with an endowment of one million marks. He wanted to make some of his wealth available for the "general welfare" and, more specifically, for the "great needs of the time." His "personal inclination and predilection for scholarship" led to this type of support but his national feelings also played a role because he thought such an exchange could lead to peace among nations in their political and economic relations. In the fall of 1910 Koppel had made a contribution of 700,000 marks for the establishment of an institute for physical chemistry. His comments to the Emperor on this gift illuminate his motives as a businessman and industrialist in taking part in this new enterprise. The Emperor, he wrote, had helped business and industry by "founding big new research institutes that will open new paths for German science. . . . For German industry is unthinkable in her present advanced state without fertilization through German science." Koppel was especially interested in the advancement of physical chemistry because it most directly affected industry, with which he was associated.[27]

Krupp von Bohlen und Halbach, on the other hand, had slightly different motives for his gift of 400,000 marks for a biological institute. He was the son-in-law of Friedrich Alfred Krupp, who had a longstanding private interest in biology and had sponsored the Krupp Prize for work in eugenics in 1900.[28] When Rudolf Valentini, head of the civil cabinet, requested contributions to found scientific research institutes on the occasion of the centenary of the University of Berlin, Krupp von Bohlen und Halbach, along with his mother-in-law and wife, agreed to donate 400,000 marks for the creation of a biology institute, which Friedrich Krupp had hoped to do for the University of Berlin.[29]

Although some donors required that the contribution be used to advance a particular discipline, very few attached conditions to the grants once they were awarded. Oftentimes a contribution to a certain scientific area was made as a result of personal interest of the donor; other times the condition attached to a gift was that the donor's name not be made known, or that it ought not to be made public (as in the case of Dr. Richard Fleischer). Biology was the most favored by the donors who required that their money be used for a specific discipline. At least six donors fell into this category: the bankers (Carl von der Heydt, Arthur von Gwinner, director of Deutsche Bank, Berlin, Paul Mankiewitz, director of Deutsche Bank) and the industrialists (for example, Krupp von Bohlen und Halbach, Verein der Spiritusfabrikanten, Institut für Gemeinwohl).[30] Three donors stipulated that their contributions be used for chemical research (Dr. Leo Gans, Professor C. Harries, and Leopold Koppel for physical chemistry). Of the 10,328,000 marks pledged by the donors at this meeting only 1,850,000 marks had conditions attached.[31]

The constitutional meeting to inaugurate the Society took place at the Royal Academy on 11 January 1911. Of the 139 donors invited about 90 came. It is interesting to note that at this formative meeting no scientists were present, except for Emil Fischer, who gave the featured lecture. In addition to the donors, Harnack, Theodor Lewald, Valentini, and von Eisenhart attended; the two other scientists invited—J. H. van't Hoff and Paul Ehrlich—could not attend.[32]

This first assembly marked the founding of the Kaiser Wilhelm Society and the drafts of the statutes prepared during the previous fall were presented and approved. Trott zu Solz, from the Ministry, chaired the meeting and spoke of a "fully free" Society with no "official influence" on its decision-making bodies. Yet simultaneously he obsequiously acknowledged (which was probably standard form) the "protection" of the Emperor, who blessed the Society with his benevolence.[33] The statutes were created by Harnack and Fischer, by industrialists, bankers, and representatives of the government. The most interesting and debatable part of the document set forth the goal of the Society: to advance science by founding and maintaining scientific research institutes. This purpose caused some quibbling among the various donors who had other ideas on how the Society should be characterized. Dr. Leo Gans, who had donated a sum for chemistry, thought the Kaiser Wilhelm Society for the Advancement of Science was a nice title, but he argued that the goals should be made broader and more flexible in order to adapt to the changing times, because the Humboldtian ideal of combining research and teaching may not be applicable later as new ways of supporting science emerged. Therefore, he thought that scientific research should be advanced in "every way," especially by creating research institutes. This proposal found no supporters. Instead the Society acquired an umbrella administrative function under which individual scientific research institutes were founded and operated.[34]

Although the specific disciplines to be housed at the institutes were not discussed in detail at the meeting, the urgency to create a biological research institute was reiterated: "Krupp von Bohlen und Halbach and other donors would like an institute for biology because, according to them and to the judgements of specialists, it ought to be at the forefront."[35] They advised that, because the field is large, a number of institutes ought to be created after consultation with a commission made up of leading German biologists.

By the time of this foundational meeting the organizational structure of the Society had been established: the major executive bodies of the Society were the executive committee, the senate, and the plenum at the annual meeting. The first ten senators were voted in at this meeting and came from the ranks of industrialists and bankers from the list of donors.[36] The executive committee consisted of Harnack as president, Krupp and Delbrück as first and second vice president, respectively, Franz von Mendelssohn and Böttinger, treasurers, and Arnold and Fischer as first and second secretary, respectively. In fact, with the exception of a few scientists, the members of the Society were drawn from the long list of donors among Prussia's superrich; a good many of them became senators and members of the executive committee. Since these bodies were the major decision-making organs of the institution, the industrialists had the opportunity to determine the shape of research agendas and nominally control the affairs of the Society. After the inaugural meeting, the plutocratic character of the membership of the Society was criticized by the social democrat H. Ströbel, who thought such a creation of funds at the "Kaiser-Wilhelm-Foundation" "extremely dangerous," from mammon's grace, even if it were for the good of science. He inveighed in a Marxist tirade that the power of the "money bag is all-powerful" and that science is already under the power of Caesar Mammon.[37]

For intellectual fare, Emil Fischer, the main scientist involved in the founding of the Society, gave the featured lecture, "Recent Successes and Problems of Chemistry," in the presence of the Emperor and the assembled donors. This stimulating experimental lecture sketched the problems motivating the foundation of a research organization independent of teaching and discussed recent work in chemistry, offering experimental demonstrations. After referring to the enormous changes occurring in the sciences and the growth of mass education at the universities, Fischer turned to some interesting new results in chemistry. He emphasized new research on synthetic materials which helped to make Germany independent of other countries' raw materials. He used two examples from the work of Otto Hahn and Fritz Haber, both future directors of Kaiser Wilhelm institutes. Hahn, who had been working at Fischer's Berlin University institute, had discovered mesothorium, a viable and cheaper substitute for radium. Germany had no raw material from which radium could be refined. By studying high temperatures, scientists had also solved the problem of synthesizing nitrates from atmospheric nitrogen in order to use them for agriculture and explosives. Haber had synthesized ammonia and BASF patented the technical application. Finally, Fischer came to the problem of coal technology and conserving energy; he also foresaw a future Kaiser Wilhelm Institute for Coal Research. Thus Fischer's vision for the new institutes combined an interest in theoretical research with practical applications useful for the nation.[38]

First Creations

Plans for the chemistry institutes were well under way by the time of the inauguration of the Society in 1911. The Reich Chemical Association merged with the Kaiser Wilhelm Society, and the Kaiser Wilhelm Institute for Chemistry became the first of the institutes to be opened in the Dahlem complex. Ernst Beckmann, a pioneer in the determination of molecular weights, who had been head of the association and had had considerable experience in organizing laboratories, was chosen as the first director. He directed the unit on inorganic chemistry while Richard Willstätter, the codirector, headed the organic chemistry section. At the institute, Willstätter continued his work on chlorophyll and photosynthesis and later was recognized for his work on plant pigments when he received the Nobel Prize for Chemistry in 1915. The Chemical Association's goals had been to pursue pure and applied chemistry and its relation to industrial practice; these goals were realized, in part, at the institute, although most of the work performed was basic research carried on with the hope for practical fallout in some distant future. The importance of the recent advances in the study of radium were recognized and a radioactivity section was added to the institute, headed by Otto Hahn (chemistry) and Lise Meitner (physics), who were appointed Scientific Members. Leopold Koppel, who had contributed 700,000 marks toward the founding of a physical chemistry institute, made the gift conditional on the appointment of Fritz Haber, professor at the Technische Hochschule, Karlsruhe. By the early 1900 Haber had made a name for himself through his work on nitrogen fixation and the synthesis of ammonia. His scientific style was characterized by theoretical studies in areas of practical importance and appealed to the industrialists.

The next priority after dedicating the first two chemistry institutes was the creation of a biological institute. By 1900 chemistry was a well-established discipline, and the choice of which branches to institutionalize and who to appoint to direct such an institute did not require prolonged discussion. Biology in Germany, by contrast, was a young science; it was splintered, and it was not clear what to institutionalize within the field as new areas such as genetics began to emerge. The need for this institute was broached in the first Krüß memorandum and was reiterated many times. Its planning was a chief concern of the Society from the beginning; the steps that followed, however, were both unusual and unprecedented in German science organization. Since the Society was not composed of scientists, except for the influential Emil Fischer, a commission of specialists in the area was recruited in order to decide who to appoint as director and what fields to represent. These events and discussions are notable as they offer a fascinating glimpse into the decision-making process for the institutionalization of a field with foundational problems. While the steps for the formation of the chemistry institutes required financial and organizational planning, the formation of the biology institute required protracted discussion about the discipline itself, which led to a printed report on the opinions of twenty-nine leading experts in various branches of biology.

Interest in creating a biological research institute emerged as early as 1904 when Otto Jaeckel submitted his memorandum to Althoff outlining the need for an independent biontology institute. Jaeckel, who later disappeared from any of the activities concerning the Kaiser Wilhelm Institute for Biology, suggested an all-encompassing institute for "problems of organic development" including four subinstitutes: a morphological, an anatomical, a biological, and an anthropological one.[39] As the scientific community heard about the creation of the Kaiser Wilhelm institutes more suggestions arrived on Harnack's desk.[40] Soon after the dissemination of Harnack's essay, Friedrich Schmidt-Ott, then an assistant in the Prussian Ministry, asked the Heidelberg biologist Otto Cohnheim to write about the needs of biology. Cohnheim noted that in the period 1904–8 there was great progress and success at American institutes. Not only did the American institutes surpass those in Germany, but the funding for the "research institutes" was greater and they were better organized. In the area of "biology"—a term and concept not widely used in Germany—the Americans had had the lead for many years.[41] Specifically, this advance was led by men such as Jacques Loeb, T. H. Morgan, Ross Harrison, and H. S. Jennings, at institutions he visited such as the Rockefeller Institute in New York, the Carnegie Institution, and Charles Davenport's Institute in Cold Spring Harbor. Echoing views voiced in many German newspapers at the time, Cohnheim argued the only way to stop the threat to German science was to establish research institutes in certain areas difficult to develop within the teaching context, and to create a flow of practically unlimited funds for animal experiments.[42]

Soon after the inauguration of the Kaiser Wilhelm Society in January 1911, plans began anew with urgent preparations for biology. In April the general secretary of the Society, Ernst Trendelenburg (1912–1920) sent out requests to the leading biologists in Germany asking for their expert opinion on the question at hand. In a circular, he explained that biological institutes had been at the forefront of the plans since the founding of the Society. In order to decide which one of the diverse areas of biology to advance, the Society wanted to study the views of competent experts in different areas of biology. By the fall, most of the twenty-nine reports had been collected from biologists ranging from the Berlin contingent (the largest pool, consisting of fourteen biologists) including Oscar Hertwig, W. Waldeyer, Max Rubner, Oscar Vogt, and August von Wassermann, to Wilhelm Roux of Halle, Max Verworn of Bonn, and Anton Dohrn in Naples. What emerged from these proposals was diverse. Of course, each representative of a certain specialty argued for the advancement of that area, and biology in Germany at 1900 had, indeed, become specialized. Rivalries also existed between various schools of thought. Some consensus, however, did emerge. Because of the differences of opinions and suggestions, the Minister of Education called a day-long meeting with twenty-seven of the advisers, along with some members of the Society, representatives of the Ministry, and Harnack.[43] The areas discussed were chiefly experimental biology, including botany, experimental zoology, heredity, microbiology, physiology, experimental medicine, brain research, and experimental psychology and anthropology. Despite the diversity of opinion, some uniformity did emerge: Everyone agreed to support the study of heredity because it was an area in urgent need of attention.[44]

Although the field of heredity was an area to be included, this did not necessarily mean a support for Mendelism. In fact, despite the rediscovery of Mendel's laws by Carl Correns, Erich von Tschermak, and Hugo de Vries in 1900, Mendelism found its greatest early support in America, France, and England. Part of the reason for the success of Mendelism in America lies in the receptiveness of the scientific community at large. There had already been interest in the study of heredity in America by breeders, but after 1900 this interest flourished at agricultural and medical institutions as well as at the universities.[45] The study of genetics also found large-scale support at the Carnegie Institution and at Cold Spring Harbor. Individual schools such as the Morgan school advanced the study of Mendelian genetics on a scale not attained in Germany. The reasons, on the other hand, for the cautious and slow acceptance of Mendelism in Germany are more difficult to discern.[46] During the interwar years the genetic research program was dominated by interest in the cytoplasm and in physiological genetics.[47]

Some of the industrialists showed interest in biologists who were at the periphery of the traditional biological community such as Jakob von Uexküll, whose unorthodox interests were based on the holistic living organism, ecology, and plants. When the American biologists were asked to comment on von Uexküll's qualifications, the chemist T. W. Richards used the opportunity to suggest a research program that ought to be supported in Germany:

> The general impression seemed to be, however, that there is no one in Germany now working in the line which is especially necessary for such an institution [as] you propose. Apparently the newer school (based on the Mendelian doctrine) has not been fruitful in Germany and the tenets of this theory have been developed much more effectually in America, England, and France. One of the zoologists suggested that the best thing for the Institution would be to invite one of our three most prominent investigators of heredity for several years to start a school in Berlin. These three men are William E. Castle, of Harvard, C. B. Davenport, of the Carnegie Institution, and Thomas Morgan, of Columbia University, New York. They are all very able men, and in the midst of interesting experimental investigations.[48]

After the deliberations the Society decided to create an institute for "Heredity and Developmental Mechanics." Soon after, Theodor Boveri, the eminent zoologist who had done important work on chromosomes, wrote a report outlining a research program and organizational plan for the institute. Although he would have become the director, Boveri withdrew on 21 May 1913 with the excuse of illness, but there were also other reasons for his reluctance to accept the position, including fear of abandoning the Würzburg university setting. Boveri, wrote Richard Goldschmidt, "had always lived in the quiet atmosphere of a small university town, was an idealist and no match for Berlin officials, who tried to drive as hard a bargain with him as possible, according to the old traditions of the ministry of education." He also "feared that he would be driven in his work, forced to produce quick results."[49] Boveri's decision was a great blow for the Society because

there were hardly any other senior or distinguished biologists in Germany
to meet this need. The four candidates for division heads—Hans Spemann
(experimental embryology), Max Hartmann (protozoas and the biology of
lower forms), Otto Warburg (cell physiology), and Goldschmidt (genetics)—
were too junior to be in such a leading position in German science. Despite Boveri's physical absence at the head of the institute, when it was actually created under the directorship of Carl Correns, Boveri's influence on
the research direction and selection of scientific members remained considerable.

At first most members of the Society thought that botanically oriented
genetics could be pursued at university-based institutes with their botanical
gardens, but then Richard Goldschmidt had the idea that Carl Correns ought
to be appointed to this post. He later recalled that he thought the grandi-
ose plans for Berlin had been abandoned but then heard from Hertwig that
the plan would be carried through if a director could be found. The emphasis had been on choosing a zoologist, but because no one in the proper
age group was available, Goldschmidt suggested that a botanist—Carl
Correns—be included in the group.[50] In the end, even the zoologists heartily
agreed to the distinguished choice. Despite the step taken in 1913, it was
not until 1915 (during the war) that the institute opened and work began.

The three institutes discussed above were at the core of the Dahlem
complex for basic research, but another institute in the biomedical complex
had already opened about a year and a half after the biological meetings on
28 October 1913: the Kaiser Wilhelm Institute for Experimental Therapy
headed by the bacteriologist and serologist August von Wassermann (one
of Harnack's advisers), who had become famous for his diagnostic test for
syphilis. Carl Neuberg, who later became director, headed the chemical section.

The first four Dahlem institutes became the hallmark of the Kaiser Wilhelm Society by the end of the Weimar Republic, and it was these institutes
in Dahlem, along with the still to be created Kaiser Wilhelm Institute for
Physics, that established the international reputation and prestige of the
Society. But during these early years, one more institute was opened outside of Berlin in the industrial area of Germany—an institute oriented
toward applied research on coal in Mülheim in the Ruhr. Franz Fischer, a
student of Emil Fischer, became director when it opened on 27 July 1914.[51]
Just as the chemistry institute had been, in many ways, the fulfillment of
Fischer's ideas for the Reich Chemical Association, so too did this institute
fill the need Fischer saw for combining pure research with a focus on
analyzing raw materials important for industry and for the nation.

World War I

Fischer's vision for the new Society, however, was transformed and realized
earlier than expected when World War I broke out several weeks later in

August 1914. The war also transformed the meaning of Harnack's prewar phrase: "Military strength and science are the two strong pillars of Germany's greatness." In 1916 Harnack referred back to his earlier words, recognizing that as a scientist one had a duty to serve the nation as the military did, but earlier he had thought the fruits of science would serve the military only indirectly. Now the enemies had "brought science and military strength together" in a way the founders of the Society had not foreseen. "Create, organize, use discipline," he encouraged the Society's members; in this way military strength and science will be brought together.[52] Thus during World War I a new war-born relationship emerged whereby military strength was supported and advanced by scientific developments in chemical weapons, in synthetic raw materials, and in meeting nutritional needs. Four out of the five new institutes were either integrated into the war effort or contributed expertise in other ways. The fifth institute for biology, which was more theoretical in its interests, did not contribute scientific expertise to the war effort but was turned into a barracks during part of the war. In addition, most of the scientific personnel at all the institutes were drafted. The most celebrated case of a scientist who willingly and enthusiastically contributed to the war effort was Fritz Haber, a German patriot and director of the Kaiser Wilhelm Institute for Physical Chemistry. Haber, in fact, together with his friend and colleague Richard Willstätter, asked Harnack immediately after the war broke out if the government needed their services, but no use could be made of them.[53] Instead, the initiative to use science for the war effort came from the scientists themselves.

In an August 1914 meeting convened to discuss the war, Harnack stressed that the Society would continue to exist in these serious times and would work for the "good of the Fatherland." Several institutes had already begun to work on the solution of problems with direct importance for the war. For example, August von Wassermann reported on his contractual work for the army at the institute for experimental therapy. Other scientists like Emil Fischer and Ernst Beckmann spoke of new tasks in chemical-physical research needed to change the way in which Germany would meet new needs for raw materials.[54]

In the area of raw materials research the coal institute contributed to the war effort in a major way. Although initially drafted, Franz Fischer was called back from the Russian front by Emil Fischer, who used his governmental connections at the War Ministry to obtain his release. When Franz Fischer arrived back at his institute in November 1914, Emil Fischer discussed a wartime program involving coordination between the War Ministry and the cokeries, which would be given technical support by the institute when needed. By 1916 the institute was also studying the synthesis of gasoline from coal and the extraction of oil from coal tar.[55]

During the early years of the war, the personnel of Haber's institute had dropped to 5 people, but by 1917 it had been transformed into a center for military science and the personnel swelled to 1,500, including 150 scientists. Space for work expanded to meet the increase and the budget was fifty times greater than it had been in peacetime. Haber voluntarily placed the institute at the disposal of the government and orchestrated a vast war effort in gas production and gas protection; it became the center for chemical warfare research in Germany.[56] Haber had joined the War Ministry in 1916 and was in charge of Section A 10, chemical warfare supplies. Between 1915 and 1918, Haber's institute was divided into ten sections under section heads in charge of research on respirator face pieces, respirator drums, enemy chemical warfare, offensive research, new gases, pharmacology, shell cases, proofing and issue of gas, trench mortars, and particulate clouds. Haber and his group in Dahlem accomplished a great deal in the development of gas warfare and protection against it. Haber developed poisonous chlorine gas, which was to be used in the trenches when the proper wind conditions prevailed, and Willstätter created a three-layer gas mask. The institute began to resemble an industrial laboratory and Haber faced mounting administrative tasks.[57] The transformation of the institute was to remain, however, a "pure war measure," and not a permanant change.[58]

Haber's enthusiasm for creating a vast organization for war technology was shared by Emil Fischer and Walther Nernst, and they set up a new Kaiser Wilhelm Foundation for War Technology in 1916, sponsored by Haber's faithful benefactor Leopold Koppel. During the war, the foundation worked closely with the War Ministry and was created in order to coordinate war-related work in Germany.[59] In addition, Haber campaigned to create an institute for gas research, which would continue after the war. Although the Prussian War Ministry initially supported the idea, both institutions, which fostered the connection between the military and science, failed to continue after the war ended in 1918.

With the changing needs of science at the turn of the century new institutional forms began to emerge in many countries where science was highly developed. America took the lead in offering full-scale support for the advancement of science in newly created research institutes funded by wealthy patrons and foundations. As Germany began to face deeply rooted structural flaws in its organization of science, the need for creating new research institutes modeled after those in America and other highly developed countries became obvious. The beginning of the twentieth century saw the emergence of cost-intensive, specialized, large-scale research requiring a new form of institutionalization outside of the traditional university-based context. Germany exhibited an institutional lag in meeting the needs of science and creating new scientific disciplines, but the Kaiser Wilhelm Society redressed the lack. The developments for the planning of the Kaiser Wilhelm Society exhibit features peculiar to the German context and to the Wilhelmine environment, yet they also display breaks from traditional German science organization. The role of the state, embodied by the Prussian Education Ministry, was considerable. In many senses the founding of the Kaiser Wilhelm

Society was a Prussian affair. This meant that certain traditions peculiar to the university–state relation in the nineteenth century continued into the early twentieth. Despite attempts by the scientists to loosen state control, the government retained its influence in making appointments. Other new influences also emerged as Germany became prosperous in a period of late industrialization: The wealthy bourgeoisie found a new expression for their economic and social power.

2

The Weimar Years

The Kaiser Wilhelm Society (KWG) emerged from World War I facing a wholly different socioeconomic, political, and cultural environment from the one in which it had been founded. After the military defeat of Germany in November 1918, the Empire collapsed and was replaced by a republic. But defeat was soon followed by humiliating peace terms and reparations, along with the devastating hyperinflation. Although Germans faced harrowing hardships, the Weimar Republic also created an atmosphere of freedom of expression and encouragement that artists and intellectuals had missed in previous regimes. Many of the movements we associate with modernity— expressionism in art, the Bauhaus in architecture, the physics of relativity— found fertile soil and blossomed during the Weimar period. In the world of science and scholarship the Weimar period consisted of conflicting elements. Many professors at the universities were notoriously conservative and a feeling of cultural pessimism, decline, uncertainty, and crisis often entered into the content of their work. Democratic educational reforms were often met by rigid opposition. All these changes in society touched the Kaiser Wilhelm Society at a time when its foundations were secure and it was ready for further growth and expansion.[1]

The Poverty of German Science

With the dissolution of the monarchy, the Society lost its monarchical patronage; with the abdication of Kaiser Wilhelm II, it had to find a new patron. The state revolution of 1918 affected the Society's relation to the political order. By February 1919 Rudolf Valentini, the head of the civil cabinet, announced he would no longer attend the senate meetings because the state revolution no longer allowed the Kaiser's protectorate to exercise its power. The Society, however, remained loyal to its old ties and considered its "bonds" with Valentini as "not broken off." Consequently, he was made a senator at the Society's next meeting in June 1919.[2]

Harnack, referring to the changes, announced that "as a result of the state revolution a change of the Kaiser Wilhelm Gesellschaft's statutes is necessary." The Society would have to decide who would replace the "all mighty protector." Harnack suggested discussing the question of whether a change in the whole structure of the Society was necessary as a result of the revolution because the Society's protector no longer existed.[3] Of course, Harnack was not only concerned about abstractions, but he also wondered whether the revolution had an effect on the Society's institutes and the science done there. Somehow, rioting in the streets of Berlin and other signs of revolution never reached the idyllic environs of the posh Berlin suburb of Dahlem, where most of the institutes were situated. Carl Correns's reply to Harnack's inquiry was typical of other institutes: "The days of revolution have not been marked by any incidents within the institute."[4]

Even these days it is hard to imagine how rioting and disruption in the center of urban Berlin could reach the suburb of Dahlem. After about a twenty-minute subway ride (the subway already existed by the twenties) from the center of Berlin one reaches Dahlem-Dorf, the subway stop and business center of the district. Just one stop further, a visiting scientist could get off at Thielplatz and reach Harnack House (the Society clubhouse built in 1929) within minutes. A brief walk around the environs would reveal a community more like a college campus than an urban center. But instead of ugly dormitories one finds large villas with well-manicured gardens and large modern institute buildings within a few minutes' walk of each other. Sitting in Otto Warburg's library today, the hustle and bustle of urban Berlin fades from view as one becomes absorbed in the task at hand with only an occasional whish of a car driving off in the distance. It is indeed hard to imagine riots or, for that matter, storm troopers or brown shirts disrupting the peace of Boltzmannstraße. But there were of course other ways in which the new social and political order entered into the functioning of, and activities at, the Society.

Simultaneously with the changed sociopolitical environment, economic problems also began to emerge. During the first few months of 1920 the Society began to feel the effects of the brewing economic crisis and reported in its first executive meeting of the year that prices were rising in every area of life.[5] Because of its increasingly difficult financial position, the Society turned to the Prussian state and the German Reich government for help.[6] It recognized that, like most other scientific institutions established with foundation funding and private contributions, it would have to close if the state did not contribute.[7] Like many private or semiprivate institutions, the

Society could no longer draw on the interest of resources accumulated through private sources. With the devaluation of the mark and the resulting inflation induced by the postwar reparations imposed by the Allies, the Society lost much of its capital.

In the summer of 1920, the Society approached the Prussian Ministry for Science (Learning), Art, and National Culture, describing its difficult financial position and the destitution of German science. The Ministry replied that it did not consider the Kaiser Wilhelm Society to be in a desperate position that would justify "special and urgent measures" allowing it to continue its operation. Nevertheless, it was ready to support the Society in conjunction with the finance minister.[8]

To evaluate the situation, a conference took place in August to examine the financial position of the Kaiser Wilhelm Society. State Secretary Carl-Heinrich Becker, Hugo Krüß from the Prussian Ministry, several financial officers from the Reich and Prussian ministries, Harnack, Friedrich Glum, the general secretary of the Society as of May 1920, and Franz von Mendelssohn, its treasurer, all attended. Becker and Krüß reviewed the origins and meaning of the Kaiser Wilhelm Society and showed that private funds had been gathered to support independent research institutes, although the state had taken part in the founding of several of the institutes.[9]

The industry-related institutes, created on the prototypical Dahlem institutes, were characterized as appendages to various industries that needed research institutes for certain areas of the applied sciences. Because of its successful activity with its original institutes the Society became a fiduciary for these institutes. Industry asked the Society to assume the scientific supervision and organization of the institutes and to incorporate them into the circle of Kaiser Wilhelm institutes. By 1920 these industry-related institutes included a coal research institute in Mühlheim-Ruhr, a coal institute in Breslau, an institute for iron research in Düsseldorf, one for textile chemistry in Dahlem, and a metal research institute in Neubabelsberg. Most of these institutes received their support from sources outside the Society (primarily industry) and therefore did not need the funds requested from the state. Thus funds were needed only for the maintenance and continuation of the old institutes for pure science.[10]

To gain support, the Society stressed the close and old relation it had with the Prussian state. But after the dissolution of the monarchy, the Prussian state claimed it also did not have much money to contribute to important areas such as science.[11] It too urged the Society to seek funding from the private sector. Becker informed the minister that without support the Society would eventually have to close its institutes, and this would damage not only science but also the practical applications of science, which could be of use to the Prussian state. He reminded the minister of Prussia's close relation to the Society and argued it would not be in Prussia's interests to allow the Reich to undertake this responsibility.[12] Even so, by March 1921, a month before the Allies set Germany's reparation payments, Harnack wrote to the Prussian Ministry thanking it for a million-mark contribution: "The

Kaiser Wilhelm Gesellschaft welcomes it if the traditional working relation between itself and the Prussian state can be made stronger through increased cooperation and joint responsibility, and it is ready to include this willingness to cooperate in its statutes."[13] The Society had stressed its early ties to the Prussian state in order to gain government support, but now the question was whether the Emperor could be replaced by another political figure if the statutes were to remain the same. The Society considered the person of the Emperor irreplaceable. A "new carrier of state power" would not do because there were certain "personal and state elements" that tied the Society and the Emperor together. Therefore, Harnack suggested the Society establish a wholly new relation to the state.[14]

As a result of these considerations, the senate decided to keep the name "Kaiser Wilhelm Society," to abolish the protectorate, and to remove the right of the Emperor to name members and senators to the Society. With the new bylaws, fifteen senators were to be elected by the Society, and fifteen, of whom five were already members of the Society, were to be named by the state on the condition that it contribute financially. In addition, two directors of institutes would also be in the senate, and a total of one-third of the senate in the categories noted would be made up of scientists.[15]

Within a year, in March 1922, the Society had changed its statutes; the protectorate no longer existed, and the Reich government and Prussian state became "organic" parts of the Kaiser Wilhelm Society. The Prussian state, however, was not to impair the "freedom and autonomy of the Society" but would always "respect this freedom."[16] Carl-Heinrich Becker, the new Prussian Education Minister, emphasized the early trustful relationship between the Prussian Education Ministry and the Society. He further characterized the Society as a working group with the state, science, and industry.[17]

Just as the political transformations affected the structure of the Society, so too did the economic and financial crisis alter its functioning. The Society reported in December 1923 that it was able to continue operating because of the help of the state and of industry, although they too had had their own financial difficulties. The inflation did, however, limit the institute's procurement budget for such things as chemicals and animals, and the institutes for physical chemistry and electro-chemistry, biology, and experimental therapy were faced with closing down altogether.[18]

To combat the hardships science had to face as a result of the war and the inflation, the Emergency Association for German Science (NGW) was founded in 1920 with the help of Fritz Haber, who was, in many ways, its spiritual founder. Friedrich Schmidt-Ott, formerly a state minister from the Prussian Education Ministry, became the president, and Carl-Heinrich Becker, Max Planck, and Adolf von Harnack were on the founding committee of the German funding organization. As the title indicates, it was a response to the "poverty" of German science. As a result of the twin shocks of World War I and the inflation, German science suffered; scientists became increasingly isolated from their foreign counterparts because of the boycott of German science after the war; budgets were the same as they had been in 1913—even though inflation had reduced the value of the money considerably. With funding for the NGW coming primarily from the Reich and in part from industry, a German-style foundation was established in March 1920. Despite the government's large debts at home and impending reparations abroad, it was expected to contribute over 20 million marks. The NGW supported science by administering research fellowships and travel grants, supplying printing costs for books and articles, lending instruments and apparatus, supplying funds for chemicals and experimental animals, and by paying research assistants.[19]

In his official announcement, Haber emphasized the role science had to play in reviving Germany as an intellectual and scientific great power: "The destruction of our country as a great political power will remain what it is today: a reminder that our existence as a people depends on the maintenance of our great intellectual power position, which is inseparable from our scientific enterprise."[20] This certainly supports Paul Forman's findings that after the war the advancement of science became a *Machtersatz*—a substitution or surrogate for the lost war and for the loss of political great-power status.[21]

The Kaiser Wilhelm Society and the Emergency Association both became integral parts of German science organization during the Weimar period. They also complemented and supported each other. While the Society undertook scientific research, the Association financially supported it. The leaders of each institution overlapped and interacted with each other; Schmidt-Ott, for example, who was president of the Association, was also second vice president of the Society. Haber, too, continued to be active in both organizations. Both experienced problems with the state in the course of the 1920s as Becker urged the priority of the state in matters of science policy. Both institutions were major parts of the general advancement of science in Germany.

Becker had introduced innovative university reforms into the educational system. But despite the perceived danger and threat of an increasingly active state in relation to the Kaiser Wilhelm Society, Becker himself acknowledged a new organizational form of the Society consisting of cooperation and independence. The funding for the Kaiser Wilhelm Society had originally come from private sources—industry and commerce—and the state offered some of the land and paid for the positions of key directorships. Despite the changed relation between the Society and the state after World War I with the Reich and Prussia undertaking to supply half of the Society's financial support, the original form and authority of a private Society survived. Becker considered this an anomaly. Even with the increased financial support, "the government's influence on the use of the money did not change."[22]

At the end of March 1929, Harnack responded to one of Becker's lectures on "Problems of Science Organization." He agreed with Becker that "in Germany the state must retain the leadership in science policy," but with regard to the Kaiser Wilhelm Society he had some reservations. Although Becker stated that the Society had the form of a private society, Harnack considered it to be a "private Society, which is in the middle of the state." He told Becker that the Kaiser Wilhelm institutes were "private institutes and state institutes at the same time." Harnack wanted to emphasize the Society's close relation with Prussia and the state while dampening the "emerging tensions" between the Society and the state because he also praised Becker for all his help and advice over the years which advanced the "life and growth of the Society." It was because of this help that the "emerging tensions" did not grow larger, he claimed.[23] Harnack, however, was unwilling to take the step of creating an entirely new and separate category for the Society in its state relations.

Scientists Take Control

Fritz Haber, the director of the Kaiser Wilhelm Institute for Physical Chemistry in Berlin-Dahlem and the leader of chemical warfare in World War I, quickly emerged as a leading science organizer and influenced the policymaking of the science administrators at the ministries after the war. His scientific abilities were widely recognized, and he received the Nobel Prize in 1919 for his work on nitrogen fixation. He also became one of the most active scientific leaders in the Berlin-Dahlem complex of institutes. It was therefore not surprising that he took the first move to increase the role of scientists in the decision-making process at the Society. With the immense growth of the Society from prewar times—by the end of the 1920s there were thirty scientific institutes compared to the initial four in prewar times—more formal bodies were needed to make decisions at the Society. Haber wanted to ensure that these decisions would originate with the scientists and not with the administrators.

Haber had already campaigned to elect a scientist to the administrative council in 1925, when it had been proposed by the senate that Hugo Krüß, the general director of the state library, become a member of the council. Although Haber greatly respected Krüß and his support of the Society, he thought that the administrative council needed a scientist. Max Planck, thought Haber, was the most suitable person, and his appointment would fill the hole created by Emil Fischer's death. Haber argued that half of the senate consisted of men from the economic/industrial sector, while the other half consisted of administrators and representatives of the sciences. By comparison, representatives from the sciences were absent from the administrative council.[24]

It was therefore not surprising that Haber wrote to Adolf von Harnack on 4 June 1928 outlining his ideas on creating a new administrative body uniting all the scientific members of the Society. He argued that the creation of a scientific council made up of the scientific members of the Society would guarantee their "coherence" and fit into the goal, set forth by Harnack in the 1928 handbook of the Society, which was to strengthen the institutions of the Society as a "task [of the] future." He emphasized that it ultimately was the scientific members who "bring the success and prestige" of the Society's institutes into the world.[25] Previously the senate, which was composed of government officials, industrialists, and corporations, had been making the decisions.

During the early years of the Society, related Haber, the number of institutes and their scientific members were so small that personal contact with one another, and a "paternalistic relationship" of each member with the administration, was enough to fulfill the Society's needs. Meanwhile there had been an "enormous growth." Thirty institutes existed now and there were seventy scientific members. Haber and the twenty-three other scientific members who signed the letter to Harnack asked him to make a change and to "unite the scientific members into a corporate body."[26] The seventy members divided themselves into twenty-six chemists and physicists, twenty-eight biomedical scientists, and nine humanists. A majority of the members—forty-one—lived in Berlin. The primary tasks of the body would be to make and suggest appointments of scientific members and directors and to advise the administration on scientific matters and the needs of the discipline. In his application to Harnack, Haber argued that the scientific members wanted to influence matters at the Society as a group and not as individuals.[27]

During the last half of 1928, Haber began to take all the necessary steps to meet Harnack's conditions for the scientific council. For example, Harnack required that all the scientific members, not just those in Dahlem, vote on the question. The scientific members almost unanimously agreed on creating the council. One exception was Ludwig Prandtl, director of the Kaiser Wilhelm Institute for Aerodynamics, who was "content" with the "paternalistic way" in which the Kaiser Wilhelm Society had been run. He thought that the scientific members could "increase their influence" by electing some more scientists to the senate of the Society rather than by creating a new organization. He would rather have too little organization than too much.[28] But he was in the minority. By the end of July Haber had tallied up the votes: out of seventy members, sixty-two approved of Haber's proposal, three rejected it (Carl Correns, Hans Spemann, and Martin Wolff), three were undecided (Viktor Bruns, Ludwig Prandtl, Ernst Rabel), and two did not vote (Martin Ficker, Friedrich Glum).[29]

The executive committee of the Society discussed and approved the creation of a scientific council at its meeting in November 1928 and proposed a change in statutes to the senate. The council was divided into a biological-medical section, a chemical-physical-technical section, and a humanities section. It would suggest the appointment of other scientific members and directors to the senate. The scientific council could suggest institutes to be created, while the senate could actively solicit recommendations.[30]

International Relations

Another sign of the growth and maturation of the Society during the Weimar years was the creation of a clubhouse (like American faculty clubs) in Dahlem to house foreign guests, hold lectures, receive guests, provide lunch for the Society's members, and host major dinners with dignitaries and scientists. It provided a central meeting point for scientists in Dahlem. Although Haber's colloquia in his institute had become famous, no other meeting place existed for such scientific gatherings. With a concentration of basic research institutes in Dahlem a central meeting point would provide a place for interdisciplinary contact and exchange. Another problem to be met was the growing number of guests from abroad who came to Dahlem for a short- or long-term visit.

Friedrich Glum, the general secretary of the Society, suggested the idea of an institute for foreign guests (Harnack House) in 1926. He thought it was necessary to reciprocate the hospitality German scientists had enjoyed after the war in foreign countries where some of them had given lectures or lived for a short time.[31] In addition, it was a way of reestablishing ties with estranged colleagues who had taken part in the postwar boycott of German science. But aside from the Society's own contemporaneous conception of Harnack House, it reflected the growing internationalism of science during the twenties.[32] The creation of an "Institute for Foreign Guests," as it was originally conceived, was one manifestation of this trend.

The research institutes of the Kaiser Wilhelm Society in Berlin-Dahlem, especially the institutes for biology, experimental therapy, biochemistry, chemistry, and physical chemistry, enjoyed the "greatest prestige in the international scientific world."[33] Since World War I these institutes had developed into the core of the Society and the "common man" thought of the Dahlem institutes as "the Kaiser Wilhelm Institute."[34] It was therefore the logical place to "found a scientific research center in Germany for international scientific cooperation."[35] Harnack House opened on 7 May 1929, Harnack's birthday.

Harnack House was located in the idyllic and plush surroundings of Berlin-Dahlem. It had large and small halls, with names like the Goethe-Saal, Helmholtz-Saal, Duisberg-Saal, and Liebig-Saal. It also had a Leibnitz Library and a Mozart room. There was a cafeteria where workers met for lunch, and bedrooms for visiting scientists. Scientists could relax over a game of chess or converse about the latest findings in various fields. The institutes for physical chemistry, biology, physics, textile chemistry, and cell physiology were all within a few minutes' walk. It was an ideal setting for the cooperative research that had already begun to emerge among the scientists at the various institutes. It is not surprising, for instance, that Warburg was indebted to the physical methods developed at the neighboring physical chemistry institute for his work in cell physiology. Within months after the founding, a lecture series was developed featuring lectures by prominent institute directors. A Dahlem Medical Evening began to be held regularly by scientists from the biological and medical disciplines. Adolf Windaus gave the first lecture in this series on "Considerations on the Biological Meaning of the Stars" at the end of June 1929. It was then followed by a social evening with a cold buffet and beer. Other lectures in this series for the period 1929–31 included Max Hartmann on "Relative Sexuality," Eugen Fischer on the "Human Genetic Factors," Adolf Butenandt on hormones, and Hans Fischer on chemistry. A biological evening began in November 1930 with Viktor Jollos, a geneticist.[36]

In November 1929 the Haber colloquium moved to Harnack House and met every two weeks on Mondays. In March 1930 there was an extended Haber Colloquium with the American Professor Irving Langmuir and 450 guests. In addition, members of Haber's institute—Michael Polanyi and Rudolf Ladenburg, for instance—scheduled teas and other social events at the house. From time to time various directors of institutes gave major lectures in the winter with audiences of 300–400. Professor Fritz von Wettstein gave the second winter lecture in December 1930 and Richard Goldschmidt another in March 1931. Other major lectures included one by Albert Einstein on "The Nature of Space Problems" and Ernst Rüdin on "Practical Results of Psychiatric Hereditary Research." In fact, between 1929 and 1933 there were a number of lectures on eugenics. The Berlin Society for Eugenics and Anthropology sponsored a few, including one by Hermann Muckermann, which had an audience of 600![37] The Kaiser Wilhelm Institute for Anthropology, Human Genetics, and Eugenics had been founded in 1927, and this institutionalization mirrored the growth of interest in, and establishment of the discipline of eugenics.[38]

In addition to scientific events, the House was also used for "Beer Evenings" by the Dahlem scientific community as well as by other groups for teas, dinners, and other social gatherings. The senate and executive council held some of their meetings in the conference rooms, and any important conference or meeting with a dignitary also took place at Harnack House. By 1937, a swimming pool was built next to the tennis courts, while the *Berliner-Zeitung* featured an article called "Between Logarithms and Experiments—A Dive into Cool Water!"[39]

What's in a Name?

By the end of the 1920s, the Society and its institutes had established a prestigious image for themselves in the international world of science. The Society's scientists were winning Nobel Prizes, making discoveries, and attracting students from home and abroad to work in their labs. Amid the success of its scientists, the Society faced many difficulties with the state. Because of the inflation, the Society had established closer ties with the government in order to improve its financial position, but over the years, the government, and especially the Prussian Education Ministry, began to expect more in return for its financial support. Despite public help, and the pressures that went with it, the Society managed to preserve its autonomy; it did not become a state institution. But during the last few years of the twenties it was not always easy to maintain its principle of self-government. Attempts began to be made by the government and parliament to meddle with the Society's administration and politicize it. The Social Democrats and the Communists hated the name of the Society, and there were numerous attempts to change it.

There were calls to change the name of the Society as early as 1918, but they quickly faded. Strident voices from the left resurfaced in 1926 when a Dr. Schwartz from the Berlin Communist party proposed a "Society for Scientific Research." Harnack dismissed this opposition in a humorous and sarcastic manner. He related a short story to Dr. Schwartz:

> When a Kaiser Wilhelm Gesellschaft institute was dedicated four years ago, the director stood by his window in the morning and heard two workers talk: The one said to the other: "We can no longer work here; it is still called the Kaiser Wilhelm Gesellschaft, in spite of the revolution." The other one answered: "You are still called Piefke, in spite of the revolution."[40]

This kept the leftists at bay for a time, but by the beginning of 1929 interest in changing the name arose again. The Prussian Minister of the Interior thought it would be misunderstood if the name of the Emperor was kept. The Society, however, argued against renaming for four reasons. First, the Kaiser Wilhelm Society represented a special type of scientific research institute, which was known under its present name at home and abroad. The renaming would not simply mean a change of name but would also abolish the characteristic name for a special kind of institute. The Society further argued that its funding had come from private sources—primarily industry— until after the war, and the effect of a name change might be the withdrawal of its members and financial supporters. Third, because of Harnack's generally conservative political attitudes he might raise objections to a change and threaten to resign. Finally, what was decisive for the members of the Society was that there was "pressure" exerted by the chief funders—Reich and Prussia—to change the name.[41] Thus the issue of changing the Society's name was more than just the pervasive conflict between self-government and control by the state—a conflict characterizing the whole Weimar period. The Society tenaciously clung to tradition, and many of its members' attitudes mirrored the general conservative attitude academics exhibited at the universities during the Weimar period.

With the death of Adolf von Harnack on 10 June 1930, both the Social Democrats and the Prussian Education Ministry once more took advantage of an opportunity to implement their goals. Just weeks after Harnack's death, Gustav Krupp von Bohlen und Halbach, the vice president of the Society, reported to a Reich Minister that the Berlin city council (with a majority vote cast by the Social Democrats and the Communists) informed the Society that it could "expect a future grant" only on the condition that it changed its name. Although Krupp believed the city council might "revise its decision" by the following year, he also warned against the danger that other grant-making public bodies supporting the Society might also demand a change of name. Krupp made it very clear to the minister that with the "new order of state relations after the war," the Society had as its "sole purpose the advancement of science, uninfluenced by, and independent of, political trends."[42]

Theodor Leipart, a senator of the Society and chairman of the German Trade Union, immediately wrote to Krupp von Bohlen und Halbach about changing the name. Leipart had not suggested a change in name for the Society before Harnack's death because he knew that Harnack had been closely associated with the Society since its founding and would therefore oppose a change in the name out of "reverence." He thought the change in leadership at the Society was an appropriate time to make a change. He proposed the Society be named the "German Society for the Advancement of Science."[43]

According to Leipart, when the German trade union became a member of the Kaiser Wilhelm Society there had been much resistance against joining a Society with such a "shocking name." The trade union assumed the name would change over time and expected this to happen after Harnack's death. Leipart also claimed that republican circles found the name "incomprehensible" or "anachronistic." He found no reason to keep the name since the protectorate of the former Emperor had been abolished twelve years earlier. The Emperor, wrote Leipart, was not even the "spiritual father of the idea that led to the founding of the Society." Moreover, during the founding period, the Kaiserreich contributed no financial support to the Society, he added, while during the Weimar period it was industry, the Reich, and Prussia that financed the effort. According to Leipart, half of the institutes of the Society were created in the postwar period. These facts, he concluded, suggest that the "German republic" has made many more "financial sacrifices" than did the Kaiserreich.

> The change of name is, therefore, only a logical consequence of the changing times. It is the people and Reich, industry and workers, that have made the Society's pure work in the service of the German people possible. This fact must be unequivocal and clear in the name of the Society. Especially now with the death of the great representative of German intellect, who governed the Society for two decades . . . [the name] must be careful to convey [the Society's] essence and goals. . . : "German Society for the Advancement of Science."[44]

Also in 1930, the Communist member of parliament, Malowski, characterized the Kaiser Wilhelm Society as supporting a "highly reactionary bourgeois science"; it was a "flight from reality."[45]

The Society opposed this name change yet again in its executive council meeting of October 1930. The president explained that after the protectorate of the Emperor was abolished over ten years ago and the Society decided to continue under the same name, there seemed to be no new reason to alter the decision. He thought that a name change would lead to a "crisis" at the Kaiser Wilhelm Society because members (probably the paying members as opposed to the scientific members) might resign and this would lead to financial disaster. He was quick to add, however, that the Society still had a "loyal attitude towards the state in every way," and that the retaining of the name did not imply lack of loyalty. He argued, as the Society had done before, that the name did not have a "historical meaning" but it marked a "special type of scientific institute," and that it was known as such all over the world.[46]

By 1930 rumors had already spread that Becker was aspiring to the presidency of the Society and wanted to force Harnack to resign.[47] Within several weeks after Harnack's death, Friedrich Saemisch, a senator of the Society, wrote to Krupp calling a meeting to discuss the future of the presidency. He emphasized that the senate was the most important body of the Society and that he wished the election to run smoothly—"with as much consensus as possible."[48] Soon after Harnack's death the newspapers began to gossip about possible successors. They knew that Planck was being considered, but so was Becker. For the latter, the newspapers wondered about the opposition that Becker would face from the senate. A lively fight took place in the senate over Becker, although there was little opposition to Planck. Becker's political point of view offended some; other senators considered him to be "an exponent of a clearly emphasized political direction," and as a minister he was considered too politically involved. The newspaper *Berliner Lokalanzeiger* commented that the KWG "senate's attitude . . . shed strange light on the inner structure of the Society" because, after all, Becker had served the republic so faithfully for years.[49]

But the gossip failed to reveal that four candidates had been considered for the post: Gustav Krupp von Bohlen und Halbach, Max Planck, Richard von Wettstein, the botanist from Vienna, and the former Prussian Education Minister Carl-Heinrich Becker. Once more there was opposition to the Becker candidacy, especially because "science had become a playground for political machinations," and the Society wanted to "maintain its free, apolitical position." A Becker presidency would mean a "politicization of the Society." Planck was characterized as a famous physicist, Nobel Prize winner, and the rector of the University of Berlin, who had retired in 1926 and was a "totally independent personality who guaranteed an impartial leadership." Wettstein was an energetic scientist who had also led scientific expeditions. Finally, Krupp had done a lot for the Society and had contacts with industry. From these evaluations it was no surprise that Planck was finally elected president on 14 July 1930.[50]

Spawning Industry-Related Sciences

During the twenties, there had been many attacks on, and some changes in, the general structure and organization of the Society. As a result, tensions grew between the Society and the state. Although the Society had to struggle to maintain its existence, under these adverse conditions the scientific research of its institutes managed to flourish, and science experienced the same period of explosive creativity that characterized the arts and literature during the Weimar period.[51] In addition, many new institutes were founded or adopted by the Society during and after the war. By successfully appealing to both the state and the industrial sector for financial support it managed to experience a period of great expansion.

The new institutes created both during and after the war departed from the classic basic research Berlin-Dahlem institutes built, or conceived of, before the war. Not only did the Society expand the location of its institutes to the Rhine river valley—the industrial area of Germany—but there also was a postwar spawning of institutes in the industry-related or applied sciences. As a result of the war, the society recognized the importance of developing the manufacture of raw materials, and with the poverty of the postwar economy, it welcomed the contributions of wealthy industrialists. During the war a coal research institute opened in Mühlheim-Ruhr (1914) and an iron research institute in Düsseldorf (1917). Between 1918 and 1933, two major industry-related institutes were created outside of Berlin for coal (1918) and leather (1922) research. Institutes for textile chemistry (1922) and silicate (1926) research opened in Berlin, as did one for metal research (1922) in Neubabelsberg.[52]

To claim with the East German historian Heike Reishaus-Etzold that during the Weimar period the Kaiser Wilhelm Society was "totally integrated" into the "state monopolistic research organizations" and in particular the "chemistry monopoly" is to underestimate the increasingly influential role that German industry played in founding scientific research institutes during the war and in the immediate postwar period.[53] In some cases it also determined or influenced the research activities of the institute. The industrialists' role in founding new institutes was not a surprising development since university chemists and industrial chemists had already taken part in the founding of, and contributed to the financing of, the Society from its earliest years.

The first industry-related institute for coal research had been conceived of and created during the first half of 1912 soon after the chemistry and physical chemistry institutes had been established. There was lively interest from the Rheinland-Westfalian industrialists to found another, more practical, chemistry institute in western Germany, outside Berlin. This circle of industrialists already had clearly in mind the creation of an institute which would do research on coal with an emphasis on chemical problems. Emil Fischer, a university chemist and one of the spiritual founders of the Society, supported the project and defined the institute's research objectives as transferring the methods of studying mineral coal, and the experience gained from this research, to other combustible materials such as brown coal, peat, or even wood.[54] The research goals of the institute remained the study of different kinds of combustible materials. Unlike the Dahlem institutes, the research was intended to help the coal industry directly or indirectly and to meet the needs of science and practice.

The Silesian coal research institute of the Kaiser Wilhelm Society in Breslau was established in 1918 primarily because of a very large contribution of 3 million marks by Fritz von Friedländer-Fuld, a leader in the coal, iron, and steel industries.[55] Although the original funders intended to undertake basic research in the field of the components and products of coal, by 1923 the Silesian coal and steel industry increasingly influenced the scientific research. In part because the state was not prepared to finance the industry-related institutes, industry took advantage of the economic crisis by offering more financial support and simultaneously increasingly influencing the research directions.[56] By 1923 the coal and steel industry received free licenses for all discoveries at the institute and assumed all patents; by 1936 industry appointed a researcher director who did not meet the Society's qualifications, but who was willing to undertake industrial research.[57]

The institute for iron research in Düsseldorf was founded in 1917 by the "Club of German Iron Works People" (Verein Deutscher Eisenhüttenleute) at an assembly of representatives of the German steel and iron industry. To remain free from the influence of various interest groups, it was incorporated into the circle of Kaiser Wilhelm institutes. Its research program included the study of the metallurgical, chemical, and technological bases for the production of iron and steel. Interestingly, Albert Vögler, general director of United Steel and a senator of the Society, was also an active leader in the association.[58]

The other major industry-related institute for metal research was opened in 1921 in Neubabelsberg under the direction of Emil Heyn. After his death in 1922, the institute moved to Berlin-Dahlem and was administratively part of the Material Testing Office. Just as the coal and iron institutes studied a particular raw material, so too did the institute for metal focus on the study of metallurgy and research on metal.[59]

The leather research institute opened in Dresden under the directorship of Max Bergmann in September 1922, but it had been conceived of as soon as the war ended in 1918. In many ways the institute was a child of the war; it had been recognized by leaders in political and industrial circles that the chief way to rebuild a strong Germany after the war was to generously support scientific research. But more concretely, the Society had been given a contribution of 700,000 marks by the War Leather Company, after the latter had been dissolved in 1918, for the construction of a leather research institute. A council made up of Society members, including Harnack and Glum, and members of the leather industry like Ernst Ammer, a factory owner, was created in 1920 and was responsible for planning and finding a site for the institute. Many different cities in Germany from Mülheim/Ruhr (Westfalia) in the west to Dresden in the southeast (Saxony) competed to undertake the building of the institute. The institute was finally built in Dresden (the first institute to be built outside of Berlin and the Ruhr/

Westfalia area) and supported by the city, the Saxon state, and the Central Association of the German Leather Industry. It studied the material of the leather industry—protein substances and the tanning of animal hide to produce leather—and provided the results to the leather industry and to business.[60]

Two industry-related institutes for textile chemistry and silicate research were also founded in Berlin after the war. Emil Fischer and Fritz Haber advised creating a textile institute because they considered fibrous materials to be one of the most important raw materials, along with coal, created by "human technology." The Kaiser Wilhelm Society agreed to allow a textile institute to be built under its auspices with the condition that it preserve the Society's "essential principle of scientific freedom" and that it receive external financial support. Because of Harnack's reservations, and a host of other problems relating to personnel and the creation of other textile research institutes in Germany, a textile department was first created at the Kaiser Wilhelm Institute for Physical Chemistry in 1919. An independent institute for textile chemistry then opened in 1920 with Reginald Herzog as director.[61]

The silicate research institute opened in one of the textile chemistry institute buildings in 1926 with Wilhelm Eitel, a professor of mineralogy at the university of Königsberg, as director. The institute was founded as a result of interest by the German Glass Technology Society in reestablishing Germany's preeminence in optical glass. During early negotiations in 1925, however, Harnack found the area too narrow and suggested including ceramics and cement research in the program of the institute. The institute became unique because it undertook theoretical research while maintaining the interests of a big industry. As the silicate industry became more automated in the twenties and thirties there was a shift from manual labor to mechanization. Basic research could not find all the answers to practical and technological problems and more input came from industry. The institute's tie to practical work was institutionalized by the creation of an advisory committee for technical science.[62]

The proliferation of industry-related institutes at the Society during and after the war naturally raises the question of why research institutes were created under the auspices of the Kaiser Wilhelm Society rather than in research laboratories within each specific industry from coal, iron, and metal to leather, silicates, and textile chemistry. Although no single reason exists for this phenomenon, it seems that various industries had recognized the success of science organization at the existing Kaiser Wilhelm institutes and saw the Society as an effective body to administer and organize the various disciplines for them. Another reason for this new symbiosis was the growing cross-fertilization between industrial and academic research. The existence and success of this newly forged relationship has been nicely described by L. F. Haber for the case of the chemical industry and its relations to academic chemistry.[63]

In the final analysis it is not surprising that many industry-related institutes were created by the Society. After all, many industrialists had been involved with the Society's founding and sat on its board or senate. Krupp von Bohlen und Halbach was the vice president and Wilhelm von Siemens, Carl Duisberg, and Albert Vögler were all members of the senate. Many managers and industrialists in Germany had been trained in the sciences and were therefore interested in basic research and its application to industry. Vögler is a prime example of this pattern. He was trained as an engineer and took a genuine interest in advancing basic and applied research. Furthermore, it was Emil Fischer, the scientist who was responsible for charting many of the initial research directions for the Society, who recognized the importance of including an institute for coal among the basic research institutes.

That "Very Empyrean of Science"
in Berlin-Dahlem

While the Society created new industry-related institutes in the period before the severe inflation of 1923, the older Berlin-Dahlem institutes were becoming a world center of science. From chemistry, physics, and physical chemistry in Hahn's chemistry institute and Fritz Haber's physical chemistry institute to biology and biochemistry in the institutes for biology, science in Berlin-Dahlem flourished; it had become part of what made Berlin, in the words of Erwin Chargaff, "the very empyrean of science."[64] It was, however, somewhat paradoxical that science should experience this extraordinary period after the lost war, the revolution, and a time of severe financial crisis and inflation in Germany. Somehow much creativity was stimulated in the aftermath of this drama.

Many scientists who worked in Berlin-Dahlem at one of the Kaiser Wilhelm institutes have reminisced about Dahlem in the twenties in order to characterize this period of great creativity. Hans Krebs, who worked in Otto Warburg's laboratory, not only wrote about Dahlem in the late twenties, but also produced a biography of Warburg. Hermann Blashko and Fritz Lippmann, both former students of Otto Meyerhof, wrote sketches for a commemorative volume on biochemistry. David Nachmansohn, a respected biochemist who emigrated to America, also worked in the Meyerhof lab and wrote a book about German-Jewish pioneers in science. Even the young band of American scientists who flocked to these laboratories have discussed the cast of characters in somewhat less glowing terms.[65] All these works by the scientists themselves seem to share the view that much of the success of the period was due to the scientific personalities of the time, and the fact that the Kaiser Wilhelm institutes gave researchers complete freedom to pursue whatever they wished without any teaching obligations. While a great-men-and-their-discoveries view of the history of science tends to simplify the convergence of factors in a period of great scientific activity, there is much support that would help explain this burst of activity through a combination of scientific genius and personality, the institutional and national context, and the developments in the various fields at the time.

Of course, other intellectual areas such as literature and the arts also blossomed; perhaps this was part of the Zeitgeist, with its daring experimentation and modernity. Whether or not insularity existed between the arts and the sciences, the fact remains that both spheres of activity experienced an unusually lively period. While I am not sure how much time was left over after a demanding day in Warburg's laboratory, scientists too might have inhaled the exuberance of the times as they visited the theater or the art galleries or cafés on the Kurfürstendamm. As Laqueur has reminded us, however, "Weimar culture was conceived outside the schools and universities and it never penetrated the academic establishment to any depth."[66] This might be less true of a research establishment like the Kaiser Wilhelm Society, but because the Society was still very young by the Weimar years, most of the scientists there had come from the universities and academia. Indeed, science receives only passing attention in the classic accounts by Gay and Laqueur; there was nothing "specifically German" about the discoveries, adds Laqueur dismissively. Clearly, more work needs to be done on science and Weimar culture (not just on financial support and internationalism) and whether science is of the same fabric as culture. In a lesser known study, Döring has examined the "Weimar circle" and the political affiliations and beliefs of university professors loyal to the constitution in the Weimar Republic.[67]

The example of the practice of biochemistry at the Kaiser Wilhelm institutes is of particular interest. Three pioneers in twentieth-century biochemistry worked at the Kaiser Wilhelm institutes in the 1920s and 1930s, Carl Neuberg, Otto Warburg, and Otto Meyerhof; the latter two of these leaders were Nobel laureates in physiology or medicine; all three scientists were Jewish. All three were also influenced by, or studied with, Emil Fischer. During the early twenties biochemistry was institutionalized at the Kaiser Wilhelm institutes for experimental therapy and biology. As Warburg's and Meyerhof's work became increasingly recognized, they became the heads of independent institutes for cell physiology and medicine, respectively. Carl Neuberg eventually became director of the institute for experimental therapy and biochemistry.

Otto Warburg had the oldest ties to the Kaiser Wilhelm institutes. He had become a scientific member of the institute for biology and head of its chemistry department in 1913, at the age of thirty. As the son of the Berlin physicist Emil Warburg, he had met many well-known scientists from the Berlin community when he was growing up, including Max Planck and Emil Fischer. He completed his doctoral degree in chemistry in 1906 with Fischer at the University of Berlin, and it was Fischer who supported and promoted Warburg's appointment at the Kaiser Wilhelm institute. After receiving his doctorate he studied medicine in Heidelberg and worked under Ludolf von Krehl in the Department of Internal Medicine; he then received his M.D. degree in 1911.[68]

It was at Krehl's clinic that Otto Meyerhof met Warburg. Meyerhof had studied medicine at various universities in Germany in typical peripatetic fashion before receiving his doctorate in 1909 with a specialization in psychiatry. This interest was, in fact, just one of many other interests including philosophy, archeology, and history. Under the influence of Warburg, however, Meyerhof became increasingly interested in cell physiology and began to devote himself more exclusively to biochemistry. In 1912 Meyerhof became a member of the Department of Physiology at the University of Kiel. There his work focused on the energetics of cell processes (now called bioenergetics), a field which used concepts from thermodynamics and energetics to study cell processes. In 1918 Meyerhof began work on the biochemical basis of muscular contraction. It was this work that won him the Nobel Prize in 1922 (awarded in 1923) together with A. V. Hill.[69]

The scientific achievements and discoveries of the Warburg and Meyerhof laboratories were staggering. Several of the major breakthroughs in the Warburg laboratory were the aerobic glycolysis of tumors, the general occurrence of the Pasteur effect, the accurate quantitative measurements of cell respiration and cell glycolysis, and the carbon monoxide inhibition of cell respiration. Meyerhof's laboratory made the essential contributions to the Embden-Meyerhof pathway of glycolysis. Karl Lohmann, who also worked there, discovered adenosine triphosphate (ATP). Equally important was the creation of new methods such as manometry and the tissue slice technique.[70]

Life in the Warburg and Meyerhof laboratories was not easy. Many of the scientists who worked there, such as Hans Krebs and Fritz Lipmann, have depicted long, hard working hours and minimal, if any, salary. A scientist was expected to work six days a week in the laboratory from eight in the morning to six at night. The evening was a time to catch up on the literature and write papers. There were no coffee breaks and lunch was simple and brief.[71] Most scientists who worked in Warburg's laboratory agree about his autocratic rule and idiosyncratic personality, but they seemed to endure it because of his greatness. His students who actually won Nobel Prizes later, however, such as Krebs and Erwin Negelein, may have needed the freedom of another laboratory, free from his rule, to achieve that honor.

Carl Neuberg began his ascent at the Society as a scientific member and head of the chemical department at the institute for experimental therapy when it was headed by August von Wassermann. He became second director in 1922, when the institute was renamed the Kaiser Wilhelm Institute for Experimental Therapy and Biochemistry. After Wassermann's death in 1925, Neuberg became director. His most famous contribution was the discovery of the enzyme carboxylase; his work was a turning point in the history of enzyme chemistry because alcohol fermentation then began to be seen as part of a complex interaction of several enzymes.[72]

In addition to the "Big Three" in biochemistry, pure biology had a galaxy of stars in Dahlem. Working primarily at the Kaiser Wilhelm Institute for Biology, Carl Correns, Hans Spemann, Richard Goldschmidt, and Max Hartmann made significant contributions to the fields of genetics, developmental mechanics, and protozoology. It was also during the Weimar period that an institute for breeding research under the directorship of Erwin Baur was founded, as was one for anthropology, human genetics and eugenics headed by Emil Fischer. Important work in biology took place at the genetics department (headed by the Russian N. Timoféeff-Ressovsky) of the Kaiser Wilhelm Institute for Brain Research as well. The German work in genetics had found its major institutional home at the biology institute and was characterized by studies of cytoplasmic inheritance rather than classical Mendelian genetics, which was flourishing in America, primarily at the Morgan laboratory.[73]

Finally, the areas of physical chemistry, chemistry, and physics were also enjoying a lively and vibrant period. Fritz Haber, Herbert Freundlich, and Michael Polanyi worked at the institute for physical chemistry; Otto Hahn and Lise Meitner enlarged our understanding of the chemical elements at the institute for chemistry; Max von Laue and Albert Einstein did theoretical work in a yet to be built institute for physics. In the aftermath of his success with ammonia synthesis and the controversy surrounding his work in gas warfare during World War I, Haber worked on other areas in physical chemistry which were at the intersection of theory and application. During this period his published papers showed interest in the architecture of metals, the clinging of materials to solid surfaces, the burning of gases, chain reactions, and the role of light and heat for chemical reactions. By the end of the twenties his institute had produced over 700 publications in scientific journals.[74]

Another postwar project for which Haber gained notoriety was his search for gold in the sea. After the war, the Allies had demanded $33 billion in reparations from Germany to be paid over 120 years. Haber predicted this would require about 50,000 tons of gold. Svante Arrhenius, the Swedish chemist, had once suggested to Haber that gold existed in the ocean and that it might be possible to extract large amounts. Despite doubts from colleagues, Haber went ahead with the project, which in some ways resembled his previous effort to extract wealth from the air; perhaps he could also extract wealth from the sea. Haber mobilized some help from industry, and laboratories were set up in ships. He also convinced some students and one senior colleague (J. Jaenicke) of the merit of the project, and they too went along. In the end, however, it was a failure because the estimates of gold content had been too high.[75]

Haber had become a central figure in this Berlin community of scientists. His presence at the biweekly colloquium was such an attraction that people would telephone to make sure he was coming. His quick grasp of difficult and complex scientific material became a legend. In his memorial lecture J. E. Coates wrote that "in the Colloquium Haber was at his best.

Here came out one of his most brilliant qualities, the capacity to grasp
quickly the essentials of a subject not his own, to perceive their true bear-
ings beyond the details, to discover errors, to indicate the lines of advance."[76]
Chargaff thought he had a "marvellously Socratic skill of drawing the best
out of speaker and audience."[77] It was no wonder that Chargaff characterized Berlin as that "empyrean of science."

The Weimar years saw a transformation in the relationship between the state
and scientific institutions. With the postwar inflation and resulting "poverty" of German science, sources of support became increasingly scarce, but
the Emergency Association of German Science was created to combat this
hardship. There was a general tension between the need for academic
autonomy on the one hand and the need for governmental and industrial
support on the other. In the case of the Kaiser Wilhelm Society, this meant
a shift from its original relatively independent status vis-à-vis the government to financial dependence and tensions. Throughout the twenties the
Society sought to gain financial support while maintaining its principle of
self-government. An autocratic Prussian Education Minister, Carl-Heinrich
Becker, tried to extend his reforms of education to the realm of research
and science. There was even the threat that he might become president of
the Society and politicize it, but instead the Society upheld its autonomy
and elected a scientist, Max Planck.

The Weimar years were also a period of growth and expansion for the
Society. New forms were created, such as the scientific council and Harnack
House, to meet new needs. From the initial four institutes in 1914 it had
expanded to about thirty by the early thirties, in spite of the inflation and
financial crisis. This included a host of industry-related institutes created
primarily in the industrial region of Germany. The success of its earlier pure
science research institutes in Dahlem had impressed the industries enough
to seek out the Kaiser Wilhelm Society to organize and maintain the institutes in a trustee relationship. The second half of the twenties witnessed a
remarkably lively and vibrant period for science in Berlin-Dahlem, and it
was there that many of its scientists worked and made the discoveries that
had given the Society its prestige and fame by the time of the Third Reich;
many of these scientists were Jewish. Success was not, however, always the
case for other aspects of the scientific enterprise. For example, at the level
of the state–Society relationship, Friedrich Glum, complained in 1936 that
it was "not always easy to maintain the self-governing character of the
Society" during the Weimar period.[78] The rest of this book will examine
the extent to which the Society upheld its principle of self-government during
the Third Reich, retained high-caliber scientists, and maintained the quality
and integrity of its scientific research.

II

NATIONAL SOCIALISM

3

From Accommodation
to Passive Opposition
1933–35

Writing to Otto Hahn, who was traveling in America during the first months of the National Socialist regime, Lise Meitner, his friend and colleague at the Kaiser Wilhelm Institute for Chemistry, characterized the new Germany as "totally under the spell of the political revolution." In a letter written on the day of the Reichstag's opening celebration in Potsdam, she reported that "last week [scientists] received instructions" from the Society's leaders "to raise the swastika flag next to the black-white-red one" [From the Empire]. Moreover, she added, the Society "paid for the flag."[1]

The juxtaposition of the flag imagery and the observation that Germany was "under the spell of a political revolution" aptly capture the omnipresence of the new totalitarian regime. But the external symbols and atmosphere of those spring months in 1933 were only a few manifestations of the changes occurring in German society at the time. There were a number of other critical features of the new Germany that had an impact on major institutions of learning and research. The process through which the National Socialists attempted to gain total control is called *Gleichschaltung*, which literally means "putting into the same gear or line"; it was the attempt to place all of life on one track. For scientific and educational institutions, *Gleichschaltung* was the process by which the new regime attempted to take control by aligning them with the ideals and practice of National Socialism.[2] For the National Socialists, it meant the use of "legal" means to transform and align institutions into one unified Reich.

The process of *Gleichschaltung* and the concomitant transformations took place rapidly, efficiently, and thoroughly at the universities, institutes of technology (*Technische Hochschulen*), and even at the prestigious Prussian Academy of Sciences. Although similarities exist, there was a different pattern of stimuli and response at the Kaiser Wilhelm Society. In many respects, it retained more professional autonomy well into the Third Reich.[3]

The effect of the political revolution on the Society as a whole—on the level of its administration, its institutes, and its scientists during the National Socialists' first year of power—was a dramatic one. There were a number of measures enforced at the Kaiser Wilhelm Society by the party and state. For the Society, and for science in general, the most dramatic impact of the new Nazi legislation was the implementation and the consequences of the Law for the Reestablishment of the Career Civil Service (Das Gesetz zur Wiederherstellung des Berufsbeamtentums). The aim of this law was to purge Germany of Jews, communists, and others perceived as politically undesirable or unreliable in the civil service. It was stage one of the *Gleichschaltung* process and an instrument for its implementation. A crucial point to recall here, however, is that this law was promulgated as part of a political agenda and was *not* directed specifically at *scientists*. When Max Planck, the president of the Society, appealed to Adolf Hitler on behalf of able Jewish scientists, Hitler singlemindedly replied: "Our national policies will not be revoked or modified, even for scientists. If the dismissal of Jewish scientists means the annihilation of contemporary German science, then we shall do without science for a few years!"[4] At least during the early years no distinction was made between scientists and other people; scientists were not immune to dismissals on political grounds.

The events of the year 1933 at the Kaiser Wilhelm Society tend to radiate out of one or another aspect of the dismissal policy—its dissemination, the Society's reaction and response, and the consolidation process, in which follow-up measures were implemented. These processes reflect the characteristic control and surveillance of life in the Third Reich. Other transformations that occurred as a result of National Socialist policies include the reduction of the senate, the main decision-making organ of the Society. The public stance of Planck and the Society toward National Socialism is reflected in the annual meeting held in the spring.

The Haber Memorial Ceremony of 1935, where Fritz Haber, who had died one year earlier, an exile in Switzerland, was memorialized for his contributions to German science and chemistry has sometimes been characterized as the only act of resistance by scientists during the Third Reich.[5] I prefer to analyze it as an act of passive opposition and, given new evidence, we can better understand the *intentions* of the ceremony. Although not intended as an act of resistance, the National Socialists perceived it as a provocation against the national state but still allowed it to be held. By honoring a Jewish scientist who emigrated because of the dismissal policies, the Kaiser Wilhelm Society performed an act of passive opposition—passive because it was not a planned act of resistance against the National Socialists, but rather an honoring of a Jewish scientist who had made extraordinary contributions to German science in times of war and peace.

Forced Transformations

During the spring months of 1933, the Kaiser Wilhelm Society experienced the first stage of *Gleichschaltung*: the implementation of the Law for the Reestablishment of the Career Civil Service. The law, couched in euphemistic language, was enacted on 7 April 1933 in order to "reestablish a national career civil service and to simplify the administration" by firing civil servants who did not meet certain requirements. The crux of the law was summarized in paragraph 3—what came to be known as the "Aryan Paragraph"—which stated that civil servants who were not of "Aryan descent" were to be "retired." This did not apply to civil servants who had served before 1 August 1914 or who had fought in World War I or whose father or son had died in the war. The law explicitly stated that other exceptions could be made by the Reich Minister of the Interior. Policy toward politically undesirable people was described in paragraph 4, which stated that civil servants who could not show that they would defend the "national state" through their previous political activity could also be fired.[6] There were several major revisions in the months following which cleared up ambiguities and made the law more general to include workers and employees.

The law could be applied to employees working at institutes of the Society receiving more than 50 percent of their funding from the state. This 7 April decree coincided with the universities' spring vacation and with Max Planck's vacation. Therefore, Friedrich Glum, the powerful general director of the Society (and a trained lawyer), and his staff in the administration of the Kaiser Wilhelm Society, had to act in Planck's absence. The decree reached the institutes quickly: Ludolf von Krehl from the Heidelberg medical institute reported by 7 April that the Jews in his institute would have to leave.[7] Ernst Telschow and Major Lukas von Cranach reported to Planck on the new developments but assured him there was no need to shorten his vacation and come back, although many of the scientists and professors were worried, including Max von Laue, who urged him to return.[8] Planck therefore did not perceive the situation as acute and did not immediately return from his vacation in Sicily. Planck had often advised worried professors to take a vacation in Italy: When "you return," he said, "all the troubles will be gone."[9] After Planck's return from Italy, however, the troubles had magnified and he was criticized for contributing to the loss of some scientists during the first months of the consolidation of power. Hans Kopfermann, a member of Haber's institute, writing to Niels Bohr a few weeks after the passage of the Civil Service Law, attributed Haber's resignation and those of his colleagues Herbert Freundlich and Michael Polanyi in part to Planck's absence and the lack of leadership at the Kaiser Wilhelm Society.[10]

The Education Ministry considered the "Jewish question" to be "acute" at the Kaiser Wilhelm Society. During the first months it monitored Fritz Haber's Institute for Physical Chemistry and Electrochemistry, where more than a quarter of the personnel was Jewish, more closely than any other institutes.[11] Haber's institute had become a magnet for young physical chemists and enjoyed an international reputation. However, according to Glum, it had an abnormally large number of Jews, in part because the universities had refused to employ Jewish chemists and they were therefore attracted to the institute.[12] It had also been transformed during World War I into a center for gas warfare, from which Fritz Haber orchestrated the German effort and emerged as a heralded patriot.

A second important characteristic of the Haber institute was its financial and administrative relation to the state. Although initially funded and created by the Koppel Foundation with the stipulation that Haber be appointed director, his position was tied to the Prussian government's budget, as were six other institute directorships. His salary, therefore, was paid through the Prussian Ministry, which had veto rights concerning his appointment, although up until the National Socialist period it was never used.

The Ministry informed the Society that there was a possibility of keeping leading scholars if it took immediate steps, but it required that Haber's institute change the composition of its personnel. If this change did not occur immediately, the minister threatened, the "greatest danger" existed not only for the Haber institute but for the whole Society.[13] Haber could not tolerate this intended "forced transformation"[14] of his institute because it required dismissing his closest collaborators and assistants, nor could he tolerate the resignations of Freundlich and Polanyi; therefore he resigned in a now well-known letter of 30 April 1933 to the Minister of Science, Art, and Education, Bernhard Rust:

> My decision to request dismissal is a consequence of the opposing tradition with regard to research in which I have lived until now, and to the changed views which you and your ministry represent as bearers of the present great national movement. My tradition requires that I select the staff for a scientific post based only on their qualifications and character without asking about race. You cannot expect that a sixty-five year old man will change this way of thinking which has guided him for thirty-nine years of university-life.[15]

Haber's "sensational resignation"[16] created fury in the Ministry and drew alarmed attention to the famous institute from abroad. In some ways this was a bold and courageous act by a German patriot with integrity who, himself a Jew, could not in good conscience dismiss fellow Jews. But in some ways Haber simultaneously fell into the hands of the government by opening the way for the new regime to occupy an empty institute.

Other Jewish institute directors responded in different ways to the dismissal policy. Richard Goldschmidt, codirector of the institute for biology, pointed out to Glum that he himself could be dismissed according to the law. Unlike Haber, Goldschmidt actually dismissed Jewish personnel at his institute.[17] Otto Meyerhof, director at the institute for medical research in Heidelberg, wrote one of the few critical letters to Glum, reminding the general director of the "moral duty" one had to employees who had served the Society for many years. He admitted that the Society and its scientists could not change the law, but he thought the utmost should be done to "modify the brutality" that lay in the ruthless application of the law.[18]

Within a few weeks, Glum, as acting president, sent all the directors of the Kaiser Wilhelm institutes a circular informing them of the Ministry of Interior's orders: the law is to be applied to Kaiser Wilhelm institutes receiving more that half of their financial support from public funding. In particular, civil servants who were not of "Aryan" descent were to be "retired." Civil servants who had shown through their earlier political activity that they could not guarantee they would unreservedly join the national state should be dismissed together with communists, stated the circular. The law also applied to employees and workers. Because the Society's industry institutes were privately supported, they were not required to implement the law. Institute directors received a questionnaire designed by the administration of the Kaiser Wilhelm Society and modeled after the questionnaires from the Ministry, which included questions on the scientists' position at the institute, their country of citizenship, and finally the key question on race, where information was solicited about the heritage of all four grandparents.[19] But this form, created by the Kaiser Wilhelm Society itself, failed to include questions on the political activities of the scientists, a factor that prolonged the process of implementing the law well into the fall months of 1933 and continued to cause problems into 1934 as the general *Gleichschaltung* process in all of Germany reached its completion.

Soon after his return from Italy Planck responded to the measures of the new National Socialist state by calling a meeting of all the Berlin institute directors to discuss the relationship of the Kaiser Wilhelm Society to the national state and the intended changes expected in the structure of the Society. Aware of the presence of a member of the Ministry (Richard Donnevert) and of sympathizers to the regime, Planck claimed the Society had "placed itself at the disposal of the national government" and that Planck or Glum had contacted figures from the government such as Wilhelm Frick, Bernhard Rust, and E. Milch. The government looks upon the Kaiser Wilhelm Society benevolently, he reported, and no special wishes have been expressed. The government demands only "a transformation and reduction of the senate, but no changes were demanded at the leadership level."[20]

At this meeting on the position of the Society under the new regime there seemed to have been a split between Haber, Richard Goldschmidt, and Carl Neuberg, on the one hand, and sympathizers of the regime such as Wilhelm Eitel, Erwin Baur, and Eugen Fischer, on the other.[21] The end result was that the Society would not be transformed into a Reich institute, but rather its "complete independence" would be preserved "under the supervision of the Reich." In order to guarantee the "unity of the Society" all questions usually considered by the directors would have to be considered by the presidial office. At this point the Ministry did not have special plans for the Society, but it ominously intimated that after return to normalcy it might turn to the Society with great interest.[22]

These measures demonstrated the differentiated transformations occurring at the Society. On the one hand, it was not forced to introduce into its statutes and structure a number of changes such as the leadership principle; on the other hand, there was an attempted restructuring of responsibility at the top whereby the administration was to be answerable to questions traditionally handled by institute directors. This was a somewhat modified version of the "leadership principle" combined with the National Socialist attempt at unification, yet there is no evidence that this intended transformation took place.

Wilhelm Eitel, an enthusiastic supporter of the new regime, thought the Kaiser Wilhelm Society should place itself at the disposal of the national government in questions of defense, and he wrote a long memorandum on a new orientation supporting this stance. It is not possible, he wrote, to keep the Kaiser Wilhelm Society in its present form as part of the "national state" because of the disunity in the institutes and the unclear legal position of the staff. He called for a "reorganization of the administration, the senate and, eventually, the whole structure of the Society" in order to make it a "German national affair." He wanted the institutes to be reorganized in order to "serve the German people."[23]

After the war, Eitel characterized his attraction to the "'Programm' of the National-Socialist Party" and especially its role for the Kaiser Wilhelm Society:

> I was confirmed in this conception by the apparent perplexity and helplessness in which the scientific circles of our Dahlem center of Research Institutes of the Kaiser Wilhelm Gesellschaft were living in those days. Nobody had a clear understanding [sic] what could happen in the near future. The danger of disorder if the SA [Sturmabteilung, Storm Troopers] would invade our Institutes and offend our numerous Hebrew colleagues and co-workers was growing from week to week. . . . The official Kaiser Wilhelm Gesellschaft did nothing for those people, and nobody had contact with the new regime, in order to ask for protection against coming troubles. . . .
>
> Since neither the president of KWG (Professor Dr. Max Planck), nor the General Director (Dr. Friedrich Glum) were present in those critical days in Berlin (they stayed in Italy), I took the risk of personally recommending to the new Minister of Interior Dr. Fricke, [sic] a special protection for maintenance of order in the Dahlem Institutes. In the presence of two of my co-workers as witnesses I answered the Minister's question as to whether there had been any financial irregularities in the Kaiser Wilhelm Gesellschaft, decidedly in the negative. Really, in the following months we had absolute order and no troubles in Dahlem. As long as Dr. Fricke protected us, there was no persecution, and no disorder. . . . Unfortunately, some months later, the new Minister for Science and Education, Dr. Rust, changed the policy of the Government. He changed the Senate of the Kaiser Wilhelm Gesellschaft and organized his "leadership" of Scientific Research in Germany.[24]

The Kaiser Wilhelm Society was spared some of the measures implemented at other institutions enacted to put them in line with National

Socialist ideology and goals. For example, the universities, academies, and the Emergency Association for German Science were severely affected by the implementation of the Civil Service Law, the introduction of the leadership principle, and a change in the leadership whereby the personnel was replaced by party members. In educational institutions coordination included a redirection of education along racial and Nazi ideological lines.[25]

On 16 May 1933 at 11 a.m. Planck gained his audience with Adolf Hitler to discuss the Haber affair and the future of the Kaiser Wilhelm Society. The dating of the celebrated meeting is particularly important because it came soon after the Haber resignation, the directors' meeting, and the measures taken against the Society by the National Socialists.[26] Except for Planck's (1947) own short reminiscence of this meeting, and some hearsay, little is known about what happened. Planck seems to have initiated the contact after Hitler sent him birthday greetings on the occasion of his seventy-fifth birthday. Planck thanked Hitler for his birthday wishes and used the opportunity to request a meeting in order to "report to" Hitler on the "present position and on the future plans of the Society." As president of the Kaiser Wilhelm Society, he wished, he claimed, to "place scientific research . . . at the service of the fatherland" and he hoped to find the support and protection of the Reich government.[27]

At the meeting Planck used the opportunity to support his colleague Fritz Haber, to which Hitler replied he had nothing against Jews, but "Jews are all communists and they are the enemy I am fighting against." Planck pointed out that one must make a distinction among Jews. Hitler responded: "A Jew is a Jew; all Jews hang together like burrs. Whoever is a Jew gathers other Jews around him" (a veiled reference, perhaps, to the high number of Jews in Haber's institute). Finally, in his effort to save German science, Planck added characteristically: "It is self-destruction to force valuable Jews to emigrate because we need them for our science. These Jewish emigrés will, above all, benefit countries abroad."[28] Planck's words, however, fell on deaf ears.

Rifle at Rest

Despite his failed attempt at reasonable negotiations, Planck sent Adolf Hitler a telegram from the twenty-second annual meeting of the Kaiser Wilhelm Society at Harnack House on 23 May 1933 with best wishes and a pledge that "German science is also ready to collaborate in the restoration of the new national state."[29] At the Society's first major public event after the seizure of power, senators, scientific members, and government officials gathered for a social and business meeting to report on the activities of the Society over the year, to hear lectures by scientific members, to socialize, and specifically to change the statute about the election and number of members in the senate. There was to be an "agreed upon" transformation and reduction in the senate; Planck's public response, reflected at this meeting, was to cooperate with the new regime. He announced that no one in Germany could be allowed to "stand aside 'rifle at rest.'" He declared that there was only one watchword: "The consolidation of available forces for an active contribution to construct our fatherland."[30]

But behind this rhetoric, plans had been made for the reduction of the senate through negotiations with Hans Pfundtner, the Secretary of State at the Ministry of the Interior. They were formally announced at the meeting.[31] Such a measure would allow more control by the government and the opportunity to install its own people, yet three Jewish senators were still allowed to stay. The senate was reduced from the previous forty-four members to thirty-two. Fourteen members were elected from and by the Society at the annual meeting, seven each were to be named from the Reich and Prussian government, respectively; the three chairmen of the scientific council and the general director belonged to the senate.

The whole senate resigned and simultaneously the new senate selection process was introduced into the statutes of the Society. The "politically tainted" and as many "non-Aryans" as possible would be "removed." Through negotiations with the Ministry, the Society was allowed to retain three non-"Aryan" senators who were long-time members and had made major contributions. Because the Society was dependent on funding from industry to maintain its institutes, the three members—Franz von Mendelssohn, Paul Schottländer, and Alfred Merton—were allowed to stay.[32] The Ministry did not, of course, appoint these Jewish members of the senate but allowed the Society to include them among their fourteen elected members.

Most of the fourteen senators elected by the Society were reelected. One of the Society's choices, Walter Darré (Agricultural Ministry), was newly elected and everybody else was renewed. Three senators from this last category who had been selected earlier by the government's votes were transferred into this category, and two of the Jews—Schottländer and Merton—were renewed by the Society. The biggest turnover came from the senators named by the government. Of the fourteen members named by the Reich government and the Prussian state, three were renewed and eleven were newly elected. Most, if not all, were party members or were trusted by the party, or they were industrialists such as Fritz Thyssen.

Planck has sometimes been criticized for not taking a more active stand against the National Socialists during the Third Reich. In evaluating this public meeting of 23 May 1933 one could turn around Planck's phrase and claim that Planck stood with his "rifle at rest" rather than actively resisting the new measures of the new regime. I would argue, however, that after he saw the futility of negotiating with Hitler, it made more sense for him to outwardly cooperate and to work behind the scenes on behalf of German science and scientists by using the exception clauses and negotiating with the various ministries rather than openly resisting. Furthermore, this behavior is hardly unique to Planck; it characterized the apolitical behavior of many university leaders and professors in general. These outward signs of cooperation cannot be interpreted as condonement of, and complicity with, the National Socialist policies at this stage of the Third Reich.

A Breeding Ground for Jewish Exploiters, Oppressors, and Marxists?

Meanwhile, the Society faced other attacks and measures designed to help carry through the National Socialist program and to identify undesirable people. Just days before the annual meeting, Ewald Reche, a member of the National Socialist Factory Workers' Association (Nationalsozialistische Betriebszellen Organisation, NSBO)—one of the many National Socialist organizations used for surveillance and control of public life—had written a denunciatory piece about the Dahlem Kaiser Wilhelm institutes. He branded the institutes a breeding ground for Jewish exploiters, oppressors, and Marxists. He accused the Society of employing primarily Jews as institute directors and he further showed that these Jewish directors exploited assistants by using their results without acknowledging them. The "German scientist," he concluded, has been degraded to a "slave of this vampire." Reche focused on Reginald Herzog's Institute for Textile Chemistry, where he created a "factory cell"—three German assistants who reported on the activities of the institute to the National Socialists. According to Reche, Herzog cheated a German assistant out of the financial rewards of the assistant's discovery. Therefore, concluded Reche, a "German institute" in such a form must disappear. Such institutes are only "parasites" on the German body politic, "vampires at the highest cultural centers," he continued.[33] This kind of antisemitic diatribe was common among National Socialist groups like the NSBO.

The Consolidation Process

By the summer, and some weeks after the annual meeting, Planck sent a report on the implementation of the Civil Service Law to the Ministry of the Interior, in which he ranked the personnel slated for dismissal into three groups: (1) those to be unequivocally dismissed; this included nineteen employees from eight different institutes, primarily scientific or technical assistants and secretaries; (2) questionable cases, which included three employees; and (3) "cases of hardship." The latter were five employees from four institutes and included cases such as the relatives of the famous scientists Heinrich Hertz and Emil Du Bois-Reymond.[34] Planck requested an exception from the Minister for the last two groups in applying the dismissal law. The exception clauses were used by the leaders of the Society as a strategy for working around the laws.

From this grouping and from Planck's request, it is evident that the Society agreed to dismiss nineteen out of twenty-seven assistants. This list did not include any directors, scientific members, or professors with the exception of Professor Karl Weissenberg from the Kaiser Wilhelm Institute for Physics, who was leaving on 30 September with the termination of his contract. In these early stages, then, no directors were given notice. Some director positions, however, were vulnerable since they were directly tied to the Prussian state budget. For these cases Planck simultaneously wrote to the Prussian Minister of Science enclosing five questionnaires filled out by the directors Erwin Baur, Franz Fischer, Richard Goldschmidt, Reginald Herzog, and Friedrich Körber. No questionnaire was enclosed for Fritz Haber because he had resigned; nor was any information provided for the three newly vacant director positions. In the case of Richard Goldschmidt, Planck tried to use the exemption clauses for civil servants and, in his effort to maintain the quality of German science, added that Goldschmidt was highly regarded and enjoyed an international reputation in the field of genetics, in which he had made pioneering contributions.[35] By the end of July, Planck had to inform several institute directors that his efforts to obtain an exception for special cases from the Reich Minister of the Interior had failed.[36]

By mid-September Glum wrote to about ten institutes as a result of pressure from the Ministry informing them that he was required to write a report to the Ministry of the Interior on the implementation of the dismissal law. The Kaiser Wilhelm Society, he added, did not want to see further employment of dismissed personnel even if they were paid with foundation funds. Holders of private fellowships, especially Rockefeller Fellows, were allowed to work until the fellowship ran out.[37] Soon after, the chairman of the Berlin-Dahlem National Socialist Factory Organization ordered a conference with institute directors and their respective informants from the organizations. Only institutes with more than 50 percent public funding were required to undergo this process and a meeting was arranged on short notice at Harnack House with Glum, Lukas von Cranach, and Franz Arndt from the administration, the institute directors, Eitel, Hahn, Hartmann, Herzog, and Walther Horn, and the representatives from the factory organizations.[38]

The purpose of the meeting was to determine whether the dismissal policy was thoroughly implemented and to review whether other personnel working in the institutes ought to be dismissed. What emerged instead was that the administration had addressed the "Aryan question" but had neglected to use the ministries' questionnaires to identify the political unreliables. Therefore, the emphasis of the meeting was on ferreting out the political unreliables from each institute. The chairman of the National Socialist Factory Organization, Hecker, argued that these people could be identified only by his informants associated with each institute, not by the institute directors.[39] These informants were spies planted in many public institutions and were designed to be the "eyes" of the National Socialists to find people who they perceived as undesirable. Once the eyes found information, it was passed on to the "head" of the organization. Once found they would be replaced with National Socialists.[40]

The personnel change planned for the Kaiser Wilhelm Society was established after the meeting. Thirteen members of seven different institutes were entered onto a list of "civil servants" and "employees" who must be "removed" in order "to safeguard the goals of the National Socialists."[41] In addition, they found that three members of the administration, including Glum, who had been assiduously implementing the law, were considered politically unreliable. By far the most cases—six—came from the Kaiser Wilhelm Institute for Physical Chemistry. Although most of the institute personnel on the lists were mechanics or staff members, the directors of two institutes were also included—Carl Neuberg (Kaiser Wilhelm Institute for Biochemistry) and Reginald Herzog (Kaiser Wilhelm Institute for Textile Chemistry).

The case of the eminent biochemist Carl Neuberg is of particular interest. Not only was he Jewish, but he was also accused of insulting Hitler, stating that he conducted foreign policy "like a bull in a china shop."[42] This statement was attributed to him by the informant at the institute, Kurt Delatrée-Wegner, who Neuberg in turn designated a psychopath. Despite his eminence as a biochemist and his eligibility for exemption under the exception clauses, this display of political criticism played a role in Neuberg's dismissal in 1934.

That Glum supported Neuberg may have caused him, Cranach, and Arndt to be added to the politically unreliable list. The cases of the administrators dragged on into 1934 when Giersch, a former employee of Harnack House and the 1934 chairman (Hecker's successor) of the National Socialist Factory Organization, wrote threatening denunciations against the administrators and called for their dismissals. At least until 1934, Glum was still writing statements denying an alleged "democratic/pacifist attitude before the National Socialist revolution." Glum was also accused of writing a subversive book called *The Secret Germany*.[43]

After the Harnack House Meeting, Glum reported to the Reich Minister of the Interior, Dr. Rudolf Buttmann, on the implementation of the non-"Aryan" clause of the dismissal law at the administration and the institutes of the Kaiser Wilhelm Society. His statistics were based primarily on institutes receiving more than 50 percent public funding. According to his figures, out of 1,007 personnel, 54, or 5.09 percent, were non-"Aryan."[44] These figures do not, apparently, include the political unreliable cases. Of the 54 non-"Aryans", 12 alone came from the Haber institute, for almost a quarter of the whole institute was Jewish. It is not easy, however, to determine the exact number and names of the non-"Aryans" actually dismissed, for the various statistics and figures generated often do not agree. For example, I have found a total of 19 scientists from Haber's physical chemistry institute who actually emigrated, which would suggest more than 12 were dismissed.

Glum sent a copy of these figures to the Minister of the Interior and to Albert Vögler, the industrialist and long-time senator of the Society, who later became president. The industrialists and industry protected the Society by serving as buffers and intermediaries in its relation and dealings with the National Socialists and the government. As a result of Vögler's important meeting with Minister Frick on science and research policy in the new state (see Chapter 4), he had an opportunity to broach the "Aryan question" with ministry officials. Vögler argued it was necessary to create exceptions for outstanding scientists and pointed out that countries abroad were getting the best scientists because of a strict application of the "Aryan paragraph"; this was disadvantageous for German science.[45] This was a frequently used argument in negotiations that seemed to impress the National Socialists.

Other interventions came from Max Planck, who quietly supported prominent institute directors and, in special cases, assistants. The director positions in the Prussian state's budget included two Jews—Richard Goldschmidt, the second director of the Kaiser Wilhelm Institute for Biology, and Reginald Herzog, director of the Kaiser Wilhelm Institute for Textile Chemistry. Herzog, the less well known of the two, was dismissed without, as far as the evidence shows, a fight from Planck. Planck fought to keep Goldschmidt through the exemption clause for civil servants appointed before World War I, and simultaneously praised Goldschmidt's achievements and prestige abroad: "Professor Goldschmidt is a personality with much scientific prestige and international reputation who has made pioneering studies in his field of heredity."[46] Planck also wrote to the Reich Minister of the Interior on behalf of Max Bergmann, director of the institute for leather research in Dresden, asking him not to dismiss Bergmann from his position. Planck considered Bergmann to be a world-renowned protein chemist who was irreplaceable, and he therefore urged the minister to use the exception clauses in the law whereby regular employees hired before 1914 were exempt. By July Bergmann had been "retired" by the Saxon government effective 1 October 1933.[47]

There are two cases of Planck assiduously using the exception clauses to protect and retain lower level personnel at the institutes who were relatives of famous scientists: Mathilde Hertz was an assistant at the Kaiser Wilhelm Institute for Biology and daughter of the famous physicist Heinrich Hertz; and Fanny Du Bois-Reymond was a gardener at the institute for breeding research and the granddaughter of the famous physiologist Emil Du Bois-Reymond. Both women had been listed as "cases of hardship" in Planck's early report to the Ministry, and since that time, he persistently served as their advocate appealing either to their scientific lineage or to ways in which they were exempt from the dismissal law.

In July 1933, Planck proudly "Aryanized" Mathilde Hertz in a letter to the Minister of the Interior where he pointed out that Hertz's great-grandparents were baptized Protestants. He acknowledged that her grandfather Gustav Hertz was Jewish (baptized as a Protestant) but he had been a member of the church executive board in Hamburg. Planck was "especially pleased" to be able to allow Hertz to continue her work in this way (i.e., by Aryanizing her) because a "dismissal of the daughter of the famous physicist would cause, undoubtedly, a very unfavorable impression at home and abroad."[48] The process continued, however, and by the fall, Hertz had undergone a "genealogical check" by the race department at the Ministry of the Interior and the expert report, based on Hertz's genealogical table, found her to be a "non-Aryan."[49] Despite this foreboding event, Planck continued to find various clauses in the law which would allow her to stay. He also argued that she was doing animal psychology experiments in an institute created for this purpose; therefore, he thought that she should be allowed to continue her work using a revised decree. By 3 January 1934, the minister allowed her to work by revising the law to apply to her case.[50] She emigrated to Cambridge, England, in 1935.

The case of Fanny Du Bois-Reymond developed in a similar way, but the outcome was different. As early as May 1933, Erwin Baur, director of the institute for breeding research, had pleaded for Du Bois-Reymond's retention. On 21 March 1934, the Reich Minister found her to be "non-Aryan." B. Husfeld, Baur's successor, dismissed her days later. Du Bois-Reymond wrote a farewell letter to Glum describing her attempt at "outer calm" and how hard it would be for her to leave the "community" at the Society; even in her modest position she too "breathed the air" of the great scientific tradition of her family; she did not understand how she would exist outside of the community. She hoped Glum would be able to "keep the tradition of the KWG nice and clean in the Third Reich," and she signed the letter with a "Heil Hitler!"[51]

Jewish Scientists Who Stayed or Delayed Departure

Despite the exodus of many talented Jewish scientists as a result of the discriminatory legislation, there were a few cases of Jewish scientists who either stayed during the entire period of the Third Reich or who, protected by various circumstances, could or did delay departure until about 1938 or the outbreak of war. The only Jewish scientific member of the Society I know of who stayed and worked at a Kaiser Wilhelm institute for the entire Third Reich period is Otto Warburg, the Nobel Prize–winning biochemist and director of the Kaiser Wilhelm Institute for Cell Physiology. There has been speculation and rumors among scientists, scholars, and the public as to why he was able or allowed to stay in spite of his Jewish heritage. One explanation that has gained currency is that he had connections in the Reichswehr and that Hitler, afraid of getting cancer, thought Warburg was on to a cure.[52] These explanations may very well be true, but there are a few other reasons grounded more firmly in the documents: It appears as though Warburg was immune to the dismissal law during the first year of purges because his institute was built by the Rockefeller Foundation and supported primarily by the Gradenwitz Fund.[53]

As events progressed in the Third Reich there were, indeed, inquiries from the Ministry as to why Warburg was still at his institute. By the fall of

1937 Telschow wrote in response to a circular requiring a list of Jewish members from Rudolf Mentzel, by then head of the office for science in the Reich Ministry for Science, Education, and People's Education (Reichserziehungsministerium, REM), listing two Jewish institute directors: Warburg and Otto Meyerhof. The reasons, Telschow explained vaguely, these scientists were not dismissed had been reported to the Ministry in 1933 and there had been no objection then.[54] Finally, by 1941, Warburg was given notice by the Kaiser Wilhelm Society. Mentzel wrote to the general director of the Society ordering him to dismiss Warburg because of his part non-"Aryan" blood. Mentzel envisioned occupying the institute for the use of the Reich doctor, Kurt Blome. In order to help preserve the quality of German science, one of the members of the board of directors of the Kaiser Wilhelm Institute for Cell Physiology, the industrialist W. Schoeller, turned to the high-ranking Reich leader Philipp Bouhler to "apply for Professor Warburg's 'Aryanization.'"[55] Warburg's later testimony almost matches the contemporary account:

> The Kaiser Wilhelm Institut for Cell Physiology, whose director I was since it was founded, was built, equipped, and partly maintained with funds from the Rockefeller Foundation. Because of this I was able to keep my position until 1941 although I am half-Jewish.
>
> I was dismissed by the Kaiser Wilhelm Gesellschaft in 1941. The head of the Reich Chancellery, Philipp Bouhler heard about this dismissal and ordered his chief of staff Viktor Brack to appeal my case.
>
> In a few weeks Viktor Brack achieved the withdrawal of my dismissal and thereby probably saved my life. The world-famous medical research institute was used for purely peaceful purposes.
>
> "I did this," Brack said to me on 21 June 1941, "not for you, nor for Germany, but for the world."[56]

By 1941 many of the officials around Hitler had begun to realize the importance of science for the war effort, but this was unusual because Warburg's institute and the science done there were not used for the war effort. Also astonishing is the intervention of Bouhler and Brack, the two key figures in the T 4 euthanasia action in which over 50,000 Jews, gypsies, and mentally ill people were killed. Undoubtedly, one of the major reasons Warburg was allowed to stay was because of good personal connections. An industrialist turned to Bouhler, who in turn considered the Warburg case on three levels: first, he sent out for the opinions of leading German scientists to obtain information on Warburg's importance; second, Warburg's mother was pure "Aryan"; third, Warburg was an officer in World War I. In addition to having a powerful man supporting him, Warburg's own exceptional achievements saved him.[57]

Others who remained in Germany were not able to stay as long as Warburg. The second round of dismissals began soon after the Nuremberg laws of 1935. In much more explicit language these laws marked the radicalization of antisemitic policy. Felix Plaut, department head at the German Research

Institute for Psychiatry, an institute of the Kaiser Wilhelm Society, was dismissed in October 1935 by Ernst Rüdin, with the authority of the Ministry of Science through the "German Citizenship Law of 15 September 1935,"[58] but managed somehow to live in Germany until about 1938, when it became extraordinarily difficult for a Jew to obtain a passport. Lise Meitner, who had been protected by her Austrian nationality, fled to Sweden via the Netherlands and Denmark after Anschluss with Austria in 1938. In 1936 Otto Meyerhof "realized that his position was untenable" and that he would soon have to leave.[59] He first found a position in France (1938) but a year later the war broke out, and after the Germans invaded France Meyerhof and his wife fled to the United States via Lisbon in October 1940. To this list we can add Carl Neuberg, who was forced to resign as director of his institute in 1934 but managed to work there until 1936, when Adolf Butenandt agreed to accept the director position. Neuberg arrived in the United States in 1939 after traveling through Palestine, Iran, Hawaii, and other countries. He later bitterly related: "I did not emigrate in 1933 because of Planck's bad advice—he said I was protected as an old civil servant of the Kaiserreich—and because I did not listen to Nernst's better advice. Later I was forbidden to leave the country."[60]

It was finally possible for Neuberg to receive an exit visa two weeks before the outbreak of war because he had served in World War I. Neuberg was also one of the special cases Planck fought for behind the scenes. In July 1934 he wrote a long letter to Minister Rust in support of Neuberg, who had just been forced into "retirement" by the sixth paragraph of the dismissal law. In addition to praising Neuberg's scientific accomplishments, Planck outlined three chief reasons why this "decision would be very unpleasant" for the Kaiser Wilhelm Society: (1) he was not in the position to explain the reasons to the members of the Society's institutes where much personal worry would arise; (2) it would make a bad impression abroad; and (3) the Rockefeller Foundation would withdraw its grant for the Kaiser Wilhelm Institute of Physics for which Planck was negotiating. It would be unpleasant if institutes built or supported by the Rockefeller Foundation were disturbed in their scientific work.[61] Perhaps Neuberg was too harsh in his retrospective judgment of Planck's advice, but Planck's goal was to do everything possible to maintain the quality of German science and this hope blinded him to some more realistic aspects of life during the Third Reich. Planck could hardly predict that the troubles would grow progressively worse, especially with an attitude that the events were like a "thunder storm that would soon pass away."[62]

Storm Troopers and Communists

It was not only Jews, however, who were hounded out of their jobs or harassed by the National Socialists. During the night of 15–16 March 1933, before the implemention of the dismissal law, storm troopers raided Oscar

Vogt's villa on the property of the Kaiser Wilhelm Institute for Brain Research in Berlin-Buch, ordering him to "open up." Storm troopers, armed with pistols, entered the villa by breaking a window on the ground floor. Vogt was accused of a number of activities, including maintaining connections to Russia, allegedly making payments to the Communist party, being a member of the German Socialist party, dismissing National Socialist staff members, tolerating communist staff members, and earning a double income.[63] The surprise attack seems to have been provoked by the denunciation of a physiologist at the institute, M. H. Fischer, who wanted to rise in the NSDAP; Fischer called a storm trooper leader the night before and then submitted a denunciatory report, which went through the SA hierarchy and landed at the Nuremberg central party office where the order to attack was given. The SA also demanded that the Hungarian revolutionary Béla Kun, who was allegedly in hiding at the institute, be surrendered. Such searches occurred several times in the course of the year and culminated in July as storm troopers raided the institute and seized five staff members, who were taken to an SA barracks and interrogated. During the interrogation they were insulted, threatened, and beaten. Under such conditions peaceful work at the institute was impossible and the director and staff were very disturbed. It gave Vogt and his wife a nervous shock. The Kaiser Wilhelm Society even tried to have the Reich Ministry of the Interior arrange police protection for the institute. Finally, the SA wanted to take Vogt to a concentration camp and labeled the institute a "communist nest."[64]

Over the course of the year scientists and assistants at the institute were threatened with dismissal because of Jewish heritage or Communist party membership. Two non-"Aryans" were paid with funding from the Rockefeller Foundation and were therefore allowed to stay until their fellowships ran out. The central administration of the Society was reluctant to allow this and reported to Vogt that the administration had "strictly applied" the dismissal law and would not allow already dismissed non-"Aryans" to continue with private funding. It was only because the foundation would be very angry if fellowship holders were to be dismissed that two members of the institute were allowed to stay until their fellowships ran out. By 13 March 1934 their time was also up.[65]

In March 1934, Vogt received, as he described, "a totally unexpected order" to dismiss employees at the institute if they were or had been members of the German Communist party or its related organizations. In a letter to Planck, Vogt announced, without any written protest, that he had given four institute members notice. He also gave this information to the Berlin-Buch/Karow branch of the NSDAP.[66] Not all institute directors followed orders, however. On 13 March 1934 Ludwig Prandtl, director of the institute for aerodynamics in Göttingen, wrote to General Director Glum that he did not see himself in a position to comply with the demand to dismiss a coppersmith at his institute because he had been a Communist party member in his youth, although he could see that one could force someone to leave the institute if he was not an able worker.[67]

The Balance Sheet:
Quantitative and Qualitative Losses

Despite Planck's efforts on behalf of the Society's scientific and staff members, many scientists were forced to leave their positions at the institutes and members of the senate had to resign. It is difficult to arrive at an exact and accurate numerical count of directors, scientific members, assistants, members (including senators), and secretaries dismissed as a result of their race or political convictions. The information has to be pieced together from incomplete lists compiled by the emergency committee for displaced scholars in 1936, from scattered archival evidence that sometimes shows only that a scientist or assistant ought to be dismissed or was placed on a list.[68] It is also difficult to track down Jewish or communist assistants who were not reported by the institute director.

Based on the evidence available, the following quantitative list of scientists dismissed (this does not include secretaries and senators) can be generated: As a whole the Society seemed to have lost about seventy-one scientists. This group breaks down into six directors and sixty-five department heads, assistants, researchers, and scientific members. (See the Appendix for complete listing with data on position, birth date, institute affiliation, field, dismissal date, and new country.) The institute for physical chemistry lost the most scientists, with nineteen emigrating after 1933. The institute for medical research in Heidelberg and the Dahlem biology institute each lost ten scientists, textile chemistry seven, and the others three or fewer. It is interesting to note that, in contrast to the Haber institute, the institute for breeding research seemed to have only one non-"Aryan" out of 180 staff members. In fact, breeding research, with its relation to agriculture, seemed to employ a high percentage of conservative or National socialist staff members.

The number of emigres in proportion to the total scientific staff of the Society can only be approximated because disparate figures exist. According to lists in the Society's archives, it employed 1,052 staff members including cleaning ladies, workers, technicians, and administrators. The scientific personnel, consisting of directors, department heads, and assistants made up 318 of the 1,052. If my figure of 71 emigres is correct, this would mean that 22% of the Society's scientists emigrated. But because my list includes research fellows, researchers, and scientists not included in the Society's records of initial dismissals, one cannot determine exactly if all the scientists in my list match all those included in the Society's. Furthermore, according to the Society's figures, there were only 55 non-"Aryans" out of the 1,052 staff members, which is considerably lower than the figure I have generated. I have found that at least a total of 86 staff emigrated or were dismissed, i.e., 8.1% of the total staff.

But these numbers do not reflect the caliber of scientists dismissed or driven from their land. Biochemists such as Carl Neuberg and Otto Meyerhof, despite their pioneering contributions to the development of twentieth-century biochemistry, ended up in America with positions far beneath their accomplishments. Fritz Haber, who had contributed so much to his "fatherland," was forced to leave and die in exile. Felix Plaut, Richard Gold-schmidt, Lise Meitner—the names speak for themselves—had to rebuild their careers at a late stage in their life. The assistants who left early in their careers had more of a chance abroad: Michael Polanyi, Curt Stern, and Hermann Blaschko, for example. But established emigrés must have shared Neuberg's sentiments after the war, when he lamented: "So you see, dear Mr. Bute-nandt, in toto, my twilight years are no bed of roses—but perhaps that is not the meaning of life."[69]

Despite the loss of great scientists because of the dismissal policy, many scientists of high caliber remained. One can point to Max von Laue, Otto Hahn, Werner Heisenberg, Carl-Friedrich von Weizsäcker, and Karl Wirtz in physics or to Adolf Butenandt in biochemistry, Richard Kuhn in chem-istry, or Max Hartmann, Hans Stubbe, and Fritz von Wettstein in biology, and even Otto Warburg in biochemistry. It will be the task of later chapters to examine and evaluate the type, quality, and nature of the science done under the conditions of the Third Reich.

Passive Opposition: The Haber Memorial Service

Fritz Haber, one of the first Jewish scientists who chose to resign and leave Germany, died "a broken man"[70] in exile on his way from Cambridge, England, to a health spa in Switzerland on 29 January 1934. No mention was made in the German press of Haber's passing; only Max von Laue had the courage to write an obituary notice in *Die Naturwissenschaften* where he compared Haber to Themistocles: "Themistocles is not remembered in history as an exile from the Persian King's court, but rather as the victor from Salamis. Haber will go down in history as the brilliant discoverer of the binding of nitrogen and hydrogen."[71]

This brave step led to defamations from the *Deutsche Physik* duo—Philipp Lenard and Johannes Stark—to the Nazi party. While the so-called Einstein circle—Planck, Heisenberg, and Arnold Sommerfeld—tried to create a posi-tion for Laue at the Prussian Academy of Sciences, Lenard blocked it by accusing Laue of making Haber, whom he considered a "scientific fraud," a "martyr of the 3d Reich." Moreover, Laue's article focused the party's attention on the journal *Die Naturwissenschaften*, which the deputy of the Führer thought should be *gleichgeschaltet* because it was founded and edited by the Jew Arnold Berliner and published articles such as Laue's.[72]

Other scientists were more cautious in their defense of Jewish scientists. When Otto Hahn suggested to Planck early in 1933 that professors "pro-test the treatment of Jewish scientists," Planck replied "if 30 professors appealed the measures 150 would counter them because they wanted the new positions."[73] Protest was not Planck's style; quiet diplomacy and behind-the-scene action was. Nor did Planck conceive of the Haber ceremony as an act of resistance; he organized it at the suggestion of General Director Glum, wishing finally to "satisfy the duty of the piety";[74] a year after Haber's death was the last opportunity to do so.

Just as there has been mystery and rumor surrounding Planck's meeting with Hitler, so too have scholars and scientists been unclear about the motivations behind the Haber ceremony. The major secondary source accounts, Haberer (1969) and Beyerchen (1977), rely heavily on Hahn's (1966) description, but some hitherto undiscovered archival material sheds new light on the preparations for the event. Planck's personal experience in preparation for the meeting shows that there was no intention of public protest, but that the service was conceived as a memorial service for an institute director.

Planck took charge of the preparations, and the invitations for the affair went out at the beginning of January; the event was co-sponsored by the German Chemical Society, the Physical Society, and the Kaiser Wilhelm Society. Everything seemed to progress smoothly, but then on 15 January the Education Ministry sent out a circular to all university rectors that "exploded into the preparations like a bomb,"[75] because it forbade state employees from attending the ceremony, which the minister characterized as a "challenge to the National Socialist state." The minister accused Haber, in his letter of resignation, of making clear his "attitude against the present state" and the "public must have seen [it] as a critique of the measures of the National Socialist state."[76]

Before replying to the minister, Planck wrote to Krupp von Bohlen und Halbach, most likely in Krupp's capacity as vice president of the Society, but also because of his role as an industrialist with close connections to the ministries, asking for advice on a way in which to answer the Ministry while preserving the prestige of the Kaiser Wilhelm Society. Planck noted that the Society had had a memorial service for every director of an institute without receiving permission from the Ministry. Although Haber's friends and students had come to Planck with a request for a memorial during the last year, he did not comply with their wish because he wanted to let some time pass between Haber's resignation and the memorial service.[77] Because Krupp's reply, if he answered in writing, is not preserved, and because there is no evidence of contact with the Ministry, it is impossible to know the nature of Krupp's advice or of any overtures made to the Ministry.

Planck, nevertheless, replied to Minister Rust the next day vigorously denying any intention of "provoking" the National Socialist state by organizing a memorial service. He explained it simply as an "old custom," without any political connotations, honoring a dead member's contribution to German science, economy, and war technology. Planck also pointed out that the Prussian Academy of Sciences, which is directly tied to the Ministry, had held a memorial speech in the preceding year without any objections from the Ministry. He closed by drawing attention to the "positive attitude of the Kaiser Wilhelm Gesellschaft" to the state and its "loyal belief in the Führer and his government," which had already been shown in "word and deed."[78]

The Ministry sent a staff member to Planck's house to discuss a way to "settle the awkward business," and Planck convinced him that the 15 January ministerial decree should be withdrawn because the event would be a private one in pure scientific circles; now he had to convince Minister Rust of this solution.[79] Rust replied in writing by justifying the memorial *talk* at the academy on the grounds that it was an international organization without consideration for "nationality or race." He characterized the Kaiser Wilhelm Society as the principal organization for *German* research and therefore every public action must harmonize with the principles of the National Socialist state. Although Rust acknowledged Planck's positive attitude toward the National Socialist state, he thought the Haber ceremony could call forth the opposite impression. He did, however, allow the service to take place as a pure internal and private affair of the Society which the daily press was not allowed to report on.[80]

Two days later Planck visited Rust at his villa in Dahlem and tactfully defended the Haber service. The minister seemed to have found the idea of a memorial service disagreeable because Haber criticized the principles of the National Socialist state. Planck admitted that "it was a fact if a Jewish director ruled, it was easy over a period of time for more and more employees to be Jewish and this [was] unpleasant." He still defended Haber's scientific work and asked whether Haber had accomplished enough in his life for a scientific society to honor him, as is a matter of course for a scientific member. Planck was certainly not antisemitic, but he was being diplomatic by trying to convince Rust that he was not criticizing the policies of the government. Rust's reply was that he knew "Haber has done a lot for science and for Germany, but the NSDAP has done a lot more."[81]

Planck soon recognized the futility of discussing these general issues and asked specifically if Professor Karl Friedrich Bonhoeffer would be allowed to participate and deliver his talk. As a university professor in Leipzig Bonhoeffer was forbidden to go to the ceremony, but Rust assured him in a telegram that permission to take part in the ceremony was on its way. Planck, according to his own words, was "surprised and delighted" by this accommodation but, wary of such promises, asked the minister if he could "count on it." Rust assured him, and Planck thought "everything was okay." As the date of the ceremony approached, Planck became anxious because Bonhoeffer had not received a telegram from the Ministry. It soon became clear to him, however, that the promised telegram would never arrive. Apparently "trouble had been brewing in the Ministry," because the secretary of state did not approve the telegram and it was therefore not sent out. Hahn, who was no longer a member of the university faculty, however, would be allowed to read Bonhoeffer's talk. The only action remaining, thought Planck, was the "sabotaging of the ceremony either through the use of brute force . . . or a malicious throwing of a stink bomb."[82]

On the morning of the ceremony, 29 January, everything went smoothly. Planck had taken Telschow along in his limousine because as a "party comrade" there would be more of a chance to be let through if Harnack House were to be closed. Despite Planck's fears, there were no incidents and the ceremony was the most "dignified memorial" ever held.[83]

Planck gave the introductory remarks at the meeting attended by a full house of guests—largely women (wives of professors forbidden to come), Carl Bosch and other important men from I. G. Farben, and members of Hahn's institute like Max Delbrück and Lise Meitner. Hahn delivered the main eulogies by Bonhoeffer and himself on the human side of Haber and the importance of his famous institute and scientific work. No photographs were made of the event and the German press did not report on the memorial service,[84] although a few days beforehand *The New York Times* had publicized the forced silence on the part of the German press: "Nazis Gag Haber Services."[85]

In light of the new evidence it would be difficult to interpret this event as an act of political resistance. It would be advisable to save such designations for activities of the Kreisau Circle and the White Rose, for example— organized groups planning a coup against the existing regime—or, better yet, groups directly involved in the assassination plot of 20 July 1944 in an attempt to "bring about the overthrow of the Nazi regime."[86] It was surely an act of intellectual defiance that the Society honored a Jewish scientist given the attitudes of the existing regime; in this sense, also, one can interpret the service as passive opposition.

The first eventful year of National Socialist Germany produced changes in the structures of the Society and its institutes and, more important, great transformations in the composition of its scientists. Although in some ways a victim of National Socialist policies, the Society implemented them in what can be characterized as obedience to authority. While many of the scientists and directors were uneasy about, and disturbed by, the new legislation, the administrators were almost overzealous in their strict application of the dismissal law. As a lawyer, General Director Glum clung to the legal details without seeming to realize the human implications and the resulting impact on the scientific community.

Rather than openly resisting—in 1933 as in 1935—the Society's leaders, and most of the scientists, pursued a path of accommodation. Planck's way was of diplomatic tact in public and behind-the-scenes maneuvering, and he did all he could within his capacity to preserve the quality of German science by encouraging eligible and qualified Jewish scientists to stay in their posts; he manipulated the exception clauses to work within the system. Other signs of adaptation at the Society on a daily level included flying the swastika flag and signing official letters with a "Heil Hitler."

The dismissal law was primarily applied to institutions receiving more than 50 percent of their funding from public sources. From its founding period the Kaiser Wilhelm Society had never loosened itself from the German tradition of state support. Had it been more privately organized it could have preserved more of its autonomy, at least for a time. That it was not transformed into a National Socialist–controlled organization seems to be due to its semiprivate character, its prestige, Planck's influence, and to the help of powerful industrialist members. Because it was an institution devoted to research, and not to education, it had less utility for the National Socialists' goals in the early years of the Third Reich. During the first year of the political revolution the structure and personnel of the Society were the aspects of the scientific enterprise most heavily affected, but this had been a byproduct of National Socialist policies and was not part of a policy for science. The place of the Kaiser Wilhelm Society in National Socialist science policy shows that in the early years the National Socialists had few set plans to implement in the world of scientific research.

4

National Socialist
Science Policy and the Kaiser
Wilhelm Society

During the early years of the Third Reich social and racial policies were implemented by the National Socialist regime that affected the composition of the
scientific community by eliminating scientists because of their race or political
convictions. Scientists who stayed attempted to gain support from the state,
but apart from some who worked on race studies or gas warfare, and other
military-related science, these pleas fell on deaf ears until about 1936–37.[1] This
lack of interest by the state was partly ideological but, more important, there
was, at the time, no coherent and separate policy for the natural sciences. (In
Germany, *Wissenschaftspolitik* usually encompasses both scholarship and science.)
A posture toward science finally emerged around 1937 and reflected the social,
economic, and political policies as they were promulgated in the course of the
Third Reich. The reorganization of Weimar science institutions, which were
embodied by the various governmental ministries and the Emergency Association for German Science (Notgemeinschaft der deutschen Wissenschaft, NGW),
and the creation of new organizations for science such as the Reich Research
Council (Reichsforschungsrat, RFR), neatly reflected the stages of economic
and political transformations, from the early attempts to create a centralized
bureaucracy in 1933 through the implementation of the Four Year Plan in
1936–37, to the outbreak of war in 1939, and its turning point in 1942.

Universities

Although there were few clear-cut ideas for a transformed scientific landscape to be implemented after the seizure of power in 1933, a vision for

National Socialist education had already begun to develop during the Weimar period among old fighter (early members of the NSDAP honored for their role in the rise of the National Socialist Movement) National Socialists such as Ernst Krieck and Alfred Baeumler. While some argue that a coherent policy for education was also missing after the seizure of power, many ideas that existed before 1933 were implemented, and universities and other educational institutions were nazified and transformed as a result of National Socialist policies. This is not surprising. In a totalitarian regime educational establishments are the first to be targeted for several strategic and obvious reasons. By seizing power at the universities one can educate a new generation of students in the reigning ideology and worldview. At these National Socialist universities students could be educated in race science, military science, new population policies, and any fields which became cornerstones of National Socialist ideology.

Unlike the developments at the major research institutions, students played a key role in the transformation of university structures and the spread of National Socialist ideology and worldview. The National Socialist leaders also had high hopes for using them as civil soldiers on campus. Soon after the Civil Service Law was passed in the late spring and summer of 1933, students actively attacked Jewish and socialist professors and students. They outwardly supported the regime by adopting its paraphernalia from the brown shirt to the martial tone. In Berlin, the student body *(Studentenschaft)* presented "twelve points against the non-German spirit of the university" to the rector. These points included strident attacks against Jewish professors, demanding that they publish their work in Hebrew and that any German edition be considered a "translation." The students' early revolutionary fervor culminated in the burning of books of fifteen authors at the main square on Unter den Linden opposite the university on the evening of 10 May 1933.[2]

Within the first year of the new regime there were several measures enacted to coordinate the universities along National Socialist principles. Common to all German universities was the introduction of the leadership principle to replace academic self-government in the university constitution. The rector became the leader *(Führer)* of the university and was named by the Reich Minister. The most radical incision at all German universities, however, was the purge and transformation of faculty and staff members. The instrument for this process was the 7 April 1933 Civil Service Law. The National Socialists were open about their intention to intervene at the universities in order to implement the National Socialist "spirit." More than in any other area of life in the Third Reich, they accomplished this through the dismissals and through changes in positions, suspensions, and transfers of staff to other universities. These measures also allowed the National Socialists to install their own politically acceptable candidates and start rebuilding a National Socialist university. By 1939, at least 2,000, or one-third of Germany's university teachers, had been dismissed, and 45 percent of all positions were newly occupied.[3]

Those professors who stayed in Germany were not as active as the student body in the new construction of the universities, but professors who were appointed as a result of vacancies due to forced emigration were often political appointees. More importantly, the procedure to achieve professor status through the *Habilitation* and *Dozent* process changed to include political training of the candidate. Once the candidate submitted his *Habilitation* (a second dissertation needed to qualify for a professorship) to the committee he underwent some of the pre-1933 procedures, such as faculty examination, but new requirements included proving "Aryan" ancestry and serving in a Community Camp and Teachers' Academy. At the camp and the academy, the candidate attended lectures and was observed by the National Socialist Teachers' Association in order to determine his personal and political qualifications for teaching youth in the new Germany.[4] Because the Kaiser Wilhelm Society was a research organization, scientists there did not have to go through the same process. At times, scientists who were shut out of a university career for political reasons could work at the Society instead.

The National Socialist program for the universities was first developed by theorists such as Krieck and Baeumler, and then expanded upon, or further articulated by, National Socialist rectors such as Eugen Fischer and Martin Heidegger and the Education Minister Bernhard Rust.

By 1936, National Socialist leaders from the world of science and education responded to the claim that National Socialist ideology was hostile to science with denial. For example, in his speech at the University of Heidelberg anniversary celebration, Rust claimed that the ideology had achieved a reversal of a long process of fragmentation in the sciences. According to Rust, state ideology was not hostile to science because objectivity is not an integral part of science and there is no value-free scientist. National Socialist ideology believes that there never has been any science without underlying values and preconditions. The premise of the liberal positivistic era was that man was separate from the world and could therefore approach the world as premiseless and value-free. The result of this worldview was a scientist living in a fragmented reality. National Socialist ideology rejects this fragmentation of reality, continued Rust, by asserting that man, although an observer, is still part of a natural and historical order; it returns the lost unity. The reform of scientific life at the universities must therefore begin with the idea of science.[5]

Rust also somewhat elliptically repudiated the accusation that the National Socialists had turned the sciences into a servant of state ideology by stating that the National Socialist state must not profess any "false tolerance" toward the enemy of German self-confidence (Marxist liars). This is the reason, continued Rust, the state has removed from positions of influence people who have disseminated unvölkisch doctrines and those who are different by blood, and thus unable to shape the sciences in a German spirit.[6] The official attitudes toward science were still ambivalent and unstable during the early years.

The transformation of the universities, and of science and scholarship there, was entrusted by those in power to proven National Socialists such as Krieck and Baeumler, who were the chief theoreticians of National Socialist university policies. They were given professorships and made rectors of the leading universities. While Krieck believed that the universities should be dissolved and replaced with vocational training, Baeumler advanced the idea of the organization of science in "Male Houses" to suppress the feminine democratic elements. Militarization and the transformation of the student–teacher relationship to one of leader and follower were prominent characteristics of their early Weimar plans. Finally, Martin Heidegger's celebrated Rector's Speech called for the unity of science based on the spirit of the National Socialist worldview and the sweeping away of isolated specialists.[7]

Franz Bachér, who was head of the university department at the Reich Ministry of Education, addressed the question of the role of the German university in implementing the goals of the Four Year Plan at a rally of the NSDB-Teacher's Association in 1937, where he also defended Germany against charges that the National Socialist government was hostile to scientific innovation and especially against criticism of the dismissal of Jewish faculty members. He introduced the metaphor of mountain peaks and valleys to convey the idea that before the seizure of power the diverse sciences were mountain peaks lacking in unity, while under National Socialism, scientific life returned to a valley for the purpose of regrouping into a "common peak" of ideological concord and racial purity. (Non-Germans had to be "left behind" on this new ascent because their weakness would have prevented the German nation from reaching its goal.)[8]

To achieve this ideological concord it was necessary to centralize the organization of higher education by transforming and centralizing the Ministry for Science, Education and People's Education. To mobilize science for the purposes of the state, it was vital for the "idea of science" itself to be reformed. Finally, he called upon the older faculty members to be tolerant of their younger colleagues because their sight into the "new future" might be longer than that of their predecessors.[9]

Ministries Transformed

By 1933 there were two ministries responsible for, and associated with, the Kaiser Wilhelm Society: the Prussian Ministry for Science (Learning), Art and People's Education and the Reich Ministry of the Interior.[10] These ministries were the organs through which the government dictated and implemented its policies. They had had close ties to the Society since its founding in Wilhelmine Germany, and even in those days there had already been discussions on the precise nature and role of the ministries' relationship with the Society. Not only Harnack but Reich Minister Theodor Lewald and the Prussian Minister Friedrich Schmidt-Ott had proposed that the Society remain organizationally independent from the state. In addition to the obvious reasons of autonomy, the ministers argued that it would be easier to gain private support by introducing self-government.[11] There had been debates from the Wilhelmine period through the Weimar years about the sort of cooperation that would exist. The Society ended up being supported by the state, industry, and wealthy patrons; thus it was not entirely dependent on any one.

But the participation of the Prussian state in the founding of, and later support for, the Society was considerable. It financially supported and maintained a half-dozen director positions and continued to support various institutes. Representatives of the ministries sat in on board meetings of the administration and institutes. Despite the presence of Ministry officials, the ministries exerted comparatively little control over the Society, and they had never been active in formulating policy or influencing research agendas; their representatives often did not attend the meetings. More indirect influence was exerted by the ministries' senatorial appointments to the Society. By the Weimar years tension had arisen between the Kaiser Wilhelm Society and the ministries because of the Society's increasing dependence on the state for financial support as a result of the inflation. The inflation of the twenties had wiped out the Society's capital, and industrial support had also decreased; therefore, the Society had to turn to the state and other sources, even as far as the Rockefeller Foundation in America, for financial support.

In 1925 Carl-Heinrich Becker, a distinguished orientalist, had become the Prussian science minister, and in 1930 rumors had spread that he was aspiring to the presidency of the Society and wanted to force Harnack to resign.[12] Harnack, however, died in 1930, and although Becker resigned his post at the Ministry, he continued his travels in the Orient until his death in 1933. Although the Prussian state had strong ties to the Society early on, it was not until about 1921 that the Reich began to support the Society on a large scale; during the Weimar years their contributions were equal. From the name of the Prussian Ministry it is clear that science was a major activity under its jurisdiction. Although not as large, the Reich Ministry of the Interior had a cultural department—"Department III"—which included the sciences within its domain. Rudolf Buttmann and Richard Donnevert were the ministers for science and attended the senate meetings of the Society.

During the years 1933 and 1934 there was much flux and reorganization in the ministries as party members assumed key positions. In the first year after the Nazis' seizure of power the ministries were actively implementing the Law for the Reestablishment of the Civil Service, and it was not until the spring of 1934 that official plans for the reorganization of science took place at the Prussian and Reich ministries. As part of the Nazi attempt at centralization and federalization, the Reich and Prussian ministries were united and renamed the Prussian and Reich Ministry for Science, Education, and People's Education.[13] Within sixteen months after the National Socialist regime took office, the cultural department of the Reich Ministry of the Interior had been dissolved and the Reich Ministry of Education

(Reichserziehungsministerium, REM) took its place; the name was officially changed to REM in 1936. Bernhard Rust was named Reich Minister for Science and Education on 1 May 1934 and the Ministry was now officially transformed from the old Prussian Cultural Ministry; in 1937 the ministries were united into one Reich Ministry, thereby eliminating any Prussian state influence on science and education policy. It was through the founding of this new Reich Ministry that the National Socialists thought "the conditions were created to unify and control all of German science by the Reich both within and outside the universities. It was with this creation that the Reich itself took over the control and methodical shaping of all of scientific life especially at the university."[14] As the Ministry emphasized in its own history, the most important task for the new National Socialist Reich was in the area of education. In fact, in the early years science and research had been neglected by policymakers. Even though the Ministry consisted of departments for *Wissenschaft* (Scholarship and Science), *Erziehung* (Education), and *Volksbildung* (People's Education), scientific research was overshadowed by the shaping and control of education at the universities. The Kaiser Wilhelm Society was under the jurisdiction of the office for science— Amt Wissenschaft—at the Ministry, which had two sections: W I, responsible for universities and technical colleges, headed by Theodor Vahlen (later by the chemist Franz Bachér), and W II, the section for scientific research, headed by Erich Schumann, but run by Rudolf Mentzel, who became head of the whole office in 1939.[15]

Theodor "Papa" (he was already sixty-five in 1934) Vahlen was an Austrian-born mathematician who started his career as a professor in Greifswald in 1904. In 1927 he was dismissed from his position because of his political activities. It had been unusual to be open about one's political preference for National Socialism during the Weimar period, and even more dangerous to voice one's political views as rector of the university. As an "old fighter" who entered a substitute NSDAP organization in 1923 in Pommern, where the National Socialist party was forbidden, he simultaneously became Gauleiter of Pommern; he finally entered the NSDAP in 1925. He was also in the SS, like many of the staff members in the REM. In addition to working in a number of areas in pure and applied mathematics he specialized in ballistics and made numerous contributions to journals for military science. After 1933 his career took off again and he was appointed director of the REM in March 1933; in 1934 he was named professor at the University of Berlin as the successor to Richard von Mises, who had emigrated. As director of the REM, Vahlen had been involved to some extent in the process of dismissing scientists from the KWG, but it was not until he became president of the Prussian Academy of Sciences in 1938 that his antipathy to the Society became public. That the Society was a rival, and therefore an unwanted organization, was reflected in his remarks in the Academy's yearbook. He branded the KWG a "democratic remnant of disorganization," which threatened the prestige of the Academy because the Academy members' research results increased the prestige of the Society, which only administered, while scientists themselves belonged to the Academy.[16]

Despite his position at the REM, Vahlen was not active and often not present at the offices of the Ministry. Otto Wacker, the Baden State Minister, was appointed provisionally as a substitute for the "missing" Ministerial Director Vahlen by Minister Rust on 1 January 1937; as Wacker recalled in 1939, the REM "borrowed" him. Wacker, however, took the post only on the condition that he could continue as Minister for Culture and Teaching in Baden. Like Vahlen, Wacker was also an old fighter (he entered the party in 1925) and SS-man. After two years, however, it became clear that Wacker would have to move to Berlin if he were to keep the position. In April 1939 he resigned his post effective 1 May 1939; within half a year, in February 1940, he died.[17]

Erich Schumann, who headed the office for research in a pro forma way, was also interested in military science and his major post was in the Army Weapons Office. Both contemporaries and postwar commentators have caricatured his dual interest in physics and music. It has been alleged that he wrote march music for military parades, and, after the war, Samuel Goudsmit characterized him as an inferior physicist.[18] To be fair, one should be reminded that Schumann did write a *Habilitation* (1929) on the physics of tones and was a Privatdozent at the University of Berlin in 1931. Prominent physicists who were members of his *Habilitation* committee for experimental and theoretical physics include Walther Nernst, Max von Laue, and Max Planck. Soon after the seizure of power he was named professor at the University of Berlin for physics and music. As a professor he taught courses in military physics, military music, and in his research areas of acoustics and explosives. By the time of the outbreak of war he had a number of other positions including director in the research department of the Reich War Ministry. It has been noted that he had five offices in Berlin but could not be reached in any of them. Friedrich Glum reported, however, that he could always be found at the Telschow Konditorei (Ernst Telschow's family bakery). He did not enter the party until 1933.[19]

During the Third Reich, Rudolf Mentzel emerged as a powerful and key figure in National Socialist science policy as well as in the affairs of the Kaiser Wilhelm Society. He had an impressive Nazi profile. He was born in 1900 and studied chemistry in Göttingen, where he received a Ph.D. He entered the NSDAP early on, in 1922, earning a "Golden Party Badge"; he then also joined the SA and the SS and played an important role as Kreisleiter (Circuit Leader, one step below Gauleiter) of the party in Göttingen. Rust had been his Gauleiter (District leader, highest-ranking Nazi party official below top Reich leadership) and had brought him into the university department of the Ministry in 1934 as an officer for the natural sciences. His scientific career was controversial even to contemporaries. In 1933 he received his *Habilitation* in Greifswald in military chemistry although the faculty was not allowed to read it because it was considered secret. The commission characterized Mentzel as an empiricist with a primitive understanding of science.[20] It was because of his background in military chemistry that he joined Gerhard Jander, with whom he had worked at the Reich Armed Forces Ministry, as a staff member and later department head at the Kaiser Wilhelm Institute for Physical Chemistry.

As a representative of the Reich Ministry, Mentzel attended the Kaiser Wilhelm Society's senate meetings in his black SS uniform, with a brown shirt and a revolver in his belt.[21] He succeeded Johannes Stark as president of the German Research Association (Deutsche Forschungsgemeinschaft, DFG; formerly called the Notgemeinschaft der deutschen Wissenschaft) in 1937 and rose in the ranks at the Kaiser Wilhelm Society, becoming second vice president with Albert Vögler's assumption of the president's office in 1941.

Another important figure in the science policy arena for the area of agriculture and biology was Konrad Meyer. Meyer, an agricultural scientist and party member since 1931, started his career in Göttingen as an assistant at the plant institute. Just as the military scientists tended to be on the conservative side of the political spectrum, so too were the agricultural scientists, especially in Göttingen. Not only did they take part in the "42-Statement" (forty-two professors and teachers protested against the eminent Jewish physicist) James Frank's resignation but they were actively engaged in the political transformation of the university. Meyer, for example, held lectures during the spring of 1933 calling for the construction of a political university with a German face. During the Third Reich Meyer's career blossomed. In October 1933 he took a leave from his Göttingen duties and became a staff member at the Prussian Ministry for Science and Education. In April 1934 he was appointed a professor (Ordinarius) at the University of Jena and moved to the University of Berlin as full professor in December of the same year. While maintaining his duties at the Science Ministry he became director of a new institute for agriculture and agricultural policies at the University of Berlin in 1935. But his ascent did not stop there. He was also chairman of the Research Service (Reich Worker's Community for Agriculture), an organization founded in 1934 for the centralization and control of all agricultural research. The goal of the Research Service was to make agriculture National Socialist. Meyer was also active in a number of other organizations, becoming head of the subject area for Agriculture and General Biology at the Reich Research Council in 1937. As an SS member he enjoyed a great deal of influence, and the section's budget increased substantially during his tenure as subject director. Kaiser Wilhelm institute scientists had frequent interactions with this section of the Reich Research Council; Alfred Kühn and Fritz von Wettstein were referees for it, and Kaiser Wilhelm institute scientists received substantial research support as a result. During the war Meyer's responsibilities expanded, and he gained even more influence in formulating agricultural policies when he was named director of the Planning Office "General Plan East" by the Führer of the SS Heinrich Himmler. In this office his task was to plan a settlement program for the occupied territories of the Soviet Union.[22]

Unification, Nationalization, and Control

Although the now unified Prussian/Reich Ministry for Science was responsible for the Kaiser Wilhelm Society on the day the Ministry officially opened under its new name in May 1934, the Ministry of the Interior maintained close ties to the Society at least into the fall of 1933. In May 1934, Rudolf Buttmann (Reich Ministry of the Interior), who had been attending the Society's senate and yearly meetings since the Weimar years, wrote to Planck that he would no longer be attending the meetings because the administration and care *(Betreuung)* of the Society had been transferred to the new Reich Ministry for Science and Education.[23]

Soon after the implementation of the Civil Service Law, the Ministry and leaders from science and industry, including Johannes Stark and Albert Vögler, began to conceive a master plan for German science. Although the Reich government envisioned that the Society would become integrated into a "Reich Ring" of German science, the German Research Association and the universities were the major institutions focused on by government policymakers. The main feature of this plan was the unification of science under the Führer with the Reich Ministry of the Interior managing it. The goal was to advance scientific research, to regenerate the economy, and to support national defense.[24] Stark, the most zealous proponent of *Deutsche Physik*, was asked by Reich Minister Wilhelm Frick to head the program. Stark was already president of the Imperial Physical-Technical Institute and was also about to become president of the newly coordinated Emergency Association for German Science under its new name, German Research Association.

Stark believed that a plan for a strong scientific program would serve to "dispel the severe alarm that had arisen in scientific circles because of the alleged rape or disregard for science." To Stark the great discoveries of the last fifty years indicated that "progress in the economy is dependent on the progress of scientific-technical research." Although the Imperial Physical-Technical Institute, a Reich institution, was successful in securing the economic benefits of science, Stark saw other tasks awaiting the Reich government in the advancement of scientific research: the maintenance of the Kaiser Wilhelm institutes. The Reich government considered financially supporting the Society and taking part in the administration of the Kaiser Wilhelm institutes. But these plans for increased care and control (*Betreuung*) never materialized.[25]

The Reich government envisioned that the Kaiser Wilhelm Society, the Emergency Association for German Science, and the Imperial Physical-Technical Institute would be the chief players in a new organization of science. The increased participation of the Reich, argued the government, justified a change of name from Emergency Association for German Science to Reich Research Service (Reichsforschungsdienst).[26] In sum, then, the Reich government set three tasks for German science: the building and maintenance of big scientific-technical Reich institutions, the care of the

Kaiser Wilhelm institutes, and the organization and administration of the
Reich Research Service.

Physics, including chemistry, technology, and military and industrial technology, would be supported at the scientific-technical Reich institutions, and
the organizational and administrative arm would be the Imperial Physical-
Technical Institute. Plans were made to organize biological-technical research,
including botany, zoology, and breeding research, under a soon to be created
biological-technical Reich institution under the leadership of the Kaiser
Wilhelm Institute for Breeding Research.[27] As part of an intended takeover,
the Reich Ministry envisioned that the Kaiser Wilhelm institutes matching
the subject matter of the analogous Reich institutions would be incorporated organizationally within them. The plan was to allow the senate of the
Society to continue in its present composition, but the names of the institutes would change, and the administration was to be dissolved and replaced
by administrators from the Reich Ministry.

In these plans for the unification of German science it was clear that the
newly coordinated Emergency Association for German Science would play
the key role in Nazi science organization. Rudolf Buttmann, Johannes Stark,
Erwin Baur, director of the Kaiser Wilhelm Institute for Breeding Research,
Erich Rothacker from the Ministry, and Erich Schumann at the Reich Armed
Forces Ministry fashioned a set of principles contained in a report on the
Research Community and Research Service (Forschungsgemeinschaft und
Forschungsdienst). The Emergency Association for German Science was to
be integrated into the National Socialist structure and was to support fundamental National Socialist slogans: "In the fight for the renewal . . . of the
German folk an overview of the intellectual forces available for research is
indispensable. The National Socialist state needs a mobilization of research
energy." Science should serve the whole, and not the individual; the interests of research should not be contrary to those of the state and the government, as was the case in the Weimar period; and the Emergency Association for German Science will contribute not only to theoretical sciences
but also to the welfare of the people and the economy.[28]

Another important figure who initially seemed ready to collaborate in
the plans for the new organization of science was Albert Vögler, the industrialist, director of United Steel, and senator, treasurer, and later president
of the Kaiser Wilhelm Society. Although never a party member, Vögler had,
at least in the Weimar period, financed Hitler and the NSDAP; therefore,
he had the trust and cooperation of the National Socialists, and as a leading
industrialist he commanded respect and wielded authority. Vögler envisioned
adapting some of the Kaiser Wilhelm institutes to the purposes of national
defense. Because the five institutes for chemistry, physical chemistry, iron
research, aerodynamics, and physiology of work were already well-outfitted
for tasks related to military research, and in some cases already working for
the Wehrmacht, Vögler thought a scientific clearinghouse could be set up
to exploit the facilities and scientific talent. According to Vögler's plan, the
institute directors would assign work to the institutes or have an institute

solve problems. By sending representatives from their staff to the Kaiser Wilhelm institutes, military organizations like the Reichswehr, the marines, and the Aviation Ministry could exploit the results or assign problems which could be used later for problems relating to the war economy.[29]

The Reich Ministry of the Interior responded positively to Vögler's ideas, and in an 8 November meeting the idea was expanded to include a national policy whereby a clearinghouse would have full authority in assigning research work to the institutes of the Society, to Reich institutions, the university institutes, and to big industry. And by the end of November this plan was brought to the attention of Reich Minister Wilhelm Frick, the industrialist Gustav Krupp von Bohlen und Halbach, and Planck. The intended transformation in the organization of scientific research was presented as a military-style structure consisting of a general staff with the chancellor at the head of the pyramid. The staff's task was to monitor the national organization of science and influence government funding of research projects.[30]

Vögler refined the idea further and proposed a "leaders council" with members chosen by the government from scientists at the universities, independent research institutes, and various industries. This type of agency was to strive towards achieving an overview of scientific research at the universities and other institutions while also advancing a research program in the production of raw material for Germany. Vögler thought that, at this early stage, the tasks of the university in the "new Germany" had been limited to "national-educational" goals but they could benefit the nation by developing military technology in preparation for war.[31]

Vögler's ideas on the organization of German science were similar to those of Stark and the Reich Ministry in that the military and economic benefits of research were stressed. The desire for a unified center for organizing this research was also common to both plans. One fundamental and important difference, however, was the intended function and use of the Kaiser Wilhelm institutes. In the discussions emanating from Stark, the Kaiser Wilhelm Institutes would, in effect, be coordinated and integrated into the Reich Research Service. Vögler, however, called for avoiding a nationalization of institutes but did offer some of the application-oriented institutes for the service of national defense.

Despite this early interest and support from the Reich Ministry of the Interior for a Reich Ring of German science, no concrete organization had materialized by the spring of 1934. It is surely no coincidence that the Reich Ministry's responsibilities for science had ended in the spring, thereby making it impossible for the plans emanating from the ministry to come to fruition. The Reich Ministry's department for culture had merged with the Prussian Education Ministry and was transformed into one unified Prussian/Reich Ministry for Science.

Another all-encompassing plan for research came in the following year from Rust's Ministry. The idea was to create a Reich Academy of Research by transforming and coordinating the Emergency Association for German

Science. These plans resembled the later Reich Research Council but much infighting accompanied them as Rust and Stark clashed over competing interests. Opposition to this academy also came from the Kaiser Wilhelm Society. Planck wrote a remarkable letter of protest together with the president of the Emergency Association for German Science, Friedrich Schmidt-Ott, criticizing this Reich organization. Planck addressed Minister Rust, "out of responsibility towards the Führer, towards German science and towards the German people." As leaders of the two major research organizations for German science they felt it was their duty to oppose the reordering of German science into a Reich academy:

> Scientific and technical research can fulfill the great tasks that the Führer has outlined in his plan for a restoration of Germany only if it can develop unfettered by the chains of any kind of bureaucracy and on the basis of the free initiative of individual researchers and principles of self-government by reliable researchers. This is all in the best interests of the German economy, the country's defense and for Germany's prestige in the world.[32]

Planck's plea seems to have had some influence, because in Rust's draft of bylaws for a Reich Academy in February 1935, he explicitly stated that the "composition of the Kaiser Wilhelm Gesellschaft would not be affected by the new order." He perceived the "preservation" of the Kaiser Wilhelm Society as necessary, not only because of its prestige both at home and abroad, but because of the connection between research and industry.[33] These failures to create a new organization for German science reflected the lack of cooperation among competing agencies and, at this early stage, the lack of understanding that research could be of great use for the state. This was not fully understood until well into World War II; but the use of science for economic and political purposes was recognized in 1936–37 with the passing of the Four Year Plan and the creation of a new Reich organization for science.

Military Science

In 1935 the military program of the National Socialist regime became more visible to the population of Germany with the announcement of universal military conscription and the restoration of the armed forces; but this was only the latest manifestation of an early program for rearmament, military preparedness, and a stated ideal of defensemindedness. Military science began to be incorporated into the student curriculum early on, and the Storm Troopers on campus were given the task of training students in defensemindedness. A new field began to be founded for military science and discussions of the concept and its incorporation as a field of study at the university enter the gazette of the Ministry of Education by 1935.[34] The concept, ideology, and practice of military science also entered the world of research early on, but in the case of the Kaiser Wilhelm Society, the forced introduction of this new science met with stiff resistance.

On 30 April 1933 Fritz Haber had resigned his position as director of the Kaiser Wilhelm Institute for Physical Chemistry and Electrochemistry effective October 1933. Although he would have been allowed to stay as a war veteran, he could not watch silently as his co-workers were dismissed. In many ways, this step allowed the National Socialists to take over the institute because it created a vacancy at an institute supported financially by the Prussian state.

Dramatic events occurred between the two milestones of Haber's sensational resignation in 1933 and the memorial service in his honor in 1935. Soon after he resigned, Haber began to make provisions for a possible successor at the institute, but the Prussian Ministry of Education and the Reich Ministry of Defense had already filled the now open position. On 12 May 1933 Haber had written to Karl Bonhoeffer asking him to attend a meeting with Planck to discuss the possibility of his return to Berlin after Herbert Freundlich and Michael Polanyi left in September. He later wrote to James Franck about this meeting where he proposed the idea of transforming the institute into one for physics and physical chemistry provided that Laue would become the first director and Bonhoeffer the second, with James Franck as a guest.[35] Finally, by the beginning of the summer Planck had named Otto Hahn acting director of the institute.

The question of Haber's successor was accompanied by the issue of equipment purchased with the help of a Rockefeller Foundation grant that had been authorized for specific people and projects. With the changed political conditions, however, the question arose of whether the equipment would be taken by the director abroad or if it would stay at the institute to be used by his yet to be appointed successor. The implications became even more difficult when Haber proposed the following scenario: "Now it seems to me, that there is a silent condition; namely that if it keeps any gifted piece [sic] the Institute remains devoted to the same scientific purpose. . . . But now please consider what you would think right in my case supposed that my institute would be devoted to the study of chemical warfare?"[36] The scenario became a reality, Haber's nominee as successor thwarted, and a "perfectly unknown man from Göttingen who" was "ordered to study chemical warfare" was appointed by the ministry.[37]

Although he was the leader of chemical warfare during World War I and was "proud to work for the military authorities with the Institute as experimental base," after the armistice Haber vowed never to do such work again. He wanted the Rockefeller Foundation to tell Planck that the instruments would never have been given to the institute had it known that they would be used for the development of chemical weapons; it would be better, advised Haber, for the equipment to follow Haber to Cambridge or Freundlich to London. Despite Haber's warnings, Lauder Jones, the officer in charge, did not think the Foundation should change its usual policy even though the scientific equipment might be used later for experimentation in connection with chemical warfare.[38] Jones wrote to Haber that it was up to the Society officials to decide. Despite Planck's ruling that Freundlich could take his equipment to England, "some authority, higher than the officers of the KWG, has decided to the contrary."[39]

A few days later, on 16 October, Otto Hahn wrote to Planck that "for political and human reasons, these points seem important." He was discussing the issue of the release of the Rockefeller apparatus:

> In case the institute should be placed in the service of national defense any apparatus in the institute should be given back . . . the repercussions abroad would be intolerable, if the impression is given that military work is undertaken here with foreign support which had been appropriated for wholly other goals. Not only would German science be damaged, but the entire German people would be damaged as well.[40]

It was clear by the middle of October that in the future the institute would "be used for military-technical purposes that lie in the framework of the Versailles treaty. Herr Prof. Jander already has earned special merit in this area."[41]

Although not known to many at the time, Jander had been appointed acting director by the Prussian Education Ministry on 4 August 1933. In a startling letter, Telschow reported to the vacationing Glum that he was ordered to a conference by Gerullis, a minister at the Ministry who had monitored the Haber institute during the implementation of the dismissal law. The matter was a simple one; the Ministry wanted to fill Haber's position right away. Professor Gerhard Jander, formerly from the Chemistry Institute of the University of Göttingen, was ordered to take Haber's place. The Ministry knew that Hahn had been appointed by the Society but claimed they had never approved it. Telschow told the Ministry that Jander could not be appointed without the approval of the Kaiser Wilhelm Society; the Society and its senate must discuss the appointment, he continued. Vahlen, however, argued that the Ministry's demand was authoritative and asked for a contract between the Society and Jander.[42]

Planck quickly responded to this unprecedented step and to this violation of the Society's autonomy by the Ministry. On 11 August he wrote to Vahlen from his vacation in Tegernsee "in shock." He tried to persuade him that this was not a suitable institute to use for the purposes of the Ministry because, with Haber's "sensational resignation," not only were the eyes of Germany focused on the institute, but "above all those of countries abroad." If Jander's appointment was the intention of another ministry (i.e., the Reich Ministry of Defense), he would comply, but he urged the education ministry to consider using another institute, lying outside of the Dahlem complex, for such purposes. Furthermore, state director positions at the Kaiser Wilhelm institutes, he forcefully reminded the minister, must be filled "with the approval of the Kaiser Wilhelm Gesellschaft." The "modus procendi" has always been "a vote" of the appropriate section of the scientific council and a resolution of the senate. Planck urged the minister to wait until his return so that the appointment of an acting director could be decided at a meeting of the executive committee and, he repeated, only "with the approval" of the Kaiser Wilhelm Society. Planck also pointed out that before a decision could be made, the opinions of both the Reich government and private industry would have to be obtained because they both financially supported the Kaiser Wilhelm institutes.[43] Just as the Ministry had used the spring vacations in April 1933 to implement the dismissal law, so too did it take advantage of the absence of leadership at the Society to fill the director position.

Hans Pfundtner, from the Reich Ministry of the Interior, wrote to the Prussian Ministry in defense of Planck's view. Before Jander was to be named Haber's successor, Pfundtner thought the case should be discussed democratically with all the ministries involved and with the Society, in order to reach an agreement: "A one-sided appointment of the director without the approval of my ministry and without contacting the Kaiser Wilhelm Gesellschaft would, in my opinion, neither adhere to the practice until now, nor to the legal position, and is therefore unacceptable."[44]

Despite these letters of protest, Jander was appointed acting director effective 1 October 1933, for one year. Planck, however, made it clear in a forceful, if not angry, statement to the Prussian Minister for Science that the Society did not approve of the intervention. "The final decision about the future" of the institute would take place with the approval of the Kaiser Wilhelm Society senate and of the Reich Ministry of the Interior, he wrote. He referred to the importance of the institute and emphasized that the Jander selection could be justified only with regard to the "special needs" of the Reich Defense Ministry but not in "general scientific" competences.[45]

The Prussian Ministry had, in fact, already become interested in advancing Jander's research interests by early April 1933, shortly before Haber's resignation. The plan was to appoint him to a position in Berlin where he would have better staffing and funding than in Göttingen. In April Jander had already visited another research institute where he could carry out his chemical work. Even at this early date the state had been considering Haber's institute as a possible workplace for research on defense. Haber also seems to have become aware that someone would be carrying out "chemical work in the interest of the state."[46] Karl Becker from the Reich Ministry of Defense and the Army Weapons Office in Berlin had heard of the Prussian Ministry's plans and supported Jander, who had already "worked closely" with Becker's agencies on the most "urgent questions of defense."[47] Therefore, Jander's call to Berlin was planned before Haber's resignation and very soon after the National Socialists' seizure of power; it was compatible with the Reich Defense Ministry's military science research interests.

By December 1933 Planck was still trying to persuade the government to return the institute to the Kaiser Wilhelm Society. He even offered a compromise solution whereby an "especially qualified worker" would be sought who could combine the research interests of the Reich Defense

Ministry with other worthwhile projects.[48] He suggested Jander remain as head of a department at the institute where "gas research" would be done. In this way, Pfundtner explained (on behalf of the Society), the "goal of camouflage" would be reached and the institute would be directed by an outstanding scientist. The Ministry of Defense decided that such plans were impossible, however, and Jander would continue as director while the institute would be "placed at the service of the goal of military science in the Reich Defense Ministry's sense."[49]

When Planck saw that Jander's term was coming to an end, he tried again to assert the rights of the Society in the appointment of its own director. On 11 April 1935 he wrote a persuasive letter to Bernhard Rust reiterating some of his old arguments about protecting the "prestige of the Society abroad" and added new arguments to the old theme. By allowing the Society to select an outstanding scientist of its own choice the "Minister could make a great contribution to German science by destroying the false conception abroad concerning the National Socialist state's attitude towards science," wrote Planck.[50] Aside from these broader issues, Planck reacted negatively to the Ministry's new appointment of Peter Adolf Thiessen, who had been head of the physical chemistry section of the institute, as temporary director. Planck rightly feared that the Ministry would yet again appoint its own director. Once more the Ministry made Planck believe that this was only a temporary solution. Therefore he proposed Hans Fischer, a Nobel Prize winner from the College of Technology in Munich, as Haber's successor; Planck's proposal was approved by the executive committee of the Society. He had already had numerous conferences with colleagues, representatives of industry, and the Wehrmacht arguing that an outstanding and leading scientist should be offered the position. The attitudes and actions of the competing agencies involved in these negotiations reflect the polycratic nature of National Socialist Germany. Not only did the Reich Ministry of the Interior disagree with the Reich Ministry of Defense, but two military agencies—the Army Weapons Office and the Reich Ministry of Defense—supported different candidates.[51]

At a meeting of the executive committee Mentzel announced that the Reich Ministry of Defense wanted to continue "practical work" in "military chemistry" for some years; therefore, only Thiessen was suitable as Jander's successor and this would be a final, not temporary, appointment. Planck meekly agreed, as he did in 1933, to "yield to the wishes of the Reich Defense Minister," out of an "obvious duty."[52] As commentators have reiterated again and again, in other contexts, there was little or no protest to such imposed decisions during the Third Reich. Planck responded to this latest measure as he did to the dismissal of Jewish scientists—through diplomacy. In this case, however, he also tried to work within the rules of the Society whereby it had the right to appoint the director of an institute; apparently these were rights the Society no longer possessed. Unlike the Society's response to the dismissals, Planck actually wrote angry letters trying to resist the government's intrusion into the Society's personnel policies, but when the final decision was made he acquiesced.

On 1 May 1935, Professor Peter Adolf Thiessen was named director of the institute. Thiessen, who had studied chemistry, became a Privatdozent and professor of chemistry in Göttingen. He received his doctorate under Richard Zsigmondy, a Nobel-prize–winning colloid chemist. He had entered the National Socialist party in 1925 and received a golden party badge, but he left in 1928. He reentered the party on 1 May 1933.[53] In Göttingen he worked closely with Mentzel, who also came to the Kaiser Wilhelm Institute for Physical Chemistry in 1933. Mentzel, in fact, shared an apartment (Haber's former apartment) with Thiessen on Faradayweg in Dahlem.

When the board of directors of the institute for physical chemistry met on 19 June 1935, Planck reported that Thiessen was appointed in an "unusual way. The Kaiser Wilhelm Gesellschaft had intended to appoint another man. Now that the minister has made his decision the Kaiser Wilhelm Gesellschaft will obviously work together with the director of the institute."[54] He asked Thiessen to report on future plans for the institute. This institute, responded Thiessen, would do the kind of work that the Reich Army Ministry thought most important.

Although few documents remain, one can piece together the general research direction and character of the institute through some vague remarks in the published reports of the Society's activities in its journal *Die Naturwissenschaften,* through reports to the funding organizations that sponsored the work, and through some hints that remain in the surviving archival material. In the annual report for October 1935–March 1937, Thiessen reported that new facilities were being built and expanded. A new department for x-rays and electron methods had been built with a Dr. Wittstadt as "group leader"; here x-ray methods were applied to chemical questions. New high-voltage equipment and x-ray tubes were installed. The physical-chemical section worked on metallurgical problems and Winkel's department studied the constitution and characteristics of aerosol (work that can be used for chemical and biological warfare). Much of the work was related to the goals of the Four Year Plan and therefore could not be published. Following the scientific report, Thiessen wrote that the aim of the institute was to "form a community." He reported that comradeship evenings had been instituted and that the whole institute had visited one of the Minister of Education's camps.[55]

By 1940 the institute was so successful at adapting to, and functioning along the lines of, National Socialist ideology it had been named a "National Socialist model institute" and was awarded a golden flag by the Führer.[56] In times of peace the institute worked on science indirectly related to war research while in times of war it served the fatherland; to paraphrase Fritz Haber's dictum: In times of peace science serves humanity, in times of war, the fatherland. But the new direction the institute took, with a director not approved of by the Society, met with vigorous but ineffective opposition.

One area in which a science policy had been developing during the early years of the Third Reich was in military science or the science of defense. During the first year after the seizure of power the Kaiser Wilhelm Society made it a point to trace the history of the relationship of the Reich Armed Forces Ministry to the Society. The Society had wanted to disprove the rumor that it was withdrawing from work on the science of defense which had arisen because of the Society's disapproval of the seizure of Haber's institute by the Prussian Science Ministry to work on military research. Historically, the industry-related institutes had already worked on military research. For example, the institute for coal research directed by F. Hoffmann reported that it had worked together with, and received funding from, the Reich Armed Forces Ministry between 1926 and 1929. Five other industry-related institutes had connections of some kind with the army: the institutes for leather research in Dresden, for textile chemistry in Berlin-Dahlem, for silicate research in Berlin-Dahlem, for workers' physiology in Dortmund, and for iron research in Düsseldorf. By the middle of December 1933 Planck wrote to General Werner von Blomberg, the Reich's army minister, suggesting the creation of a committee made up of administrators from the Ministry and directors of institutes working on problems of defense. Planck thereby stressed the way in which the Society wanted to intensify its relationship with the War Ministry and displayed its willingness to work on urgent problems of national defense.[57]

Mobilization for War

It was not until about 1937 that discussions and plans began anew on the creation of a central Reich organization for scientific research. By this time, the Nazi regime had consolidated its forces, and its leaders began to recognize that scientific research could be of use in realizing and implementing economic, political, and military goals like the Four Year Plan. Therefore, some months after the announcement of the Four Year Plan in the fall of 1936, Minister Rust proclaimed the creation of a Reich Research Council in March 1937: "The great tasks ahead in German science for the Four Year Plan require that all resources in the area of research contributing to the fulfillment of these tasks be unified and brought into action."[58]

In this decree, which appeared in the Education Ministry's official gazette, Rust argued that, despite this goal of serving the Four Year Plan, freedom of research would remain untouched. The new organization was under the jurisdiction and control of the Ministry of Education (REM), but it would not dissolve other similar organizations.[59] For example, the German Research Council was closely tied to the Reich council and provided funding and administrative support. In 1936 Rudolf Mentzel, the much maligned but omnipresent figure in National Socialist science policy, had become president of the German Research Association and played an important role in the Reich Research Council as well—becoming director of the administrative advisers to the council. Rust, however, appointed General Karl Becker, head of the Army Weapons Office (Heereswaffenamt), president of the council. Becker was also dean and professor in the faculty of defense technology at the Technische Hochschule, Berlin. This appointment further illustrates the way in which the military was involved in shaping science policy.[60] The Reich Research Council was a culmination of Rust's earlier aborted attempts, including the plans for a Reich Academy of Science, to create a central organ for the advancement of science; it also embodied some of Stark's and Vögler's early ideas on the organization of science in the National Socialist state.

In addition to its stated goal of supporting the Four Year Plan, a new feature of the Reich Research Council was the creation of a board of specialists responsible for different areas of science from chemistry to nonferrous metals; eighteen scientists from all of Germany were appointed section heads. These scientists included three directors of Kaiser Wilhelm institutes—Peter Adolf Thiessen, the Nazi-appointed successor to Fritz Haber at the Kaiser Wilhelm Institute for Physical Chemistry, Richard Kuhn, head of the chemistry department at the Kaiser Wilhelm Institute for Medical Research in Heidelberg, and Werner Köster from the Kaiser Wilhelm Institute for Metal Research in Stuttgart. Thiessen was named head of the chemistry section, Kuhn, head of organic chemistry, and Köster was named head of nonferrous metals. But the most significant and active member of this body was Thiessen, who was part of the Mentzel–Schumann group.[61] In addition to the scientific specialists, the council's presidial members included high-ranking and old card-carrying National Socialists. The names speak for themselves: Reich Minister Dr. Bernhard Rust; Ministerial Director Professor Dr. Rudolf Mentzel, president of the DFG; Reich Minister Dr. Fritz Todt; Ministerial Director Dr. Erich Schumann; Dr. Leonardo Conti, Prussian State Secretary until 1939 and later Reich Health Leader; Professor Dr. Carl Krauch, Reich Office for Economic Construction; and State Secretary Herbert Backe.[62]

In May 1937 the Reich Research Council was officially inaugurated at the REM's opening celebration. Adolf Hitler, Hermann Göring, and Wilhelm Keitel, among other prominent National Socialists, attended the meeting but did not speak. Swastika flags and laurel wreaths hung in the Ministry's banquet hall as Rust delivered the opening speech: "The National Socialist awakening has called science to where the decisive battle will be fought."[63] Becker, the new president, also spoke and outlined the important tasks of the council, which included using research for urgent state needs and the regulation and coordination of research institutions.

But this new Reich-led and supported research institution proved to be ineffective under the leadership of Becker. Soon after the outbreak of war in 1939 Rust used Hitler's decree on the unification of administration to unify the German Research Association and the Reich Research Council under his office. When Becker died in 1940, Rust took over the presidency. Under Rust's leadership the council remained weak and was on unsure political ground. It was not until 1942 that a great change occurred in the National Socialists' attitude toward science, leading to a major reorganization.

In June 1942, Hitler issued a decree ordering the founding of an independent Reich Research Council under the leadership of Reich Marshall

Hermann Göring and financially supported by the Reich.[64] Now the Reich Research Council's original goals of advancing the Four Year Plan and supporting Germany's rearmament and self-sufficiency in raw materials were transformed and radicalized in order to support the war effort. The council's organization was similar to the earlier Reich Research Council, but it was no longer under the jurisdiction of the Reich Ministry of Education. Because of its war-related status it gained significant support and interest from the government.

Albert Speer, who was named Armaments Minister when Fritz Todt died in February 1942, stimulated the creation of this new Reich Research Council. The most significant change in the organization of the Reich Research Council was in this shift in jurisdiction from Rust's Ministry to Speer's Ministry. Speer envisioned appointing Albert Vögler, by this time president of the Kaiser Wilhelm Society, head of armaments research.[65] Despite its stated independence, the Reich Research Council still remained tied to Mentzel's German Research Association because the grants were approved and paid through it. Changes were made in the presidial council and heads of the research areas. The new organization of the Reich Research Council took place at a time when it was realized by the Germans that weapons research and development could make a decisive difference in carrying out the war. The Reich had belatedly mobilized German science for the final victory.

About a month after Hitler's decree on 6 July, an important secret meeting took place under the chairmanship of Hermann Göring at the Reich Aviation Ministry. The function of the old Reich Research Council was discussed and the agenda of a new research council was planned. Göring, in a rambling, lengthy introductory speech, announced that the Führer had empowered him to organize research for the war effort. This research, he announced, should be weighted toward weaponry development and advances in nutrition and health. Albert Vögler attended the meeting and made important suggestions about the organization of science. Other participants included Rust, Conti, and Alfred Rosenberg.[66] This meeting reflected a turning point in the National Socialists' attitude toward science. It was recognized only at this late date that the policy toward Jewish scientists had been a mistake and that the state needed their expertise. In a remarkable speech, Göring outlined some of his reasons for making these belated exceptions for Jewish scientists:

> The Führer rejects a regimentation of science as such . . . yes, this product is very valuable, exceptionally valuable and would take us a long way, but we cannot use it because a man happens to be married to a Jew or because he is half-Jewish . . . this must be avoided . . . I have just discussed this with the Führer. We have just kept a Jew in Vienna, and another photographer two years longer, because they have certain things that we need and that we absolutely have to complete at this moment. It would be crazy to say here: he has to go! He was a great researcher, he had a fantastic head, but he has

a Jewish wife and cannot stay at the university. The Führer has made exceptions for artists in cases like this. He will make exceptions even more gladly
if it is a question of an important research project or researcher.[67]

Much of this meeting involved discussion between Göring and Vögler.
Vögler, in his capacity as president and long-time associate of the Kaiser
Wilhelm Society and as a leading industrialist, offered organizational suggestions. He drew a sketch illustrating a plan whereby the Reich Marshall
was at the top of a pyramid with the two ministers Rust and Speer beneath
him. The Speer Ministry was to be in charge of research on defense, and
research emanating from the army, navy, and air force would be under its
jurisdiction. According to this plan, the Rust Ministry controlled the universities and a presidium presided over a senate which topped the other scientific sectors: the Reich institutions, the Reich trains, and the post office,
on the one hand, and the scientific-technical clubs, the Reich Research
Council, and the Kaiser Wilhelm Society, on the other. Vögler emphasized
the role of the Wehrmacht columns and argued that the chairman of each
sector should be a civilian—someone like Ludwig Prandtl, director of the
Kaiser Wilhelm Institute for Aerodynamics in Göttingen, could head the
air force section, for example.[68]

Except for this reference to Prandtl there was little discussion about the
role of the Kaiser Wilhelm Society and its institutes in this new order. Vögler
remarked that nutrition research was firmly anchored in the Kaiser Wilhelm
institutes and thanked General Friedrich Fromm for freeing many Kaiser
Wilhelm institute scientists from military service. Without this UK-Stellung
(Uk = *Unabkömmlich* = indispensable; military deferal) most of the institutes would have remained inactive, and therefore Vögler urged Fromm to
retain it for the duration of the war and not just for a year.[69] After the
meeting Vögler nominated many Kaiser Wilhelm Institute directors and
scientists to membership in the council. Seventeen institute directors and
three administrators—Vögler, Planck, and Telschow—were listed as intended
members.[70] But the most active members of the Kaiser Wilhelm Society
remained the leaders of the scientific specialties—Thiessen, Kuhn, and Köster.

By the end of July, a presidial council had been formed consisting of a
who's who of National Socialists: Albert Speer, Erhard Milch, Martin Bor-
mann, Alfred Rosenberg, Bernhard Rust, and Hermann Backe, among others.
Vögler, who had the confidence of high-ranking officials such as Speer, was
also appointed to join the presidium by Göring.[71] The presidium, however,
seemed to be a circle without much weight and did not meet during the
course of the war. The most important organ of the Reich Research Council remained the group of scientific specialists.[72] Vögler emerged in these
changes, however, as a nonofficial science adviser to Speer.

Göring outlined the new goals and tasks for the council. The chief
message was that a central place had to be created to answer the basic questions: Who is researching what, where, how and under whose contract?
Organizations requesting research contracts would have to be willing to share

this information in order to achieve a composite overall view of research in Germany. Moreover, the state must have the opportunity to lead and direct the research and to give orders for research projects. To achieve this centralization of research, Göring wanted to establish an "information center" with a director whose task was to gather this information from officers of various institutions including the armaments industry, the army, air force, universities, and research centers.[73] Soon after the creation of the second Reich Research Council Mentzel began to build up a card index file and information center for the Reich Research Council. The card file index stored information on scientists and institutions and served the function, outlined by Göring, of having a place to centralize information on the who, what, and where of ongoing research. Each index card had information on the scientist's institutional affiliation, area of specialty, research contracts, and personal data.[74]

Another feature of the second Reich Research Council was the creation of a Planning Office. In the middle of 1943, Göring had named Werner Osenberg director of a Planning Office in the Reich Research Council. Osenberg, an engineer, was the director of an institute for machine tools at the Technische Hochschule in Hannover. Since the beginning of the war he had worked for the navy and initiated a program of releasing researchers and technicians from military service so that they could do research for the navy. Researchers had begun to complain that they were losing workers to the army. Osenberg had joined this chorus of criticism and campaigned to leading figures from the party, state, and Wehrmacht referring to the Reich's neglect of using research for war purposes.[75]

On 29 June 1943, Göring wrote a decree announcing the creation of the Planning Office under the direction of Osenberg as one of the measures for "intensifying German research." Göring empowered Osenberg with executing the release of scientists for research important for the war effort. He was required to "negotiate with all the agencies of the Wehrmacht, the state, the party and industry" and to stay in contact with the members of the Reich Research Council presidial council. Finally, Osenberg would have to ensure that solved research problems would lead to practical results.[76] His chief task, however, was to integrate science and technology with the goal of building a healthy weapons technology.

One of Osenberg's most important accomplishments was the freeing of 5,000 scientists from military service in December 1943. On the order of Hitler and the Wehrmacht, 5,000 scientists under the catch phrase "Research" were called back from the front.[77] By the end of the war, Osenberg had been responsible for freeing over 15,000 scientists from military service.[78] Many of these scientists came from the Kaiser Wilhelm institutes.

The Kaiser Wilhelm Society and its institutes had contact with the war-inspired Reich Research Council, but the Society's role itself in National Socialist science policy was much more peripheral. After the creation of the second Reich Research Council, Friedrich Körber, director of the Kaiser Wilhelm Institute for Iron Research, became section head for steel and iron.

Another personal connection was Mentzel, who became second vice president of the Society in 1941 and who, as head of the office for science at the Education Ministry, had much contact with the Society. In addition, because the Society received support from the German Research Association, Mentzel had some influence on what projects received funding at the Society. Finally, Mentzel was head of the Reich Research Council and was part of the group around Schumann and Thiessen. The final personal connection was, of course, with Albert Vögler, the president of the Society, who had been a candidate for the presidency of the Reich Research Council when there was no apparent leader. Vögler had, in fact, been considered because he was "neither a party man, a ministry official or in the military."[79]

Industrial circles had been instrumental in changing government policy toward science at the beginning of World War II. While in the early years of the Third Reich *Deutsche Physik* or *Mathematik* seemed to be the kind of ideologized science the Reich would sanction, by 1942 military power took precedence over ideology. To many in the party, for example, the *Deutsche Physik* debate was, finally, an internal conflict between the Lenard school adherents and the theoretical physics school led by Werner Heisenberg; by the war years it had no utility for the National Socialist state.[80]

But important for science policy and for the preservation of science was Carl Ramsauer's plea to the REM to address the perceived decline in physics. At the time Ramsauer, an industrial physicist, was president of the German Physical Society. Although he had studied with Lenard, Ramsauer did not necessarily agree with his stance on politics and physics. Instead, he became a strong advocate of reversing the decline of physics. In the fall of 1941, Ramsauer together with other opponents of the Aryan physics movement, drafted a memorandum, which they sent to Bernhard Rust on 20 January 1942. In his cover letter, Ramsauer argued that German physics had been overtaken by Anglo-Saxon physics and enclosed six reports supporting this claim. He also documented attacks on theoretical physics while stressing the importance of theoretical physics for general physics and eventually applied work as well. In addition, Ramsauer enclosed a statement by Ludwig Prandtl, Director of the Kaiser Wilhelm Institute for Aerodynamics and Germany's most respected and well-connected aerodynamics expert, decrying the appointment of a *Deutsche Physik* adherent (Wilhelm Müller) to the coveted Munich professorship originally intended for theoretical physics; he considered this move sabotage for the continued development of physics.[81] Although the Rust Ministry did not respond to this memorandum, it did lead to the meeting between Göring and Vögler outlined previously. Prandtl's input and contacts with both Milch and Göring facilitated the contact between the academic physicist's concerns and the Aviation Ministry. Thereafter, Göring and the Speer Ministry began to see the importance of keeping science free from party political interference while mobilizing science for the war and the fatherland. This could not be done if science, in all its institutional manifestations from education to research, was not supported and nurtured.

In contrast to the sciences in general, the area of technology received large-scale support from the government early on, especially in weapons technology. During the Third Reich the first military ballistic missiles—the V 1 and V 2—were built and successfully deployed. The Army Experimental Station in Peenemünde was built in 1936 at a cost of 550 million Reich marks; the total cost of the project came to over RM 1 billion and therefore even exceeded the Manhattan Project in its scale. By 1943 Peenemünde had 15,000 staff members and was larger than all of Germany's other scientific projects combined.[82]

Contrary to the expectation that a totalitarian system would have a centralized, unified science policy, the Third Reich instead displayed a disunified policy made up of rival institutions. Although the Reich Research Council, the German Research Association, the science ministries, the Four Year Plan organizations, the Armaments Ministry, the Army, the Aviation Ministry, and the SS at times overlapped with each other organizationally or through personnel, there were continual quarrels and territorial squabbles which led to a polycracy in science policy.

In a 1939 conference with Mentzel, Karl Krauch, the plenipotentiary for the Four Year Plan, argued against using a Kaiser Wilhelm Institute as a Four Year Plan institute and stated that the Kaiser Wilhelm institutes had been "neglected by the Reich."[83] This statement is applicable also to the position of the Kaiser Wilhelm Society in the science policies of the National Socialist state in general. From the failure to integrate the Society into the Reich Ring of science, to its role in the weak research council, it was not used as much as it could have been by the state. This was due, in part, to the general developments in the government's attitude toward science and its belated recognition of the usefulness of science for the war effort, but it was also because of the special character of the Society. Recognizing its national and international prestige, the National Socialists were reluctant to interfere with the Society's affairs; moreover, with its primary emphasis on basic research, its goals were not compatible with a policy interested in the practical application of science. This did not mean, however, that the Society was immune from the changing political and economic context as it evolved in the Third Reich.

5

The Turning Point
1936–39

The Last Stand

On 10 and 11 January 1936, amid lectures, internal business, and receptions, the Kaiser Wilhelm Society celebrated its twenty-fifth birthday. The Society received two hundred guests, including representatives from the ministries, the Wehrmacht, and the party at Harnack House in Berlin-Dahlem. The official celebration began with a reception at the city hall, where Julius Lippert, the State Commissar for Berlin, characterized the Society as "the general staff of German science in our peaceful campaign for the spiritual, cultural and material development of our people."[1]

Max Planck spoke and reviewed the work of the Society. While acknowledging his gratitude to the government for its support, he opposed the collectivist tendencies of the National Socialists: "New scientific ideas never spring from a communal body, however organized, but rather from the head of an individually inspired researcher who struggles with his problems in lonely thought and unites all his thought on one single point which is his whole world for the moment."[2]

But any underlying criticism of the state by the Society was softened by praise and obeisance in a telegram sent to Hitler: "Science and business stand faithfully by your newly created German Reich knowing that they can only perform useful work under your leadership and under the protection of the armed forces."[3]

Despite this diplomacy on the part of the leaders of the Kaiser Wilhelm Society, the *Völkischer Beobachter*, the organ of the party, attacked the

Society, characterizing it as a "playground for Catholics, Socialists and Jews" that only "slowly made friends with National Socialist principles."[4] The paper argued that the National Socialist state needed its own organization for German science and threateningly asked if there was "room in the National Socialist state for the Kaiser Wilhelm Gesellschaft in its present form."[5] These threats from the press, however, did not result in any change in the shape of the Society by the party or the state. Nor did government officials such as Rust and Lippert make any announcements of impending changes. The anniversary did, however, symbolize German science's "last stand in defending the integrity" of the Society.[6] Yet another National Socialist newspaper, *The Black Corps* (*Das Schwarze Korps*), the organ of the SS and the Gestapo, ridiculed the Society, describing it as a "restricted circle" that still reflected the "aristocratic splendor" of the imperial crown as revealed by its name. It also mocked Planck and the exclusivity and social pretensions of the Society that originated with its founding in Wilhelmine Germany.[7]

Philipp Lenard thought that Planck had a "big propaganda instrument in his K.Wilh.Ges.," which first became apparent to him during the twenty-five-year celebration. He even went so far as to observe that this instrument had found its way into the *Völkischer Beobachter*. Lenard had found "unsuitable" contributions to the *Völkischer Beobachter* since December 1933, including a picture of the "typical Jewish Professor Fritz Haber." Haber, he wrote, is "typically Jewish in his science; his renown was created largely by Jews." To Lenard, this and other examples from the *Völkischer Beobachter* made it appear as though the "totally un-National Socialistic spirit of high finance and big industry had placed its hand (through M. Planck with the K. Wilh. Ges.) on the V.B., thereby cultivating the still ruling un-German spirit in science." Therefore, he thought it would be a "freeing act" for Alfred Rosenberg to "abolish" the Society in the future.[8]

Shortly after the celebration, Planck announced that he would not serve beyond his term, which ran out on 1 April 1936. This term had already been extended for three years by Wilhelm Frick in 1933, and Planck did not plan to renew it again.[9] This opening posed a threat to the integrity and independence of the Society. It was unclear who would succeed Planck, and the Society wondered if this would be the end of its self-government. The power vacuum might allow the National Socialists to appoint their own people to head the Society. Soon after the celebration, on 3 February 1936, Reich Minister Bernard Rust wrote to Reich Chancellor Adolf Hitler, as suggested by Krupp von Bohlen und Halbach (then vice president of the Society), announcing that Planck's term had run out and that leading members of the Society as well as Rust agreed that Planck would "retire" with the end of his term. "The question of his successor is not easy," continued Rust. Planck, Vögler, and Krupp von Bohlen und Halbach had already suggested Carl Bosch from I. G. Farben as a successor to Planck. Rust in turn informed the Society that this decision could not be made by the senate of the Society alone, but that the NSDAP's and the Führer's opinion had to be "obtained . . . in such an important matter." Krupp von Bohlen und

Halbach asked Rust to arrange a meeting with Hitler in order to discuss the issue personally. Rust complied with Krupp's wishes and received an answer a few days later from Hans Heinrich Lammers, the Secretary of State and head of the Reich Chancellery and Hitler's right-hand man, informing him that the "Führer und Reich Chancellor" wanted to refrain from a decision and delegated it back to Rust.[10] It was rare and unusual for Rust to write directly to Adolf Hitler, but the industrialists had power and influence during the early years of the Third Reich and could motivate a minister like Rust, who has also been rightly characterized as a weak leader. By 1936, the question of who would lead the Society was both decisive for the Society's further development in the Third Reich and of central importance in the general organization of scientific institutions and science policy.

Contrary to widespread belief, Johannes Stark and Philipp Lenard did not personally strive after the presidency at the Kaiser Wilhelm Society, although they had thought about a possible successor to Planck as early as 1933, when it was still not clear whether he would be forced to resign.[11] The question arose again in 1936, when Planck was reaching the end of his second term.[12] Stark had asked Lenard if he would consider taking over the presidency in 1933 should Planck be forced to resign. Stark promised the post would not be too much work, but the chief goal would be to "bring in a new spirit [*Geist*] to the Kaiser Wilhelm Institutes." Lenard flatly refused the offer with the remark that he was too old for the position.[13]

It was plausible that Stark would aspire to the presidency of the Society as he had become president of the Emergency Association for German Science and the Reich Institute for Physics and Technology. Both Lenard and Stark sought to influence the filling of key positions after 1933, and the Kaiser Wilhelm Society presidency was one of the most important posts in science administration. Soon after the seizure of power in 1933, Lenard wrote to Stark that "finally the time has come when we can realize our conception of science and research."[14]

In 1936, with the imminent vacancy of the presidency, neither Lenard nor Stark still wanted to lead the Society. The only alternative course they saw was to dissolve the Society completely. After all, in Lenard's eyes, it had been a "Jewish monstrosity" from its founding, with the chief goal of making Jews "socially acceptable" and bringing them into powerful positions as "researchers."[15] Stark thought all the institutes supported by Prussia and the Reich should be dissolved and transformed into Reich institutions such as the Reich Institute for Physics and Technology. The remaining institutes, privately supported with the money of "Jews, democrats, and Freemasons," could continue to be maintained by the Society. When it was clear that the Society would survive undissolved, possible candidates for the presidency suggested by Stark were Theodor Vahlen, then still director of the Reich Ministry of the Interior, and the physicist Rudolf Tomaschek, a Lenard student and disciple.[16] By the end of 1936, however, Stark had resigned the presidency of the Emergency Association for German Science, claiming that he had fought enough against the bureaucracy and wished to return to his scientific work. This also marked the end of the discussions between Lenard and Stark on the topic. On 29 May 1937 the senate nominated Carl Bosch to succeed Max Planck as president of the Society; he assumed office on 15 July 1937.

The Change in Leadership

Negotiations leading up to this nomination, however, lasted about half a year, although the Society had begun to think about a replacement soon after the twenty-five-year celebration, when Planck announced that he would not continue as president. A battle had to be won, or a compromise negotiated, before the Society's choice could be approved by the Rust Ministry (REM). Moreover, the Rust Ministry used the transition time to require changes in the statutes of the Society—changes it had spared the Society immediately after the seizure of power in 1933. The Ministry demanded the inclusion of the leadership principle and required that the Society be placed under the supervision of the REM. In addition, the executive committee, initially composed of a smaller circle of senators, was transformed into an advisory board consisting of many industrialists.[17]

The proposed changes in the statutes were discussed in a series of covert meetings that stretched out over the spring months of 1937; no written minutes exist of the discussions. In an invitation for a conference of senators, Planck announced that "questions will be treated that are of central importance for the Society" and that a draft of the new statutes would also be discussed.[18] Further details are not documented. The meetings were often delayed because Carl Bosch was frequently ill and unable to attend. This illness was also to plague his presidency; therefore, the general director played a stronger role than usual from 1937 to 1940.

Bosch negotiated directly with Otto Wacker, the head of the Science Office at the REM (from 1937 until his death in 1940), about the changes in the statutes; the matter was then discussed in a small circle at the Kaiser Wilhelm Society.[19] The forced changes seemed in fact to have been drafted by Wacker himself, who acted as a representative of the Ministry. There seems to have been some protest to the introduction of changes into the statutes and to the precise language used, but only one indirect reference to such a protest exists. Wilhelm Groh, a lawyer and administrator from the REM, wrote on 12 October 1937 that "the new formulation of the statutes has created many difficulties; not only because every representative from the Society who [is] a scientist will interpret any attempt to use the principles of the National Socialist state on the Society as an infringement of the rights of the researcher," but it will give rise to great protest among non-German scientists, who would refer to the damaging effects of such a measure abroad.[20] Therefore, one had to wait for an appropriate time for such a change—presumably Planck's resignation. No other evidence exists documenting the general reaction among the leaders and scientists at the Society. Planck, however, turned to the senate, asking powerful figures such as Hjalmar Schacht to exert their influence in order to forestall the change.

The key change required in the bylaws was the introduction of the leadership principle. One of the first drafts read: "The president of the Society is nominated by the senate and *named* by the Reich Minister for Science, Education and People's Education. He is the leader [Führer] of the Society."[21] The old statute had had no separate paragraph on the president, nor was he designated the "leader," but the major distinction in practice was that he had been *elected* by the senators. The final version of the changed bylaw had a softer tone to it: "The president is nominated by the senate and named by the minister for six years. The president is the responsible director [Leiter] of the Society."[22]

These statutes were approved at the senate meeting on 29 May 1937 and were then given their final approval at the yearly meeting in June. Bosch could now be named president. Although the decision had already been made by the senate meeting, the minutes of the meeting reveal the extent to which Wacker bullied the Society into accepting his way. It also displays the new active role which the Ministry attempted to play in determining the Society's shape and agenda. Planck began the senate meeting with the issue of the presidential election. Before he even began his discussion, Wacker interrupted him and stated that he was ordered by the Ministry to defer this first point until after the second point—the changes in the statutes— had been disposed of. The minutes then laconically reported that Planck "expressed objections" but withdrew them after a "short discussion."[23]

In order to install Bosch as president, the Society had to change the statutes and dismiss Friedrich Glum along with his staff assistant Lukas von Cranach. Both had had their difficulties with the National Socialists, and their names were on the list of politically unreliables. Ernst Telschow, who had worked in the administration since 1931, replaced Glum and became general director. Telschow had received a Ph.D. in chemistry in 1911 and had written a dissertation on the element actinium under the direction of Otto Hahn, then a young Privatdozent at the University of Berlin. He was an assistant at Emil Fischer's chemistry institute until 1913, when his military service began. He was in the service until 1918. After that he entered his father's business—a famous bakery—the Telschow Konditorei.[24] But more important for the position, Telschow, a "party comrade" (Parteigenosse), had become a party member in 1933 and enjoyed the trust of the state and party. Otto Wacker, a staunch National Socialist from the Ministry, was named first vice president of the Society.

Friedrich Glum had suggested that Bosch become president, but this was no guarantee that he would continue as general director. Bosch had been a long-time senator of the Society, he was "half a scientist, had a great international reputation, was a Nobel Prize winner, and above all was head of I. G. Farben."[25] Given the times, this was an appropriate choice to ensure the Society's survival.

The great changes occurring at the Society in 1937 did not go unnoticed. A newspaper from Prague featured an article entitled "Research and the Leadership Principle," in which the "strongest and most independent organization for German science" is characterized as having "fallen into the hands of the state and party." Basing its information on the yearly meeting, the newspaper noted that the new president and the new senators of the Society were not elected but named. Under the leadership principle no elections existed; the only criterion for appointment was the responsibility to the Führer. It is unknown, continued the paper, who named them or where the changes in the bylaws came from.[26]

Research and the Four Year Plan

The change in leadership at the Kaiser Wilhelm Society coincided with changes and crises in the political and economic sphere at large. The motivation for a change in leadership did not stem, however, from these changes in society, although the choice of a successor mirrored the emerging influence of industry and I. G. Farben. The economic and political changes did, however, have an impact on the shape and research agendas of several scientific institutes of the Society.

At the party rally in September 1936, Hitler officially announced the establishment of the Four Year Plan. He claimed the plan was created to make Germany self-sufficient in the development of raw materials and to save on foreign exchange. But the covert goal was to prepare Germany for war in four years; what was in fact occurring was a massive rearmament and autarky program. Hitler's announcement had been precipitated by a shortage of foreign exchange, which in turn made it difficult to buy raw materials from abroad. Also, tensions arose with Hjalmar Schacht, the economics minister and president of the Reichsbank. Schacht, who was in charge of managing the foreign exchange, did not wholeheartedly accept autarky—the idea of self-sufficiency or independence in a country's economy—and was soon ousted from his position as Reich Minister of Economics. Reich Marshall Hermann Göring, the second in command after Hitler, became commissioner for the Four Year Plan in the spring of 1936. Soon after his appointment, Göring created the Office for Raw Material and Foreign exchange on 4 April 1936 under the auspices of the Four Year Plan.[27]

It did not take long before his office began to mobilize science in support of the manufacture of raw materials. Chemistry and the chemical industry both profited from and contributed the most to the plan. Karl Krauch, chairman of the board at I. G. Farben, headed the department for research and development. Krauch, who ended up as chief defendant for I. G. Farben at the Nuremberg trials, had ambitious plans for the department and set forth the task of creating a special organization consisting of all state and private institutes, including the Kaiser Wilhelm Society, in order to have an "overview of the leading scientists in all the areas . . . and the possibilities for working on certain problems which could be available for use in normal times and in times of crisis."[28] I. G. Farben, now notorious for its cooperation with the Nazi regime, participated so heavily in the Four Year Plan that it became known as the "I. G. Farben plan."[29]

As Hayes brought to our attention, one cannot overestimate I. G. Farben's contribution to the Four Year Plan. In addition to synthetic fuel and rubber—the key raw materials developed by Farben—steel and metal concerns also played a major role in helping to advance the Reich's autarky plans.[30] Other raw materials needed by the Reich were fat for nutrition and technical purposes, protein, textiles, rubber, leather, mineral oil, and substitutes for metal. The Reich did not hesitate to turn to the appropriate Kaiser Wilhelm Society institutes to fulfill Germany's needs, but one has to be careful to distinguish among various kinds of institutes in order to evaluate to what extent the Kaiser Wilhelm Society cooperated with Reich agencies in advancing the Four Year Plan. The Four Year Plan spawned the creation of new institutes at the Kaiser Wilhelm Society; these were precisely called "Four Year Plan Institutes" and were supported by the Reich Agency for Economic Construction.

Contact between the Society and Göring's Office for Raw Material and Foreign Exchange, the first agency created for the Four Year Plan, was mediated by Ernst Telschow, the Society's general director, who was still only a staff member of the administration in 1936, when the connection first began. It seems that Telschow, who joined the NSDAP in 1933 and had the confidence of the party and state, had a second job at Göring's office and used this contact when turning to various directors of applied institutes asking them to accept research contracts for the Four Year Plan. When Göring's office was dissolved, it was transformed into the Reich Office for Economic Construction, and several Kaiser Wilhelm institutes had research contracts to fulfill. Two institutes were designated "Four Year Plan Institutes," which meant they had lost their autonomy and worked chiefly for the Reich.

Soon after the creation of Göring's office in the spring of 1936, Telschow contacted the institutes for metal and steel and explained the work of the new office. In July 1936 he had already written to Körber, the director of the Kaiser Wilhelm Institute for Steel Research, that "the question of substituting natural raw material in order to save foreign exchange, will be a focus of the Reich Office." A special department for "Research and Testing" was created because the Office recognized the importance of research institutions for its work. "The president of the Kaiser Wilhelm Gesellschaft gave me permission to work with the Minister president's staff," related Telschow. "I took over the work gladly," he continued, "even though I am perfectly aware of the difficulties one can expect. I think, however, that it is worth it to work with them and I especially think that the Kaiser Wilhelm Institutes can contribute to this work in an important way."[31] Telschow explained to Körber that certain institutes and researchers would be given the task of doing research in designated areas of raw materials research. "Obviously," he wrote, "no force should be used" to do this, but according to the various ministries, it will be done as a matter of course. Telschow's coercive letter ended on a forceful note: "I know that you cannot suppress a certain amount of criticism and many 'buts.' I ask you, however, to hold these objections back and to cooperate. Everything else will follow."[32]

Telschow's pressure resulted in some research contracts with Göring's Office for Raw Materials from several Kaiser Wilhelm institutes. Körber agreed to work on "especially urgent problems," and General Löb, the head of the office, marveled at the "exceptionally well equipped institute" for steel research that had been doing "valuable work" for years on questions of raw material development for the "fatherland."[33] Positive answers also came in from three other Kaiser Wilhelm institutes as well. Eitel, director of the institute for silicate research, Köster, the director of the institute for metal research, and Thiessen, director of the physical chemistry institute, were all ready to cooperate.[34] One of the most active institutes to cooperate in this program was Peter Thiessen's physical chemistry institute. He suggested four areas within which he was willing to work: the production of fat from coal, research on the characteristics of soap, detergent, and softeners, research on the solid condition of organic chemical substances, and, finally, work on the tempering of metals and alloys.[35] It is therefore not surprising to find that Thiessen actively took part in the meeting of the National Socialist Teacher's Association at the University of Berlin in January 1937 on the topic of "Science and the Four Year Plan."

In his lecture Thiessen addressed the question of Germany saving its own natural resources and acquiring new ones. Germany lacks most metals necessary for producing bronze-based alloys of copper and tin and is also deficient in great quantities of leather, fossil fuels, and rubber. Therefore, Thiessen advocated autarky in the production of machinery indispensable to modern-day "motorized culture"—and, implicitly, to modern warfare. In addition, he extolled the results of modern chemistry which made it possible to replace natural resources with synthetic substances like artificial fiber, rubber (*Kautshuk*), and leather, for example. Thiessen also used this occasion to demonstrate the National Socialist regime's positive view of science, in order to defend it against claims that it was hostile and adverse to science. The National Socialist state, he argued, allowed a new cooperation to develop among science, industry, and the state through ideological concord. The political and economic benefits of this "goal-oriented" and applied science will allow Germany to acquire foreign resources once autarky is achieved.[36]

Most of these institutes were still Kaiser Wilhelm institutes doing some contract research on the side. The institute for leather research and Thiessen's physical chemistry institute were the only Kaiser Wilhelm Society institutes actually designated "Four Year Plan" institutes. The Four Year Plan institutes were creations of the Göring office as well as the Reich Agency for Economic Construction, its successor organization. In 1941 there were at least twelve such institutes in the Reich focused primarily on research in chemistry, but also on other practical areas such as plastics, engines, and clock technology; by 1943 thirty-five Four Year Plan institutes were supported by the Reich Office for Economic Construction.[37] But there were still only two full-fledged Four Year Plan institutes at the Society, while other institutes undertook some contract work on the side.

In 1941 research contracts existed between the Reich Office for Economic Construction and the Kaiser Wilhelm Society institutes with the leather research institute, Dr. Isolde Hausser from the medical research institute, Heidelberg, and Professor Wilhelm Rudorf, director of the institute for breeding research. All these institutes had formally written contracts with the Reich. They included information ranging from the amount of financial support and length of the research contract from the Reich, represented by the Reich Office for Economic Construction, to more mundane aspects of a legal contract such as giving notice.[38] Professor Rudorf received RM 21,500 to continue his research on plants containing rubber (*Kautschuk*), which he had begun between 1937 and 1939 with a contract from the Reich. Dr. Hausser received RM 8,000 for research on physiological-medical effects of ultra–short waves, and the physical chemistry institute received RM 18,000 to continue research on soap, fat, and oil.

From the examples cited it is clear that the Kaiser Wilhelm institutes supported by the Four Year Plan were primarily from the field of applied or, as aptly called in German, "goal-directed" research. However, the importance of the Four Year Plan in its effect upon the scientific work taking place at the Kaiser Wilhelm Society as a whole should not be overestimated. In fact, the number of the Kaiser Wilhelm institutes that were supported by the Four Year Plan was proportionally small when measured against the total number of Kaiser Wilhelm institutes (thirty-four to thirty-six in 1938); and the proportion seems even smaller when compared to the much greater ratio of universities and technical colleges cooperating in the Four Year Plan. A majority of Four Year Plan institutes were actually supported by or related to I. G. Farben, and the effort was concentrated there; but for an institution priding itself on advancing basic research the amount of work done was more than that undertaken in normal times.

International Exchange and Isolation

By 1936 German science had been losing its status as a link in international science, and German scientists were becoming increasingly isolated from other scholars abroad. This change manifested itself in several ways. At the Kaiser Wilhelm Society a major development was the decline in visitors at Harnack House, the Society's guest house created in 1929 to promote international contact. As Alan Beyerchen has pointed out, however, this decline came from Western and, in particular, American scientists, whereas visits from scientists from other countries like Romania, Bulgaria, and Hungary increased.[39] The records of visitors to Harnack House from 1929 to 1939 chart the decline in foreign visitors. Although the total number of visits

actually increased to a high point in 1934–35 of 359 visitors in toto, 71
percent were German and 29 percent were foreigners, of whom only 3 percent were American. Another important development was the official
denunciation of international exchange in 1936 and its reversal by 1938–
39 with the changed political constellations and foreign policy aims whereby
certain international exchanges were stimulated and sanctioned by the
National Socialist government. Three examples from the late 1930s illustrate the little-known phenomenon of international exchange at the Kaiser
Wilhelm Society in the Third Reich: scientific exchange with Soviet Russia
and England and research visits by foreign guests.

In response to a directive by the Reich and Prussian Minister for Science, Education and People's Education, Planck wrote to all institute
directors on 27 June 1936 asking them to report on the extent and nature
of any exchange relationship with Soviet Russia. By February 1937 the minister's circular had led to a prohibition of scientific exchange with that country.[40] The director's responses produced a differentiated picture of contacts
with Soviet Russia. From the twelve institutes answering the circular in 1936,
six had varying degrees of contact with institutes in the Soviet Union or
exchanged journals. Some Kaiser Wilhelm institute scientists seemed to have
considered Soviet contributions in certain areas to be important enough to
retain scientific exchange in the form of journal-swapping and other contacts with specific institutes. For example, August Thienemann, the director of the hydrobiological institute, reported that his institute "naturally had
very strong exchanges with Russia" and listed seven institutes in Russia with
which his institute had personal contact.[41] On the other hand, Wilhelm
Rudorf, director of the institute for breeding research, simply traded the
Zeitschrift für Induktive Abstammungs- und Vererbungslehre for the *Bulletin of Applied Botany of Genetics and Plant Breeding* with the Leningrad
Academy.[42]

About half a year after the initial query from the Ministry, the Kaiser
Wilhelm Society received another letter marked "confidential," in which the
REM forbade scientific exchange with the Soviet Union: "As a follow-up
to my circular of 17 June 1936 concerning the distribution of articles and
the maintenance of exchange relations with Soviet Russia . . . I forbid every
scientific written contact between German scholars and scholars or scientific institutions in the Soviet Union."[43] In cases where the contact could
be construed to be in the "interest of the state" the minister had to receive
a report in order to make the final approval of such contact.[44] A few weeks
later the requests began to come in. The minister wrote to the Kaiser Wilhelm Institute for Leather Research refining its definition of the "interest
of the Reich": "If it appears desirable to observe the development of certain research branches in the Soviet Union or if special areas of research in
Germany can profit from the results."[45]

At the end of November 1939, two months after World War II broke
out, Mentzel sent out yet another circular on the resumption of scientific
relations with the Soviet Union and asked to what extent it was in the

interests of the Germans.[46] A few weeks after Mentzel's circular had come out, Telschow announced the Reich Education Minister's intentions at a meeting of the Society's advisory council: The Reich Minister encourages the scientific members of the Kaiser Wilhelm institutes to "take up" relations with countries abroad for the "purpose" of "influencing neutral countries." The Ministry particularly encouraged scientific relations with Soviet Russia; most of the institutes had in fact highly supported this.[47]

In contrast to the sparse reply in 1936, in 1939 twenty-three institute directors responded to the question of scientific relations with Soviet Russia in the form of letters or reports. This occurred during the ill-fated non-aggression pact between Adolf Hitler and Joseph Stalin from 23 August 1939 to 22 June 1941. In 1939 fourteen institutes admitted to having contacts with Russian science. Most of the respondents strongly supported contact with Soviet Russia in the form of exchanging journals or increasing knowledge of a particular specialty.[48] Soviet science seemed to offer worthwhile contributions in many areas. Although I do not believe the reports provide enough information to gauge the Russians' scientific level,[49] they do show that the Kaiser Wilhelm Society scientists valued the research enough to find it useful for their own work. Indeed, the worthiness of scientific contact was often conceived of in these terms. For example, Wolfgang Graβman, director of the leather research institute, thought this contact was in the "interests of the German leather economy."[50] Fritz von Wettstein, director of the Kaiser Wilhelm Institute for Biology, wrote that "maintaining scientific exchange with Soviet-Russian biologists was in the interest of German biology."[51] Walther Bothe, director of the physics section of the Kaiser Wilhelm Institute for Medical Research, wrote that it was timely because of the present situation. There was a possibility that German science could collaborate in the exploitation of Russian mineral reserves. Bothe thought this could be an aid in finding radioactive ore for his work. Furthermore, he thought it would be "very advantageous" to establish an exchange of scientific reprints because of the difficulty in obtaining foreign journals in Germany at that time.[52] On 21 October 1940 the resumption of scientific relations was officially approved.[53] But this state of affairs did not last long, and political affairs shaped the course of events yet again with the German invasion of Russia on 22 June 1941. The minister belatedly revoked his earlier order one year later on 18 June 1942.[54]

Another attempt at scientific exchange with a neutral country began in 1938 shortly before the war broke out. While the Science Ministry forbade exchange with Soviet Russia in 1937, the Foreign Office encouraged and stimulated exchange with England. A cultural exchange with the Royal Society originated in an inquiry by the Foreign Office in July 1938 asking if the Kaiser Wilhelm Society had a "representative" in England. The Foreign Office intended to "expand its activity in the area of cultural policies in England and to give this activity a pronounced scientific character." It would have liked to see the Society itself act as a representative. The Ministry of Education also supported the expansion of cultural policies (*Kultur-*

politik) with England.[55] While the Society rejected this idea, it did begin to explore the possibility of creating a Kaiser Wilhelm institute in England and sent Hugo Andreas Krüß, the vice president of the Society, there. Krüß negotiated with the German ambassador and with the head of the Royal Society, Sir William Bragg, in the fall of 1938, and these discussions quickly led to an exchange agreement between the Kaiser Wilhelm Society and the Royal Society. Carl Bosch, by then president of the Society, discouraged creating an institute for the humanities in favor of an institute in the natural sciences, because the former would "easily create the impression of a purely political party effect."[56]

The initial form of exchange in a generally conceived cooperative relationship between the Kaiser Wilhelm Society and the Royal Society was that of a Guest Lecturer Series. F. G. Donnan, emeritus professor of chemistry at the University of London, and A. J. Clark, professor of materia medica at the University of Edinburgh, were the first British professors chosen to speak, and a dinner was held in their honor at Harnack House on 24 February with guests from the Foreign Office, the Ministry of Science, and leading institute directors from Berlin-Dahlem.[57] The British professors thought the visit had been a great success, and Donnan wrote to Krüß thanking him "most heartily" for his "splendid hospitality" and for the "efficiency of all arrangements made." He was also "impressed with everything" he saw in the "new Germany," from the laboratories to the new institutions.[58]

Conversely, in June 1939, the Royal Society hosted four German scientists. They were Otmar von Verschuer, then at the University of Frankfurt, Richard Kuhn, director of the chemistry section of the Kaiser Wilhelm Institute for Medical Research, F. Wever, of the Kaiser Wilhelm Institute for Iron Research, and Otto Hahn of the Kaiser Wilhelm Institute for Chemistry. In the first exchange lecture, Verschuer spoke on his research on twins and the role of heredity and environment in the development of the individual. Two days later Kuhn spoke on the chemical bases of the biological actions of light.[59]

The final example of a cultural exchange in the late thirties at the Kaiser Wilhelm Society was the program established to invite guest scientists to the Kaiser Wilhelm Insitute for Biology. At the end of 1937 Bosch had approved RM 10,000 for an exchange of scientists to occur in 1938. In the fall of 1938 Fritz von Wettstein, director of the institute, invited Sir Vincent Brian Wigglesworth, a British professor from the London School of Hygiene and Tropical Medicine, who he considered to be "one of the best representatives of Developmental Physiology in the Anglo-American world."[60] Telschow liked the idea and invited Wigglesworth to be a guest of the Society so that they could "advance the necessary and desired exchange of scientific methods and achievements of both our countries."[61] In addition, Dr. Philip White, a research associate at the Rockefeller Institute for Medical Research, Department of Animal and Plant Pathology, who was considered to be the best representative for the study of tissue culture in the world, was scheduled to come in July 1940.[62]

The generalization most applicable to international exchanges is their *nationalistic* and political motivation. These dual motivations originated in the examples cited either from the government or from the Kaiser Wilhelm Society. Nationalism and political constellations played a role in the scientists' reasons for maintaining contact with the Soviet Union; by using valuable results or having access to journals unavailable in Germany, German science could be made much stronger. The exchange with the Royal Society had been stimulated by the foreign office and motivated by changing political alliances. Germany and England were still on good terms diplomatically in 1938. But the foreign office wanted to camouflage this political motivation by giving any contact, whether it be a Kaiser Wilhelm Society institute abroad or an exchange, a "scientific character." The guest scientists' agreement at the Kaiser Wilhelm Institute for Biology had its origins in the growing isolation from scientists abroad and attempts to remedy this deficit by reestablishing contact with scholars abroad. Through this contact, scientists could exchange new methods and techniques; the biology institute also benefited from the presence of two leading biologists in the world in a field rapidly gaining ground in America and falling behind in Germany.

There were clearly multifaceted reasons and motivations for scientific exchanges in the late thirties. By the war years these motivations became increasingly political as the Reich expanded to include "Greater Germany." The three themes explored here—the change in leadership, research and the Four Year Plan, and internationalism and scientific exchange—highlight the changing administrative context and the Society's seemingly increased subordination to the state and its step toward industry. In order to examine all the different levels of activity taking place at a scientific research institution one also needs to examine the transformations in scientific research at the Society.

6

The Survival of Basic
Biological Research

Virtually no one outside Germany, however, thought that Schramm's story was right. This was because of the war. It was inconceivable to most people that the German beasts would have permitted the extensive experiments underlying his claims to be routinely carried out during the last years of a war they were so badly losing. It was all too easy to imagine that the work had direct Nazi support and that his experiments were incorrectly analyzed. Wasting time to disprove Schramm was not to most biochemists' liking.[1]

James Watson, *The Double Helix*

The science done at the Kaiser Wilhelm institutes was differentially affected by National Socialist ideology and the state's policies, but generally excellent research continued—and pathbreaking discoveries were made—throughout the period of the Third Reich. One of the most widely known discoveries is that of nuclear fission in 1938 at the institute for chemistry. Some of the great scientists who stayed in Germany at the Kaiser Wilhelm institutes include Werner Heisenberg, Otto Hahn, and Carl-Friedrich von Weizsäcker in physics and Otto Warburg, Adolf Butenandt, Alfred Kühn, Fritz von Wettstein, N. Timoféeff-Ressovsky, and Richard Kuhn in the life sciences and chemistry. Berlin was hardly a scientific wasteland, and even throughout the war high-quality work was done in basic and applied science. One can capture just that variation in the type of research done in the Third Reich by examining the fate of the life sciences, including branches that were obviously politicized such as eugenics or race hygiene as well as basic research in genetics, radiation genetics, endocrinology, and virus research.

The passage quoted from James Watson's book *The Double Helix* is not only applicable to Gerhard Schramm's work on virus research, but also to scientific research in general at the Kaiser Wilhelm institutes. Many people both during and after the war found it hard to believe that normal research continued in Germany without "direct Nazi support" and that the "German beasts" allowed research to continue at the Kaiser Wilhelm institutes. Innovative and excellent research took place at the Kaiser Wilhelm Institute for Biochemistry (headed by Adolf Butenandt) and Biology (codirected by Fritz von Wettstein, Alfred Kühn, and Max Hartmann) and the genetic department of the Kaiser Wilhelm Institute for Brain Research, headed by N. Timoféeff-Ressovsky. That high-quality and innovative research was recognized and continued during the thirties is illustrated by the fact that three Nobel Prizes were awarded to Kaiser Wilhelm institute scientists during the Third Reich. Adolf Butenandt was awarded the Nobel Prize in Chemistry jointly with Leopold Ružička in 1939 for his work on sex hormones and Richard Kuhn, head of the chemistry department at the Kaiser Wilhelm Institute for Medical Research in Heidelberg, was awarded the Nobel Prize in 1938 for his work on vitamins and other physiological substances. Otto Hahn was awarded the Nobel Prize in 1944 for his work on nuclear disintegration. All three were forced to decline the prize by the German government (it was boycotting the prize after Carl von Ossietzky, a Jew, was awarded the peace prize) and only received the diploma and medal after the Second World War.

Because the postwar historiography on science during the Third Reich focused attention on the decline and destruction of science, the general public and scholars were often not ready to see conceptually other aspects of scientific development in National Socialist Germany. While in general Nazi Germany did not provide an especially favorable environment for the practice of scientific research, pockets of innovation existed, and some institutional arrangements provided support for normal science. By identifying and describing the Berlin-Dahlem community of scientists in biology at the Kaiser Wilhelm Society, by examining the issue of whether new personnel was politically or scientifically qualified when institute director vacancies were filled, and by explaining the nature, type, and increase in financial support one can reconstruct a vibrant scientific community. In addition, two disciplines in the life sciences—the institutionalization of virus research and the practice of radiation genetics—illustrate two areas of highly productive research. All these elements at the Kaiser Wilhelm institutes show the way in which science at these institutes was less affected by factors traditionally hostile to the development of science in totalitarian regimes and help explain the reasons for its survival.

The Berlin Biological Community

One of the least politicized institutes of the Society was the Kaiser Wilhelm Institute for Biology, which was codirected by Fritz von Wettstein, Alfred Kühn, and Max Hartmann. None of the directors was in the party or other National Socialist associations, and despite the political potential of their research in heredity, they were able to continue along pre-1933 lines. This does not mean, however, that they withdrew from the community and did not continue to participate in scientific organizational activities.[2] If there were any compromises made they manifest themselves in willingness to serve as leaders or advisers to organizations in science which were led by National Socialists.

Friedrich (Fritz) von Wettstein (1895–1945) was the son of Richard (Ritter von Westersheim) Wettstein (1863–1931), the well-known botanist from Vienna who wrote the successful *Handbook for Systematic Botany* (which went through four editions) and believed in Lamarckian evolution.[3] Richard von Wettstein had also been considered for the Kaiser Wilhelm Society presidency in 1929. His son Fritz was born in Prague in 1895, where his father had been a professor of botany since 1892. Fritz von Wettstein's specialty was also botany, and he was an assistant in Carl Correns's department at the Kaiser Wilhelm Institute for Biology from 1919 to 1924. He became a professor of botany at the University of Göttingen in 1925 and later at the University of Munich in 1931. His area of specialty was plant genetics, and he wrote his dissertation on cytoplasmic inheritance in moss.[4] After lengthy negotiations, Wettstein joined the Kaiser Wilhelm Institute for Biology in the fall of 1934 as first director and department head succeeding Carl Correns, who died in February 1933. He worked there until 1945, when he died of pneumonia. In Berlin he continued his work on plant genetics but also took on many organizational functions, becoming a senator of the Society and head of the biomedical section of the scientific council. He seemed to be quite suited to this work as well as skilled in dealing with the National Socialists. Several scientists have commented on his diplomatic skills. Georg Melchers, a student of his, referred to his "elegant diplomatic methods" as an institute director and as an enemy of the National Socialist system. Karl Zimmer, a radiation biologist, also referred to him as a "diplomat." Finally, he himself wrote to Alfred Kühn during the Third Reich and said that he had to "play diplomat" when dealing with the Springer Verlag.[5]

Max Hartmann also continued his previous work which focused on protozoa and fertilization, reproduction, and sexuality, but he withdrew to Buchenbühl (Allgäu) in 1938 to write. He was involved in organizing the German-Greek Institute for Biology in Greece during the late thirties and early forties and spent much time in Greece. In addition to his scientific work he wrote on philosophical issues in biology as he had done in the 1920s.[6]

Alfred Kühn joined the Kaiser Wilhelm Institute for Biology in 1937 as the successor to Goldschmidt, who had emigrated in 1936. A prominent zoologist, he had spent most of his professional career at the University of Göttingen (1920–37), where he had attracted a large number of students because of his stimulating teaching and important research. Although Kühn's scientific work embraced many different fields, including embryology, cytology, and the physiology of sensation, by the time he came to Berlin-Dahlem he was concentrating almost entirely on genetics and early development. His major research object was the meal moth *Ephestia kühniella*, and the central problems of his research concerned the formation of patterns and the effect of genes. In his investigations of eye color mutants, he found that ommochrome pigments in the chain of biochemical processes were set off by genes. It was with this project that he began collaborative work with Adolf Butenandt, then also in Göttingen, and found that genes achieved their effects because of a specific enzyme.[7] Kühn was particularly known for his textbooks on zoology and heredity. His *Grundriss der allgemeinen Zoologie*, also called the "small Kühn," had gone through seventeen editions by 1969. While both Kühn and Wettstein were in Göttingen, students experienced a "general biology" because of Kühn's (a zoologist) and Wettstein's (a botanist) collaboration.[8] In Göttingen they held joint seminars where they tried to break down the traditional barriers between zoology and botany and joined forces on research in basic physiological questions.

Wettstein, who was ten years younger than Kühn, did not forget his mentor after he became first director of the Kaiser Wilhelm Institute for Biology in 1934. By 1936, soon after Goldschmidt's emigration, he wrote a long letter to Planck very strongly supporting Kühn's appointment as second director at the institute before he could be lured away from Germany with attractive offers abroad. Wettstein argued that although the Germans had created the science of heredity, the Americans had taken over the leadership during the last few years. In order to allow optimal conditions for experiments and research, Wettstein wanted Kühn to be able to work in a pure research institute; in this way the field would be made much stronger. Moreover, because genetics had become a varied discipline, he thought the collaboration of a zoologist and botanist was essential, and by bringing Kühn to Berlin they could work together again. With the loss of Correns, Baur, and Goldschmidt, Wettstein thought it would be a "catastrophe" if Kühn were to go abroad. He therefore urged Planck to lure Kühn to Berlin with an attractive offer. By doing so Wettstein thought one could build up a center of biology in Dahlem of which the whole world would be "jealous."[9] Alfred Kühn did come to Berlin-Dahlem in April 1937, and the three biologists/biochemists—Wettstein, Kühn, and Butenandt, who had all collaborated at some point—became Göttingen transplants in Berlin-Dahlem.

Another significant appointment in Berlin-Dahlem in the life sciences during the thirties was that of Adolf Butenandt, the Nobel Prize–winning biochemist who left the Technische Hochschule in Danzig to become director of the Kaiser Wilhelm Institute for Biochemistry in October 1936. Butenandt had already made many breakthroughs in the field of sex hormones starting with the isolation of estrone—the hormone which determines sexual development in females—in pure crystalline form in 1929. Within a few years he had also isolated androsterone (1931), a male sex hormone, and progesterone (1934), a hormone important for the biochemical processes involved in pregnancy. Between 1931 and 1933 Butenandt was head of the organic and biochemical department of the chemistry laboratory at the University of Göttingen. In 1933 he received an appointment as professor for organic chemistry and director of the organic-chemical institute at the Technische Hochschule in Danzig. In 1935 he turned down an appointment as professor of biological chemistry at Harvard University, opting to "stay and save" in Germany rather than emigrate. In Dahlem Butenandt took his work on the isolation and purification of sex hormones one step further, and he began work on hormone synthesis. He also worked on virus research, cancer research, and the relationship between estrogenic hormones and tumors, on eye pigmentation in insects, and on the study of insecticides.[10]

In Dahlem, there was much opportunity for cooperative research and Butenandt continued his collaborative work with Alfred Kühn, with whom he had studied and worked in Göttingen. The work was considered so important that it was supported by the Rockefeller Foundation from 1934 to 1937. It was remarkable because this was a period when the Rockefeller Foundation had been withdrawing from Germany in response to the new totalitarian regime. The one case in which an exception was made in the general withdrawal policy was with Kühn's and Butenandt's work. In August 1934 Wilbur Tisdale, an officer from the Foundation, thought "however uncertain the political situation might make a large or longtime project, [they were] safe in dealing with sound men as Kühn on a year to year basis— Nowhere in the continent or England [could one] find chemists, embryologists, and geneticists willing to cooperate among themselves as are these German scientists."[11] Their work—hormone studies on meal moths—combined developmental physiology and genetics and the chemistry of endocrine functions. Kühn already had a group working on the production of eye color in the meal moth *Ephestia kühniella*, while Butenandt and his group succeeded in identifying the eye pigment "kynurenine" in 1940. Kühn had found that there were two races of moths, those with red eyes and those with black eyes; if the testes were transplanted from one race to another in the larval stage there was a corresponding change in eye color. He believed that a hormone was responsible for controlling eye color and for causing the development of the pupae of butterflies.

Butenandt also collaborated with a long-time Berlin-Dahlem biochemist —Otto Warburg. Warburg was one of the few Jewish scientists who stayed in Germany for the whole National Socialist period. From the end of World War I until 1931 he had been head of one of the four sections at the institute for biology and was director of the institute for cell physiology since 1931. One of the chief architects of modern biochemistry and biology, Warburg is usually associated with his elucidation of the mechanism of oxidation—the process responsible for the energy source for cell functions. He was a pioneer in the field of enzymes and introduced new methods for analyzing enzymatic reactions. He won the Nobel Prize in 1931 for his work in enzymology. He continued his pioneering work relatively undisturbed during the Third Reich, publishing over one hundred papers between 1933 and 1945.[12]

Scientifically or Politically Qualified?

As a result of death or emigration, three scientists from the institute for biology and for biochemistry had been appointed to their positions after 1933. The leaders and scientists at the Society were understandably fearful that their autonomy in making appointments might be threatened because of the new political constellations. In particular, Max Planck, primed with his fresh experience of the government seizing the Haber institute and installing its own candidate, was eager to preserve the integrity and scientific excellence of the Society.

Carl Correns's death in February 1933 left the first directorship of the institute for biology vacant. Because the Society wanted to appoint a director without the interference of the government, it moved quickly to find a successor. In March 1933 Planck asked Eugen Fischer, the chairman of the biomedical section of the scientific council, to solicit suggestions from the council for directorship candidates.[13] By the end of March Fischer had called together a meeting with Richard Goldschmidt and Erwin Baur in which Otto Renner and Fritz von Wettstein were proposed to succeed Correns: "Every biologist knows of the personality and achievement of both candidates; any further justification is superfluous. It would be in the interest of the institute to choose the younger one."[14] Wettstein quickly emerged as the Society's leading candidate, and Planck accordingly sought the approval of the various ministries, as had always been the custom.

After preliminary discussions with the Society and the various ministries, including a visit to Berlin with Theodor Vahlen, a minister at the Prussian Ministry for Science and Education, Wettstein "thought very carefully" about the research direction the institute might take. He planned on building upon Correns's work and taking it in new directions, not simply continuing it. He envisaged an institute where the "stiff American competition" would be swept away by first-class work. Wettstein planned to model the institute on the Morgan school in America, which featured working groups. Finally, he emphasized that becoming a professor for genetics (*Vererbungslehre*) and developmental physiology at the University of Berlin was very important to him.[15] This was a condition which most Kaiser Wilhelm institute directors requested if they were to accept an offer at the Society. Despite the freedoms and attractions of research unfettered by administrative and teaching duties, most scientists were reluctant to break their ties with the university. As a result, most Kaiser Wilhelm Society scientists were made honorary professors, usually unpaid, with the right but not the duty to lecture.

Wettstein's call to Berlin-Dahlem, however, met with the resistance of the Bavarian Ministry, and with Wettstein's colleagues and students. Wettstein reported that they were "moving heaven and earth" to keep him in Munich. Therefore, he urged Planck to push the Education Ministry in Berlin (in the person of Vahlen) to speed up the process there because the longer the attempts in Munich lasted, the harder it would be to leave, explained Wettstein.[16] While the Prussian and Bavarian ministries were competing over Wettstein, the Prussian and Reich ministries in Berlin had begun to undergo major organizational and personnel changes in the wake of the National Socialists' seizure of power, thus delaying any negotiations and decisions. By February 1934 everything had come to a stand still because of the change in the responsibilities of the Reich and Prussian ministries. Although both Vahlen and Donnevert, from the Prussian Ministry, planned to approve the Wettstein appointment, the Ministry could not make the official decision until the new Reich cultural/educational ministry was created.[17]

Because of the long delay of half a year since Wettstein's candidacy was submitted to the Ministry, he began to find it harder to leave Munich. Even though the Ministry had finally sent its written approval to the Society, Planck sensed that he was losing Wettstein for the Berlin-Dahlem post and wrote him a persuasive letter putting moral pressure on him to come to Berlin. With the death of Correns and Erwin Baur (KWI for Breeding Research) and the specter of the Ministry filling the position with its own candidate and a probable suspect research direction, Planck persisted, and coaxed Wettstein: "If your decision should now change you will have to pay for the sins of the cultural ministry that could take place at the Correns Institute."[18] It is likely that the "sins" of the Ministry would be research on race hygiene or eugenics. Wettstein was not only a qualified botanist who would work on pure genetic research untainted by the needs of the government, but Planck also saw in him someone who could help preserve the basic research tradition of the Society.[19]

The Wettstein appointment was one of the first successful appointments made by the Society where pure scientific merit, and not political considerations, led to an appointment. Whereas in the early years of the Third Reich the appropriate science ministries played a role in this process, by the mid-thirties it was often the case that party offices vetted candidates for positions. At the universities party membership was often a criterion for selection, while at the biology institutes of the Kaiser Wilhelm Society it seems to have played no role in the final decision. Two more cases of directorship appointments in the life sciences in 1936–37 illustrate opposing choices made by the scientists regarding political affiliation and show the type of evaluation made by party officials at the university. It should be noted that this sort of scrutiny was not typical of other Kaiser Wilhelm Society appointees but appears to be characteristic of the Göttingen University setting from which both scientists were coming; Göttingen was one of the more politicized universities in Germany during the early years of the Third Reich.

Scientist 1, who eventually became a party member in 1936, was characterized in the following way by the university group of the National Socialist teachers association in Göttingen where he had previously worked:

Scientifically. [Scientist 1] is considered to be undisputably terrific in his field. His work is chiefly in the area of [. . .] and here he has made outstanding contributions.

Pedagogically: Pedagogically I have heard nothing negative about him. He has a good reputation.

Character: Kind, flexible, soft, smooth man of the world.

Politically: [Scientist 1] has to be evaluated very carefully. His attitude before the seizure of power is to be judged as democratic, and it fit in well with the whole personnel of the [. . .] institute in Göttingen. After the seizure of power he did not have any contact with National Socialism, and it is as totally foreign to him as before the seizure of power. A colleague from the teachers association from [. . .] told me that in Altrhese [scientist 1] rejected National Socialism in every way and has tried to sabotage National Socialist institutions like the SA-service. He does it in such a clever way that it is impossible to catch him.

In spite of all this we cannot do without [scientist 1] as a scientist.[20]

Despite this negative judgment of his political reliability it was recognized that he might emigrate to the United States if a good position was not found for him;[21] and despite his apparent negative attitude toward National Socialism, scientist 1 had already joined the party in May 1936. Not only that, but in his 1939 questionnaire on party membership or National Socialist affiliations, he checked off that he was a member of the NS-Dozentenbund, the Deutsche Arbeitsfront, the NS-Volkswohlfahrt, the NS-Lehrerbund (entered 1 July 1934), the NS-Bund der Technik, and the NS-Altherrenbund der Deutschen Studenten.[22] It would seem that scientist 1 joined the party out of opportunistic reasons—just months before his appointment as director of a Kaiser Wilhelm institute he joined the party even though he seemed democratic and hostile toward National Socialism. Because he was not considered to be "politically reliable" during his years in Göttingen he might have thought it expedient to join the party to compensate for his earlier opposing political convictions.

Alfred Kühn, on the other hand, did not seem to consider it expedient to join the party. There was also a check done on his political background before his appointment at the Kaiser Wilhelm Society. By 1935 the NSDAP had established that Kühn was not a member of the German Communist party and that his behavior toward the party was not negative but was "without interest." They also found that he was a member of the Democratic party before the seizure of power and that his political attitude remained liberal. The head of the NSDAP personnel office in Göttingen wrote to the Propaganda Ministry that Kühn was a "very talented" and knowledgeable researcher. He was also a "masterful speaker" who "casts a spell" over his audience through the "logical construction of his lectures, stylistic skill and an impressive liveliness." Kühn rejected the National Socialist Weltanschauung but was clever enough to mask this and not to come across as an enemy of the National Socialist movement. The head of the personnel office thought it would be "dangerous" and "damaging for the party" to invite him to speak on heredity.[23]

About three months before his appointment to the Kaiser Wilhelm Institute in 1937, the University Group in Göttingen of the NS-Dozentenbund wrote a report on Kühn which was similar in format to the report on scientist 1:

> *Scientifically*: Kühn is a scholar of undeniable world-wide renown. His present area is genetics and there are only a few scientists in the world of his equal.
>
> *Pedagogically*: Kühn is terrific here also.
>
> *Character*: Kühn is kind and agreeable; otherwise he has the characteristics of a scholar of the old school. He is highly demanding of his students and assistants.
>
> *Politically*: Kühn was no friend of National Socialism before the seizure of power and was closely associated with the democratic party. . . . Today Kühn acts reservedly to politics in every way. I know him personally and I have the impression that he is no longer an active enemy of National Socialism. His appointment to the KWI can therefore be approved of.[24]

The head of the regional personnel office concluded in another report that Kühn projected the impression of a "loyal man" in his outward behavior in social relations and on the streets. He was "smart enough" to refrain from "rashness" and "provocative public attacks." Nevertheless, there was no proof that Kühn had "honestly transformed inwardly" in his thinking. Therefore, his "political reliability" could be affirmed only with much reservation. At least it was affirmed, unlike scientist 1. From this evidence it would appear that Kühn was the stereotypical apolitical scientist who did not see the need to join the party to further his career, as scientist 1 did. There was, in fact, no need for him to join.

Viruses, Sex Hormones, and Mutation Genetics

One example of the emergence of a research specialty during the Third Reich at the Kaiser Wilhelm institutes untainted by racist or ideological conceptions is the institutionalization of virus research. In 1935, Wendell Stanley's crystallization of tobacco mosaic virus in its pure form was hailed as a revolutionary discovery and sparked much research all over the world.[25] Interest was especially lively in Germany. Adolf Butenandt was among those present at a meeting of the Gesellschaft Deutscher Naturforscher und Ärtzte in 1936 where the topic of virus research figured prominently. Here, he recalled, K. Herzberg and O. Waldemann spoke about filterable virus types as infectious agents in humans, animals, and plants. It was at this point that Butenandt realized virology would no longer be regarded simply from a medical point of view; a new type of research had been born which combined biology and chemistry and became a part of basic research in biology.[26]

Interest in virus research burgeoned on the eve of Butenandt's move to the Kaiser Wilhelm Institute for Biochemistry in October 1936. Having just completed his major work on sex hormone research, Butenandt considered virus research to be a new fruitful research direction to be undertaken in Dahlem. At numerous colloquia the idea that nonliving forms could exhibit the phenomena of life was discussed. Alfred Kühn, who shared this enthusiasm for virus research, joined Butenandt in organizing a cooperative group of biologists and biochemists.[27] By 1938 discussions and colloquia had begun among the senior scientists and junior scientists from the institutes of biology and biochemistry on the topic of virus research. In preparation for the work Gerhard Schramm, an assistant from Butenandt's institute, was sent to Sweden to study modern protein chemistry and the technology associated with it. He visited both Theodor Svedberg's and Arne Tiselius's laboratories and studied the characterization of pure protein substances with Tiselius's electrophoresis technique and sedimentation constants with the ultracentrifuge. One of the first achievements of the research group in Dahlem was to design, develop, and construct an air-driven centrifuge because none was on the market.[28] In addition to the use of a centrifuge machine and the electrophoresis apparatus, the group used one of the earliest electron microscopes built by Manfred von Ardenne.

By 1939 Wettstein, Kühn, and Butenandt had written a memorandum rationalizing and summarizing their plans for a "Branch for Virus Research of the Kaiser Wilhelm Institutes for Biochemistry and Biology." Here they suggested the creation of a formal "workshop" (*Arbeitsstätte*) for the existing working groups. They referred to Stanley's pioneering work at the Rockefeller Institute for Medical Research in Princeton on tobacco mosaic virus in which he claimed that the infecting virus was a protein (this was found to be erroneous later) which could be isolated and crystallized. They characterized the discovery as a "new land" for chemists and biologists and for understanding viruses. Aware of the innovations in the United States, the senior scientists consciously developed an organizational form in Dahlem where a group of young, suitable scientists would be selected to do virus research. They considered virus research to be a model example of the modern organization of science where the work could be done successfully only with the cooperation of biochemists, botanists, and zoologists. They were also aware that new, modern instruments such as the ultracentrifuge and the electron microscope were necessary for such work. The research itself would be done from a "basic research" basis, but contact and sharing of results with the practical world, in particular with breeders, was considered very important. The "model experiments" would be done at the workshop and when they were finished they would be carried out as "big experiments of practice," in particular at the Kaiser Wilhelm Institutes for Animal Breeding in Dummerstorf and for Breeding Research in Müncheberg.[29]

By 1940 the workshop for virus research was established with three working groups headed by the younger scientists who had taken part in the earlier cooperative research. Georg Melchers (from Wettstein's institute) was selected for the botany department and worked on plant viruses, Rolf Daneel (from Kühn's institute) headed the zoology department and worked on animal viruses, and Gerhard Schramm (from Butenandt's institute) headed the biochemistry department and did chemical work associated with the tobacco mosaic virus. It initially received support from H. Hörlein, an I. G. Farben industrialist, and the Schering pharmaceutical company. Telschow had in fact reported that Carl Bosch was very interested in creating a virus research institute and that it should be called "Carl Bosch Institut."[30] Later, the German Research Association supported aspects of the group's work, and by the end of the war the Reich Ministry for Food and Agriculture was also contributing.

A number of significant results, extending Stanley's work, emerged from the group. Commentators after the war have praised the German work in virus research, which was criticized abroad by some during the war. It has been recognized that "throughout the war years much significant work on tobacco mosaic virus was done both in Britain and Germany," and that although the "war years inevitably slowed down academic work in Europe, the field of filterable viruses probably suffered less than most other academic work."[31] A new form of organization at the Kaiser Wilhelm institutes was also initiated which later became a model for the institutionalization of new specialties.[32] The whole plan for the new research specialty also went beyond research on the tobacco mosaic virus and included tomato and potato viruses (Melchers' research), the fowl plague virus, and Schramm's very important biochemical work in protein chemistry.

Schramm's work was of particular significance both in itself and in the contribution it made to the postwar understanding that the virus contained mostly nucleic acid and was not protein as Stanley had claimed in 1935. This result was also connected to the identification of nucleic acids as the hereditary material rather than protein. In 1943 Schramm found that tobacco mosaic viruses decomposed into subunits when in a solution with a pH value above 9. He had also shown that tobacco mosaic virus was inactivated when its nucleic acid was removed with enzymes.[33]

In addition to the work done at the institutes for biochemistry and biology, the genetics division of the institute for brain research produced much innovative research in *Drosophila* and mutation genetics. This work was orchestrated by N. Timoféeff-Ressovsky, the brilliant and lively Russian geneticist.[34] By the early 1930s an active group of biologists, biochemists, and physicists had emerged in Berlin who met every week at Max Delbrück's home and at Timoféeff-Ressovsky's home or institute to discuss new and emerging problems in areas which crossed disciplinary boundaries. Karl Zimmer, a radiation biologist working at the Buch institute, recalls discussions that went on for ten hours or more with no break, two to three times a week. This gathering began as a group of five or six "internally exiled" theoretical physicists who had met initially at the Delbrück family house. Delbrück recalls suggesting that other people in biology and biochemistry also attend these meetings. One of these people was Timoféeff-Ressovsky, whose institute was an hour and a half away in Berlin-Buch. At that time Timoféeff was studying the induction of mutations by ionizing radiation quantitatively. Zimmer undertook quantitative dosimetry of ionizing radiation. Delbrück contributed to the analysis of this material from the point of view of a theoretical physicist. The result of this collaborative research was a joint paper entitled "On the Nature of Gene Mutations and of Genetic Structure" published in the *Nachrichten der Gesellschaft der Wissenschaften*. Known as the "three-man work" or the "green book" (because of the cover of the reprints), the major paper, recalled Delbrück, "got a funeral first class" because of the journal in which it was published. This important paper proposed the "hit" theory (*Treffertheorie*), a theory about mutations.[35]

This aspect of the study of radiation genetics had grown out of H. J. Muller's pioneering work on the artificial induction of mutations. The birth of this specialty can be dated to 1927 when Muller read a paper at the Fifth International Conference of Genetics in Berlin. Here he proved that x-rays produce mutations in *Drosophila melanogaster*. It was thought that these induced mutations would shed light on the nature and structure of the gene. If the gene was a well-defined corpuscle of a definite size, bombarding it with ionizing radiation would produce "hits" on these corpuscles and the resulting damage would show up as mutations. In the end the theory failed to contribute to a better understanding of the gene, but it was found that irradiation of the substrate might increase the mutation rate.[36]

In addition to the hit theory Timoféeff and other scientists at the biological Kaiser Wilhelm institutes produced an enormous literature on mutation genetics. Timoféeff, Alfred Kühn, and Hans Stubbe also received rich financial support from the German Research Association for this work. As early as 1934 a commission had been formed for cooperative research in the area of "hereditary damage through radiational effects." Originally proposed by Timoféeff in the fall of 1933 for the support of his work on radiation genetics, a year later it had expanded to include a number of other radiation geneticists in Germany. The commission was headed by Alfred Kühn, and at an early meeting in the fall of 1934, Kühn reported that general work had been done since the last meeting on laws of mutations on *Drosophila* (fruit flies) by Timoféeff in Buch and on *Ephestia* (*Ephestia kühniella*—meal moths) by Kühn in Göttingen. Kühn referred to the mutants in *Ephestia* and explained the effect of mutated genes on various characteristics such as pigmentation in eyes. One of the genes affected inner secretions and all mutations changed the vitality of the mutated gene.

Timoféeff also discussed his work on the "triggering of vitality mutations in *Drosophila* through x-rays." After a detailed discussion of the experiments, Timoféeff concluded that physiological mutations occur because of radiation and manifest themselves in vitality reduction. He then made the only statement I have found of a direct connection between eugenics and mutation genetics: "Such mutations in man must be characterized as especially undesirable from the race hygiene point of view."[37] This is just one instance of Timoféeff selling his science. Timoféeff was able to continue his work undisturbed during the Third Reich precisely because of his ability to secure support and interest for his work. While capitalizing on the

National Socialists' interest in genetics, he was able to create an institute
where Jews were protected and where scientific research thrived through the
war years.[38] In his reports to the DFG, Timoféeff unfailingly ended by stating that the work was successful and continued undisturbed. For example,
in 1943 he wrote that "all the work ran and runs very satisfactory, with total
capacity and without substantial hindrance, thanks, in part, to the smooth
cooperation with the German Research Association." In 1944 he also thanked
the funding organization and its economic war office for allowing the work
to continue with "very good success and without any disturbances and without any difficulty acquiring material."[39]

Hans Stubbe, the well-known plant geneticist, also worked on radiation
genetics and focused on the snapdragon, *Antirrhinum*. As a student of Erwin
Baur he had begun his career as an assistant at Baur's Kaiser Wilhelm Institute for Breeding Research in Müncheberg (1927–36). Because of the
politically charged changes taking place at the breeding research institute
after the death of Baur in 1933 he transferred to the biology institute as an
assistant to Wettstein from 1936 to 1943; from 1943 on he was director of
a Kaiser Wilhelm Institute for Cultivated Plants in Vienna. Soon after Stubbe
joined the biology institute, both Kühn and Wettstein supported his work
in radiation genetics very strongly. In fact, the German Research Council
awarded Stubbe the most funding of any junior scientist (only institute
directors understandably received more) at any Kaiser Wilhelm institutes,
totaling RM 97,236 between 1934 and 1945. Kühn and von Wettstein were
often the referees designated to evaluate his applications for funding.[40]

It was, in fact, because of Wettstein's support that Stubbe could successfully continue his work in the Third Reich. Stubbe was a scientist protected by the Kaiser Wilhelm Society while banned from the universities
because of his political past as a Marxist. As early as 1938, Stubbe had gone
to a community work camp at the Tännich Castle, a camp where scientists
and teachers were sent in order to be indoctrinated and observed. The report
on his one-month stay described an apolitical scientist entirely ruled by his
field of study. The reporter found it "astounding" that someone in such a
potentially political field as genetics did not belong to the party or other
National Socialist organizations. By 1940 the rector of the Friedrich-Wilhelm
University in Berlin rejected Stubbe's application for permission to teach
through the submission of his *Habilitation*. This decision was based on the
recommendation of the university's Dozent leader, who justified the action
by evaluating Stubbe's political activities before the seizure of power and
his involvement in disturbing the work at the institute for breeding research
in 1936.[41]

Stubbe's past political activities led to his prohibition from any position
at the universities despite the recognition of his talent as a geneticist and
the need to help advance the younger generation of scientists. He had been
considered both for a position at the German-Bulgarian institute and for a
chair in phytogenetics at the Reich University in Poland. In 1943 the head
of the Security Service (SD) had written a report outlining Stubbe's nega-

tive attitude toward National Socialism despite his entry into the SS and SA after the seizure of power. The report focused on Stubbe's Marxist activities at the breeding research institute where he helped Jews and was part of a group that disseminated Marxist literature in the institute. In 1932 Stubbe designated the NSDAP Party Badge a cloakroom ticket; in the spring of 1933, after listening to a speech, he called Adolf Hitler "pathological." After the National Socialist seizure of power, however, Stubbe acted very reservedly toward politics and assured an institute party member that he was neither a Marxist nor a National Socialist.[42] Nevertheless, the Party Chancellery banned him from university service.

Another biologist sheltered by the Society and supported by Wettstein because of her political views was Elisabeth Schiemann. Also a plant geneticist, she studied with Erwin Baur in Berlin, completing her doctoral dissertation on the induction of mutations in *Aspergillus niger* and received her degree at the Friedrich Wilhelms University in Berlin. She then joined Baur at the Agricultural College in Berlin in the department of genetics; in 1923 the department moved to Dahlem. During the early thirties she broke with her mentor Baur and joined the University of Berlin as extraordinary professor without tenure and worked as a visiting scientist at the Botanical Museum in Dahlem, a university institution. The most productive years in her career began in 1930 but ended in 1940 with her final clash with the National Socialist system. According to Anton Lang, a long-time student of Schiemann's, she was a strong anti-Nazi and never attended Hitler broadcasts, the required sessions of the National Socialist Teacher's League, or the 1 May marches. She participated in subversive activities including quoting Jewish and Russian authors, being active in the Confessional Church (a major source of opposition to the National Socialists), and supporting persecuted people. By 1940 all these activities came to a head and her professorship at the Berlin University was revoked. Wettstein helped support her in these troubled times by awarding her a German Research Council fellowship to support her work at the Botanical Museum. Just as Stubbe found a position as director of the Kaiser Wilhelm Institute for Cultivated Plants in Vienna (founded in 1943), so too was Schiemann appointed director of the division for the history of cultivated plants.

The cases of Stubbe and Schiemann were two instances of prominent scientists who were not allowed to work at the universities but instead gained a measure of professional support and security through Wettstein, who had been instrumental in creating the institute at the Society for them.[43]

Funding for Basic Biological Research

There were a number of factors which allowed basic research to continue in Berlin. One of these was the type of financial support available. Biology at the Kaiser Wilhelm institutes and other institutions received funding from the German Research Council. Although the council was controlled and led by loyal National Socialists (in contrast to the Kaiser Wilhelm Society), many of its committees and sections were headed by apolitical scientists or scientists who were interested in supporting science which was not necessarily of interest or use to the state. One of these sections encompassed agriculture and biology and was headed by Konrad Meyer, who was an agricultural scientist instrumental in designing and implementing National Socialist agricultural policies. *Within* this section, however, a committee existed for the advancement of basic research in biology. There were six divisions to this section with two Kaiser Wilhelm institute directors as heads: genetics and cytology (Fritz von Wettstein); developmental physiology (Alfred Kühn); metabolism physiology (Kurt Noack); ecology (Hermann Weber); systematics (Hanns von Lengerken); and microbiology (Rippel).[44]

In 1938 the biology section of the division for agriculture and biology was awarded RM 510,270 for research in the life sciences in the areas outlined above. All of the eighteen grants in the working group for genetics and cytology given to scientists from all over Germany were for basic research in genetics and cytology without regard for application to race issues. Half of these grants were awarded to Kaiser Wilhelm institute scientists in Berlin and Müncheberg. The subject matter of the various research projects seemed to reflect the development of the field at the time rather than the priorities of the National Socialists, although the research fields often coincided with potential fields of interest like genetics. Mutation research was also a popular topic with five out of the eighteen grants focusing on this area; many of them were Kaiser Wilhelm institute scientists. The results culled from the 1938 award period reflected the pattern for research awards throughout the rest of the Third Reich. Hans Bauer from the Kaiser Wilhelm Institute for Biology received a grant for research on the relationship between x-rays and the appearance of chromosome mutations; Edgar Knapp (Kaiser Wilhelm Institute for Breeding Research) for research on the mutational effect of ultraviolet light in *Livermoose Sphaerocarpus*; Hans Stubbe (Kaiser Wilhelm Institute for Biology) for experimental triggering of mutations through chemicals; and Timoféeff-Ressovsky for experimental mutation induction.[45]

Basic research in developmental physiology was also supported with twenty-four grants. Adolf Butenandt received a grant for developmental physiological research on "genetic substances," Joachim Hämmerling (Kaiser Wilhelm Institute for Biology) for the effect of the cell nucleus and of genes on development, Max Hartmann for work on general sex determination problems, and Alfred Kühn for research on the functioning of genes, especially genetically active substances.[46]

The Kaiser Wilhelm Society also received a block grant of RM 92,000 in 1941 for eight institute directors; seven of these were scientists in the life sciences. The Kaiser Wilhelm Institute for Biology alone received a total of RM 36,000. This block grant had, in fact, been awarded to the Society almost yearly since 1941; a grant of RM 92,000 was even approved for the year 1945. In 1941 Fritz von Wettstein received his grant for research on metabolism in connection with chromosome multiplication and on the problem of the origin of races and species. Alfred Kühn was awarded a grant for research on genetically active substances and the nature and functioning of developmental hormones; he also did work on racial bastards from the standpoint of evolution. Max Hartmann planned to work on fertilization substances in animals (echinoderms and amphibians) and on genetic and cytogenetics in the fly *Phryne*. Butenandt continued his work on hormones, genetically triggered active substances, cancer, and viruses.[47]

In addition to the grants from this program for basic biological research, Kaiser Wilhelm biologists received rich support from the council, far exceeding their university counterparts. In fact, during World War II they received almost half of all grants awarded. One can attribute this remarkable figure partly to the general continuation of basic biological research at the institutes, whereas work at the universities was curtailed because of loss of staff to the war effort. In addition, Kühn and Wettstein were the most influential biologists in Germany at the time and played major roles in the German Research Association. The increase in financial support by the council also paralleled the general increase in financial support for research at the Society during the war, from 7.4 million marks in 1937 to 14.4 million marks in 1944. There was a marked increase in work in genetics and applied botany during the war at the research institutes. Plant breeding research alone received 40 percent of all research funding. Expeditions to collect wild and primitive forms of cultivated plants were richly supported during the war and included trips to the Balkans. In addition, experimental mutation research at all the institutes received large grants.

Eugenics at the Kaiser Wilhelm Institutes

A study of the Kaiser Wilhelm institutes during the Third Reich would be incomplete without addressing the issue of research in race hygiene and scientists' participation in the Nazi eugenic program. During the last ten years there has been much interest among scholars, scientists, and the lay public in eugenics in National Socialist Germany.[48] Benno Müller-Hill's inflammatory but well-researched *Murderous Science* exposed the participation of academic scientists in the "scientific murder" of Jews, gypsies, and the mentally ill, thus reviving and extending Max Weinreich's 1946 thesis that it was ideas deriving from scholarship that made many of the atrocities in the Third Reich possible. The question naturally arises: To what extent did Kaiser Wilhelm scientists participate in this "deathly project"?

Research on eugenics was done primarily at the Kaiser Wilhelm Institute for Anthropology, Human Heredity, and Eugenics in Berlin-Dahlem (directed by Eugen Fischer from 1927, its founding, to 1942, and by Otmar von Verschuer from 1942 to 1945) and the Kaiser Wilhelm Institute for Genealogy and Demography of the Deutsche Forschungsanstalt (directed by Ernst Rüdin) in Munich. Because many of the documents from the Kaiser Wilhelm Institute for Anthropology were destroyed after World War II, it is difficult to determine the precise nature of the research activities at the institute and its services to the state.[49] From the surviving material, including publications from research activities from the years 1927–45, it would appear as though the fundamental research did not change considerably after 1933. The Kaiser Wilhelm Institute for Anthropology was deeply embedded in the Weimar social structure, the period in which it was founded,[50] and race hygiene, a term coined by Alfred Ploetz, had already emerged in the late nineteenth century. What *did* change was the degree of involvement and participation in Nazi racial policy and the newfound rich support of the Reich government.

Until 1935 the Kaiser Wilhelm Institute for Anthropology was divided into three divisions: Eugen Fischer was head of the anthropology division, Otmar von Verschuer headed the department for human heredity from 1928 to 1935, and the department for eugenics was headed by the Jesuit Hermann Muckermann until 1933, when he was forced to resign for political reasons. The race hygienist Fritz Lenz succeeded Muckermann and remained head of the eugenics division until the end of the Third Reich. In the course of the Third Reich other divisions were created such as Hans Nachtsheim's department for hereditary pathology (1941), one for hereditary tuberculosis research (1939), one for embryology, and one for race studies directed by Wolfgang Abel (1941).[51]

Fischer, previously professor of anthropology in Freiburg, had established his reputation through his work on Reheboth bastards, people of mixed blood in German South-West Africa (published in 1913). In Berlin-Dahlem Fischer focused on the genetic analysis of racial crossing before and after 1933. He was the editor of the *Zeitschrift für Morphologie und Anthropologie*, the leading journal for eugenics and anthropology, from 1917 to 1948. He was also co-author of the well-known genetics textbook of the time by Erwin Baur, Eugen Fischer, and Fritz Lenz, *Human Heredity and Race Hygiene*, first published in 1921 and on its fourth edition by 1936. This book was highly praised and remained a standard work in genetics in Germany for over twenty years. All three authors were already prominent before becoming scientific members of the Kaiser Wilhelm Society. Erwin Baur, the plant geneticist, was a professor at the University of Berlin and became director of the Kaiser Wilhelm Institute for Breeding Research in 1927, when it was founded. Fritz Lenz, editor of the *Archiv für Rassen- und Gesellschaftsbiologie*, was a prominent and prolific race hygienist, becoming the first professor of race hygiene at the University of Munich in 1923. While a student in Freiburg, Lenz attended Eugen Fischer's lectures. The Baur, Fischer, and Lenz textbook greatly influenced German biomedical thinking and was eventually used as a scientific basis and justification for National Socialist policy.

Verschuer, Fischer's successor in 1942 (after a brief period in Frankfurt where he helped establish an institute for hereditary biology and race hygiene from 1935 to 1942), studied the inheritance of normal and pathological traits and the inheritance of disease, intelligence, and behavior. His main area of interest was twin studies. In the eugenics division the main research area before and after 1933 seems to have been in the differential birth rates of various social groups.[52]

While the pure research activities of many race hygienists at the Kaiser Wilhelm institutes continued along pre-1933 lines, some used their positions to enhance their prestige by turning to the National Socialist state and offering their services; others were coerced into providing services of use to Nazi racial policy; others simply agreed to place their science at the service of the state. In July 1933 Dr. Arthur Gütt, a Reich official, attended the Kaiser Wilhelm Institute for Anthropology board of directors meeting as a guest. He recognized the importance of the work of the institute and asked that it devote itself to the "work of the Reich government." He specifically asked for help in carrying through the Sterilization Law. The Reich government put a lot of weight, continued Gütt, on the "competent advice of the institute." Not only this, but he also suggested that the whole Kaiser Wilhelm Society "place itself systematically in the service of the Reich."[53] The Fischer institute was therefore expected to help the government apply its racial laws and measures. Two years later the institute reported that it had tried to follow through with all of Gütt's wishes "unreservedly."[54]

Just days after the *Machtergreifung* Eugen Fischer gave a lecture on 1 February 1933 at the Kaiser Wilhelm Society's Winter Lecture Series at Harnack House on "Racial Crossing and Intellectual Achievement." Here he argued that the racial mixing of Nordic with non-Nordic types from Europe—Alpine and Mediterranean, for example—was not harmful and was indeed responsible for many of the spiritual achievements of present-day people. He even went as far as to say that when the Nordic race did remain pure it produced "no great cultural achievements."[55] Ernst Rüdin gave a lecture on "Empirical Hereditary Prognosis" in May 1933 at the Society's yearly meeting, thereby preempting Otto Warburg's talk, which had already been scheduled in December of 1932 to be given in May 1933.[56] Here Rüdin characterized the race hygiene program as "maintaining healthy hereditary [material]" through "family planning of carriers of good hereditary characteristics and the eradication of sick hereditary [material]" by "preventing the reproduction of humans with sick hereditary" characteristics. By using Mendel's laws Rüdin argued one could predict the probability of inheriting diseases such as manic-depression, schizophrenia, and epilepsy.[57] It was Rüdin who had, in fact, helped design the Sterilization Law for the prevention of genetically diseased offspring.

Archival evidence also shows that the Kaiser Wilhelm Institute for Anthropology provided courses for state-employed physicians and SS doctors and that it helped carry out the Sterilization Law by providing *Gutachten* (expert opinions) in preparation for cases in the genetic health courts. By 1935, over 1,100 doctors had taken courses at the anthropology institute and between 50 and 185 doctors took a year-long course in "genetic and racial cure."[58]

A year-long hereditarean biology and race hygiene training course was provided at the Dahlem institute from 1 October 1934 to 1 August 1935 by the Ministry of the Interior. According to the Race Policy Office of the NSDAP, the purpose of the course was to ensure that enough scientific progeny was secured for the future and that young, interested men and women were "familiarized" with "National Socialist race policies." These students would then be available later to work in the staff of the Race Policy Office. The scientific training lay in the hands of the Kaiser Wilhelm Institute while the political Weltanschauung training was to be provided by the Race Policy Office.[59] Twenty young doctors participated in daily lectures, seminars, and colloquia by Fischer, Lenz, and Verschuer on hereditary doctrines, race science, and race hygiene. They also took part in all of the scientific research at the institute.[60] Fischer and the department heads of his institute also began to attend many meetings and advisory sessions in ministries and committees between 1933 and 1935. Fritz Lenz was a member of the Expert Committee for Population and Race Policies, Verschuer was a member of the Hereditary Health Court, and Fischer was a member of the Hereditary Health Superior Court.[61]

Both Fischer's and Rüdin's institutes provided racial testimonies and genealogies for the Ministry of Interior. The Fischer institute considered these *Gutachten* a great "burden" and refused to provide any private *Gutachten*. It did, however, provide evaluations for three offices: the Chamber Court of the Berlin District for questions of paternity, mostly in alimony cases; the Hereditary Health Courts; and for the Reich Ministry of the Interior *Gutachten* on racial purity and paternity with unmarried couples with doubtful or unknown fathers.[62] In 1936 Fischer had asked for a pay increase for the racial *Gutachten*, which the Reich Office for Genealogical Research had wanted to be done free of charge. By 1939 Fischer complained that his institute was receiving requests for four times as many evaluations as it was possible to process.[63] By 1940 not only did this advisory role continue in questions of race policy, population policy, and resettlement, but there were also evaluations and advice for health offices, both official and private. There were many genetic paternity *Gutachten* for courts and race *Gutachten* for the Reich Office for Genealogical Research. Institute members also took part in many training courses of the State Medical Academy and the Academy for Doctors' Continuing Education. They went to conferences abroad, race hygiene courses in Budapest, and congresses in Paris, Copenhagen, London, and Edinburgh. Race hygiene prospered in the Third Reich. All these new activities seemed to take so much time, that as early as 1935 Fischer reported that since he had been rector of the University of Berlin for the last two years, scientific research had been impossible for him because of his heavy administrative duties.[64]

Ernst Rüdin's Institute for Genealogy and Demography became one of the leading centers for race hygiene in Germany. Rüdin, a psychiatrist, co-authored a book with Arthur Gütt and Falk Ruttke, a lawyer, which was a commentary on the Law for the Prevention of Genetically Diseased Offspring passed on 14 July 1933—the Sterilization Law. The law stated that an individual could be sterilized if he or she suffered from a "genetic" illness including feeblemindedness, schizophrenia, and epilepsy. What began as legislation in America had finally also been realized in Germany. The Sterilization Law was just the first step in measures to eliminate a whole group of people considered to be either genetically defective or racially inferior.[65]

Thus the Fischer and Rüdin institutes played important advisory roles in Nazi racial policy. Although race hygiene made the extermination of the Jews, gypsies, and mentally ill possible, neither of these institutes was directly involved with mass extermination or concentration camps. None of their members were "Nazi doctors," although the Fischer institute probably trained a number of them, and Joseph Mengele, the notorious Auschwitz death camp doctor, had been an assistant to Otmar von Verschuer in Frankfurt and maintained contact with his mentor when Verschuer returned to Berlin-Dahlem. This is indeed the most damning of connections that has been found concerning the institute for anthropology. Mengele apparently sent to the institute "material" stamped "War Material—Urgent," and the "directors of the Berlin-Dahlem Institute always warmly thanked Dr. Mengele for this rare and precious material."[66] Finally, in a March 1944 report to the German Research Council, Verschuer refers to Mengele's work at Auschwitz on the "protein body and eye color project," from which blood samples were being sent back to Verschuer.[67] Conclusive evidence has not yet been found that Verschuer knew about the origins of these materials, but the little evidence that does exist seems to show that he must have known.

The departments of brain anatomy of the Kaiser Wilhelm Institute for Brain Research in Berlin-Buch and of psychiatry in Munich also used materials from questionable sources. For example, Julius Hallervorden, department head at the brain research institute, used brains from murdered feebleminded patients for his research. By 1944 Hallervorden had obtained thousands of brains from various mental hospitals, including one in Görden where he had previously worked; the Görden hospital also had close connections to an extermination center. In reports to funding organizations and colleagues he reported dissecting 500 brains from feebleminded patients and preparing them for examination; he himself resected many brains of victims immediately after they were killed.[68]

In discussions of eugenics it is important to make a distinction between a group of scientists who contributed to Nazi racial policies and the scientists' politics. Membership or nonmembership in the NSDAP does not seem to have been of prime importance. One could be very active in contributing, supporting, and advancing National Socialist policies without even being in the party. While race hygiene science supported National Socialist ideology, this did not automatically mean that the leaders of the movement were heavily involved in the party or were in it at all. Four Kaiser Wilhelm institute race hygiene scientists entered the party very late: Eugen Fischer did not enter until January 1940, Ernst Rüdin until 1937, Otmar von Verschuer until July 1940, and Fritz Lenz until 1937. While Rüdin quickly received the party stamp of approval and was considered "politically dependable,"

Fischer's and Lenz's applications for party membership were eyed with suspicion. While Himmler acknowledged that they both corroborated the racist part of the National Socialist Weltanschauung through their scientific
work, there were doubts voiced by the party. Himmler thought, however,
that their admission to the party was a "political necessity" because one could
not "use the energy of both men as a scientific underpinning for the party"
on the one hand, while "rejecting them as party comrades," on the other.[69]

The scientific research done at the Kaiser Wilhelm institutes was differentially affected by National Socialist policies and ideology. In the case of
biology, however, considerable quality science continued. Much of this work
took place in the Berlin Kaiser Wilhelm Institutes for Biology and Biochemistry and at the genetics division of the Institute for Brain Research in Berlin-
Buch. From Kühn's work in developmental physiology, Wettstein's in cultivated plants, Hartmann's on sexuality in protozoa, to Butenandt's work
in sex hormones and virus research, and Timoféeff's in mutation genetics,
it was a lively and productive period. There was the emergence of cooperative research among scientists in different disciplines. Even during the war,
when many other scientific institutes in Germany had to close down, much
work continued at the Kaiser Wilhelm institutes in Berlin.

But other work in the life sciences, in particular eugenics, showed a different face. While eugenics had been officially institutionalized at the Kaiser
Wilhelm institutes in 1927, when the Fischer institute opened, its potential
was fully realized by the state only during the Third Reich. It should be
remembered, however, that the cognitive content of the science of race
hygiene did not change dramatically in the Third Reich, but it was the use
it was put to that altered. Scientists served the state, for example, by writing
Gutachten which could prove whether one was Jewish. Other scientists such
as Rüdin played a major role in contributing to the Sterilization Law, which
was one of the early cornerstones of eugenic policy.

In sum, then, there was a broad spectrum of science done at the biological institutes of the Society. This depended, in part, on the nature of
the biology. Eugenics is a politicized science by its nature and content, laden
with the prejudices and emotions of the times. But by understanding its
roots and form in countries all over the world, scholars have begun to chart
its complexities and to make people aware that eugenics was not a product
of National Socialist Germany; rather, the state used the science for a scientific underpinning and rationalization of its racist policies. Some scientists
were either in the party or politically active, but many were apolitical and
anti–National Socialist. Despite a political regime which has been characterized as destructive of science and not appreciative of intellectual achievements, scientists continued to do important work in the life sciences. But
as scientists sought to continue their work undisturbed during the war, the
Society faced other challenges to its functioning and autonomy.

1.   Although Kaiser Wilhelm II was not directly involved in founding the Society, his name reflects the way in which it was a product of Wilhelmian Germany. He attended the dedication of the Kaiser Wilhelm Institutes for Chemistry and Physical Chemistry on 23 October 1912. To his right are Adolf Von Harnack, Emil Fischer, and Fritz Haber.

2.   Adolf von Harnack, the theologian, was president of the Society from 1911 to 1930.

3.   The administration of the Society was located in the Berlin Palace between 1922
and 1945. Although the bridge is still standing in East Berlin off Under den Linden,
the palace was bombed at the end of the war and razed to the ground by the Socialist
East German government because of its imperial connotations.

4.   Friedrich Glum was general director of the Society between 1922 and 1937 when he was forced to leave and was replaced by a Party Member. A trained lawyer, Glum was involved in giving notice to Jewish and Communist scientists at the Society during the first two years following the National Socialist seizure of power.

5. A swimming pool was built behind Harnack House in 1937 and scientists could now take a cool dive in between experiments and lectures.

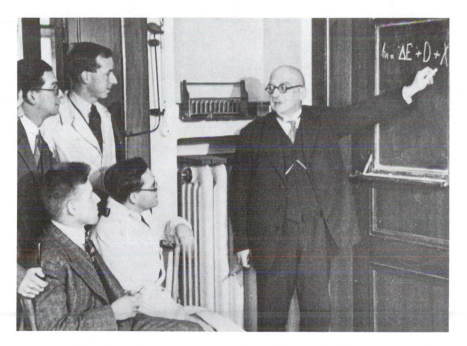

6. Fritz Haber, the Nobel Prize-winning physical chemist, holding a lecture before spellbound students during the late 1920s. In 1933 Haber, a Jew and patriotic German, resigned his directorship of the Kaiser Wilhelm Institute for Physical Chemistry because of the racial laws which led to the dismissal of his assistants and other scientists. He could have remained at his post as a civil servant appointed before 1918, but resigned in protest. He died in exile in Switzerland in 1935.

7.   An aerial view of the Berlin-Dahlem Research Institutes of the Kaiser Wilhelm Society during the early 1930s. Each director had his own private house nearby. After the Kaiser Wilhelm Institute for Physics was built in 1937, behind the Cell Physiology Institute, these institutes formed the core of the Society's institutes. Most of these institutes are still standing and are owned primarily by the Free University of Berlin. 1. KWI for Biochemistry; 2. KWI for Chemistry, 2a. Director's House; 3. KWI for Physical Chemistry and Electrochemistry, 3a. Director's House; 4. KWI for Biology, 4a. Director's House; 5. KWI for Anthropology, 5a. Director's House; 6. Harnack House; 7. KWI for Cell Physiology, 7a. Director's House; 8. KWI for Silicate Research.

8. Max Planck, president of the Society (1930–37, 1945–46), appears to ignore the National Socialist Minister of the Interior Wilhelm Frick on his left. Frick's Ministry was primarily responsible for monitoring the dismissal of Jewish or Communist members of the Society.

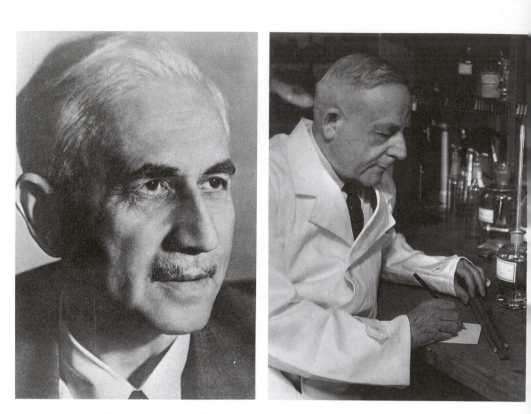

9.   (*left*) Otto Meyerhof, the Nobel Prize-winning biochemist (1922) was director of the institute for physiology at the medical research institute in Heidelberg. He was placed on leave in August 1938 and fled to the United States, via France and Spain, in 1939. He became a professor at the University of Pennsylvania.

10.   (*right*) Otto Warburg in his laboratory. Also a Nobel Prize-winning biochemist (1931), Warburg, who was half-Jewish, remained director of the institute for cell physiology and stayed in Germany throughout the Third Reich period.

11. Max Planck lecturing at the 25th anniversary celebration of the Kaiser Wilhelm Society in Harnack House, 11 January 1936.

12.   Minister for Science and Education, Bernhard Rust. This photograph was taken in 1936 on the occasion of his promotion to SA-Group Leader.

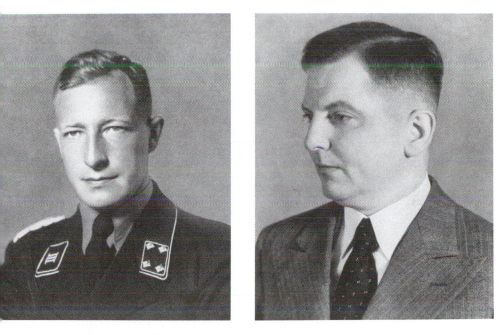

13.   (*left*) Rudolf Mentzel was an important figure in National Socialist science policy. A chemist with a specialty in military chemistry and an SS-man, he became
president of the German Research Council in 1937, and second vice-president of the
Kaiser Wilhelm Society in 1940.

14.   (*right*) Peter Adolf Thiessen, a staunch National Socialist, was named director
of the Physical Chemistry Institute in 1935 by the National Socialist government
after Fritz Haber left the government-funded institute directorship vacant with his
resignation.

15.   Carl Bosch, the industrialist and head of I.G. Farben, was president of the Kaiser Wilhelm Society between 1937 and 1940.

16. Ernst Telschow (r), General Director of the Kaiser Wilhelm Society (1937–45), listening to Otto Wacher (l), head, until his death in 1937, of the Reich Ministry for Science and Education.

17. Albert Vögler is pictured here to Adolf Hitler's right. Vögler, a leading industrialist, was a long-time member and senator of the Society and became president in
1940; as a separate power center in Nazi Germany, the industrialists helped the
Society in various ways throughout the period of the Third Reich.

18.   The Kaiser Wilhelm Institute for Chemistry. Nuclear fission was discovered here in 1938 by Otto Hahn and Fritz Strassmann.

19. Albert Vögler, president of the Kaiser Wilhelm Society from 1940 until 1945.

7

The War Years
1939–45

During the war years the Kaiser Wilhelm Society reached the apogee of its integration into National Socialist culture and society. In the course of the Third Reich the Society and its institutes had gone through changes and phases—gradually stepping into National Socialist society by 1936–37, but taking a larger step by 1940. During the war, the Society, in fact, prospered financially, as it expanded its research frontiers to areas compatible with National Socialist ideology and policy. Although the Society and its institutes worked more closely with various offices of the regime, they had to curtail much of their normal activity after the outbreak of war in the fall of 1939. For example, the yearly meetings of the Society ceased after 1939 because of the war, and the senate met only once a year until 1943, when it also stopped meeting. Although many of the scientific members and staff of the institutes were drafted during the war, many received deferments from the military (Uk-gestellt = indispensable) if the institute director could demonstrate the scientist was working on a project important for the war effort. During the last year and a half of the war, however, scientific work was also curtailed, and in some cases brought to an end by the deteriorating war conditions. Thus by the time war broke out, it was no longer a question of how the Society responded to the measures of the National Socialist state, as it had been in the early years. Instead, one must examine how it integrated itself into the societal structure, how the structures and priorities of scientific research changed as a result of the war, and to what extent it and its institutes contributed to the war effort.

Albert Vögler: The Perfect but
Reluctant President, 1941

An important sign of the changing times was the process leading up to the selection and ultimate choice of a president to succeed Carl Bosch, who had died on 26 April 1940. Although several new institutes—for biophysics, animal breeding, and bast fiber research—were founded under Bosch's short leadership (1937–40), his presidency was not a vigorous one. He suffered from depression and was often unable to attend meetings because of illness. The events of the Third Reich had taken their toll on him, and he turned to alcohol and painkillers for solace. Furthermore, much of his time was consumed by his duties at I. G. Farben, which had, in effect, put itself at the service of the state. It was during Bosch's presidency that Ernst Telschow began to be pivotal in managing the affairs of the Society.

Telschow also took charge of the steps toward finding a suitable successor for Bosch; within weeks after Bosch's death, the Society had established a short list of possible candidates. Telschow recognized the importance of speeding up the process of selection in order to avoid the possibility that the Reichsministerium für Wissenschaft, Erziehung, und Volksbildung (Reich Ministry of Science and Education, REM) would name a temporary president in the absence of a suggestion by the Kaiser Wilhelm Society.[1] By the beginning of May 1940, Telschow had already confidentially reported the three top candidates in rank order to Planck and to the second vice president, Carl Friedrich von Siemens: Albert Vögler, Karl Krauch, and Richard Kuhn. Vögler, however, was the first choice, and the others never seemed to have been considered seriously. The opinions of nine senators (including Krauch and Vögler) of the Society on the presidential candidates were telling: they unanimously agreed with the Vögler selection. Viktor Bruns, director of the Kaiser Wilhelm Institute for Law and International Law and section head for the humanities in the scientific council, "fundamentally agreed with the election of a president from the industry group and especially with Dr. Vögler." He did not think it right to elect a scientist. Siemens "totally agreed" with the Vögler selection and characterized it as the "most suitable solution that existed." Although Dr. Gustav Winkler would have liked to see a "luminary of science" selected, he considered Vögler "absolutely suitable"—especially since he had done so much for the Society over the years. Minister Saemisch was "very taken" by Vögler and was "very happy" about the choice. Both Krüß and Schmidt-Ott fully agreed with the Vögler candidacy, and the latter thought it was an "excellent suggestion." Rudolf Mentzel at first leaned toward the Krauch candidacy, but after thinking over the possible collision between the Four Year Plan institutes and the Kaiser Wilhelm institutes, he finally favored Vögler. Krauch agreed to a selection which was "dependent on the approval of Göring, the *Party* and Rust." Vögler said he was not fundamentally against accepting the offer but asked for some time to think it over.[2] Planck thought that "if we lived in normal times" one would tend to chose a scholar, as has been the tradition of the Society; but because in these times everything was less than normal, and no one knew what the next day would bring, everything should be done, he thought, to allow the Society to continue its activities. To do this no one was "more suitable than Dr. Vögler."[3]

As the consensus of opinion suggests, in ordinary times the Society would have carried out its tradition of selecting an outstanding scholar or scientist such as Harnack or Planck as its representative leader, but as a result of the changed socioeconomic and political context the Society favored expediency. This president would have the onerous task of leading the Society in times of war in a National Socialist context. As an industrialist, Vögler would serve as a mediator between the Society and various government ministries; he could use his contacts to benefit the Society. His appointment would find the approval of all of the competing ministries and personalities including Göring, the party, and the Rust Ministry. Finally, he had already helped the Society a great deal in negotiating with the National Socialists during the early years of the Third Reich and commanded great respect from the senators, the scientists, and the administrators. The final choice was therefore not surprising.

Albert Vögler, a leading industrialist, was general manager of United Steel. He was born in Borbeck, in the Ruhr, in 1877. An engineer by training, he had already become a major figure in the German steel industry by the time he was in his early thirties. In 1920 he was elected to the National Assembly as a delegate of the German People's party and served for four years. The German People's party was founded in 1919 by Gustav Stresemann for middle-class liberals; the party opposed further economic and social reforms designed to benefit the working class, but it was eventually taken over by conservative businessmen. By the end of the Weimar period Vögler seemed to support Franz von Papen over Hitler, and it was in this direction that any industrial money flowed. In fact, in January 1933 Vögler hosted a meeting at his home in Dortmund for Papen with Krupp von Bohlen und Halbach, Paul Reusch, and Fritz Springhorum in attendance. Although Vögler took part in some major meetings where Hitler or Göring gave speeches to industrialists, it is not clear how much support (if any at all) he gave to the NSDAP. By the end of the Weimar period he favored reconciling the NSDAP and the Papen cabinet. He was invited by Göring to attend the celebrated meeting of industrialists with Hitler and Göring on 20 February 1933, where future Nazi policy was outlined by Hitler to a group of leading industrialists at Göring's Presidential Palace. Hitler promised to rearm Germany and rid it of the Marxists. The industrialists then pledged three million marks to the party. Vögler, however, was disappointed that after an hour and a half, Hitler failed to address the economic policy questions that interested his audience.[4]

By the time Vögler became associated with the Kaiser Wilhelm Society he sported a close-cropped haircut framing a pallid face with prominent dark eyebrows in an expression that radiated sadness yet quiet determination. He came to meetings in a pin-striped three-piece suit and a starched white shirt with a high collar. He had been associated with the Society from its early days, and by 1917 he was a paying member as a representative of the German-Luxemburg Mining Company; the same year he became a member of the board of the Kaiser Wilhelm Institute for Iron Research, which he helped found. He had been a senator of the Kaiser Wilhelm Society since 1920. In 1925 he became third treasurer, and later, the treasurer; in this capacity he was a member of the administrative council.[5] In the early years of the Third Reich Planck turned to Vögler to mediate negotiations with Frick and the Reich Ministry of the Interior, especially when it came to protecting Jewish scientists. Like Carl Bosch, Fritz Thyssen, and other industrialists, Vögler had been openly against the National Socialist antisemitic policies. He even scolded Hitler and Göring about their attitudes toward Jews in 1932. By mid-July 1933 it was common knowledge at the Society that Vögler knew Göring very well personally.[6] Later in the Third Reich Vögler also grew to know Albert Speer, with whom he had frequent meetings and who often helped the Society receive necessary priority ratings and military deferrals for scientists. He was therefore socially acceptable to the National Socialist government while providing useful contacts to the Kaiser Wilhelm Society. In addition, he was "neither a party man, a ministry official or in the military."[7]

Despite the unanimous choice for the president's position at the outset, the process actually moved slowly. The senate meeting planned for May had been postponed because the REM canceled it. The reasons were not entirely clear, but it appears as though a third candidate was under consideration who had no connection with the Society, and the Ministry could not make a decision until the problem was solved. The events of the war, moreover, seemed to overshadow, or as Telschow described, "outshine," every aspect of life, and it was difficult for the Society's leaders to motivate the agencies to make decisions.[8]

The only way Telschow foresaw an accleration of the process was by sending the two vice presidents of the Society—Siemens and Krüß—to Bernhard Rust to discuss and resolve the impasse. Telschow thought Siemens and Krüß had a duty to take preparatory steps in the selection of a president, because the Society and the senate could later reproach them for not acting in the interests of the Society. Although a meeting took place, the only result was that Minister Rust postponed the senate's suggestion because of the "circumstances of the times," and even in the middle of November 1940, Mentzel thought it was not the right time to prod Minister Rust to make a decision.[9]

Although the process for approval of the Society's choice for president dragged, the issue of the selection of first vice president arose in the context of a May visit by Telschow with Herbert Backe, State Secretary of Agriculture and senator of the Kaiser Wilhelm Society. Backe appeared to be very interested in the state of the presidential election and reminded Telschow of the heavy financial support the Society had been receiving from the Reich Ministry for Food and Agriculture (Reichsernährungsministerium). He claimed that the contribution was greater than that from the REM. Half a year later, Backe again stressed the large financial contribution from his Ministry and the importance of agricultural research for Germany. Accordingly, Backe thought these developments required a stronger representation by Ministry officials in the governing bodies of the Society. Backe urged Telschow to consider filling the vice-presidential post with a Food and Agriculture official. Telschow told Backe he agreed with him completely and promised to offer Backe himself the post at the next meeting of the senate. Carl Friedrich von Siemens planned to resign his post of second vice president because of illness, thus creating an opening. Telschow noted to Backe, however, that he could not name him first president because the REM would resist the move.[10] Maneuvering among the competing agencies during the Third Reich was a delicate task.

By mid-December no action had been taken on the presidential candidacy. In order to prod Rust, Siemens wrote to him reminding him that half a year had gone by and it was not clear when the "circumstances of the times would change." Because Otto Wacker, named first vice president by the Rust Ministry and, according to the statutes, acting president, had died, the Society had been without a responsible leader for over half a year. Siemens thought it was irresponsible to continue in this way. If it was not possible for the Ministry to make a decision by the end of January, Siemens concluded, then another temporary solution had to be found; he could no longer function as president. Telschow therefore urged Rust to come to a senate meeting planned for the end of January 1941, a date which coincided with the thirtieth birthday celebration of the Society.[11]

Despite the seriousness of the situation, there was no senate meeting at the end of January, and the Society's birthday was not officially celebrated except for some articles in newspapers referring to the research of the Society and the anniversary. The Ministry's delays had slowed the process, but the real problem arose when Vögler declined the invitation to become president. Vögler recounted that he had had his doubts early on when speaking with Telschow about the issue shortly after Bosch's death. Now, after the developments surrounding the presidency question in the past months and after "mature reflection," he declined after repeated offers. Even if Vögler had had no doubts about taking the post, he felt unable to begin "new tasks during the war." He simply could not offer enough time to the Kaiser Wilhelm Society while covering his duties as managing director of United Steel. Instead, Vögler, unaware of the implications, agreed with Mentzel's suggestion that Mentzel take the post of vice president as a temporary solution. Vögler, however, was ready to accept the presidency only after the war was over, in case he was elected again.[12]

Rust, aware of the possibilities of this power vacuum, announced his intention of appointing Mentzel first vice president of the Society; according to the statutes of the Society, this would allow Mentzel to become the "acting leader" of the Society.[13] Rust saw Mentzel as a solution to the vacant presidential post. Despite the Society's acquiescence in other matters, it was not ready to allow such an easy transfer of leadership from the Society to the Ministry. Although the statutes had been changed to some extent in 1937, the Society's senate still had voting rights, and, according to the statutes, the president names the first vice president but not the minister. Even Telschow thought the recent developments were "unpleasant" and "not in the interests of the Kaiser Wilhelm Gesellschaft." Over the next week Telschow compiled the opinions of seven senators on the Rust move. The senators—Backe, Otto Fitzner, Krauch, Schmidt-Ott, Wettstein (the only scientist—and head of the biology section of the scientific council), Ernst Ammer, and Krüß—all agreed, with the exception of Krauch, that Mentzel could be the vice president, but they all had doubts about his assumption of the acting leadership of the Society. Ammer did not consider a temporary leadership by someone empowered by the Ministry the right thing to do because of the private character of the Society.[14]

Telschow also spoke to Siemens and Saemisch to sound them out for solutions to the Rust intervention. Siemens was reluctant to assume temporary leadership of the Society and declined Telschow's offer with the remark that he did not wish merely to offer his name for the Society to use. Saemisch, on the other hand, had some constructive suggestions. One could use the statutes as a basis for action. According to the tenth paragraph the vice president can only be named by the president; therefore, in order to appoint Mentzel, Vögler had to be "officially named president." If Vögler declined again, Krüß would then have to lead the Society until the war ended. Moreover, the vice president had to be elected from among the senators; since Mentzel was not a senator but took part in the senate meetings as a representative of the Ministry, he would first have to be elected into the senate. Saemisch officially told Telschow he would resign his post as senator if the various agencies of the government did not act according to the statutes. Wettstein thought the senate (not just the advisory council) had to be assembled to make the decision. If the senate was not to be heard in such a matter, Wettstein predicted its members would all resign or it would dissolve itself as a body.[15]

The Rust intervention had finally prodded the Society to take more active steps to protect its autonomy. The advisory council met on 20 June. The only solution the council saw was that Vögler would agree to become president, at least in name. Because of the situation, Siemens agreed, in spite of his illness, to take over the leadership of the Society if Vögler declined yet again. A week later, Telschow was called to Siemensstadt in Berlin by Siemens's secretary to meet with Vögler. Yet again Vögler declined to take the president's post before the end of the war. Vögler suggested meeting with Rust, Mentzel, Siemens, Krüß, Telschow, and himself at the end of July in order to solve the problem. Despite Vögler's repeated declinations of the post, Telschow still did not lose hope that he would decide to take on the job. The Rust meeting was scheduled for 15 July. Unfortunately, no minutes remain of the meeting, but between 15 and 29 July Vögler had been persuaded to take over the presidency. Moreover, Reich Marshall Göring approved very highly of the Vögler selection. He felt strongly, however, that Backe and not Mentzel should be named first vice president, thus reversing the original order.[16]

The senate met on 31 July 1941 and announced the decision. Vögler was named president by Bernhard Rust for six years upon the suggestion of the senate. Backe was named first vice president and Mentzel second. Rust assured the Society at the meeting that the "tradition and peculiarity of the Kaiser Wilhelm Gesellschaft would remain intact, and he would not bureaucratize or politicize the leadership."[17]

Greater Germany and the New Order
of German Science

Within weeks after the outbreak of World War II in 1939, cultural and science policies for use in foreign countries were formulated by the leaders of National Socialist Germany. Just as *Lebensraum* had its roots in imperial Germany, so too was foreign *Kulturpolitik* (cultural policy in the broadest sense) an old tradition in Germany. By the time of the Third Reich, however, the emphasis had turned to cultural imperialism with the defined goal of national expansion of power and the use of power politics to achieve this; it had become a vehicle of foreign policy.[18] The REM perceived the cultural policies of the Reich as a "war without weapons" and it was the goal of the REM to "secure and influence" similar policies in Germany's occupied territories. These policies would be implemented and spread through the German scientific institutes abroad (*deutsche wissenschaftliche Institute im Ausland*), which were founded during the war by the Reich and the foreign office to spread German propaganda to occupied territories.[19] Institutes had already opened in Bucharest, Sofia, and Belgrade, and twelve more were being built. The institutes planned and took the lead in implementing German *Kulturpolitik*.[20]

By autumn 1941 German troops had occupied almost all of continental Europe as part of Nazi Germany's expansionist policy. This territorial expansion led to a more conscious advance of cultural policies and, in particular, of science policy. Of central importance for science in this scheme was a series of secret meetings held at the REM in the winter of 1940–41 which dealt with the question of transferring international organizations from Brussels to Germany. It was also during this time that the Rosenberg Ministry for Occupied Eastern Territories, headed by Alfred Rosenberg, approached the Kaiser Wilhelm Society asking for a collaborative effort.

Within weeks after the outbreak of war, the Reich Ministry of the Interior had already announced that "scientific and cultural relations to neutral countries abroad must be cultivated even more during the war."[21] By autumn 1940 a victorious outcome of the war seemed likely for Germany; therefore plans were made for the immediate postwar world under German leadership. There were many meetings among the appropriate ministries where the "importance of scientific cooperation within the international organizations for future foreign cultural policies of the Greater German Reich" were discussed. The question of restructuring international organizations and the influence of Germany on these institutions was not considered to be an independent problem, but only part of the "foreign relations of science and its extra-political meaning, that is, its importance for cultural policies."[22]

As part of the new international politics for science, the Foreign Office began to consider the question of whether to bring international organizations, which originally had their home in Brussels or Paris, to Germany.[23] This question led to an important conference on 12 November 1940 with scientists and officials from the ministries. Among the scientists asked to participate in the meeting and advise the Ministry on the question of moving the headquarters of international organizations to Germany were six directors of Kaiser Wilhelm institutes: Fritz von Wettstein (Kaiser Wilhelm Institute for Biology), Richard Kuhn (Kaiser Wilhelm Institute for Medical Research), Peter Thiessen (Kaiser Wilhelm Institute for Physical Chemistry), Eugen Fischer (Kaiser Wilhelm Institute for Anthropology), Ernst Heymann (Kaiser Wilhelm Institute for Private Law), and Vicktor Bruns (Kaiser Wilhelm Institute for Law and International Law).

The responses of these Kaiser Wilhelm institute directors varied with regard to the role of international unions and societies, but many displayed nationalistic tendencies while conceiving of Germany as the leader of a united European science in competition with American science. Wettstein stands out as a representative of this type of thinking with this statement:

> I believe the best way [to restructure international organizations] would be to organize Europe under German leadership as a European section. We can forget about America. The struggle with America will start after the war and ability will decide whether the right to lead will lie with America or with Europe.[24]

Other Kaiser Wilhelm institute scientists had similar views. Richard Kuhn, who was vice president of the Chemical Union, thought that German leadership was possible in Europe (in other words, Germany did not have a chance to be competitive with America), but he also believed that the headquarters should be moved only if the American president of the union agreed. If he did not, it would create bad feelings between Europe and America.[25] Thiessen, who was probably the most convinced National Socialist of the group, thought that the warlike position (*Kampfstellung*) between Germany and America that Kuhn foresaw already existed, and therefore steps should be taken to limit *Kulturpolitik* to European territory.[26]

Wettstein's and Brun's contribution to *Kulturpolitik*, or cultural imperialism and exploitation, did not end with this important meeting. By early 1942 two developments occurred almost simultaneously: Wettstein and Bruns, with the support and complicity of Ernst Telschow (as the responsible representative of the Kaiser Wilhelm Society), agreed to cooperate with both the Reich Ministry for Food and Agriculture and the Rosenberg Ministry on scientific research in the East.

Alfred Rosenberg's office, a party agency, approached Bruns in February 1942 with detailed plans on a future cooperative venture between the office and the Kaiser Wilhelm Society. The agenda for this cooperation was detailed and telling:

1. Appointment of teaching and research personnel in all areas of science for deployment in the East.

2. Arranging the military deferments [Uk-Stellung] through the Reich Ministry of the East for Kaiser Wilhelm Gesellschaft scientists participating in tasks important for the war effort.

3. Scheduled deployment of scientific personnel in the East.

4. Introduction of scientists to the practical problems and tasks of the East. Research contracts for the institutes and exchange of results.

5. Financial support for the contract research in the East through the Ministry.

6. Creation of an East office within the Kaiser-Wilhelm-Gesellschaft, for the purpose of regulating business with the Ministry.

7. The support of future generations of scientists [*Nachwuchs*].

8. Cooperation with the *Hauptamt Wissenschaft* [science section of the REM] in cultural areas.

9. Deployment of teaching and research personnel at the Kaiser Wilhelm Gesellschaft for the "*Hohe Schule*" [literally "Higher Schools," run by the Nazi party].

10. Deployment of scientists in the camps of the Reich Teachers' Association [*Reichsdozentenbundes*].

11. Cooperation between the *Hauptamt Wissenschaft* and the Kaiser-Wilhelm-Gesellschaft for the deployment of scientists in the scientific work of the party and its affiliates.

12. Publication of scientific articles, especially those related to cultural areas, in the journals of the party.[27]

This plan soon led to a meeting at the Hauptamt Wissenschaft with Bruns, Telschow, and two representatives of that office, where they discussed "problems arising from research in the East, especially the maintenance and safeguarding of the Russian Institutes there." Telschow "promised the support of the Kaiser Wilhelm Gesellschaft as long as the personnel existed and as long as [the Society's] advice was needed."[28] These plans, however, seemed to have remained in the preliminary stages since no full-scale deployment of Kaiser Wilhelm institute scientists in the East occurred.

Negotiations for institutes in Russia had begun with the Reich Ministry for Food and Agriculture about the same time as the overture was made to Bruns. Wettstein suggested a plan for Nikolai Vavilov's breeding research stations, which lay in European Russia. Wettstein thought the valuable material collected by Vavilov could be used at the newly founded institute for cultivated plant research in Austria. Nikolai Ivanovic Vavilov, the distinguished Soviet geneticist, rose to prominence in the 1920s when he became director of the department of applied botany. In 1924, he reorganized the department into the All-Union Institute of Applied Botany and New Cultures, which became the All-Union Institute of Plant Breeding in 1930; he was also president of the All-Union Lenin Academy of Agricultural Sciences, which encompassed the Plant Breeding Institute, until 1935. By then the institutions maintained more than 400 experimental stations throughout the Soviet Union and employed more than 20,000 people. In 1940 he was arrested while on a collecting expedition; in 1941 he was tried, found guilty of sabotaging agriculture and other charges, and sent to prison in Moscow; he died in prison in Saratov in 1943.[29]

Vavilov maintained one of the world's best collections of wild and primitive plant forms. They were partly in German-occupied territory and partly in Russian territory. Wettstein recommended taking the stations and "caring for them through the Kaiser Wilhelm Gesellschaft in order to save the valuable material and to make further work there possible."[30] On 9 March 1942 Wettstein drafted a list of the most important places in Russia for the biological institutes in the east which would make up part of the "biological network" of the Kaiser Wilhelm Society.[31] By the end of March, however, it seems that the Rosenberg Ministry had taken care of the matter without the consultation of the Society. And by the winter of 1942, with the defeat of Germany, these plans came to nought. The SS, however, was also interested in research on wild and primitive forms of cultivated plants and had already sponsored a number of expeditions to collect primitive forms in other countries. It therefore arranged a special commando in 1943 to collect the material from the numerous breeding research stations in Russia, including parts of the Vavilov collection, which had been partly under German occupation. Heinz Brücher, head of this Russian Commando, used this material in the newly founded SS institute for plant genetics in Lannach.[32]

The Kaiser Wilhelm Society recognized the effect of the "new order" ideology on its international scientific relations and reported in 1941 that "the recent events of the war and the concomitant new order of European territory is increasingly affecting the international scientific relations of the Kaiser-Wilhelm-Gesellschaft."[33] The various cultural agreements had led to visits from foreign guests to Germany and the Kaiser Wilhelm institutes. In part independently, and in part in collaboration with the Foreign Office's new *Kulturpolitik* for the occupied eastern territories, the Kaiser Wilhelm Society created several new institutes in territories either occupied by the Reich or under its indirect control, and scientists traveled to eastern countries to deliver lectures as goodwill ambassadors.[34]

Four new institutes for agriculture and biology were founded by the Kaiser Wilhelm Society after the war broke out: one in Breslau (for agriculture), another in Sofia, Bulgaria (for agriculture), a third in Athens/Piraeus,

Greece (for biology), and a fourth in Austria (for cultivated plant research).[35]
On closer inspection, it seems as though the Sofia, Athens, and Austrian
institutes were conceived of before the outbreak of war, but the new political circumstances were more favorable to the enterprises outlined, thus
making it possible to gain government support through the Reich Ministry
for Food and Agriculture, the REM, and the Foreign Office. With agriculture and *Lebensraum* as parts of a core National Socialist ideology, projects
relating to agriculture and to the ideals of *Lebensraum* flourished.

One of the first institutes for agriculture to be founded after the war
broke out in the fall of 1939 was the Institute for the Science of Agricultural Work in the Kaiser Wilhelm Society in Breslau. It had its founding
meeting on 6 December 1940. Although Breslau was not a city in one of
the occupied territories, it was located near Poland, on Germany's eastern-
most border. Even before the war broke out natives of Breslau began to
think of the city as the "cultural center of the Ostmark [Eastern Border-
land]."[36] It was also an agricultural center. After the German victories in
Poland in 1939, the east began to assume even greater importance. For these
reasons it became a good location from which to organize agricultural activity
for the east and a place from which to look toward the southeast.

Otto Fitzner, president of the Chamber of Industry and Commerce in
Breslau, a party member since 1931, and a Kaiser Wilhelm Society senator
since 1937, approached Telschow in April 1940 suggesting the establishment of an institute for research on the physiology of work in agriculture.
Funding would come from Fitzner, the City of Breslau, and from agriculture. Initially, Telschow was skeptical about the project. Konrad Meyer, the
doyen of agricultural research, also thought other problems were more
important, and Rudolf Mentzel, head of the Hauptamt Wissenschaft at the
REM, agreed.[37]

The institute was motivated by the need to find ways to master the work
necessary for agriculture. With the rise of technical methods available since
the middle of the nineteenth century, machines and migrant workers from
abroad were used for this purpose, but no systematic methods were developed. More recently, Germany had been beset with a flight of workers to
the cities, slashing the number of agricultural workers. To remedy the situation in an efficient way it was proposed that the new institute would have
the task of researching all methods available for use in agricultural businesses.
The second task of the institute would be to advise agronomists about questions arising from the economics of work. Finally, the institute would work
closely with the agricultural machine industry to find new technical solutions. Breslau was considered to be a favorable location for the institute
because it lay in the "big agricultural area of the east and the institute could
help considerably with the expansion of the new territory there."[38]

By the fall of 1940 both the Nutrition Ministry and the REM still did
not support the founding of this new institute. The Nutrition Ministry saw
it as a rival institute to a state agricultural institute, and it is not clear why
the REM initially did not support the institute. Fitzner, however, sought

out Telschow yet again, pledging RM 100,000 for the institute. He planned to interest Mentzel and Lammers (the head of the Reich Chancellery) in the project as well. Because of the tasks for the institute in the east, Fitzner thought the institute should be called the "Adolf-Hitler-Institut." Telschow wanted to delay the Kaiser Wilhelm Society decision until the final verdict of the Reich Ministry for Food and Agriculture and of the REM, because the Kaiser Wilhelm Society could "in no way provide funding for this goal."[39] By the end of September, however, Mentzel, Meyer, and the Nutrition Ministry supported the creation of such an institute.[40] Fitzner and Gerhardt Preuschen, the future director of the institute, also gained the personal support of Herbert Backe, who wanted to sit on the board of trustees.[41] Backe, who had been a member of the Kaiser Wilhelm Society senate since 1937, now was one of the leaders of the National Socialist regime through his position as Secretary of State in the Reich Agriculture and Nutrition Ministry (by 1943 he was appointed Reich Minister and Reich Farmer's Leader by Adolf Hitler). The REM sent its official support by the middle of October with "an order" for the Kaiser Wilhelm Society to begin the preparations necessary to found the institute.[42]

The organizational stages of the institute progressed quickly, and by the founding celebration on 6 December 1940, Telschow was able to draw attention to the "exceptional quickness" with which the institute had been set up. A number of leaders from the party the state, and business showed interest in the project by joining the board of trustees, and the Society was "satisfied" that the new institute could contribute to "questions of the German east."[43]

The new director of the institute was Dr. Gerhardt Preuschen. Before taking up the position of director of the agricultural institute, Preuschen had been the founder and director of an institute for agricultural technology and workers' physiology in Eberswalde from 1932 to 1940. Because he had not yet written his *Habilitation,* Mentzel and Meyer did not believe it was a good idea to create an institute under his leadership, but perhaps his background in mechanical engineering, practical training in agriculture, and experience in the technology of agriculture compensated for this.[44] Although his political affiliation was not openly discussed in the negotiations, he had been a member of the NSDAP since 1 May 1937.[45] The appointment of a director who was not habilitated marks a change in the general policies of the Society as well as general German academic policy.[46]

Preuschen gave the opening lecture and thereby outlined the tasks and methods for the new institute: "Safeguarding the new living space [*Lebensraum*] of the victorious campaign in 1939," began Preuschen, is the task that awaits the German people in the future. He made his National Socialist views clear and brought to light the motivation behind the founding of this institute: "The territory in the east must be integrated into German living space over the next few years."[47] In his talk, Mentzel also emphasized the new tasks in the east as a result of the successful military campaign in 1939. He drew attention to the important contribution of science for these political goals. The creation of a new institute in the middle of the war "proved Germany's strength," he said, and was done through German diplomacy and recognition of the importance of science for the new Europe.[48] Backe began his talk with the oft-repeated National Socialist slogan about the "danger [of the] flight from the land." The reason for this flight, he claimed, was the "devaluation of agricultural work." Because the east was assuming great importance, this flight from agricultural work, which was primarily occurring in the eastern parts of Germany, posed a threat. By creating new technical methods for agricultural work, Backe hoped the institute could help eradicate the causes of "flight from the land."[49] Common to all three speeches was the emphasis on the Breslau connection to the Balkans or southeast Europe. Backe identified the new institute as a "bridge to Southeastern Europe." Mentzel thought the institute would have an impact not only on Germany but also on southeastern Europe, which had a longstanding relationship with Breslau. Thus foreigners from the southeast, like Iwan Bagrianoff, the Minister for Agriculture in Bulgaria, would be appointed to the Board of Trustees. Preuschen also discussed Breslau's close relation to southeastern countries and the interaction of Balkan agriculture with the German economy.[50]

Since the Kaiser Wilhelm Society had no president from the time of Bosch's death in April 1940 until June 1941, as managing director Telschow assumed the role in absentia and participated in the founding of the new institute. As a member of the NSDAP since May 1933 it is no surprise that Telschow would support National Socialist goals in agriculture. But if a strong president had been present at the time, the Society might have been able to resist the intrusion of National Socialist politics into the founding of a new institute. The Kaiser Wilhelm Society viewed the institute with reservation, as is indicated by its name: "Institut für landwirtschaftliche Arbeitswissenschaft in der Kaiser Wilhelm Gesellschaft" (Institute for the Science of Agricultural Work in the Kaiser Wilhelm Society). This institute, in fact, inaugurated a new type of institute for the Society, one under the general framework of the Kaiser Wilhelm Society.[51] Administratively it was loosely connected to the Kaiser Wilhelm Society, but the inspiration and operation of the institute came from other individuals and institutions.

Soon after the opening celebration of the agricultural institute in Breslau, another agricultural institute was projected for Bulgaria, occupied by Germany but under indirect control. Bulgaria, according to Norman Rich, a leading authority on the German occupation, "retained a greater degree of control over its domestic and foreign affairs during the war than any other country in Southeastern Europe."[52] Yet, simultaneously, it was Hitler's "self-willed ally."[53]

Just as the Breslau agricultural institute had political origins, so too did the German-Bulgarian Institute for Agricultural Research. The institute seems to be the outcome of an agreement for cooperation in agriculture made on 25 June 1940 between Konrad Meyer, the head of the Research Service and director of the section for agriculture and biology in the Reich Research

Council, and Dontscho Kostoff, director of the Central Agricultural Experimental and Research Institute in Sofia. Meyer and Kostoff agreed to deepen scientific cooperation by cultivating personal contacts between scientists through mutual invitations for research trips and lectures. According to the Kaiser Wilhelm Society, it was the Bulgarian Agricultural Minister Iwan Bagrianoff's idea to create a joint German-Bulgarian institute for agricultural research.[54] Bagrianoff had visited the Kaiser Wilhelm Institute for Breeding Research in 1940 and had, during that time, made overtures to the ministries and to the Kaiser Wilhelm Society about creating a similar institute in Sofia. Therefore, by April 1941 the Kaiser Wilhelm Society began preparations for an institute based on "strict parity" whereby there would be both a German and a Bulgarian president and director. Both countries would also share the costs; the Bulgarian government would build the institute and contribute the land, while the Kaiser Wilhelm Society would supply the instruments and other needs for running an institute.[55] Such joint efforts were not unprecedented in the history of the Society. For example, in 1931, even before the Third Reich, a German-Italian institute for marine biology had been founded. This in turn was built on a long tradition of German involvement in the Naples station and a desire for a Mediterranean center. But the context of Greater Germany and the war cannot be overlooked in evaluating the founding of a new institute in the forties. Although it seems as though a Bulgarian stimulated the project, the Kaiser Wilhelm Society was taking advantage of, and contributing to, the state's *Lebensraum* policy. *Lebensraum* had found its way to the world of science as the Society expanded its foreign relations to the southeast. The cooperative nature of the project probably mirrored the general attitude of the occupied countries (or those countries under indirect control), which saw the Germans as providers of needed equipment and instrumentation while the poorer rural countries would provide the rich agricultural resources, or whatever resources were available.

The political goals of the Bulgarian institute fit the notion of a "new Europe" under German rule: "Without a doubt, the results won here in the continental climate of southeast Europe will also have fundamental importance for the *new Europe*. Indeed, in the future the main emphasis of Europe's total agricultural production will lie in the territories of the European East and Southeast."[56]

The Kaiser Wilhelm Society planned to uphold the "basic research" tradition of its institutes in this project even though, by its nature, agriculture is primarily applied research. The memorandum on the tasks of the German-Bulgarian Institute for Agriculture paid lip service to basic research and argued that one must conceive of research in the long term. Basic research, so the argument goes, eventually leads to practical fallout. Accordingly, the institute would focus on problems of plant production not only for the "new Europe" but also for Bulgaria.

Unlike the Breslau institute, plans for the institute in Bulgaria did not develop quickly, and it was not until late 1942 that the institute celebrated its founding. Unlike the Breslau institute, however, the Kaiser Wilhelm Society, the REM, and the Foreign Office supported the project unequivocally. The role and importance of the Foreign Office in the affairs of the Society at this juncture are also significant. Not only did it support the creation of the institute financially and scientifically, but its general influence in the affairs of the Society is reflected also by the presence of Ernst von Weizsäcker of the Foreign Office as a member of the president's advisory board (as of 24 April 1942). It was at the 24 April 1942 senate meeting that Weizsäcker suggested naming King Boris of Bulgaria an honorary member of the Society. The head of the cultural department of the Foreign Office, Fritz von Twardowski, was a member of the board of trustees of the institute and participated in its founding.

The political and scientific importance of the project is reflected by the three-day program prepared by the Bulgarians for the president and his entourage from the Kaiser Wilhelm Society. On the first day the German guests visited the Bulgarian Minister President and the Agricultural Minister. The evening ended with a dinner given by the German consulate.[57] The next day, 12 September 1942, the institute in Bulgaria opened officially in the presence of Albert Vögler, Fritz von Twardowski, Mentzel, Beckerle, the German consulate in Sofia, the Bulgarian Minister President, and the Bulgarian Agricultural Minister.[58] Speeches extolled the new cooperative venture and after the "auspicious intensification and deepening of mutual political, economic and cultural ties" between Germany and Bulgaria it was clear that activity would develop in agriculture, said a spokesman for the Bulgarians.[59] After the celebration, there was time for some sightseeing. The Society entourage visited agricultural schools near Sofia the next day and ended the visit on the 14 September with more dinners with German and Bulgarian dignitaries.

The founding of a new institute in Bulgaria raised suspicion, and a few days before the official celebrations the English radio announced that "the German government is now establishing an institute for agriculture with the help of the Kaiser Wilhelm Gesellschaft which has the singular goal of exploiting Bulgarian agriculture for the interests of the Reich."[60] This statement was in part true. In fact, when Telschow outlined the origins of the project to Mentzel, he stated: "the stimulus for the founding of the institute came when the former Bulgarian Agriculture Minister, his excellency Bagrianoff, and his Secretary of State Kostoff, visited Germany. The Kaiser Wilhelm Gesellschaft, *as a representative of the German Reich,* brought the negotiations to a successful conclusion.[61] This retrospective explanation would seem to substantiate the claim that the German government was building the institute with "the help" of the Kaiser Wilhelm Society. Although the Kaiser Wilhelm Society was not a Reich institution but an autonomous organization, it became, perhaps, "a representative of the German Reich" when its administrators or scientists went abroad. The Kaiser Wilhelm Society was certainly exploiting Bulgarian agriculture, but in a reciprocal way. Another unanswered question involves the motivations of the Bulgarians. It seems that in addition to Iwan Bagrianoff, Slaw Antonoff, a Bulgarian scientist who had studied in Germany and was a Germanophile, campaigned to found the institute. As a result of his efforts, Telschow nominated him for a "German order." Antonoff's friendly attitude also earned him the name "betrayer" by the English radio. In addition to making the best of a bad situation, there were probably a number of fellow travelers from the political right in Bulgaria, as there were in other countries.

The German director of the institute was Professor Arnold Scheibe, who came from an institute for agriculture at the technical college in Munich. Scheibe had been a member of the NSDAP since 1 May 1937 and of the SS since 1 October 1933. After becoming institute director in Bulgaria on 1 April 1942 he was given a leave of absence from the university in Munich. As early as September 1940, he was exempted from the service (Uk-Stellung) because his work on plant breeding was considered important for the war effort. He had been working on a project for the Research Service since 1935 on oil and food plants. This work was, in turn, based on his participation in the German Hindukusch Expedition in Afghanistan (supported by the Reich Research Council) where he collected materials for research on plant breeding.[62] Scheibe's research received ample support from the Reich Research Council, and by 1944 he had at least two contracts for research designated important for the war and state: one for breeding and preparation of fibrous plants and the other for fruit and vegetable preservation especially for the army.[63] In addition, German agriculture could profit from his research on fat and protein, which had become a relevant topic during the war.

The Bulgarian director was to be Professor Dontscho Kostoff. But because of difficulties in gaining approval for Kostoff as a result of his activities in Russia, no Bulgarian director had been installed by 1943. The plans for equity in the board of trustees were realized, and twelve representatives from both the German and Bulgarian authorities sat on the board. On the German side there were two representatives from the Kaiser Wilhelm Society, one from the Foreign Office, one from the REM, and one from the Reich Ministry for Food and Agriculture. The Bulgarian board of trustees consisted of the Agricultural Minister, Bagrianoff, Antonoff, the director of the natural history museum, a biologist, and the director of the Bulgarian Sugar Trust.[64]

The Kaiser Wilhelm Society thought the institute would become the "leading agricultural institute for the whole Southeast"[65] and therefore it was advantageous for the Society's network of institutes abroad in agriculture and biology. Another institute to be added to the Kaiser Wilhelm Society network abroad was one for biology in Piraeus, Greece, a country occupied by Germany in April 1941.

The German-Greek biology institute also seemed to have received its initial stimulus from the foreign country participating in the joint arrangement. According to the record, it was Dr. Tzonis, the director of a chemical-biological and cancer research institute in Athens, who proposed the founding of a joint German-Greek research institute for biology.[66] Even before the war, in January 1938, Max Hartmann, a department head at the Kaiser Wilhelm Institute for Biology, evaluated and approved very highly of Tzonis's plan. Hartmann called attention to the existence of biological institutes in the Mediterranean—in Spain, France, Italy, Yugoslavia, and Egypt; yet no similar institute existed in Greece. "With its strong geographic structure, its great climatic differences, its rich coastal formations and rich island world . . . Greece is very favorable for modern experimental-biological researches," wrote Hartmann in his assessment. Therefore, German biologists had a strong interest in founding the institute. By exploring the land and sea thoroughly it would also be of great use for Greek agriculture and fishing. Finally, young Greek biologists would be better educated through their contact with German personnel.[67]

The institute was designed to create a "firm connection between Greek and German culture."[68] The "cultural goals" of the institute were also stressed in the statutes where the first sentence read: The Kaiser Wilhelm Society is building an institute, with the approval of the German Reich government and the Greek government, "in an attempt to intensify and cultivate the cultural and scientific relations" between the two countries.[69] Some scientists involved in the founding discussions also saw it in this "cultural propagandistic" way—a significant departure from the traditional pure science institutes created by the Society. Fritz von Wettstein even went so far as to say that the institute abroad would "never only have the character of a pure research institute," like those at home; rather, he thought it was an "important task" for the institute to be used as a "German cultural propaganda institute."[70]

Tzonis visited the cultural department of the Foreign Office in Berlin on 24 August 1940 to discuss the founding of the institute again. Hartmann reported to Telschow that Tzonis was in Berlin to realize his plan "under the present more favorable political conditions." Hartmann advised Tzonis to found the institute as a Kaiser Wilhelm Institute and not as a direct state institute.[71] The Kaiser Wilhelm Society wrote to the Foreign Office expressing "great interest" in the project should funding from the Reich be forthcoming.[72]

Although Tzonis sponsored the project, as preparations went on for the institute in Athens, Hartmann began to sense a dampening of interest by the Greeks toward the end of 1941. The war had begun to penetrate more deeply into Greece as German troops occupied much of Europe; Greece was invaded in April 1941. The German military had apparently taken over many scientific institutes for their own use. Hartmann reported in December 1941 he had the impression that the "attitude of Greek academic circles—also those who had been very friendly towards Germans before—had become much more reserved since the summer." One Greek scientist apparently declined to join the board of directors of the institute because the political context in Greece made it "psychologically impossible [*seelisch unmöglich*]."[73] As a result of these reservations it was not until 1942 that a contract between the Kaiser Wilhelm Society and the Greek government was signed.[74]

In addition to the agricultural institutes in Breslau and Bulgaria, another joint institute for agriculture was planned for Hungary, an agricultural country in southeast Europe. Discussions began in the fall of 1941 at a time when the Bulgarian institute was well on the way to completion; it was therefore often referred to as a model for the prospective Hungarian institute. The initial written stimulus for a joint German-Hungarian institute for agriculture came from Baron Tilo von Wilmowsky, an Austrian and president of the Central European Economic Association, on 2 September 1941. As a result of discussions with Vögler, the president of the Kaiser Wilhelm Society, German and Hungarian colleagues from the economic association, Reichsminister for Finance Lutz Count Schwerin von Krosigk, and Herbert Backe, the idea to create such an institute found great interest and warm support, especially from the latter two individuals. Wilmowsky thought that German scientific results could be used on the special climatic and soil conditions in Hungary and the Danube basin. The Hungarians were interested in such a project because they had a long interest in exporting agricultural products and importing industrial products.[75]

The Kaiser Wilhelm Society was interested in the project and financial support was available, but there did not seem to be a leading scientist on hand; after all, it had been the tradition of the Society to find a scientist to build an institute around. Telschow, the general director of the Society, approached his contacts at the Foreign Office. They also supported the project as an analogue to the Bulgarian institute, although they did not want it to become "the central agricultural station in the Southeast" because of rivalries among countries.[76]

Yet even before detailed plans could be developed for the institute, interference came from the REM. Mentzel claimed that the Society had not told him of the plans for an agricultural institute in Hungary. In a power play which reflects the changing relation of the Kaiser Wilhelm Society to the state, Mentzel wrote to the Society on 21 October 1941 claiming that in accordance with his decree of 30 July 1941, "all future negotiations about foreign questions at the Kaiser Wilhelm Gesellschaft" can be undertaken only with his prior permission. Therefore, he required a report about the founding of this institute in Hungary. Annoyed at this interference in its internal administration, Vögler wrote to remind the Ministry that the Society had reported the discussions to the Ministry in a letter predating Mentzel's and clearly the Society would contact the appropriate ministries in such questions, but the senate of the Society was finally responsible for founding such institutes. Furthermore, wrote Vögler, according to its statutes, the president leads the whole Society and is not bound to the directives of a ministry. Three months after Vögler's letter of 6 November, Mentzel replied and repeated his assertion that the Society's plans abroad had to be undertaken in agreement with him and his directives. He wrote Vögler that he did not subscribe to the basic attitude in Vögler's letter and referred to the statement in the first paragraph of the Society's statutes (as of 1937) that the Kaiser Wilhelm Society is "under the ministries' control [*untersteht . . . meiner*

Aufsicht]." He then referred to paragraph fourteen where the statutes state that the creation of research institutes can be undertaken after a hearing by the senate and scientific council in agreement with the minister. By the end of the letter Mentzel asked the Society to defer the plan because no scientist was available for the task.[77] In the end, the plan failed because no suitable scientist was found to head the proposed institute, a problem which had plagued the negotiations from the start and did not seem to be a result of Mentzel's interference.

Another institute which was founded in Austria in 1943 differs from the previous three institute foundings because foreign policy questions played a smaller role than in Sofia and Athens, for example. The Institute for Cultivated Plant Research founded in Vienna and directed by Hans Stubbe became a classic Kaiser Wilhelm institute and was created primarily because of Wettstein's planning and energy. Wettstein, however, did use the more favorable and changing political constellations to emphasize the importance of cultivated plant research. In October 1941 he wrote that "the occupation of further territories in the east, the tight connection of the German Reich with the South East, the contact with the furthest North through Finland and with the Mediterranean" have moved cultivated plant research to the forefront of essential research areas.[78] Both Backe and Konrad Meyer very warmly supported the plans, and the institute also received financial support from the Ministry for Food and Agriculture and its scientists. In particular, Hans Stubbe, were generously supported by Meyer's section of the German Research Council.

In general, cultivated plant research and plant breeding research flourished in National Socialist Germany. Richly supported collecting expeditions were undertaken in Hindukusch, Albania, the Peloponnesos, and Crete. For example, Hans Stubbe was the head of collecting expedition to Crete with a contract from the High Command of the Military and the Reich Research Council.[79] His institute also ended up receiving some of the Vavilov material from Russia.

Plant breeding was already firmly institutionalized at the institute for plant breeding in Müncheberg, which had been founded by Erwin Baur in 1927. After Baur died in 1933, there was a period of temporary leadership under B. Husfeld, but Wilhelm Rudorf, an active National Socialist, became director in 1937. Rudorf, who had seen the newly founded cultivated plant research institute as competition to his own institute, prospered in the Third Reich. His institute's work on Kautshuk—a rubber manufactured from the kok-saghyz plant (an Asiatic dandelion with high rubber content roots)—had already received support from the Four Year Plan institutions, but by the war, even the Reichsführer of the SS supported the research by donating an area—the Red Hole—near Müncheberg for this research. It also received the rich support of Backe and his Ministry.[80]

It is significant that three institutes were created, and that one was planned, in southeastern Europe. The Balkans were seen by the National Socialists as an important element of the New Order of Europe under German rule. These countries would provide agrarian products in exchange for industrial growth and would thereby benefit the Germany economy. In fact, by 1939, Germany led France and England with the lion's share of exports from southeastern countries; by June 1941 Germany's influence in the Balkans was growing.[81] But, in particular, Germany saw the southeastern European countries as providers of agricultural raw materials. During the war the most important task of German agriculture was the provision of protein and, even more, fat. Sunflower seeds from Romania, Bulgaria, and Hungary, for example, were considered to be an important raw material for oil. Walter Darré proclaimed at an exhibition that southeastern Europe could supply Greater Germany's needs for plant oil.[82]

Interestingly enough, the Kaiser Wilhelm Society had no institutional commitments in Poland, the country targeted for living space, the first country occupied by Germany during the war, and a country where other scholars and scientists set up ideologically inspired or influenced institutes. A few examples of institutions set up by other scholars and scientists show how much less the Society was influenced by, and contributed to, *Lebensraum* ideology in the east. And it should be emphasized that *Lebensraum* is generally applied to areas in the east, especially Poland and European Russia. The two most important and notorious institutes founded in Poland during the Third Reich were the Institute for German Work in the East (Institut für Deutsche Ostarbeit) in Krakow and the Reichsuniversität Posen (Poland).

The Institute for German Work in the East was supposed to become the intellectual bulwark of German culture in the east and a center for research and teaching.[83] Located in the Generalgouvernement of occupied Poland, the institute was headed and conceived by Hans Frank, who was also the governer of the Generalgouvernement. It consisted of eleven departments ranging from race and Volk research, law, history, and philology, to agriculture; it also organized conferences and published its own journal. The Reichsuniversität Posen, on the other hand, was one of three Reich universities founded in the occupied countries of the newly won *Lebensraum* (the other two were in Straßburg and Prague). The Reich universities were model National Socialist universities and were created to serve cultural, economic, and political rule in the occupied areas and to build up *Lebensraum* policies.[84] The Kaiser Wilhelm Society and its scientists were not involved in these institutions, nor were comparable institutions created by the Society. This contrast is important because it reflects the different and subtle nature of the relationship between National Socialist ideology and the Kaiser Wilhelm Society.

For the Fatherland?

The scientific research done at the Kaiser Wilhelm institutes during the war went far beyond tasks for the East and the "war without weapons." Because "Hitler's war" is known for its pursuit of "wonder weapons" and other technological developments, it is natural to consider the extent of the contributions made by the Kaiser Wilhelm Society and its institutes to the war effort. Since it was an institution committed to advancing basic scientific research, it is not surprising to find that the Society was not a major part of the war machine. Nor were there as many academic scientists drafted into military research as there were, for example, in the United States. The tradition of basic research at the Kaiser Wilhelm institutes, however, was more applicable to the older institutes in Berlin-Dahlem, whereas the institutes in the Ruhr Valley and outside of Berlin had the capacity and tendency to do applied work. These tendencies were magnified during the war as the industry-related institutes altered their research emphasis with the changed environment and sources of support.

Unfortunately, it is not always easy to determine the exact nature of the work done during the war or gain access to the papers produced, whether published or secret. *Die Naturwissenschaften*, the organ of the Society, continued to publish reports on the scientific activity of each institute until 1943, but if an institute was engaged in highly secret war work, the results of the research would not be published at all. By 1943, the last year the reports appeared in *Die Naturwissenschaften*, Telschow prefaced the presentations by the institutes with a statement that the Kaiser Wilhelm institutes were working under full deployment for the war even if the reports did not "explicitly emphasize" it.[85] Because a major portion of the war work was done after 1942, it is difficult to fully examine these activities. There were a number of other reasons that the issues of *Die Naturwissenschaften* became thin during the last two war years: many of the staff members had been drafted, the institutes were preoccupied with moving to areas protected from allied bombing, and supplies and materials—including paper—became scarce.

During the war the Society outwardly proclaimed its intended and actual participation in the war effort while believing it still maintained its tradition of basic research. Because the annual meetings ceased after the war broke out, special publications made general announcements and reported on activities to members of the Society. Publication of a yearbook began in 1939, and four editions appeared yearly through 1942, when publication ceased. In addition to Society members, Telschow sent the yearbook to "the Führer, Reichsmarshall Göring, Reichsminister Rust," and many other ministers.[86] As the war progressed, the leaders of the Society increasingly stressed the importance of research for the final outcome of the war. This readiness to contribute to the German war effort started as a willingness to offer the services of the Society to the war effort after the outbreak of war in 1939 to a rising crescendo by the 1942–43 turning point of the war, when leaders of the Society proclaimed that science could determine the outcome of the war.

Describing the year 1939, Telschow wrote in a nationalistic tone that new tasks had emerged as a result of the "outbreak of the great fight for Germany's freedom and future." He claimed it was possible for almost all of the thirty-six institutes to contribute to solving problems important for the war and a war economy without compromising the basic research tradition of the Society. Despite the Society's unique characteristic—its combination of independence from, but close contact with, various ministries and branches of the party and state—it was ready for a quick and multifaceted deployment for the fatherland.[87] Although Telschow was quick to offer the services of the Society to the state for the war effort, at this early date Germany's war machinery did not view science or scientists as decisive for the war. Rather than have them work on science, the government began to draft scientists for use in the field and not in the lab. In fact, by 1941 some 31 percent (or 330) of the Society's male staff members had been drafted. However, 412 (46 percent), were given service exemptions (Uk-Stellung).[88] By 1942, some 40 percent of the male staff was fighting in the war, but no other men were going to be drafted as a result of Vögler's personal negotiations with General Friedrich Fromm and General Wilhelm von Leeb.[89]

By December 1939, twenty-four of the thirty-six institutes of the Society were designated "Bedarfstellen 1. Ordnung," literally "first-class places of need." This designation provided for cases of mobilization and allowed the institution to continue operating in its entirety. By contrast, the University of Göttingen was "Bedarfstelle 2. Ordnung," and therefore closed at the outbreak of war, when most students and teachers were drafted. During the same year Telschow was named a Reich Defense Officer and Defense Marshall for all the Kaiser Wilhelm institutes.[90] By 1941, twenty-five of thirty-six institutes were given the special ratings of W (Wehr, Military), R (Rüstung, armaments), or SS (Sonderstufe, special rating) Betrieben—which meant that they were ostensibly doing military research.[91]

By 1941, the year of the thirtieth anniversary of the Society, the leaders of the Society continued to portray its dual character in public statements while emphasizing its readiness to undertake the new tasks induced by the war by using the outstanding technical facilities of the institutes and skilled staff. The *Völkischer Beobachter*, the party's house organ, illustrated the way in which the Society upheld the international reputation of German science through the work of its distinguished scientists. The newspaper referred to the work of the Society's outstanding institute directors Carl Correns, Erwin Baur, Eugen Fischer, and Fritz Lenz—all well-known geneticists. In addition to the traditional representatives of industry who sat on the administrative board and senate, the paper boasted that the Society now also had leading representatives from the state and the party on its boards. National Socialist Germany, it went on, had supported the biggest research society in the world more than state institutions. It claimed that the National Socialist representatives had made sure that the institutes were used for the tasks of the Four Year Plan and for the production of German armaments. The personal connection between the Society and representatives of the Four Year plan was made with Telschow. The paper also featured photographs of the physics institute's atom smasher and high-tension equipment as well as Eugen Fischer, Otto Hahn, and Ludwig Prandtl. Although the paper realized and acknowledged the emphasis of basic research at the Society, it found the processes for, and developments of, new raw materials at the more practical-oriented institutes especially interesting. For example, it referred to a process developed for enriching poor ores and the development of new steel varieties at the institute for iron research and to the achievements in improving light metals at the institute for metal research. It praised the work of Franz Fischer at the coal institute most highly, drawing attention to the institute's success in developing procedures for transforming coal into fuel and oils.[92] This positive assessment of the work of the Society by the party newspaper during the early war years was certainly a far cry from the newspaper's diatribes against it during the early years of the Third Reich.

After the failure to defeat Russia in the winter of 1941–42 Germany had to shift the war from a strategy of Blitzkrieg to one of total war. This required an enormous increase in armaments production. Every available scientific institution—whether it was affiliated with the military, industry, or a university—was tapped for a possible contribution to the development of weapons either directly or indirectly. It was with this shift in the phase of the war that the Reich began to recognize the value of science for the war effort. Albert Vögler assumed office "at a moment when total war" increasingly determined scientific work and gave it new tasks. According to Telschow, solutions for these new tasks required the deployment of all the Society's workers. With this knowledge, the new president of the staff of all Kaiser Wilhelm institutes gave them the directive in October 1942: "We expect that all of you will pursue your work with passionate devotion. You must be imbued with the belief, indeed obsessed by it, that the results of your research today will guarantee the victory of tomorrow."[93]

Reviewing the year April 1941 to March 1942 Vögler thought it was "superfluous" to remind scientists of the meaning of science for the war. The development of modern weapons, the creation of synthetic raw materials, and the health care of the soldier all relied on the results of scientific research. Vögler announced in the 1942 yearbook that the institutes were all leaders in the areas outlined above. Research, he continued, possessed only one goal: "the quickest interpretation of results for the war."[94] Vögler's directives were made at a time when the German government had belatedly realized that science could be of use for the war effort and, in fact, might determine its outcome. The idea that science could contribute to a final victory became prevalent only after Germany's 1942 defeat in Stalingrad.

As the war increasingly dominated life in Germany, the Society publicly proclaimed that even though basic research would continue, the institutes of the Society fell under the "law of total war." The changed attitude toward the role of science had become so marked by 1942 that Telschow wrote in *Die Naturwissenschaften* that the "victor in this war will be the one who delivers science and research to provide the basis for the technology of the offense and defense before" the face of the enemy.[95] He reported that there were fewer personnel and more limited materiel to maintain or even increase past production. Despite these claims, the reports of the institutes hardly mentioned this increased role in the war.

By the fall of 1943, the conditions of research at the institutes of the Society had become so critical that the leaders of the Society called a meeting of all institute directors to discuss the evacuation of institutes, the institutes' war work, the institutes' needs for funding, materiel, staff, and apparatus, and new building projects. The meeting was in partial preparation for a future conference on science to be sponsored by Albert Speer. There was concern that enemy powers had a great lead in scientific research and that Germany was falling behind. Vögler therefore asked the directors to comment on which fields had fallen behind and what to do to catch up. The Speer Ministry richly supported scientific research at the Society, contributing RM 1.5 million yearly in 1942 and 1943; indeed, the Society's access to materials and priorities seemed limitless because of Speer's strong support. When the directors' conference took place at Harnack House in November 1943 the twenty-two directors who attended signed an attendance sheet swearing to keep secret all research matters related to the war effort or other secret things reported on. Most of the meeting was spent discussing evacuation plans and very little time was spent on the secret war work; instead, institute directors were asked to submit reports to the administration on their war work. Vögler, in his attempt to boost the sagging morale of the scientists, implored them to fight against defeatist attitudes. Now was not the time to debate and question; work for a German victory was the only important matter.[96]

As the war progressed the leaders of the Society emphasized the heightened role of the Society in the war effort. During the final years of the war, Vögler began to make proscriptive statements with the expectation expressed that the scientists would help lead Germany to victory through scientific research. Like many general pronouncements, the characterizations referred to previously included much rhetoric partly designed to satisfy the National Socialists, who funded the science and occasionally sat on the Society's boards or received its publications. It cannot be assumed that the rhetoric from above reflected or articulated the thoughts and actions of the scientists below. In any country, whether a democracy or a dictatorship, a war alters the emphasis of scientific research significantly, and most people—whether ordinary laborer or scientist—are ready to serve their nation (at least they were in those days). It came as a real surprise to the Allies after the war, however, how little German academic scientists contributed in general to war work. Indeed, it was not until the Allies recognized the importance of science for the war and began to score victories that the Germans mobilized science for the "final victory."

This changed attitude toward the role of science in the war effort trickled down to individual Kaiser Wilhelm institutes differentially. The leaders of the Society claimed that both the basic science tradition and the new tasks for the Society were combined during the war, yet more often than not the Dahlem institutes continued to pursue basic research while the industry-related institutes took on more research contracts for the military. The example of the Kaiser Wilhelm Society disproves Leslie Simon's claim that "during World War II almost all German research was war research."[97] In fact, German war research in the early years of the war was confined to labs operated by the armed forces and war industries, and fundamental research in these institutions was curtailed. Conversely, the Kaiser Wilhelm institutes did little war research compared to the German war machine and to their counterparts in the United States. In the United States many academic scientists at universities undertook defense contract research and at least a quarter of all physicists in America shifted their interests to war-related research.[98] This is not to say that Kaiser Wilhelm institute scientists did no defense research at all; many institutes contributed to the war effort; a few contributed heavily. The Kaiser Wilhelm Society differed in its fate from other scientific establishments in the *degree* to which it was influenced, changed, affected by, or contributed to National Socialist policies.

The German war effort consisted primarily of weapons research and development, the building of planes, ships, submarines, and rockets, and the development of radar. Based on the evidence of contemporary documents (the immediate postwar documents must be read with care and will be used only sparingly, when no other evidence exists) some Kaiser Wilhelm institutes worked on war research, primarily in an advisory way or by taking on research contracts; others did basic research under the guise of work important for the war effort. Finally, there were those that simply continued their basic research.

It is not surprising that the applied institutes of the Society contributed to the war effort more than any of the other institutes. During World War I, the existing institutes had already contributed to the war in its search for raw materials and development of gas warfare. As early as the announcement of the Four Year Plan in 1936 the industry-related institutes of the Society had pledged their support again for National Socialist Germany's quest for raw materials. In 1936, however, it was not clear that the Four Year Plan was a step toward armaments production and toward putting Germany on a war course. As a result of these earlier developments it was a logical step for many industry-related institutes to take on war contracts.

By World War II the applied and industry-related institutes of the Society encompassed the institutes for iron and steel research in Düsseldorf, the metal research institute in Stuttgart, the two coal research institutes, the leather research institute, the institute for aerodynamics in Göttingen, the worker's physiology institute, and the institute for silicate research and the physical chemistry institute in Berlin. Prandtl's institute for aerodynamics was financially supported by the Luftwaffe and worked on research contracts for it and for the army and navy. By 1943 the institute was conducting secret work for these agencies on questions of turbulence, high-speed problems such as increasing the flight distance of projectiles (for the Army Weapons Office), experiments on shooting under water (for the navy), and questions of heat transfer and deicing of airplanes.[99] The institute for physical chemistry in Berlin was, as in the previous war, totally occupied with work for the army. Much work seemed to have been done on gas warfare and

aerosols.[100] Rather than listing the nature of the work done at all the applied
or industry-related institutes just mentioned, we consider the institute for
iron research in Düsseldorf, an institute that became increasingly associated
with war contract research.

The development of the Kaiser Wilhelm Institute for Iron Research during the war displays the ways in which the war hampered scientific activity,
on the one hand, but stimulated it in certain areas, on the other. The work
of the institute had continued relatively undisturbed until the outbreak of
war in 1939, when 20 percent of the staff was drafted. Although the institute planned to continue pure research it increased its collaboration with
metallurgical plants and industry, finding it important to combine theoretical research with experiential iron works practice. The outbreak of war did
not create a radical departure in the research program of the institute because it had already begun to do contract research in 1936 for the Four
Year Plan; the war accelerated and increased these demands on the institute
in the area of raw material creation and defense technology.[101]

During the war the institute worked in several areas of research important for the war effort. By 1941 it had taken on many military research
contracts for the navy, the army, and especially the Aviation Ministry. Most
of the work important for the war effort received the high-priority ratings
(S or SS) and thus enabled the institute to gain easier access to materials
and equipment. One of its first major war contracts was with the Aviation
Ministry in January 1941. The way in which the specific research problems
were to be used in the long run was not revealed, but the contract specified
that experimental work on steel would be done, that all the material would
be paid for and delivered by the Aviation Ministry, and that it was important for the war effort. Experiments were done on steel smelting, on the
bending of steel, and notched bar experiments were done under low temperatures. By the fall of 1941 some scientists began to be recalled from the
front or were given service exemptions to work on research important for
the war effort; by 1943, after the Osenberg action recalling scientists from
the front, the number of scientists who were back at work in the lab rose to
twenty-three.[102] Government agencies saw the institute as a resource for
solving specific problems that were part of larger questions it was looking
at; this characterized the general relationship of many of the industry-related
institutes to government and military agencies like the navy, army, Aviation
Ministry, or Four Year Plan agencies.

In the area of armaments technology, Körber and his staff developed
techniques to substitute iron or plastic for the copper on projectile rings.
In addition, the institute had many contracts from the the high command
of the army (Oberkommando des Heeres, OKH), including research on wear
and tear on raw steel in a rotating band and decreasing the emission while
activating a grenade. By 1942 contracts for the Aviation Ministry increased
and the institute did research on the behavior of steel in order to determine how it would react to low temperatures in weapons, instruments, and
planes. Comparative research was done on the behavior of steel and metal

when they were shot at in order to create more effective metal sheaths for airplanes. Between 1942 and 1945 the research contracts for military organizations increased exponentially, reflecting the government's changed attitude toward science and its appreciation of the importance of science for the war effort.[103]

The institute for iron research in Düsseldorf during the Third Reich is an example of extreme participation in the war effort, whereas the basic biological tradition in Berlin-Dahlem illustrates the other end of the spectrum. Although some institutes declared that the work they undertook was important for the war effort, they did not fall into the same category as the applied or industry-related institutes, nor did they receive or take on major war contract research by the navy, the army, the air force, or other military agencies. At the Dahlem biological institutes, in contrast to the industry-related institutes, a considerable amount of basic research continued in biology, biochemistry, cell physiology, chemistry, and the genetics division of the brain research institute. (For details of this survival see Chapter 6) It was also at the genetics division that basic research was undertaken under the guise of doing work important for the war effort. The war context certainly influenced the conditions of research at the Berlin institutes, and the sociopolitical culture of National Socialism influenced the sources of financial support and the type of research advanced, but, in part because of the nature of basic biological research, these institutes were not mobilized for the war effort, nor has any proof been found of participation in biological warfare.

Conditions of Research

Despite the deteriorating war conditions, scientific research continued with increased financial support during World War II. The general budget increased from RM 5.6 million in 1933 to RM 14.3 million in 1944. The most dramatic increase came during the turning point of the war in 1942 when government officials began to recognize the use of science for the war effort; in addition, the Society received new large-scale support from the Ministry for Food and Agriculture and the Speer Ministry during this period.[104]

Herbert Backe, the new first vice president, had justified increased representation in the Society by calling attention to the recent generous grant the Society received from the Reich Ministry for Food and Agriculture, especially for its new animal breeding research institute. Although support for the Society from the Reich government and the Prussian state had grown in the Weimar period, support for certain areas reached unparalleled levels during World War II. Moreover, other ministries contributed in addition to the REM: the Reich Ministry for Food and Agriculture, the Foreign Office, and the Reich Air Ministry all began to contribute substantially to the Kaiser Wilhelm Society. At the beginning of the war the REM led the pack with a large contribution. Large-scale support from the Reich Ministry for Food and Agriculture was announced in the senate meeting in which the Vögler appointment was formally made. From a budget of RM 10,992,000, RM 3,106,800 came from the REM and RM 2,115,644 from the Reich Ministry for Food and Agriculture.[105] RM 919,507 came from other governmental sources such as the Foreign Office and the Reich Air Ministry. In 1942, out of a total budget of RM 11,581,155, REM support decreased to RM 2,961,800 while Reich Ministry for Food and Agriculture support increased to RM 2,851,400. In addition, the amounts from both the Air Ministry and Foreign Office were substantial enough to report—RM 297,000 and RM 43,000, respectively. Telschow did not fail to add in his report that this did not include grants from the Foreign Office for the newly founded institutes in Sofia and Athens, nor did it include funding from the RFR, the Wehrmacht, and the Deutsche Industrie Bank.[106] In the November 1943 senate meeting Telschow reported that the Society actually received RM 3,518,500 from the Reich Ministry for Food and Agriculture and RM 3,386,000 from REM out of a total general operating budget of RM 14,342,165. For 1943 the figures were similar: from a total of RM 14,295,915, RM 3,501,800 from REM and RM 3,570,250 from the Reich Ministry for Food and Agriculture. In addition, Telschow announced that the Speer Ministry had contributed RM 1.5 million in 1942 and in 1943 for work highly important for the war.[107] These figures tell us a great deal about changing priorities and emphases in scientific research and about the new alliances forged by the Society during the war.

But financial support was not limited to governmental agencies. Other major sources included the German Research Association and the Promotion Society of German Industry. In Chapters 4 and 6 we already detailed the role of the German Research Association and its relation to the Kaiser Wilhelm Society, and saw that basic research survived, in part, as a result of this support. Another extragovernmental source of support was industry. As late as 1945, the Promotion Society of German Industry, directed by Hermann von Siemens, contributed RM 2 million to the Society for general purposes. The sum was expected to contribute to the evacuated institutes and to establish assets for the postwar period. Even this late in the war, institutes continued to do research. This is indicated by Wolfgang Graßmann's (head of the Kaiser Wilhelm Institute for Leather Research) approved request for an electron microscope in January 1945.[108] Hans Stubbe also received RM 60,000 for research on cultivated plants. The Promotion Society functioned, therefore, like the DFG in that it supported general research at a time when war applications were emphasized by other agencies.[109]

In the early years of the war German science seemed to "march on" despite the conditions of war. Many scientists found their work an insulator against political and material disturbances from without. This attitude is illustrated by the community of Kaiser Wilhelm institute scientists in Berlin-Dahlem, who built their haven around Harnack House and its activities.

Indeed, in 1941 Telschow noted "growing general interest" in the work of the Society as the lecture series expanded because of the successful program in the first winter of the war. For example, the number of Dahlem Biology Evenings, which were jointly sponsored by the Kaiser Wilhelm institute for Biology and for Biochemistry, doubled from the previous year.[110] At least until 1942 the lecture series, which featured many institute directors from Kaiser Wilhelm institutes and other leaders in their fields, thrived. Harnack House also offered inexpensive food for the Kaiser Wilhelm Society staff and spoke of providing vegetables from its own new agriculture institutes.

Soon after the outbreak of the war, however, Harnack House also began to be used for meetings and social gatherings by people and institutions outside of the Kaiser Wilhelm Society circle. For example, the Dahlem branch of the NSDAP had begun to hold meetings there for films and lectures attended by 400 people a few times a month before the war, and increased the use of the House during the war. In 1941 the NSDAP met three times a month on the average; by February 1942 it met five times and in May 1942 six times. In addition to films and lectures, by May the NSDAP also had some training courses and leadership meetings. In April 1944 the meetings increased to a high of seven per month (out of a total number of twelve events for the whole House). In November 1944 the *Volkssturm* (People's Militia) of the NSDAP also began to meet and in February 1945, the last month meetings were recorded for Harnack House, the Volkssturm met fourteen times.[111]

Anyone reading the preceding descriptions of scientific research during the war years might wonder how it was possible to conduct research at all under the conditions of a total war. After all, by 1943 Berlin and other major cities had been under heavy air-raid attack and allied bombing; daily life was overshadowed by the war. The world of science fared no better. During the last year and a half of the war, scientific research slowed considerably; this is reflected in thin issues of *Die Naturwissenschaften* and other major scientific journals. Despite the idyllic environs of Dahlem, which was a haven for a while during the Third Reich, it too began to feel the ravages of war. Materials and apparatus had become scarce and personnel thinned out as they were drafted and died on the front. Many institutes were damaged and a few destroyed.

By 1943, during the intense allied bombing, the greatest preoccupation and concern of the Society was the evacuation of its institutes from Berlin to southwest Germany. Through Vögler's connections with Speer, the Society received the necessary priority ratings. The institutes situated in areas in danger of air attack and ostensibly conducting work important for the war received first priority. The institutes for iron research, entomology, and cell physiology were totally evacuated. Others were partially transferred.[112]

The institute for iron research in Düsseldorf had suffered severe damage after an air attack in June 1943; it was then evacuated to Clausthal. To ensure the success of the transfer Körber thought it expedient to have some help "from above," that is, a "directive from Speer" to the new site for the institute instructing the occupants to make room for the institute. Körber would have Vögler discuss the issue with Speer, with whom he was in frequent contact. Körber hoped to have the institute back to working order in a few weeks.[113]

Of all the Dahlem institutes, Otto Hahn's chemistry institute was damaged the most. In the evening of 15 February 1944, there had been an air raid in Berlin that caused the institutes to go up in flames. At 9:30 p.m. a bomb dropped onto the left wing of the institute scored a direct hit, totally destroying that wing. As fires began to spread, the garage, the porter's house, and Hahn's office were also destroyed. Other sections of the institute were damaged by the blast. During the attack, members of the institute, notably two mechanics, began to extinguish the flames and were joined by members of neighboring institutes and the administrative staff. Fire engines soon arrived. Apparatus, books, and materials were salvaged from labs and offices as Kurt Philipp, Thiessen, Laue, Heisenberg, and even Walter Gerlach, who had been staying at Harnack House, joined the effort. Laue raced to the institute on his bicycle and saw the "red glow of a fire" standing "against the sky in the direction of Dahlem" as he approached. "The rafters and the uppermost story" of the institute were "brightly aflame, a terrible-beautiful sight." Even Mentzel from the REM helped, and Laue saw him salvaging books.[114]

Other institutes were slightly damaged by the blast of the same attack. The glass from the Kaiser Wilhelm Institute for Biology's greenhouse was 90 percent destroyed. The animal stalls were also burned, although the animals were saved. The other Dahlem institutes suffered only slight damage.[115] As aerial warfare continued, the Kaiser Wilhelm Institute for Chemistry reported another attack during the night of 24 March 1944. Incendiary bombs were dropped on the high-tension apparatus building and on the roof of the radium building. The roof of the neighboring Kaiser Wilhelm Institute for Physical Chemistry burned.[116]

Of all the Dahlem institutes, the Kaiser Wilhelm Institute for Physics was the only one with a bunker that served as an air raid shelter. But because of secret work being done there, no one outside of the uranium club could use it. After the administrative offices of the Society housed in the old imperial palace in the center of Berlin were damaged in the extensive "terror bombings" on Berlin in 1944, offices were moved to the Kaiser Wilhelm Institute for Physics. The administration soon began to make plans to move again because it was difficult to maintain communications with the newly evacuated institutes in south and west Germany. This move would also enable Vögler, who lived in Dortmund and had many demands placed on him by industry in the surrounding area, to keep in contact with the Society. Telschow's trip to southwest Germany in January 1945 showed how difficult it had become to maintain contact with the Society's institutes. Railway lines had been totally destroyed, and travel on roads was limited to a few hours a day because of continual air attacks. Although the Society failed to receive the necessary permission from the Ministry for Armaments and

Munition, it unofficially began to move part of its administration to a more centrally located town in west Germany.[117]

On 1 February 1945 the move began to Göttingen, where the administration would run its affairs from, and store its files in, Prandtl's Kaiser Wilhelm Institute for Aerodynamics, which shared the extensive grounds of the Aerodynamic Experimental Station. These large institutes offered plenty of secretarial help and space. In addition, the Society was now more centrally located than it had been in Berlin; thus it could stay in close touch with its institutes and with Vögler, the Society's president.[118] Soon after the Society's arrival in Göttingen, however, allied troops occupied Germany, and by May 1945, the nightmare of the war years drew to a close.

8

The Uranium Machine

One of the most important research projects carried out at the Kaiser Wilhelm institutes during the Third Reich was the nuclear power program. Although the project was not limited to institutes of the Society, the Kaiser Wilhelm Institute for Physics in Berlin-Dahlem became Germany's center for nuclear research, and the Kaiser Wilhelm Institute for Chemistry in Berlin-Dahlem and the physics institute (Walther Bothe, director) of the Kaiser Wilhelm Institute for Medical Research in Heidelberg also participated heavily. Werner Heisenberg became director of the Dahlem physics institute in 1942 and emerged as a leading scientific personality in the nuclear power project. In addition, the Kaiser Wilhelm Society leaders helped the scientists obtain materials, the necessary priority ratings, and exemptions from the service for personnel; they also facilitated many other aspects of research under war conditions.[1]

Uranium Fission

On 19 December 1938 Otto Hahn, director of the Kaiser Wilhelm Institute for Chemistry, wrote to Lise Meitner about the puzzling results of recent experiments he and Fritz Straßmann, an analytic chemist and his assistant, had conducted. Hahn noted a curious effect on bombarding uranium with neutrons: "It could still be a very curious fluke, but we keep coming to the frightful conclusion that our Ra[dium] isotopes do not behave like Ra[dium] but like Ba[rium]. . . . I have made an agreement with Straßmann that we will only tell you about it now. Perhaps you can suggest some kind of fantastic explanation. We know that it *cannot* burst into Ba[rium]."[2]

Lise Meitner, an Austrian Jew, had been Hahn's friend and colleague at the Kaiser Wilhelm Institute for Chemistry, where she was head of the physics department, for thirty years before she had to leave as a result of the Anschluss in March 1938. Until 1938 she had been protected from the racist laws because of her Austrian nationality and the financial structure of Hahn's institute, whereby more than 50 percent of its funding came from private sources. But with the annexation of Austria she automatically became a German citizen and was therefore subject to Germany's laws. Despite Bosch's intervention it was not possible for Meitner to receive an exit visa, but colleagues contacted Professor Dirk Koster in Holland, who persuaded the Dutch government to allow her entry without a visa. She left Berlin in mid-July 1938 and went to Stockholm via Holland. But Meitner's physical separation did not end the team's collaboration, and Hahn concluded his letter with the hope that all three of them would publish the results together.

Over the four years from 1934 to 1938, the Hahn-Meitner-Straßmann team had been investigating, on Meitner's suggestion, the so-called transuranic elements produced as a result of bombarding uranium, element 92, with neutrons, particles with no electric charge. This research program had begun with Enrico Fermi and his group in Rome and was continued in Paris, at the Joliot-Curie and Savitch laboratory, and followed up in Berlin-Dahlem.[3] While Frédéric and Irène Joliot-Curie had induced artificial radioactivity through alpha particles, Fermi had introduced the idea of using neutrons as projectiles which would penetrate heavy nuclei and transform them to produce "artificial" (induced) radioactivity. If the product of this transformation was a daughter of alpha-emitting elements, the atomic decay would lead to an isotope a few positions down in the periodic table. If it was a daughter of a beta-emitter, then it led to elements beyond the last natural element then known, uranium. These elements were called "transuranics."[4]

What had been unusual about Hahn's and Straßmann's result was that barium, an element with the atomic number 56—about half the atomic number of uranium—had been identified as the isotope produced by neutron bombardment of uranium. In other words, bombardment did not produce a transuranic. This conclusion contradicted all previous experience in the physics of nuclear reactions! It was not a transmutation into an element a few steps higher or lower in the periodic table, but a splitting of an atom into lighter elements.

Because of its novelty, Hahn and Straßmann very cautiously and tentatively wrote up their results for *Die Naturwissenschaften*. The uncertainty present in Hahn's letter was apparent also in the first article reporting the results; it essentially described the experiment:

We now have to discuss the results of some recent experiments which we publish with some reluctance because of their extraordinary results. In order

> to establish the chemical nature of the substances called "radium isotopes" beyond any doubt, we performed fractional crystallizations and fractional precipitations of the active barium salts of the type used for the enrichment of barium salts with radium. . . . We had to conclude that our "radium isotopes" have the chemical characteristics of barium. Speaking as chemists, we even have to say that these new substances are barium, not radium.[5]

They had been "speaking as chemists" during the entire article and hesitated to explicitly discuss the physical interpretation or consequences of such a result. It was Lise Meitner and her nephew Otto Robert Frisch, then also an emigré in Scandinavia, who offered a "fantastic explanation." Several weeks after Hahn's and Straßmann's publication in *Die Naturwissenschaften*, Meitner and Frisch confirmed the fission hypothesis and wrote an article for *Nature* (16 January 1939) about a "new type of nuclear reaction" in which they interpreted the results and characterized "fission," the first time the word was applied to the breaking of nuclei into large fragments, using the analogy of a liquid drop: "If the movement is made sufficiently violent by adding energy, such a drop may divide itself into two smaller drops."[6]

Other scientists soon heard of Hahn and Straßmann's discovery and Meitner and Frisch's interpretation, and a flood of work followed. By the end of 1939, a year after the discovery, more than a hundred papers on fission had been published.[7] One of the most significant commentators was Niels Bohr, who had heard about the discovery from Frisch and quickly spread the word in America, at a conference on theoretical physics held on 26 January 1939.[8] By February, the splitting of uranium nuclei into two fission fragments had been confirmed by numerous experimental methods and other scientists began to consider the possibility of a self-sustaining chain reaction. Work therefore began on the measurement of the energy actually released by the uranium nucleus when it fissioned.

Atomic Beginnings

The technical and military potentials of nuclear fission were recognized within months after the publication of Hahn and Straßmann's discovery in January 1939. In April, several scientists informed governmental offices of the implications of this discovery. Georg Joos, an experimental and theoretical physicist from Göttingen, wrote to the Reich Ministry of Education after hearing a paper by William Hanle on the use of uranium fission in an energy-producing pile.[9] The letter was given to Abraham Esau, the physics section head of the Ministry's Reich Research Council, who quickly arranged a conference at the Ministry on 29 April on "questions of a self-sustaining chain reaction."[10] At the conference, Esau announced his plan to collect all the uranium in Germany and to create a uranium research project named the Uranium Club (Uran-Verein). This was the last word scientists heard about a research project until the outbreak of war in the fall.

Two other scientists—Nicholas Riehl[11] and Paul Harteck—also contacted the army about the same possibility. Harteck, a physical chemist from Hamburg and the army's explosive consultant, wrote a letter on 24 April, jointly with his assistant William Groth, making an explicit reference to the explosive potential of nuclear fission: "We take the liberty of calling your attention to the newest development in nuclear physics, which, in our opinion will perhaps make it possible to produce an explosive which is many orders of magnitude more effective than the present one."[12] This letter reached the Army Weapons Office (Heereswaffenamt) and was forwarded to Kurt Diebner, the Army's expert on nuclear physics and explosives. Harteck and Groth, however, heard nothing in reply, but this did not mean that the army ignored the message.

In June 1939, still only half a year after Hahn and Straßmann's discovery, Siegfried Flügge, an assistant at the Kaiser Wilhelm Institute for Chemistry, sent a paper to *Die Naturwissenschaften* with the title "Can the Energy Contained in the Nucleus Be Exploited on a Technical Scale?" Here he described in a dramatic way how a cubic meter of uranium could lift a cubic kilometer of water twenty-seven kilometers into the air. In order to tame this enormous amount of energy, Flügge proposed stabilizing the reaction in a "uranium machine" by adding cadmium salts to absorb the neutrons. A few months later he published a more popular account in the *Deutsche Allgemeine Zeitung*: "The Exploitation of Atomic Energy: From Laboratory Experiment to Uranium Machine—Research Results in Dahlem."[13] These articles galvanized the interest of governmental agencies over the summer, and by the fall, interest turned into action.

In the fall of 1939, then, two rival groups emerged—Esau's (REM) and Diebner's (Army Weapons Office)—competing for jurisdiction over the new uranium research project. After the spring conference, Esau had begun to organize a group to work on the project. In order to secure some pure uranium before industry or the Reich Air Ministry seized it, Esau turned to General Karl Becker at the Army Weapons Office, who promised to grant the project military significance. Despite promises from the office an official statement on the project's military importance failed to materialize. Instead, Esau heard from a Dr. Basche, a senior official at the Army Weapons Office, that Erich Schumann ordered him to tell Esau the Army Weapons Office itself was experimenting in the area and that the promised certificate could not be issued. A few months after this happened, Esau bitterly complained to Mentzel, who claimed the Army Weapons Office had been working on the project for years and that parallel work had to be avoided. Esau angrily pointed out that the problem had only emerged in January of 1939.[14] Although Esau was pushed out of the nuclear power arena, his efforts accelerated the army's interest in nuclear power.

This development reflects the polycratic nature of science policy in the Third Reich—the competing agencies, the overlapping competencies and personalities, the reneging on agreements. Interestingly, there were also overlaps in power, positions, and titles between the Army Weapons Office and the Reich Research Council. For example, Becker, the head of the Army Weapons Office, was also president of the Reich Research Council. Schumann, director of the research department in the Army Weapons Office, was also in the Reich Ministry of Education's research department. Finally, Mentzel occupied key positions in various agencies; by 1939 he was head of the office for science in the Reich Ministry of Education, president of the German Research Association, administrative manager in the Reich Research Council, and a senator in the Kaiser Wilhelm Society. In addition to the overlapping competencies, five administrator/scientists involved in the nuclear power project—Becker, Schumann, Mentzel, Diebner, and Esau—were also active party members; many were also in the SS. Their political activity had facilitated their climb to influential positions during the Third Reich, and there seems to be a correlation between National Socialism and the type of science scientists were interested in and willing to work on. In this case, the scientists shared an interest in the military applications of nuclear fission and a previous competency in military science or work on explosives. This correlation is not surprising for several reasons. First, military science had become a cornerstone of National Socialist ideology, and those who believed in, and advocated any part of, National Socialist ideology rose to the top and became visible. Moreover, conservatives tended to favor, as they do in this day and age, a strong national defense and the apparatus necessary to safeguard the nation's security.

Soon after the war broke out in September, Diebner and Schumann summoned Erich Bagge, then an assistant at the Institute for Theoretical Physics in Leipzig, to their office in Berlin for advice and information on the feasibility of launching a uranium research project. Diebner had already offered Bagge a job in 1938 because of his work on the disintegration of deuterium (a heavy isotope of hydrogen) and therefore remembered him as an expert in nuclear disintegration when the Army Weapons Office decided to fund nuclear fission research.[15] Together they drew up a list of scientists including Walther Bothe, Hans Geiger, Joseph Mattauch (Kaiser Wilhelm Institute for Chemistry), Bagge, Diebner, Flügge, and Otto Hahn, to invite to a secret conference.[16] Bagge, who had been called up to serve in the same way as a soldier, arranged a program based on the Flügge article, and the first meeting was set for 16 September. The invited scientists also received call-up papers and attended the meeting apprehensively. Although Schumann was absent, Basche announced the Army Weapons Office's decision to explore seriously the question of atomic energy. The discussion focused on "uranium engines" and whether they would work. In order to clarify the theory of a chain reaction Bagge suggested Werner Heisenberg, the young Nobel Prize–winning (1932) theoretical physicist and director of the Leipzig Physics Institute, be drafted into the project. Many of the experimental physicists in the group assembled, however, disagreed with this suggestion. Nevertheless, after the conference, Bagge persuaded Diebner to invite Heisenberg to the next conference on 26 September.[17] After the war, Bagge recalled that it was at the 8 September meeting where all the scientists in attendance said the project "must be done at once." According to Bagge's memory, someone did say, "Of course it is an open question whether one ought to do a thing like that." But then Bothe got up and said, "Gentlemen, it *must* be done."[18]

Because it had not been unequivocally established which uranium isotope fissioned with neutron capture, although it seemed likely it was U-235, Paul Harteck's group in Hamburg was given the task of separating isotopes. By the time of the second Berlin conference Heisenberg found that there were two ways to extract energy from the uranium nucleus: in a controlled way in a uranium furnace or in a violent, uncontrolled explosion. The first possibility required some sort of a moderator to slow the neutrons, whereas the second would require the extraction of the isotope U-235. Therefore, after the second Berlin conference sponsored by the Army Weapons Office, the scientific agenda was set for the scientists involved: the development of processes for large-scale separation of isotopes, the measurement of effective cross sections, and determination of the feasibility of a chain reaction.[19]

In September 1939 Schumann announced the Army Weapons Office's intention of requisitioning the Kaiser Wilhelm Institute for Physics in Berlin-Dahlem and setting up a center for the uranium research program. The new institute, one of the few modern ones in Germany recently built with funding from the Rockefeller Foundation,[20] had excellent equipment including high-tension apparatus; moreover, the army had found an opportune time to seize it. Peter Debye, the director of the institute since it was completed in 1937, was Dutch and therefore not allowed to stay at the institute during the war. Debye later recalled that "one Saturday, after I had built the whole Institute and was just beginning—and that was quite nice . . . the administrator comes in and tells me he was very sorry but I could not go in the Institute anymore if I did not become a German citizen!"[21] Debye was told by Ernst Telschow that he had been "forced to [do this] . . . after a conference that had taken place the night before" with Telschow, Rudolf Mentzel, and some men from the Army Weapons Office. Debye found that Telschow "had taken the steps on his own and that the president of the Society R. [*sic*] Bosch was not told." A few weeks later, Debye spoke with Mentzel, who told him the Ministry could no longer contribute financially to the institute unless it conducted war-related research and the staff were residents of Germany. Mentzel suggested to Debye that he could offer a couple of seminars at the Physical Institute of the University of Berlin or write a book. Since Debye already had an invitation to hold the George Fisher Baker lectureship at Cornell University in the first half of 1940 he proposed taking this vacation and extending it until the situation changed.[22]

Under Debye's direction the institute had worked on pure research; now the government would choose the type of research to be undertaken. On 16 October 1939, Basche and Diebner appropriated the physics institute, which would now be funded by the Army Weapons Office. In the vacancy created by Debye's absence, Kurt Diebner was appointed provisional head, although the Kaiser Wilhelm Society fiercely opposed this choice. A con-

tract was drawn up by the High Command of the Army, and the Kaiser
Wilhelm Society was informed on 25 January 1940 that Diebner had been
installed as the Army's commissioner.[23] For a time, then, the physics institute became the theater for the Army's nuclear power project, and it was at
this institute that most of the uranium machine trials were held. Most of
the other research for the project, however, was undertaken at various university institutes scattered around Germany.

Although the Society opposed the takeover, there is no evidence of any
measures taken to forestall it. Unlike Planck's indignant letters protesting
the takeover of the Haber institute in 1933, the leaders of the Society were
silent. Part of the reason for this was that Carl Bosch, then president, was
sick; in fact he died about half a year later. Telschow, who supported the
kind of research to be undertaken, took charge and, as Debye related, did
not inform Bosch of the move. The National Socialists tended to take
advantage of power vacuums like these. The Society had a similar experience in 1933 when the National Socialists attempted to purge the scientists
at its institutes when leading administrators were on vacation. By 1940, however, the Society had also changed its attitude toward the National Socialist
state and acquiesced to some of its policies.

Although Diebner was provisional head of the orphaned institute, Heisenberg soon became its "scientific adviser" through the machinations of
Karl Wirtz and Carl-Friedrich von Weizsäcker, two young physicists already
working in Berlin-Dahlem. Heisenberg commuted from Leipzig to Berlin,
and within months after the project began, he found that the enrichment
of U-235 would facilitate a chain reaction and creation of an energy-
producing machine.[24]

Work on atomic energy also began in other institutes in Germany. Central to the project was Paul Harteck, director of the Physical Chemistry
Institute at the University of Hamburg. Although the Army Weapons Office
had wanted to centralize all the research in Berlin-Dahlem, this move met
the opposition of many scientists, like Harteck, who preferred to stay at their
own institutions and commute to Berlin. Harteck, one of the prime movers
behind the whole project, is dealt with only briefly here because of this
study's focus on the Kaiser Wilhelm institutes.[25] Harteck's group worked
on isotope separation and heavy water production. As the project developed
over the years at least nine groups existed in Germany working on problems of uranium machines, isotope separation, and the production of uranium and heavy water. The Kaiser Wilhelm institute complex figured prominently in this work; by 1940 Walther Bothe's Institute for Physics in the
Kaiser Wilhelm Institute for Medical Research (Heidelberg) was at work on
the measurement of nuclear constants, Otto Hahn's Kaiser Wilhelm Institute for Chemistry (Berlin-Dahlem) studied transuranic elements and fission
products and worked on isotope separation and the measurement of nuclear
constants, and the Kaiser Wilhelm Institute for Physics (Dahlem) worked
chiefly on uranium machines, heavy water analysis, theoretical study of chain
reactions, isotope separation, and measurements of nuclear constants.

In July 1940, soon after Heisenberg became adviser at the Berlin-Dahlem physics institute, work began on a small wooden laboratory near the Kaiser Wilhelm Institute for Biology and Virus Research in Dahlem to house a uranium pile. Karl Wirtz, a physicist specializing in heavy water research, who had been at the Kaiser Wilhelm Institute for Physics since 1937, was in charge of organizing the construction. The "Virus House"—so named to keep curious visitors away—was ready by October 1940 and consisted of a circular pit six feet deep with brick lining.[26] A wooden laboratory barracks about twenty feet in length and nine feet high was built around the pit. The pit was in the back part of the laboratory so that there was room for experimental work. The laboratory shared utility installations with the nearby Virus Research Greenhouse. The reactor pit could be filled with ordinary water as a reflector shield and high-speed pumps could drain it within an hour if a problem arose. A portal crane was installed in the laboratory in order to lift the heavy aluminum holder into the pit.[27] As soon as the laboratory was ready in October 1940 uranium machine experiments began. The B (for Berlin) experiments were primarily carried out by Fritz Bopp, Erich Fischer, Werner Heisenberg, and Karl Wirtz. From 1940 until 1942, three atomic pile experiments were carried out in the newly built barracks.

Nuclear Power Conferences in Berlin-Dahlem, 1942

In the fall of 1941 the German lightning war seemed to be marching on to victory and a large part of Europe was under German control, but by December German armies had suffered a great reversal at Stalingrad and the armaments economy began to take precedence over the national economy. As a result, Schumann, head of the research division at the Army Weapons Office, wrote a letter to all institute directors involved in the project, announcing a meeting on 16 December: "Given the present personnel and raw materials shortage," he wrote, the nuclear power project requires resources that "can only be justified if there is certainty that an application will be found in the near future."[28] On the sixteenth, Hans Geiger, Heisenberg, Walther Bothe, Karl Clusius, Hahn, Harteck, and Diebner attended the meeting and delivered papers. After the meeting, Schumann reported to his superior, General Emil Leeb, Becker's successor as the head of Army Weapons Office, and requested a decision on the army's future thinking on the project. By late January the Army Weapons Office decided to relinquish control of the project and gave the physics institute back to the Kaiser Wilhelm Society, Germany's traditional site for basic research.

After the conference, the Army Weapons Office issued a long, detailed report, "The Production of Energy from Uranium." It is the most explicit and detailed description and analysis of the work until February 1942. It opened with these words: "The experiments performed thus far on the applications of atomic energy show that it will be possible to build a uranium energy source." The tempo of building the uranium machine, however, would be determined by the ability to procure materials. The report dealt with the development of the uranium problem; it also contained a detailed chapter on the theory of uranium machines, a second one on experimental research with the material, and a final chapter on isotope separation. It concluded from the results of the work that the "technical application of atomic energy from nuclear fission was definitely possible." The Army Weapons Office scientists thought the "technical organization" should definitely be undertaken because the energy problem had immense importance for the economy and the armed forces.[29]

During the December meeting, Schumann also impulsively broached the question of who would succeed Debye as director of the Kaiser Wilhelm Institute for Physics. He thought Bothe was the right man—a remark that stunned the scientists into a twenty-second silence. Schumann then said he saw that everyone agreed with the appointment and asked Hahn, as the senior scientist, to write a letter to the Army Weapons Office stating that all the scientists present thought the Bothe candidacy was the right one. This was done. After the meeting everyone began to have doubts. Harteck said Heisenberg had not suggested himself out of modesty, but that he was actually most suited for the directorship of the Kaiser Wilhelm Institute for Physics. Bothe protested that everyone had voted for him and therefore the director post was promised to him. Harteck defended Heisenberg, calling him the "best theoretical physicist" while Bothe was the best "experimental physicist." With Heisenberg, "unfortunately" one could say "there is no better." Harteck thought Bothe could not be compared in rank to Heisenberg. Telschow, to whom Harteck had related the events of the meeting, preserved the president's prerogative and said that only the president of the Society could appoint a director of an institute and that it was not the affair of the Army Weapons Office.[30] A few days later, Hahn and Max von Laue spoke to Vögler about the question and Hahn said he thought Bothe was not the most suitable director for the Kaiser Wilhelm Institute for Physics because of his difficult personality. Furthermore, it did not seem advisable to move the institute to Heidelberg.[31]

But before the question of the directorship was resolved, the Army Weapons Office called together a scientific conference on 26–28 February 1942 at the Kaiser Wilhelm Institute for Physics in Berlin-Dahlem. Twenty-five technical lectures were submitted for a three-day conference. Simultaneously, the Reich Research Council also planned a popular conference at the council's headquarters, the House of German Research in Berlin-Steglitz, on 26 February. Invitations were sent to high-ranking officers, the SS, and some members of the scientific community. Rust announced a conference in which a "series of important questions in the area of atomic physics" was to be discussed and kept secret because of its importance for defense issues. These questions, he continued, were "exceptionally important for solving" problems for German armaments and industry.[32]

The Reich Research Council's lecture series began at 11:00 a.m. on the twenty-sixth with Erich Schumann's lecture on "Atomic Physics as a Weapon." Seven other lectures were delivered by major atomic scientists.

Hahn spoke on the fission of the uranium nucleus, Bothe on the results of research on energy production, Geiger on the necessity of basic research, Clusius on the enrichment of uranium isotopes, and Harteck on heavy water. Esau closed the proceedings with "The Expansion of the Research Group 'Atomic Physics' through the Participation of Other Reich Offices and Industry."[33]

Heisenberg also delivered a key lecture, "The Theoretical Basis for Energy Production from Nuclear Fission." This lucid presentation described the enormous energy-releasing potential of nuclear fission—250 million electron volts through the fission of each atomic nucleus. Heisenberg stressed the importance of obtaining pure U-235 in order to achieve a chain reaction: "Pure isotope 235 U/92 represents, without a doubt, an explosive of totally unimaginable effect. Unfortunately this isotope is very hard to obtain." His talk explored the various ways of obtaining the isotope in its pure form, such as uranium enrichment, and the alternative—creating a layered arrangement of normal uranium and a moderator in a machine. This machine could be used in many practical ways to fuel vehicles, ships, and even submarines. He introduced a concrete analogy in order to facilitate a Reich minister's understanding of the process: "The behaviour of neutrons in uranium can be compared to a population density where the fission process represents an analogy to marriage and the capture process an analogy to death." Finally, he stressed the importance of the Army Weapons Office's financial and material support.[34]

Shortly after Heisenberg's talk, the second scientific conference sponsored by the Army Weapons Office began at the Kaiser Wilhelm Institute for Physics in Berlin-Dahlem. Almost all the project scientists read papers over the next three days. The technical papers ranged from Bothe's report on the Heidelberg group's measurements on various nuclear constants, to Weizsäcker's description of an improved theory of resonance absorption in a reactor, to papers on the behavior of fast neutrons in uranium. Transuranics also received some attention. Hahn and Straßmann reported on the creation of an isotope of element 93 with a half-life of 2.3 days from uranium. Wirtz described the new model experiments at the Kaiser Wilhelm Institute for Physics which used alternating horizontal layers of uranium metal with paraffin in a spherical container. Finally, the uranium machine received the most attention during the conference.[35] The conferences showed that the atomic scientists seemed to have made progress in nuclear power research, although short-term applications were not in sight. The day after the conference a Berlin newspaper reported on the Reich Research Council meeting where "many members of the Party, the State, and Industry were present under the chairmanship of the president, Reich Minister Rust." The conference, continued the newspaper vaguely, "dealt with problems of modern physics that are of decisive importance for national defense and the German economy."[36]

As a result of the conference, Reich Minister Rust decided to take the project away from the Kaiser Wilhelm Society and give it to the Reich Research Council. Indignant about Rust's decision, Vögler wrote to the head of the Army Weapons Office, General Leeb, reminding him of their meeting several weeks earlier in which Leeb told Vögler that the "preparatory work on special questions of atomic physics under the Army Weapons Office had come to an end," and therefore the work could be done at another place such as the Kaiser Wilhelm Society. Because Leeb had violated his agreement, Vögler wrote to him that the Kaiser Wilhelm Society would withdraw from the project.[37]

The project had been repeatedly tossed from one organization to another, yet there were other organizational problems to settle before continuing the research. Bothe had been the principal candidate for the directorship of the Kaiser Wilhelm Institute for Physics before the February conferences, and at the beginning of March this was still the case. Since the Kaiser Wilhelm Institute for Physics had been led only temporarily by a representative from the Army Weapons Office it was time again to find a suitable physics professor because it did not appear as though Debye would be coming back in the near future. The Kaiser Wilhelm Society and Leeb agreed that the institute ought to continue to undertake experimental work in the area of atomic physics. But because the Reich Research Council decided to take over the project, the directorship would probably be decided by Mentzel and Esau. When Vögler met Mentzel and Schumann at the Reich Research Council meeting and asked where the future of the project would lie, Mentzel said "of course, with the Reich Research Council." This was the first Vögler had heard of the decision.[38]

Despite the fact that it seemed as though Bothe would become director, there had been discordant voices from some Berlin-Dahlem scientists about the impending appointment. Heisenberg had already become part of the working group in Dahlem, commuting from Leipzig on a regular basis, and to many he appeared to be the right choice. Within less than a month there had been a reversal of the initial decision, and Vögler announced at the Society's senate meeting on 24 April 1942 that the High Command of the Army had returned the Physics Institute to the Kaiser Wilhelm Society. Simultaneously, Heisenberg was named "Director *at* the Institute" (Direktor *am* Institut) but not *of* the Institute because Debye was still technically on leave in the United States.[39]

Heisenberg's appointment to the institute had been the culmination of many failed attempts to appoint him professor at various universities, the most famous case being the Arnold Sommerfeld successorship at Munich. In 1936, early in the Third Reich, Heisenberg had been the object of attacks by adherents of the *Deutsche Physik* movement, who labeled him a "white Jew" because of his work on theoretical physics and support of Jewish scientists like Albert Einstein. During the early years, also, the movement managed to achieve some victories in appointments at the university. For example, Wilhelm Müller, an aeronautical engineer who was sympathetic to the movement, was appointed Sommerfeld's successor in December 1939.

Soon after an attack on him in the SS newspaper *Das Schwarze Korps*, Heisenberg used personal connections and wrote directly to Heinrich

Himmler (the Reich Leader of the SS) for help with his political problems. After learning of Heisenberg's difficulties, Ludwig Prandtl, director of the Kaiser Wilhelm Institute for Aerodynamics, began to intervene on his behalf in 1938. Prandtl, who had already been an outspoken critic of the antisemitic policies against Jewish scientists in 1933, spoke and wrote directly to Himmler about the importance of modern theoretical physics and the destructiveness of *Deutsche Physik* for modern physics. By 1943, Heisenberg could write to Himmler thanking him for "reestablishing his honor" through the appointment at the Kaiser Wilhelm institute in 1942.[40] The appointment coincided with the National Socialists' shift in attitude toward science and the recognition that it could be of use for the war, but it was also the culmination of attempts by other physicists and industrialists like Carl Ramsauer and Albert Vögler to save physics and physics education through support by government sources.

The most important task Heisenberg faced as the newly appointed director (to start officially on 1 October 1942) was the celebrated 4 June 1942 meeting with Albert Speer, known as Hitler's architect, but also the successor to Fritz Todt as Armaments Minister. This was a crucial conference for the project and many of the atomic scientists met with Speer and other senior munitions officials to decide the future of nuclear research. It has also become the object of some mythology, and except for Heisenberg's testimony, supported by Telschow, the only other account by a participant is contained in the Speer Memoirs.[41]

The Speer conference was held at the Helmholtz lecture room of the Kaiser Wilhelm Society's Harnack House. Other scientists in attendance included Hahn, Diebner, Harteck, Wirtz, Thiessen, and Vögler. Three military representatives—Erhard Milch, Friedrich Fromm, and Karl Witzell—joined Speer for the meeting. Speer reported after the war that Heisenberg spoke about "atom smashing and the development of the uranium machine and the cyclotron." He also apparently complained about the project's "lack of funds and materials, and the drafting of scientific men into the services." After the lecture Speer asked Heisenberg how atomic physics could be applied to manufacturing atomic bombs. Heisenberg claimed the scientific problem had already been solved, but "technical prerequisites for production" were a long way off and it would take years to achieve the goal, thus reiterating the evaluations made at the February meetings. Nevertheless, Speer took great interest in the project and asked the scientists to present their requests for funding and necessary materials. The group asked for a sum of several hundred thousand marks, small amounts of metals, the building of a bunker, and highest priority for their experiments. Speer balked at the small amount of financial support that the scientists requested and suggested a larger sum of several million marks. Because it did not appear to Speer that the building of a bomb could influence the course of the war, he opted to support the project on a small scale. Speer even reported very briefly, as item 15 on a long agenda, to Adolf Hitler about the meeting, but the idea of an atom bomb apparently "strained his intellectual capacity." Another plausible reason Speer put forth for Hitler's failure to pursue the development of atomic weapons was ideological. Philipp Lenard, the advocate of "Aryan Physics," often referred to atomic physics as "Jewish Physics."[42]

One of the most successful outcomes of the Speer meeting was the approval of construction projects at the Kaiser Wilhelm Institute for Physics; Germany's first major, large nuclear reactor could now be housed in a bunker to be built there. The institute also received the coveted DE rating (Dringlichkeitsentwicklung), the highest priority rating in Germany. This rating greatly facilitated the institute's access to materials, manpower, apparatus, and anything else the project could need. A high priority rating was, in some ways, more important than financial support because it actually made research possible. Speer's support of atomic research at the Kaiser Wilhelm institutes was influenced by Albert Vögler, who, as Speer wrote after the war, "called my attention to the neglected field of nuclear research." It also seems that Vögler's complaints about the "inadequate support fundamental research was receiving from the Ministry of Education and Science" led to the large-scale reorganization of the Reich Research Council in June.[43] On 9 June Speer appointed Göring head of the council. It was shortly after the June Harnack House meeting that Vögler met with the same circle of military and government officials at the Air Force Ministry. At this meeting, Vögler presented the research of many Kaiser Wilhelm institute scientists to National Socialist leaders and urged Speer and his circle to support basic research.[44]

With the reorganization of the Reich Research Council, Abraham Esau remained head of the physics section but Göring also eventually gave him the title "Deputy for All Questions of Atomic Physics."[45] Esau would therefore oversee nuclear power research with the transfer of the project. After the Army takeover of the uranium club Esau had founded three years earlier he saw a chance to reassert his power. The Kaiser Wilhelm scientists were not happy about this state of affairs because they thought Esau was trying to take too much control.[46] There had already been tensions between the Kaiser Wilhelm institute groups and the government agencies from the time the Army Weapons Office seized the institute for physics at the outbreak of war. Now that Heisenberg was officially director at the institute he did not want to be dictated to by someone whom he considered an inferior physicist.

Esau had begun to assert his prerogative as early as July 1942 when friction had arisen with Heisenberg about a proposed large experiment. Esau wanted to perform the experiment in a neutral place, which excluded the Kaiser Wilhelm Institute for Physics. Esau was supported by Bothe, but Heisenberg wanted to retain the Dahlem interdisciplinary working community.[47] In November Esau was writing to Mentzel, the new managing director of the Reich Research Council, pushing him to centralize the whole project and to obtain the same coveted DE priority rating that the Kaiser Wilhelm Society enjoyed: "Personally, I would like to add for your orientation, that Geh.[eimrat] Vögler has obtained the DE-rating for construction at the Kaiser Wilhelm Gesellschaft—something not possible for ordinary mortals."[48] Some weeks later Mentzel suggested that Esau head a working group for atomic physics, which led to his appointment as Reich Marshall Göring's deputy for atomic physics. Mentzel argued that although Esau was not an atomic physicist, he was neutral, which was important because of the "oversensitive researchers." If a specialist were to be appointed, it would lead to problems.[49] Despite Mentzel's warm recommendation, Esau did not hold favor with many circles in Germany; both the Kaiser Wilhelm establishment and Speer had a low opinion of him.

Thus Esau's second reign as a responsible figure in atomic research started as problematically as the first one. To clarify Esau's role as newly named deputy, Vögler called Esau and Mentzel to a meeting at his offices in United Steel in Berlin in February 1943. The institutes for physics (Berlin-Dahlem), biophysics, physics (Heidelberg), and chemistry (Dahlem), which "enjoyed Reich Minister Speer's support," were to continue their work under the special DE priority rating. The apportioning of responsibility among Esau, Speer, and the Kaiser Wilhelm Society was as follows: Esau was administrative head of the nuclear physics group and was responsible for coordinating the various centers for nuclear research. The Society could apply directly to the Speer Ministry for any necessary construction work and any of the institutes involved with the nuclear power project were financed, in part, by contributions from the Speer Ministry. All equipment and materials—insofar as they had the DE rating—were to be claimed directly at the Reich Research Council by the Society. The Uk-Stellung of staff continued to come directly from the Society.[50] Within weeks, however, the Society complained to Mentzel that difficulties had emerged between the institutes and Esau over sharing materials.[51] As a result, the Society wanted to call another meeting with a representative from the Speer Ministry in order to make new arrangements.

Meanwhile, from the time of the February meetings through the reorganization of the Reich Research Council in 1942, the pile experiments continued at the Virus House in Dahlem using layers of uranium metal powder and paraffin wax. Between January and November 1942 three experiments were performed using between 50 and 864 kilograms of metal powder and between 12 and 44 kilograms of paraffin wax, varying the number of uranium layers from nineteen to twelve to seven while also varying their thickness.[52] The large intermediate-pile experiments seemed to be progressing well. By the beginning of 1943, however, other problems began to plague the project. Germany had lost the high-concentration plant in Vermork, its main source for heavy water, to English aerial raids at a time when the Germans had begun to rely almost exclusively on the use of heavy water as a moderator in the machine.

The Final War Years

At the end of March 1943 the army dropped out of the project and reneged on its appropriation of RM 2 million. Diebner's project was given to Esau, and the Reich Research Council was instructed to find funds for the project itself. After the army relinquished the project because it was not convinced that work on nuclear research would determine the outcome of the war, interest in the project came from other quarters in the Reich as a result of the 1942 Berlin meetings. Carl Ramsauer, a physicist and chairman of the German Physical Society, raised the specter of Anglo-Saxon physics surpassing German physics at an address given at the German Academy of Aeronautical Research in April 1943. In his speech Ramsauer charted the rise of Anglo-American "Big Science" and the decline of German physics by counting Nobel Prize winners, the most frequently read journals (American), apparatus, and other quantitative and qualitative measures. The Anglo-Saxons were emerging as a superior power and they also recognized the importance of physics in a modern war. Ramsauer had interested the members of the academy in atomic physics and as a result the Reich Air Ministry organized a lecture series on the topic for the beginning of May 1943.[53]

In his role as deputy for atomic physics, Abraham Esau led and introduced the meeting. He gave the first lecture on luminous paints, Hahn spoke about artificial atomic transformations and uranium fission, Heisenberg gave a lecture on the production of energy from atomic fission, and Bothe on the research potential of atomic physics; Clusius closed the series with a talk on isotope separation. Although Heisenberg's talk was similar to the one from the previous year, here he emphasized that the "liberation of atomic energy for technical purposes" was possible, but the "practical execution" was made difficult by the "strained economic state of the war."[54] There was no mention or discussion of a bomb and hardly a reference to an explosive, as there had been in the 1942 talk, but the manufacture of a "uranium burner," in contrast to a "machine," was broached. In the deteriorating state of the war the military potentials of nuclear fission were soft-pedaled.[55]

The war context had affected the procurement of materials, such as heavy water, uranium, and uranium plates, and the ability to carry out experiments in the quiet and safety of the laboratory. Even though Speer had approved the building of a bunker in the Kaiser Wilhelm Institute for Physics, the institute began to evacuate much of its personnel and one-third of the institute's staff was transferred to Hechingen, a town in southwest Germany. Large-scale air raids began to threaten Berlin at the end of August 1943 and the Kaiser Wilhelm Society had already begun to evacuate many of its other institutes as well.

The project's administrative personnel changed again at the end of 1943. Esau's relations with many of the Kaiser Wilhelm institute scientists and administrators had not been a good one. Moreover, he had incurred the enmity of Albert Vögler. The project scientists disliked him because he had tried to centralize the project, use materials they needed, and assume full control. Therefore, Albert Speer forced him to resign both his posts at the Reich Research Council. Although Mentzel had supported Esau's appointment as deputy for atomic physics, he abandoned him because of Speer's disapproval. Angry about the move, Esau sought the intervention of Göring's senior officials. Speer, thought Esau, had interfered with the running of the Reich Research Council, which was Göring's domain. Mentzel, however, did not budge because he believed Speer must have had a well-grounded reason for the dismissal. Esau's "departure," wrote Mentzel to Görnnert, will be met with great "joy" by the other section heads and deputies. Vögler was also "delighted" about the personnel change in the area of physics.[56]

Meanwhile, Mentzel had already chosen Walter Gerlach as Esau's replacement. In the interest of achieving a harmonious collaboration between the government agencies and the Kaiser Wilhelm institutes, it was a wise choice. Gerlach was a professor of physics at the University of Munich and won the approval of both Heisenberg and Hahn. As an academic physicist he was interested in pursuing pure research, sometimes under the guise of war research. In other respects, however, the choice was puzzling. Gerlach was not in that class of scientists with marked party affiliations and he had had no previous contact with the nuclear power project. During World War II he had worked on torpedo fuses. It seems that the Kaiser Wilhelm Society's connections with Speer, through the person of Vögler, influenced the choice, one with which their scientists could be happy. On 1 January 1944 Gerlach assumed the position of deputy to the Reich Marshall on questions of atomic physics.

Uranium Machine Experiments in the Bunker and Cave

The Berlin-Dahlem bunker laboratory was completed by the end of 1943; it was then possible to begin a series of experiments in the spring of 1944. From the spring months on, the Dahlem scientists singlemindedly pursued the goal of achieving a self-sustaining nuclear chain reaction. To safeguard against aerial attack and radiation from the uranium furnace, the laboratory was surrounded by two meters of reinforced concrete. The main laboratory contained a pit, pumps, laboratory equipment, a ventilation and heating system, and a storeroom for the heavy water tanks. Other rooms in the laboratory included a workshop and many smaller labs for research on uranium metal and on heavy water. Plans were also made for an air vacuum apparatus for the radioactivity emitted by the uranium machine.[57]

During the winter of 1943–44 the Berlin and Heidelberg Kaiser Wilhelm physics institutes collaborated in building a model pile using 1.5 tons of heavy water and about the same weight in uranium plates at the Dahlem laboratory bunker. In the spring of 1944 four pile experiments were carried out at the laboratory designated as B (for Berlin)-VI a–d. Both experiments, B-VI and B-VII, consisted of horizontal layers of uranium plates and heavy water placed within a cylindrical container to prevent the absorption of neutrons. By varying the widths of the layers one could obtain different production coefficients for the neutrons. The numerical value of the production coefficients indicate the ability to produce a chain reaction, and no self-sustaining chain reaction will occur with a negative production coefficient. The numerical values obtained by all of the piles (B-I to B-VII) at the Berlin bunker fluctuated greatly,[58] a phenomenon later found to be a result of the design of the pile.

By contrast, the competing Diebner group in Gottow had already obtained better results by using a uranium metal cube design. The cube lattices were immersed in a cylindrical aluminum container filled with heavy water. This design proved to be quite an innovative step in reactor technology and was eventually adopted by the Berlin group, but not until after the results had been obtained from the B-VI and B-VII experiments. In late summer 1944 Gerlach summarized the most important research results and progress made since his tenure as the deputy for atomic physics; the first point he made was that cube configurations were better than plate configurations.[59]

Despite his affinity for academic physicists and the Heisenberg group, Gerlach remained impartial and fair on the question of judging and supporting Diebner's work. Wirtz had wondered why Gerlach allowed Diebner's group (now in Gottow-Berlin) and Heisenberg's group to compete for the same scarce materials.[60] As Irving has pointed out, Gerlach was probably reluctant to "pass a final, and possibly wrong, verdict in deciding between Diebner's and Heisenberg's group."[61] This was a brave position. Most people are reluctant to criticize a Nobel Prize–winning professor and director of a prestigious institute. This behavior is magnified in Germany where, in the hierarchy of the institute structure, an assistant or junior person would be less likely, for example, to tell Heisenberg that he was wrong or that a cube design was better than a layer configuration. This had also been the case with accepting Bothe's measurement of the absorption coefficient in graphite.

Gerlach had even supported Diebner's *Habilitation*, a second dissertation necessary to qualify for a professorship in Germany. Diebner had been criticized by scientists and party circles because he was not *habilitiert*. Gerlach, however, thought Diebner's work on the geometry of uranium piles was significant enough to merit a *Habilitation*. Other scientists blocked this move when Gerlach took the question to the Technical University in Berlin.[62] The Heisenberg group in particular had a negative opinion of Diebner because they considered him an inferior scientist and pro–National Socialist. This antipathy is clearly shown in Heisenberg's remarks and behavior after he was in the custody of the Alsos Mission and at Farm Hall in England, where the atomic scientists were brought after the occupation of Germany.[63]

By the spring of 1944 scientists at the Kaiser Wilhelm Institute for Physics began to see the merits of a lattice cube design for increased neutron production. Nevertheless, Heisenberg reported after the war that experiment B-VI and VII still used the layer design in order to be "systematic."[64] Meanwhile allied air raids had forced both scientific institutes and factories producing uranium to evacuate, thus slowing down research activities and the production of needed materials such as uranium. Even though Gerlach seemed at first not to favor one group over the other, after the flush of Diebner's success with the cube design wore off, Gerlach gave the remainder of the heavy water and uranium to the prestigious Berlin-Dahlem physics institute to carry out the next big experiment and attempt at a self-sustaining chain reaction.[65]

After Vögler had heard about the B-VI experiment from Gerlach, he wrote to Heisenberg in October 1944 that he found the experiment "very interesting." If he could be of any assistance in procuring the "necessary material," wrote Vögler, both he and Speer were ready to aid the project in any way. He was also prepared to "talk" again to Speer, "who as you know is extremely interested in the question" and always asks about it whenever Vögler sees him.[66] At this late date, then, there was still much interest from both the politicians and the scientists in achieving a chain reaction in a pile even though the war was surely lost and no attempt had been made to shift the emphasis from laboratory experiments to large-scale industrial production of an atomic bomb.

As 1944 drew to a close, the last uranium pile experiment in Berlin, B-VII, was performed at the bunker laboratory. Karl Wirtz directed the construction of the pile, which was surrounded by a graphite reflecting shield in contrast to all the other big experiments, which had used water as a reflector. Earlier studies by Heisenberg (1942) and by Bopp and Fischer (March 1944) had shown that there was a "marked" improvement in the "increase factor" (i.e., an increase in neutron multiplication) with the same constant using a carbon reflecting mantle. Previous numerical expectations were then tested on the B-VII "big experiment."[67] The experimental arrangement consisted of an aluminum vessel 210.8 centimeters in diameter and 216 centimeters tall. The "electron" vessel used in earlier experiments was placed inside in order to facilitate the arrangements of the layers. The older vessel stood on 45 centimeters of graphite, and 43 centimeters separated the two vessels. The inner electron vessel was filled with layers and the carbon shield was built with huge graphite slabs between the two vessels. The whole arrangement was then built into the concrete tub of the neutron laboratory in Dahlem and surrounded by water. As the title of the report indicated, the machine contained 1.5 tons of heavy water and uranium. The uranium was still in the form of plates 1 centimeter thick alternating with 18 centimeters of heavy water in a layer design. The results yielded a neutron increase of 3.37 compared to a previous measure of 2.9. The group cautiously reasoned that the difference was probably a result of the graphite reflecting shield. Finally, the Wirtz group came to the conclusion that the size of a self-sustaining machine had been "over, rather than underestimated."[68]

Despite the bombing and air-raid attacks on Berlin, Karl Wirtz's group remained in Dahlem working in the protected bunker laboratory even though Heisenberg and part of the institute had fled to Hechingen. It seemed to Wirtz's group that there still might be time to build a self-sustaining pile before the war ended. In Berlin they began to work on a heavy water pile using uranium cubes for the first time. Although they had endured the horrendous war conditions until January, it soon became impossible to work there with nightly air raids, no electrical power, and often no telephone. As the Russian army approached from the east a wholesale evacuation of Berlin began, and thousands fled from Prussia to the west.

At the end of January 1945, Gerlach made the decision to move the rest of the institute to Hechingen. By the time Wirtz's group had nearly finished setting up the biggest pile experiment yet, B-VIII, with over 600 uranium cubes and 1.5 tons of heavy water, windows began to break at the Kaiser Wilhelm Institute for Physics as a result of an air raid. The scientists were more than willing to comply with Gerlach's orders. On 30 January they began to take the pile apart and were ready on the next day for the journey southwest through Gottow-Kummersdorf to Stadtilm to Hechingen. Several trucks were loaded with heavy water, uranium, and the pieces of the uranium machine. Gerlach, Wirtz, and Diebner left that evening and arrived in Stadtilm the next morning. At first Gerlach had wanted to leave the material in the trucks with Diebner in Stadtilm, but Heisenberg personally went to Stadtilm with Weizsäcker to dissuade him; after a day's discussion Heisenberg succeeded. The Kaiser Wilhelm group was not ready to let Diebner's group achieve a critical pile with their material.[69]

As fighter bombers and airplanes filled the skies, Erich Bagge made the trip from Hechingen to Stadtilm to pick up the Kaiser Wilhelm institute's uranium and heavy water. Wirtz directed another convoy of material to Haigerloch, a village near Hechingen, where a cave was prepared to house the B-VIII pile. At the end of February, Wirtz's group and the materiel arrived in Haigerloch, four weeks after they had left Berlin.[70] The scientists were now ready to reconstruct the pile in the Haigerloch cave. After Heisenberg was convinced by the results of the earlier experiments that cubes were the best form for the uranium metal in the heavy water pile, experiment B-VIII in Haigerloch could commence. According to theory, six to seven centimeters squared was the optimal dimension for the cubes, but given the shortage of materials, the institute would use the five-centimeter cubes from the Gottow group's experiments. Because it would have been impossible to produce other cubes quickly, Wirtz's group decided to create more of the five-centimeter cubes to complement those already at hand. To compare this experiment with B-VI and B-VII, the same magnesium cylinder with a carbon reflecting shield was used as in B-VII. Six hundred and eighty uranium cubes weighing 1.5 tons were hung on the aluminum lid of the cylinder in chains; they were then lowered into a reactor vessel with a neutron source at the center. Measurements were taken to determine neutron intensity.[71]

While the experiment was beginning at the end of February Gerlach was simultaneously arranging top priority and protection for the Kaiser Wilhelm Society's institutes in Berlin-Dahlem, Heidelberg, Hechingen, Haigerloch, and Tailfingen as part of Hitler's emergency program. By the time this was arranged the Haigerloch experiment was ready. As they undertook the experiment, Heisenberg and Wirtz observed an increase in neutron multiplication. But despite the best results yet, the pile emitted only 670 neutrons for every 100 pumped in. By increasing the size of the pile they thought they could achieve their goal of a self-sustaining chain reaction; they would need more heavy water, however. They had been on the "brink" of a chain reaction.[72]

Alsos, Farm Hall, and Operation Epsilon

While the Kaiser Wilhelm institute scientists worked feverishly to achieve a self-sustaining chain reaction, the Alsos Mission, the American scientific intelligence unit headed by the physicist Samuel Goudsmit, entered Germany. The Alsos (Greek for grove, and also a play on the name of General Leslie Groves, who headed the Manhattan Project) Mission was an intelligence-gathering mission created in the fall of 1943 by the Army's G-2 (Intelligence) department, Groves's Manhattan district, the U.S. Navy, and Vannevar Bush's Office of Scientific Research and Development. Its original goal had been to obtain information about the German nuclear power project, but its scope widened to include other scientific war research as well. General Groves appointed Colonel Boris Pash military and administrative head of the mission and Vannevar Bush named Samuel Goudsmit scientific head. As Goudsmit relates in his book on the Alsos Mission, he had "assets and liabilities." Among his assets, he was a physicist who had an understanding of nuclear physics, but because he was not working on the Manhattan Project, should he be captured by the enemy, he could not disclose any secrets. He also knew the languages of his former colleagues abroad. Moreover, his parents had died in a concentration camp, fueling his enormous hatred of the Germans.[73]

In mid-March 1945 Alsos officers occupied the Kaiser Wilhelm Institute for Medical Research in Heidelberg. There, Goudsmit and his staff found Walther Bothe and the organic chemist Richard Kuhn from the same institute.[74] Because the mission had already entered Strasbourg in November 1944 and had raided Carl-Friedrich von Weizsäcker's office, they were able to learn more about the nuclear power project in Germany and its various locations. In Heidelberg, Goudsmit approached Bothe with trepidation. How should he treat an old acquaintance and colleague? Bothe greeted him "warmly" and told him about the work done at the institute, emphasizing the pure research. Surprised at the amount of pure research done during the war, Goudsmit inquired more closely into the laboratory's contribution to war problems. Bothe was reluctant to discuss his war research before the war ended and told Goudsmit that he had destroyed all the scientific reports on nuclear power. After VE Day, Bothe provided Goudsmit with a report on the "uranium problem."[75]

From Heidelberg the mission moved on to Stadilm, where documents left behind by the Diebner group were seized. Also found were progress reports left by Gerlach, who had set up headquarters in Stadilm after the evacuation from Berlin. After traveling to various other locations in Germany including Celle, where they found the centrifuge laboratory, the mission still had not reached its "main objective"—the Kaiser Wilhelm Institute for Physics in Hechingen, its remnants in Berlin-Dahlem, and the cave housing the pile in Haigerloch. The mission was still waiting for these areas to be occupied so that the troops could enter and capture the atomic scientists. Unfortunately, the desired areas in southwest Germany were going to be occupied by French troops. Upon hearing this news Pash began planning a parachute attack on Hechingen, where he intended to kidnap the scientists and confiscate their documents.[76] Although no such attack took place, Colonel Pash eventually found the Hechingen institute and the Haigerloch cave. Hechingen was occupied by French troops on 22 April 1945 and on the same day Pash and his troops arrived, occupied the laboratories, removed the equipment, and interrogated the resident scientists. They had found Laue, Weizsäcker, Wirtz, Bagge, Horst Korsching, and Hahn, and took them away to an undisclosed place. They had just missed Heisenberg, however, who had already fled to Urfeld, where his family was living.[77]

The mission's next stop was Hahn's institute in Tailfingen. Hahn proved to be more cooperative than the other scientists and showed Goudsmit the scientific reports about his research. He too was arrested, joining the other physicists. Gerlach, Diebner, and Heisenberg were soon captured as well. The only place left to inspect was the Kaiser Wilhelm Institute for Physics in Berlin-Dahlem. At the end of July 1945 the mission examined what remained of the institute after the Russian troops had stripped it of all its equipment.

It did not take long before the ten captured scientists—Erich Bagge, Kurt Diebner, Walter Gerlach, Otto Hahn, Paul Harteck, Werner Heisenberg, Horst Korsching, Max von Laue, Carl-Friedrich von Weizsäcker, and Karl Wirtz (seven Kaiser Wilhelm institute scientists)—were taken to England and interned in an old country house called Farm Hall, where they lived comfortably with access to radio, newspapers, books, and a piano. R. V. Jones had suggested the scientists be taken to the house, which had been used by British Intelligence, for "safekeeping." Jones also suggested that microphones be installed so that the British could monitor the scientists' discussion of their work.[78] The recorded conversations at Farm Hall have become the most sought-after and revealing evidence of what the German physicists knew and thought about nuclear energy in 1945. As this book was going to press, the so-called Farm Hall transcripts were released by the Public Records Office in England and declassified at the National Archives in 1992. Entitled "Operation Epsilon," the transcript is actually in the form of semimonthly intelligence reports by Major T. H. Rittner with the most interesting and relevant conversations transcribed and translated into English. From the time the reports were begun on 1 May 1945 until they were completed in 31 December 1945 it appears that only Samuel Goudsmit and General Groves, who checked out the copy available at the National Archives, had access to the report in America. Groves used verbatim extracts in his book *Now It*

Can Be Told. The ten scientists, who are called "guests" throughout the reports, arrived in England on 3 July 1945 after a two-month covert journey through Belgium and France. During their eight-month period of captivity, the scientists covered a number of topics in their conversations ranging from constant worry about their families, to whom they were not allowed to write letters until 1 August, to detailed technical discussions. In addition, the scientists held biweekly lectures on scientific topics.[79]

Initially, the scientists did not understand why they were being detained, although they thought it had something to do with their involvement in nuclear power and a belief that they were dangerous, and they threatened to run away. Their captors, in turn, often noted the morale of the group and reported constant "restiveness." During the first month at Farm Hall, the group discussed their future fate in a United States of Europe and their preference for working in Russia or America. They became convinced that their release was somehow going to be decided by the "Big Three" in Potsdam and their detention was a ploy to keep them from the Russians. They discussed possible scenarios for continuing their work on the uranium machine in Germany or abroad. Bagge and Diebner, who thought of the possibility of working on uranium in Argentina, began to rationalize their party membership, often denying or minimizing it. For example, in a conversation with Hahn, Diebner claimed he suffered under the Nazis, became a Freemason in 1933 in opposition to National Socialism, and never voted for Hitler. On his return to Germany he had visions of everyone saying: "Party man. Party man!"[80]

On 6 August 1945 the news media reported the American dropping of the atomic bomb on Hiroshima. The first reaction to the news consisted of expressions of horror and disbelief that the invention was used for destruction. These initial reactions were followed by varied and incredulous responses by the scientists, who then spent weeks discussing how the Americans had built the bomb. The responses not only show how far behind the German work was on an atomic bomb, but also display the scientists' technical knowledge of the subject at the time, and the very different and individual attitude each scientist had toward working on nuclear energy under Hitler.

Karl Wirtz was glad they did not have the bomb; Weizsäcker thought it was "madness" on the part of the Americans to have built and dropped the bomb, while Heisenberg thought what the Americans did had nothing to do with uranium. Gerlach was probably the most disappointed; he felt like a defeated general and "seemed to have a nervous breakdown," with constant "sobbing."[81] Hahn, who made the discovery that set off the project, was "shattered" but was "glad not to have taken part in the construction of such a deadly weapon"; according to the major in charge, Hahn needed to be "calmed down with alcoholic stimulant." In general, "the effect of the news" on the physicists "was naturally very intense."[82]

At first there was disbelief that the bomb had actually been dropped, and the scientists thought the news was a propaganda trick. Hahn thought the Allies could have done it if they knew about isotope separation; he speculated that it must have been a small atomic bomb—"a hand one." The scientists were also incredulous as they began to speculate on the large scale of the allied effort and the amount of manpower and resources tapped to successfully develop and use the bomb. Heisenberg remarked that the Americans must have spent all of their 500 million pounds (*sic*) in separating isotopes. Wirtz commented that the Germans had only one man working on separating isotopes, whereas the Allies "may have had ten thousand." Harteck speculated that the Allies used mass spectrographs to make U-235, and Heisenberg thought 180,000 people were working on it. The scientists had been left in the dark on the allied effort, despite some intelligence work bungled by the SS and SD.[83]

It was during the period immediately following the dropping of the bomb that some of the atomic scientists began to reconstruct, in conversation and in their own minds, the German effort to harness nuclear energy and their attitude toward it. Every scientist had his own version at the time, and it is therefore not correct to refer to "*the* atomic scientists' attitude". For example, Weizsäcker had already begun to formulate his version of the story, which seems to have remained constant since the war ended: "I believe the reason we didn't do it was because all the physicists didn't want to do it, on principle. If we had all wanted Germany to win the war we would have succeeded."[84] Hahn, however, disagreed: "I don't believe that but I am thankful we didn't succeed." Heisenberg, in turn, stated: "We wouldn't have had the moral courage to recommend to the Government in the spring of 1942 that they should employ 120,000 men just for building the thing up."[85]

Even if the project scientists had gotten all they wanted from the government, Weizsäcker thought that they could not have completed the "thing" during the war. He believed the scientists did not want to succeed. Heisenberg did not agree entirely and stated that he was "convinced of the possibility [of] making a uranium engine but never thought that we would make a bomb" and at the "bottom of [his] heart" he was "really glad that it was to be an engine and not a bomb." In the Epsilon Report Heisenberg does a good job of reconstructing the allied effort and the way to build a bomb; he was aware that an explosion could be achieved with pure U-235 and fast neutrons.[86]

In his discussion with Hahn, Heisenberg guessed that the Americans had made about thirty kilograms of pure U-235 a year, but he was not sure how much pure U-235 one actually needed to produce a bomb. When Hahn asked him why he used to say that one needed fifty kilograms of U-235 to do anything and now said one needed tons, Heisenberg replied that he did not want to commit himself. Then Heisenberg said: "Quite honestly I have never worked it out as I never believed one could get pure 235."[87] Other interesting revelations from the Operation Epsilon reports show, according to Jeremy Bernstein, that Heisenberg did not understand the concept of critical mass of uranium—the amount of mass needed to produce a chain reaction—and therefore miscalculated the weight of the bomb ("about a ton," as he thought, was forty times more than the actual weight).[88] Heisenberg knew, however, the difference between the reactions in an atomic bomb and in a reactor. The bomb uses "fast" neutrons (neutrons produced in the fission process that move several million meters a second), whereas a reactor needs only "slow" neutrons (neutrons slowed with a moderator to speeds of a few thousand meters a second): "I always knew that it could be done with 235 fast neutrons. That's why 235 only can be used as an explosive. One can never make an explosive with slow neutrons, not even with the heavy water machine as then the neutrons only go with the thermal speed, with the result that the reaction is so slow that the thing explodes sooner, before the reaction is complete."[89]

There was further disagreement on whether the scientists thought it could be done and whether it ought to be done. Weizsäcker claimed "in our case even the scientists said it couldn't be done." Bagge flatly contradicted him: "That's not true." Bagge then reminded Weizsäcker of the 8 September 1939 conference in Berlin, which he attended, where everyone said it "must be done at once." Some thought it was an open question whether it ought to be done, but Bothe and Geiger thought it "*must* be done." Weizsäcker persisted: "I don't know how you can say that. 50% of the people were against it." According to Harteck, those scientists who did not understand it were against it, and because 90 percent did not understand it, 90 percent were against it.[90]

In addition to discussions of the nuclear power program, the scientists made prescient and insightful comments about the emergence of America and Russia as superpowers and the role of the atomic bomb in achieving a victorious status for one or the other country. Heisenberg thought that the "uranium business" would give the Anglo-Saxons so much power that Europe, including Germany, would become a bloc under Anglo-Saxon domination. Weizsäcker remarked in conversation that it was the Americans and English who actually made and dropped a bomb, while the Germans, "working under the Hitler regime, produced a workable engine." While the Germans worked on the "peaceful development of the uranium engine," the Americans and English developed a "ghastly weapon of war."[91]

Although Laue had not participated in the project, he was close enough to the physicists as a member of the Kaiser Wilhelm Institute for Physics in Berlin-Dahlem to have a basic idea about what they were working on. More important for the historian is that he was probably one of the most courageous and outspoken critics of the regime. In addition to the Farm Hall transcripts the historian has several statements made by Laue during and after the period of imprisonment which illuminate and contextualize the motivations of the scientists. After the war was over, and a year before he died in a car accident, Laue wrote to Paul Rosbaud, Britain's master spy who had been in Berlin during the war, responding to Robert Jungk's new book

Brighter Than a Thousand Suns, which started the myth about the human-
istic German scientists who probably could have built the bomb but had
the "moral fortitude to resist." The relevant passage from Laue's letter reads:

> Later, during our table conversation, the version was developed that the
> German atomic physicists really had not wanted the atomic bomb, either
> because it was impossible to achieve it during the expected duration of the
> war or because they simply did not want to have it at all. The leader in
> these discussions was Weizsäcker. I did not hear the mention of any ethical
> point of view. *Heisenberg was mostly silent.*[92]

The fact that a "version was developed" has hindered somewhat the historians quest for the truth on the matter of the German nuclear power project
and the scientists' attitude toward it. But it seems clear from the evidence
presented in the foregoing treatment of the project that, although much
headway had been made on isotope separation, heavy water production, and
the uranium machine or pile, a gulf still remained between the laboratory
experiments and the industrial development of nuclear power in the Third
Reich. Moreover, the scientists' goal by 1943 was the creation of an energy-
burning machine. It is because of these considerations that the scientists really
made no decision to develop an atomic bomb.[93] They were therefore also
spared the moral dilemma.

It is also evident from the foregoing narrative of the development of
the nuclear power project at the Kaiser Wilhelm institutes that many obstacles
stood in the way of making quick progress on the development of an explosive or a self-sustaining energy-burning machine. In addition to the deteriorating war context, the lack of resources, and the attitude of the government, conflicts existed between the various groups that hindered effective
cooperation, centralization, and sharing of the scarce materials. The prestigious Kaiser Wilhelm institutes, traditionally sites for basic research, were
reluctant to cooperate with what they considered to be inferior scientists.
With their emphasis on theory and pure research, practical steps were not
taken to develop the research into a large engineering-style project like the
one that existed in America. Under the protection and support of the
umbrella Kaiser Wilhelm Society the institutes received top priorities through
Albert Vögler's connections with Speer, but despite Vögler's and Speer's
interest, the academic scientists did not take advantage of all the financial
support available to them, nor did they appeal to government officials to
undertake nuclear research on a large scale, as was done in America. Finally,
their drive to achieve a self-sustaining chain reaction in Dahlem and Haigerloch during the closing days of the war seems to have been motivated by
the desire to see the technical part of the project to its end, and not to build
a bomb before the war ended.

Epilogue

After World War II ended in May 1945, defeated Germany was left in ruins, with major cities destroyed and 7 million dead. The victors had already been planning occupation policies as early as 1943–44, and by May 1945 the Allies agreed on some ways to treat a defeated Germany. The first task was to demilitarize Germany and to destroy its war industries. Those responsible for World War II and for perpetrating war crimes would be brought to justice. All Germans would be denazified. Whether Germany would be divided or treated as a whole was the subject of a number of wartime conferences among Franklin Roosevelt, Winston Churchill, and Joseph Stalin. Because there was no agreement on this issue, they fell back to the Yalta Conference of February 1945, which had divided Germany into zones of occupation. The French took charge of the southwest; the United States, Bavaria, Württemberg-Baden, and Hessen; England, northern Germany and the Rhineland; and the Soviet Union, the eastern provinces. Berlin was divided into four sectors. In June the Allies assumed supreme government authority in Germany.[1]

With the conviction that everything must be done to prevent Germany from rising as a military power again, the Allies drew up directives to implement policies enforcing this belief. More specifically for the world of science, U.S. Secretary of the Treasury Henry Morgenthau thought that there were strong connections between science and war:

> Germany has made a great many notable contributions to science, and especially in the warlike discoveries. It must be one of the aims of Allied policy to circumvent the plans of German leaders to organize hidden laboratories for war under the guise of studying peaceful sciences whether pure or applied.[2]

Because modern research is organized on a large scale, Morgenthau thought "the teeth" could be "drawn from Germany's scientific war machine by

forbidding the organization of the elaborate laboratories of her past."
Morgenthau's point of view was incorporated into the Joint Chiefs of Staff
directive 1067; the occupation forces were instructed to enforce the directive after Germany's capitulation:

> a. prohibit initially all research activities and close all laboratories, research
> institutions and similar technical organizations except those considered nec-
> essary to the protection of public health;

> b. abolish all those laboratories and related institutions whose work has been
> connected with the building of the German war machine, safeguard initially
> such laboratories and detain such personnel as are of interest to your tech-
> nological investigations, and thereafter remove or destroy their equipment;

> c. permit the resumption of specific research in specific cases, only after
> careful investigation has established that the contemplated research will in
> no way contribute to Germany's future war potential and only under
> appropriate regulations . . .

Other unofficial proposals on how to "control" German scientists were
discussed among members of the Office of Scientific Research in Washington. A startling proposal was made by a Dr. Frueniel who considered "round-
ing up all German scientists in concentration camps."[3]

Several offices were founded by the Allies within the jurisdiction of the
military governments in order to implement directive 1067 for educational,
cultural, economic, and scientific affairs in occupied Germany. Three of these
were of importance for the fate of the Kaiser Wilhelm Society: the Office
for the Military Government, US (OMGUS), including its educational,
cultural, and economic departments, its Military Security Board, its Field
Information Agency, Technical (FIAT), headed by Carl Nordstrom; the
Research Branch, Britain, headed by Bertie Blount; the Office for Research
and Development (OSRD) also played an indirect role in its plans for the
"control of Germany." Finally, the U.S. High Commissioner for Germany
(HICOG) succeeded OMGUS in 1949, primarily as a civilian organization.

By the middle of 1945 the Kaiser Wilhelm Society and its institutes had
lost their central location in Berlin as they were forced to evacuate the
administration and many institutes to west and southwest Germany. In mid-
1945 the administration was still operating from the Aerodynamic Experimental Station in Göttingen. Albert Vögler, however, had been captured
by the Americans in Dortmund in April 1945 and had committed suicide,
leaving the Society leaderless. Ernst Telschow assumed the responsibilities
of the president until the eighty-seven-year-old Max Planck was brought from
Magdeburg to Göttingen (in the British zone) on 16 May 1945 by
G. P. Kuiper, a scientist and member of the American military government.[4]
Planck then assumed a figurehead role until a president was elected from
among the scientific members. It was a wise move. Planck would serve to
protect the Society and it could use Planck's prestige when negotiating with
the occupation powers.[5] Planck quickly saw that Otto Hahn, an active and

prominent scientific member of the Society since its founding in 1911, would be unanimously suggested for the position of president by the Kaiser Wilhelm institute directors.[6] Hahn, who was still in captivity at Farm Hall in England, received a "great shock" upon receiving this news and initially found it difficult to accept the post with the justification that he had become tired in the last few years, was "never a diplomat," and was never clever as a negotiator.[7] Nevertheless, other colleagues persuaded him to accept the "election." He officially assumed office on 1 April 1946, just three months after his return from Farm Hall.

Meanwhile, in Berlin, the Soviet Military Administration and the Berlin City Council began to stake out their cultural and scientific territory. In April 1945, before Germany's capitulation, the "Ulbricht Group," a group of German communists, had returned to Berlin from their exile in Moscow and were asked by the Red Army to help construct a new German administration.[8] Initially, Peter Adolf Thiessen (director of the Kaiser Wilhelm Institute for Physical Chemistry, 1935–45) was offered the presidency of the Kaiser Wilhelm Society by the Mayor, but he declined the post because he had agreed to take on a ten year contract in Russia. The Lord Mayor (Oberbürgermeister) and the city council then appointed Robert Havemann, a chemist who had worked at the Kaiser Wilhelm Institute for Physical Chemistry in 1932–33, leader of the Society. On 6 July 1945 Havemann, who had already had close contact with the Ulbricht Group, announced his appointment in a circular. Because he was an opponent of the National Socialist regime, founded the resistance group "European Union," and had communist sympathies, he was imprisoned in 1943 in the Brandenburg prison and sentenced to death. He was freed by the Russians in 1945. This choice met with the disapproval of many scientists still working at the Berlin institutes:

> It was an "achievement" of the Third Reich, in the area of science also, to make dispositions without listening to the "parties" and to appoint "leaders." The undersigned scientists take up the rights of the statutes which state that the president and other leading personalities are appointed by free elections in the senate and scientific council.[9]

The communist *Deutsche Volkszeitung*, on the other hand, praised Havemann for possessing "all the qualifications of a scientist, and simultaneously being a proven anti-fascist."[10]

Unlike the American occupation government, Havemann and the Soviet Occupation Administration recognized the scientific and political value of scientific organizations early on. They strongly supported the immediate reconstruction of the German Academy of Sciences and the integration of the Berlin and the Soviet zone Kaiser Wilhelm institutes into their sphere of influence. Havemann also received the support of Dr. Naas in the department for People's Education of the German Administration. Havemann thought the "political meaning" of the Society should be considered on the level of the influence the communists could have within it and the extent to which it could be useful to their "enemies." Because the Society was a Germany-wide enterprise, he thought it would be the ideal institution to use for politically molding the "German bourgeois intelligentsia." Because the Americans were fighting against any kind of regeneration of scientific life, Havemann thought his "enemies"—the Göttingen administration—would have a hard time founding the Society. He did not want the communists' "political work" to become known, however, because then the Americans' attitude toward the Kaiser Wilhelm institutes might change and hinder their work.[11]

The Kaiser Wilhelm Society was now split, with one leader in the British zone and one in the Russian zone. In the West, however, the Society did not recognize Havemann's leadership, and Planck wrote to the institute directors that Havemann's rule was limited to the Soviet zone of occupation.[12] Havemann remained in his position until January 1948 when the American occupation forces dismissed him for "lack of cooperation" and for failing to submit his reports.[13] Between 1945 and 1947, however, the Society was threatened with graver problems.

Because of their policy toward scientific research just outlined, the American occupation forces wanted to dissolve the Society completely. During much of 1945–46 the Society negotiated with and tried to persuade the Americans that the Society was not a Nazi organization, that it was private, and that it undertook no war research during the war. Planck had already started on this path by assuring the Allied Scientific Commission in June 1945 that "since its founding the Society has been able to preserve its scientific reputation, and to maintain its total independence and scientific autonomy under the National Socialist government." The institutes of the Society, he went on, were well-staffed, well-equipped, and financially healthy at the beginning of the war. Moreover, during the war they could "carry out their" original "task of advancing basic research" without being "diverted" by the "demands of the war." He urged the scientific commission to allow the Society's work to continue.[14]

By the summer of 1945 Telschow sent institute directors a directive informing them that "the fact that the Kaiser-Wilhelm-Gesellschaft is a private institution is of great importance for its further existence." The president and the administration, he continued, were independent during the Third Reich, and the institute directors had the freedom to choose their own problems. He stressed that the "leaders" of the Society rejected taking scientific equipment from occupied countries, and that it owned all its scientific materiel.[15]

In some further remarks prepared in January 1946 on research at university institutes, industrial laboratories, Reich research institutes of NSDAP organizations like the SS and the armed forces, and at the Kaiser Wilhelm Society, Telschow stressed the high quality of research done at the latter. It could maintain this "especially high standard" under the National Socialist regime and during the war, he argued. "Political influences," he wrote, were felt "by the NSDAP at the beginning of the seizure of power, but could almost always be repulsed afterwards." It was known that many scientists who were politically unacceptable at the universities were able to work at the Kaiser Wilhelm Society after being forced to leave the universities, he continued. Telschow referred to Werner Heisenberg and Erich Regener as examples. Another element that differentiated the Society from other sectors of research, he argued, was the "unbureaucratic way of administration" which allowed it to have "totally free use of the funding at the institutes." For the future, Telschow suggested unifying many scientific institutes under one Kaiser Wilhelm Society. A copy of this statement was given to Colonel Bertie Blount, who was responsible for research in the British zone.[16]

In order to make the Society's claim that it was politically clean during the Third Reich more believable it turned for help to Dr. E. Respondek, a staff member at I. G. Farben who worked with the Allies. Respondek later recalled that the Soviet and French delegation applied to the American delegation in the Allied Control Council to dissolve the Kaiser Wilhelm Society. The reason for this was that the scientists had allegedly worked on "mass extermination weapons." To help the Society, Respondek wrote a report for Ambassador Robert Murphy, the head of the political department at OMGUS, which was then sent to the State Department. In this report he guaranteed that the "scientific research in the KWG institutes was absolutely free, and none of the professors bowed before the dictator Hitler." They did not work to kill men but rather to help them live. He described the various presidents of the Society, stressing Harnack and Planck, whose sons were active in resistance movements and were killed as a result of the 20 July 1944 assassination attempt on Hitler. He mentioned that many of the scientists were Nobel Prize winners. Finally, he referred to a story about Carl Bosch, the third president of the Society. Hitler apparently had ordered a group of industrial leaders to a conference to develop and produce mass extermination weapons, to which Bosch answered "science does not follow orders."[17] Although Murphy's report was positively received, it did not change the occupying powers' dissolution order.

Meanwhile, the English saw the Society in a more favorable light. The Society was lucky it had sympathetic Englishmen in Germany in charge of the Research Branch. The physicist H. P. Robertson was the director of the department for science in the British zone and had studied in Göttingen in the twenties. Brigadier Frank Spedding was the director of the Research Branch. Colonel Bertie Blount was on the staff of the British Research Branch in Göttingen and had received a Ph.D. in 1931 with Walther Borsche; he was therefore also sympathetic to Germany.[18] As soon as Telschow met Blount in the fall of 1945 he was helpful to the Society in every way.

Within three months of Hahn's assumption of the president's office the Interallied Control Council passed a resolution to dissolve the Kaiser Wilhelm Society on 11 July 1946. The reasons for the liquidation of the Society, insofar as they were released, were that (1) it was a state institution, (2) it undertook war work, and (3) the administration assigned research contracts to individual institutes; it therefore existed in the form of a "research trust."

Hahn, who had first heard the news on the radio, replied to these accusations in the following way. (1) The Kaiser Wilhelm Society was always a "pure private institution"—an "*eingetragener Verein*," which literally means a "registered association." Although he admitted the Society received part of its financial support from the state, there were no conditions attached and much support also came from private sources. (2) During the war, claimed Hahn, the Society continued its tradition of cultivating basic research. He conceded that tasks were undertaken which were important for the war economy, but they were foremost of scientific importance. He reported that the numerous scientific commissions of the Allies which visited him directly after the occupation were "amazed" how much pure research was done, and how little war work was undertaken. (3) Finally, the administration had no influence on the scientific work of the institutes, and the institute directors were totally free to determine their own research problems. The Kaiser Wilhelm Society, wrote Hahn in the memorandum, was not National Socialist. He illustrated this by showing that none of the presidents were party members, and that Planck and Bosch were, in fact, sharp opponents of the Third Reich[19]—without mentioning, of course, that the managing director, Telschow, was a party member. For more support he quoted a passage from a diary entry made by Ambassador William Dodd, the American consul in Berlin, in 1937:

> Tonight I went to a dinner party at the Kaiser-Wilhelm-Institute. The new president taking his place, my friend, the former president, PLANCK, retiring. This organization is not Nazi and some outstanding businessmen who were present made their attitude plain. They had no Hitler decorations on their coats and they did not say "Heil Hitler" when others came up to them and shook hands.[20]

As a final sign of the political cleanliness of the Society, Hahn wrote that a measure of the prestige of the Society was that it was supported by the Rockefeller Foundation during the Third Reich—without, of course, mentioning that it had been a controversial grant promised before the National Socialists' rise to power.[21]

After the allied directive to dissolve the Kaiser Wilhelm Society, Hahn fought tenaciously to save the Society. He received the most cooperation and support from Bertie Blount, who counseled him on strategy. In a meeting with Hahn and Telschow on 11 July 1946, Blount reported that the "Society will be dissolved. (Not 'should be,' but 'will be.')."[22] Although Blount had tried to persuade the Americans otherwise, they had been "obstinate" and said the Society was a "dangerous organization with disgraceful predecessors and with much war potential."[23] Indignant and resentful of the Allies' use of force, Hahn even threatened to resign his post. He also contemplated writing an open letter to German and foreign newspapers, or of writing a collective letter with other German scientists to President Harry Truman. Blount discouraged Hahn from writing to Truman, who, he said, probably had never heard of the Kaiser Wilhelm Society, and instead suggested he write a letter to Sir Henry Dale, a scientist who was active in many British consulting organizations. Hahn followed Blount's advice and wrote a letter to Dale describing the fate of the Society in the Third Reich and asking for a revision of the Control Council's decision. He referred to the attempts by leftists to change the name Kaiser Wilhelm in the 1920s, and to Harnack's success in keeping it. After all the struggles of the last years, Hahn was frustrated that he had "suffered shipwreck as president even before" he had "the chance of saving the little that ought to be saved."[24] During a visit to England, Blount also used the opportunity to talk to Sir Henry Dale: "He did not take it too seriously. 'It is only the name which they have something against,' he said, just the words 'Kaiser Wilhelm' conjures up a picture of rattling sabres and maritime expansion. Name it the Max Planck Gesellschaft and everyone will be happy."[25] So it was that a "new" Society would be founded in the British zone, with the name the Max Planck Society. It was officially founded in Bad Driburg on 11 September 1946 in the British zone only.

During the early postwar years, 1945–49, competing impulses came from all four zones of occupation and Berlin, which only emphasized the virtual dismemberment of the Society and the chaotic situation. Research was forbidden in the French and American zones of occupation, including Berlin. During this time, there appeared to be little communication between Berlin and Göttingen as Havemann tried to organize the institutes in Berlin and negotiated with the American military government, which had occupied five institutes and the Harnack House to use as headquarters. The institutes in the Soviet zone of occupation, including East Berlin, gradually became integrated into the German Academy of Sciences. For example, the Berlin-Buch Brain research institute with its division for genetics was transformed into a biomedical research institute of the academy, as was the animal breeding institute in Rostock. Discussion also began with Dr. Fritz Karsen, who wanted to create a "Research-University" out of the institutes in West Berlin patterned on American centers for advanced studies; the successful completion of the plan was announced in the local newspaper.[26] But more importantly, the Society was able to gradually expand its operation as the Max Planck Society in the American and the French zones as it became a bizonal then trizonal research organization. Its second founding therefore occurred on 26 February 1948 for the English and American zones of occupation. In order to continue to exist, the Society had been required by the occupation forces to reduce the influence of the state and industrial circles on the Society while transferring the leadership and functioning of the Society from the administrators to the scientists themselves.[27]

It is clear from the course of events in the immediate postwar period that the Society exaggerated somewhat the extent of its independence during the Third Reich in order to preserve its existence. By drawing a general picture of the Society, it failed to consider deviations by some individuals or institutes. By concentrating on the extent of its war work, it failed to mention one institute's involvement in eugenics, for example. It was true that Erich Regener was ousted from his position at the Technische Hoch-schule because his wife was Jewish, and he found refuge at a laboratory for physics of the stratosphere. And the Society could have produced more examples from the life sciences. Although Heisenberg had been attacked during the early years of the Third Reich, by the time of his appointment in 1942, his career at the university seemed problem-free. And finally, although the "leaders" of the Society rejected taking equipment from occupied countries, some projects, such as the uranium project, might have procured material (ore) from Belgian mines. One could go on with specific examples, but it must be said that in general the Society's claims were true.

The Allies, on the other hand, uniformly applied a policy without tak-ing into consideration the differentiated nature of the various institutions they were dealing with. The American occupation forces were the most inflexible while the English were the most flexible. In the end the Society was officially dissolved, but it experienced a rebirth under a new name. The traditions of the Society, however, were carried on well into the postwar period and beyond. There was continuity in the leadership of the Society with the appointment of Hahn as president and Telschow as general director.

Telschow, whose activities as a strong and powerful general director I have documented, was, not surprisingly, a controversial administrator to keep in a leading position. As a party member he had been merely labeled a "fol-lower" by occupation officials, but a group of biologists protested his reap-pointment. In 1949, when the biological institutes, which had been evacu-ated to Tübingen in the French zone in 1944, were faced with becoming part of the Max Planck Society, they initially agreed only if Telschow did not remain on as general director. Alfred Kühn recalled that this "old Nazi" had taken part in the Science Ministry's machinations in 1937 to oust Friedrich Glum. He also thought that Telschow had achieved a position of such strong authority in Planck's and Hahn's postwar presidencies that it could only lead to the misuse of power. In the end, Telschow kept his position, but the Tübingen group was promised that a change in the Society's statutes would limit Telschow's power.[28]

As the Society negotiated over its status and functioning with the occu-pying powers, there was a general purge followed by a reeducation program, known as denazification, in the Western zones. Its aim was to remove the men and women who played an active role in National Socialist institutions and attitudes, replacing them with reeducated liberal democratic people. "Nazi mentalities and institutions" would be "eradicated." As part of this program every German over eighteen had to complete a questionnaire about past political affiliations and activities. On the basis of this questionnaire (per-haps also checked against Berlin Document Center files) people were cat-egorized as major offenders, offenders, lesser offenders, followers, or exon-erated. People in one of the first three categories lost their jobs, their pensions, and even their property. Initially security officers from the occu-pation forces processed the forms, but because cases piled up and the pro-gram was criticized, its administration was given to the German *Länder* governments by March 1946. Because the process was taking so long general amnesties were periodically given and up to two-thirds of 6 million cases heard were given amnesty. Some 1,700 people were designated major offenders, 23,000 offenders, 150,500 lesser offenders, 1 million as followers, and 1.2 million as exonerated.[29]

In the case of the Kaiser Wilhelm institutes, the existence of strict denazification laws and time pressure did not allow Roger Adams, the scientific advisor to the Deputy Military Governor of Germany, to differentiate among the status of German scientists. He admitted this in a report on his activities in which he stated the "status of German scientists presented a complex picture." The often arbitrary denazification laws included a law which "required mandatory arrest" of Kaiser Wilhelm Institute directors "regardless of their political affiliations." This produced a great deal of confusion and many injustices. As late as 1947 there were still "non-Nazi scientists of eminence" who were in detention camps.[30]

The denazification procedure was not applied uniformly, and, after the initial arrests, most scientists at the Society were either quickly rehabilitated by the courts or else their institute director guaranteed that the scientist was in no way involved with National Socialist activities. The American zone of occupation was the strictest; anyone who had a high position and was a party member was immediately arrested and could not publish. This was the case for Ernst Rüdin (Kaiser Wilhelm Institute for Psychiatric Research, Munich), who had helped formulate the Sterilization Law.[31] Many other scientitst were issued what had become known as a *Persilschein* (Persil was a popular detergent like Tide)—a "laundering certificate" absolving them of any crimes or complicity. If a scientist reached a tribunal, various witnesses were called to argue that the defendant had resisted the Nazi regime or was a victim. Very quickly everyone became an opponent of the regime, and as Berghahn has rightly pointed out, this was as "untenable as the American view that everyone had been a Nazi."[32]

Because the denazification files at the archives of the Max Planck Society have not been made available, I submitted every institute director's name to the Berlin Document Center in order to investigate party membership and other NSDAP-affiliated membership. Of forty-eight scientific members of the Society who were at one point directors of institutes or department heads, nineteen (39.5 percent) were members of the National Socialist party. Of these nineteen, three—including Jander and Thiessen—entered the party before 1933 (*Alte Kämpfer*), three entered in May 1933 (*Märzgefallene*), one in 1935, one in 1936, the most, seven in 1937, one in 1938, and three in 1940. Thus the majority entered the party late, when the membership polls reopened in 1937 after a period between the spring 1933 and 1937 when they were virtually closed. A higher percentage of scientific members were in the NSLB (Nationalsozialistische Lehrerbund) or NSDB (Nationalsozialistische Deutscher Dozentenbund)—the National Socialist teachers' associations. Out of forty-eight, twenty-one were either in the NSLB or NSDB. Those in one of the teachers' associations joined early; two joined in 1933, nine in 1934, and the rest joined between 1935 and 1938. Thirteen members of the NSLB or NSDB were also in the NSDAP, eight were only in the teachers association, and eighteen were not members of any NSDAP organization.[33] Although no comprehensive formal count of all scientists at the Kaiser Wilhelm institutes has been made, from the material examined, I have found that it was very common for an ambitious young assistant to join the NSDAP or one of the teachers' associations upon qualifying for a teaching position by writing a *Habilitationschrift*. Although the Kaiser Wilhelm Society was a research organization, many of its scientists had been recruited from the university, had affiliations or held honorary positions there. This explains the high number of scientists who joined the teachers' association. The percentage at the universities, however, is much higher. Indeed, such membership was almost a requirement for a career at the university.

Party membership, however, has little meaning in itself. One must examine when the person joined, the motivation, and the political profile. Narratives have been reconstructed in the preceding chapters on specific cases, but a few more points can be made here. If one was a party member in the *Kampfzeit* (between 1919 and 1933) and an *alte Kämpfer* (old fighter—fighters for the National Socialist revolution) one was usually a convinced National Socialist. Of the three institute directors who joined before 1933, two of them—Jander and Thiessen—were active National Socialists who had been installed as directors against the Society's will. At the institutes of the Society as a whole by 1934 there was a high of nine old fighters (this includes laboratory assistants, technicians, and secretaries) at the Jander/Thiessen institute, but it was more common that no old fighters were employed at institutes. For example, the biology, workers physiology, and medical research institutes reported no old fighters in response to a circular distributed by the Kaiser Wilhelm Society on how many old fighters were employed at the institute.[34] If one joined the party after 1933 new categories of belief, involvement, and motivation need to be identified. It was common to join in the spring of 1933 out of opportunism, fear, and enthusiasm for the new movement. These new recruits were called *Märzgefallene*. After 1933 there was a period of time when one could not join until 1937 when the polls were open again. This explains, in part, the large number of joiners at this late date.

But this was only the beginning for German science. Exploitive programs had been established by the American government to extract reparations or war booty in the form of scientific knowledge, expertise, personnel or equipment. In addition to the well-known Project Paperclip program, other missions and mechanisms for the transfer of technical know-how existed including the work of the Field Information Agency, Technical (FIAT). Many Kaiser Wilhelm Institute scientists wrote up reports on their war-time work for FIAT which were published in numerous volumes devoted to different scientific specialties.

During the second phase of the occupation period, between 1949–52, American agencies began to grant the Society more freedom of movement. HICOG (and its Military Security Board), the successor organization to OMGUS, even returned the occupied physics institute of the Medical Research Center in Heidelberg to the Society. In response to Hahn (as president of the Max Planck Society) and Heisenberg's (as president of the German Research Association) request to release the institute occupied by the fourth medical laboratory, John McCloy, the United States High Commissioner for Germany, even wrote to Germany's Federal Chancellor Konrad Adenauer on 5 May 1951 with the good news that the requisitioned institute was returned to the Society. The institute, whose scientists had worked in nuclear physics, could now return to work with the approval of occupiers who early had wanted to prohibit any research which may eventually be militarily useful. By October 1952, Carl Nordstrom, chief of the Scientific Research Division of OMGUS, announced that the division would be dissolved on 15 October 1952. He left with the hope that they "had contributed to the rehabilitation of German research and restoration of normal international relations in scientific matters." He seemed to have warm relations with Hahn and the Max Planck Society because he closed his letter (unlike a similar letter to another organization) recalling the pleasant personal and professional association, and that he would "treasure memories of many evenings" in Göttingen and Berlin.[35]

In the immediate postwar period many scientists also began to be lured away by attractive offers from the Soviet Union and the United States. While the sources to determine the number of scientists from the Society who left Germany for the Soviet Union and America are not available, one can say, in general, that most of the scientists for the American Project Paperclip, for example, did not come from the Society, but many came from Peenemünde, the rocket research center, and other Reich science establishments. Wilhelm Eitel, who had been a staunch National Socialist, emigrated to the United States with a contract from the Navy under Project Paperclip, as did several technicians.[36]

At least ten scientists, most of whom were from the former institute for physical chemistry, went to Russia. This included the Nazi-appointed director Peter Adolf Thiessen, who took on a ten-year contract with the Russians. After his return to Germany, Thiessen lived in East Germany and was instrumental in rebuilding science there along communist principles. He created the East German Research Council (which bore a resemblance to the National Socialist Research Council) and was considered one of East Germany's leading scientists. Thiessen, the cagey opportunist, had changed his allegiance from the Golden Party Badge National Socialist to an influential communist policy-maker and scientist.

Hans Stubbe, who had already been a Marxist in National Socialist Germany, also lived in East Germany after the war and was instrumental in rebuilding East German science. He became a leading biologist, director of the Academy of Sciences's Cultivated Plants Institute, and warded off Lysenkoist genetics in favor of solid basic biological research; he also continued his own research on mutation genetics.

After the end of the initial reconstruction phase of the Kaiser Wilhelm Society, the line dividing Germany began to harden as the cold war accelerated. This situation led to a deepening of the zonal boundaries established in the transitional period. It was not until 1954 that occupation law was lifted and the Society's affairs were no longer controlled by the allied forces.

Conclusion

How can we account for the anomaly that science in National Socialist Germany not only survived but often thrived? After all, according to popular wisdom and widely accepted sociological arguments, science requires a specific type of social structure and political regime—a liberal democracy—to function effectively and to survive. There is no doubt that science suffered in Germany and even at the Society, but the situation is certainly more complex than early descriptions have portrayed. When the terms of discussion were "decline" and "destruction," historians tended to focus on those aspects of the scientific enterprise and on the ideology/science dichotomy. But by shifting the discussion to other unexplored areas, more can be learned about the science/society interface working under extreme conditions.

Certainly some general reasons for the continued strength of science in National Socialist Germany—and more often at the institutes of the Society than at other institutions—lie not in the structure and character of the regime, but in the status and prestige of the pre-1933 German scientific community. The momentum had built up before and was strong enough to maintain the community through the war years. In many ways German science was riding on its previous successes and it was not until the late war years and the post-war period that the delayed effects were felt. On the other hand, it must be kept in mind that German science was already beginning to lose its international position during this period with the rise of America as a scientific world power.

Because of its elitist ethos, the institutes of the Kaiser Wilhelm Society contained the cream of the scientific community, and they too were riding on the success of their pre-1933 prestige and status in the international community of science. While university institute personnel were replaced with party members when scientists were hounded out of their jobs or died, the Society often found other leading scientists in Germany to replace them.

199

For example, when Richard Goldschmidt emigrated to America (University of California, Berkeley) in 1936, Alfred Kühn was found to replace him. Adolf Butenandt replaced Carl Neuberg and Fritz von Wettstein was the successor to Carl Correns who died in 1933. In addition, Werner Heisenberg became director at the institute for physics when Peter Debye left for America. In the Society's case the purges did not decimate its strengths as may have been expected; except for one case (Fritz Haber's successor), the Society found high caliber scientists to continue the Society's traditions.

If Nobel prizes are another indicator of quality science, the Society also did well during the thirties and forties in this arena. In addition to the Nobel-prize winning scientists who worked there, three prizes were actually awarded to active KWS scientists during the 1930s and 40s: Richard Kuhn in 1938 for his work on carotenoids and vitamins, Adolf Butenandt in 1939 for his work on sex hormones, and Otto Hahn in 1944 for his 1938 discovery of nuclear fission. While none of these scientists was allowed to accept the prize because the German government forbade them to after Carl von Ossietzky, a Jew, was awarded the peace prize, it reflects the high-quality work being done and was a vote of confidence in the scientists who worked there.

But, more specifically, this book has argued for the resilience of science at a particular institution and it is therefore useful to highlight the main narratives running through the book while illustrating the central themes.

Ultimately, the purpose of this book is to contribute to a more complex picture of the fate of science and its organization in National Socialist Germany, to understand the dynamics of the interaction of a normal but prestigious scientific research organization with a totalitarian regime, and to bring to popular attention the fact that scientists who stayed in Germany during the Third Reich represented a broad spectrum of beliefs. Few were "Nazis" (whatever value this epithet might have), but many were serious scientists attempting to continue their work undisturbed. The means used to achieve this varied from collaboration and complicity to apolitical withdrawal; the middle ground, however, of outward accommodation and withdrawal into one's scientific work was most common.

To understand the variegated nature of the scientific enterprise in National Socialist Germany, it was necessary to uncover its many different layers at the Kaiser Wilhelm Society, a society not necessarily typical of general developments for science at the time. The layers of the scientific enterprise included a general survey of the Society's development in the context of National Socialist Germany down to case studies of research projects at individual institutes such as the nuclear power project and the survival of basic research in the life sciences in Berlin-Dahlem.

Horizontal layers of analysis in one period are not sufficient to understand the continuities and discontinuities with the periods before and after. It is therefore useful to identify three general themes that emerged from this analysis of the Society's transit through four contrasting political regimes in the drama of the first half of this century in Germany. One of the most dominant issues the Society faced before, during, and after the Third Reich was the question of the control of the state versus the autonomy of science. Because of its special nature, which had already developed during the founding period, the Society thought itself to be exempt from the demands of the state and used this status as an argument, especially during the Weimar years. Second, the organization of scientific activity passes through phases closely related to the socioeconomic context and political winds. Finally, scientific research is differentially affected by the demands of society depending on the type of science done and the scientists who do it.

From the Society's earliest days the founders sought to form a private organization patterned on the American model. Although they succeeded in creating a semiprivate research institution, the strong German tradition of state support entered into its organization in a variety of ways. For example, the Ministry was heavily involved in its founding and some of the directorships were state-supported. As a result of the inflation and economic crisis, during the Weimar years the Society turned increasingly to the state for financial support. This often led to tensions between the Society and the state as the latter attempted to influence and control the affairs of the Society. This encroachment manifested itself in the demand that the Society change its Wilhelmine name to something more democratic. Because of this increased dependence on the state, by the end of the Weimar years more than half the Society's financial support came from the state, thus reversing the Wilhelmine figure whereby most of the financial support came from industry and private sources. Although the sources of support changed, the Society protected its autonomy by referring to its special nature in Germany's scientific landscape; it did not become a public or state institution.

Because of the altered socioeconomic and political context and the changing fortunes of the Society during the Weimar years, there was a proliferation in the establishment of industry-related or applied science institutes, thus diverging from the general pattern of the earlier period with its stress on basic research. It was here that the demands of industry determined the nature and direction of the research done. The basic research tradition of the Society, however, continued to exist in those institutes already established in Berlin-Dahlem, such as the institutes for biology, chemistry, physical chemistry, and biochemistry. For these institutes, which became the hallmark of the Society and established its international prestige, it was a vibrant and lively period. It was here that Fritz Haber, Otto Warburg, Carl Correns, Richard Goldschmidt, Carl Neuberg, Otto Meyerhof, Otto Hahn, Lise Meitner, and Albert Einstein, among other scientific celebrities, worked.

By the middle of the Third Reich six of the foregoing nine scientists either had emigrated or were forced out because they were Jewish. This did not all happen during the first year of the seizure of power by the National Socialists. Max Planck attempted to protect many of the distinguished scientists (although not necessarily the ordinary assistants) by behind-the-scenes maneuvering. His lobbying allowed Neuberg, Meitner, Meyerhof, and others to stay until about 1938. It was because of the Society's semiprivate and prestigious nature that this could occur. But by 1938 the Society no longer had the leverage to maneuver and protect as the racial laws became more radicalized. The Society's semiprivate status both protected it *and* prevented it from achieving more autonomy. It protected it, in part, for example, during the implementation of the dismissal policy. As was shown in Chapter 3, the law was applied only to those institutes receiving more than 50 percent of their financial support from the government. Because the Society never achieved a totally private character, however, it was not immune from the influence of the state.

In other ways, too, the Society responded to the measures of the National Socialist regime by accommodation and passive opposition. There were few, if any, public protests, although during the early years Planck wrote several strong letters protesting measures that infringed on the autonomy of the Society. There was a display of defiance when the Society organized a Memorial Meeting on the anniversary of Fritz Haber's death in exile. Haber, who would have been able to stay under the exemption clause, refused to watch the dismissal of his co-workers and resigned in protest. But by resigning he allowed the National Socialists to take over his vacant institute, where the directorship was state-supported. It was precisely this elimination of opponents that the National Socialists desired. It was at Haber's institute, despite the written protests of Planck and the Society, that the "old guard" National Socialists set up an institute for military science and worked on gas warfare. It remained a Kaiser Wilhelm institute in name only; after all, Gerhard Jander and then Peter Adolf Thiessen were appointed by the government.

But the Society managed to preserve its autonomy in other appointments during the years 1935–37 as it sought to replace scientists who had died or emigrated. By the mid-thirties another lively and productive group emerged in Berlin with transplants from Göttingen including Adolf Butenandt, Fritz von Wettstein, and Alfred Kühn. Party membership played no role in the appointment of these and other scientists at the Society. In fact, in the life sciences much innovative and important work continued with N. W. Timoféeff-Ressovsky's group working on mutation genetics, with Butenandt's group on virus research and sex hormones, Kühn's and Butenandt's collaborative work on developmental physiology, and Otto Warburg's work in biochemistry. With support from the German Research Association's program in basic research in the life sciences many projects at the biological institutes of the Society could continue. It was at Timoféeff's institute that several Jews were sheltered and protected for the whole period of the Third Reich. It was also possible for Otto Warburg, who was half-Jewish, to remain in a visible position as director of the Kaiser Wilhelm Institute for Cell Physiology for the entire period. In addition, Wettstein protected several scientists at the Society who could not pursue careers at the university for political reasons.

The survival of basic biological research at the Society, and the fact that scientists who were barred from the university could find a niche there, are only several examples of the differences among the patterns of development at the Society and other institutions in National Socialist Germany. While complete coordination and nazification have been the hallmarks of change at the universities, academies, and science-funding organizations, this book has documented the different pattern of response and transformation at the Society. That the Society survived the nazification process more intact than the universities was attributed to a number of factors—including its prestige, its place within the German scientific landscape, and its structure. Yet these factors are not all necessarily due to the initiatives of the leaders or the scientists themselves. While purges of Jewish or communist personnel occurred at the universities and the Society, more Jewish scientists could stay on at the Society than the universities. During the early years of the regime, the Society was spared the attention, interest, and intervention of the National Socialists because of its research character. The universities as educational institutions were targeted as the place to implement policies designed to penetrate society and to indoctrinate a new generation of students to the National Socialist ideology. The students themselves had, in fact, played a key role in the transformation of university structures and in the spread of ideology and a world view. However, scientists at the Society—a semi-private research organization—could often bypass political training that had become a necessary complement toward achieving a professorship at the university. By the war years, of course, the National Socialists had begun to realize the importance of science for the state and for warfare and their attitude changed concerning governmental support of science.

Certainly another main feature of science and university policies in National Socialist Germany was centralization of, and control over, science. As I have shown, however, while centralization did take place at the government level with the merging of science departments at the appropriate ministries and the overlapping personnel at the most influential institutions, a polycratic science policy existed in the composite of science institutions. The Kaiser Wilhelm Society maneuvered itself among these competing agencies.

During the mid-thirties, the Society took a step closer to the industrial power block and elected presidents from industry out of expediency. Thus Carl Bosch, head of I. G. Farben and long-time senator of the Society, succeeded Planck in 1937, and after Bosch's death in 1940, Albert Vögler replaced him in 1941. The choice of Albert Vögler as president during the war reflected the needs of the times rather than the tradition of the Society. It was industry that had helped the Society in its early years while it negotiated with the National Socialists, and it was industry that acted as a buffer between the state and the Society in the later years. This ability to adapt and achieve advantageous measures accounts, in part, for the Society's resilience during the Third Reich.

But in a larger sense, this alliance with industry allowed scientists to retrieve some of the profession's losses. During the early years of the regime, social policies had changed and reduced the composition of the scientific community at universities and research institutions. Although the Society managed to preserve a higher degree of autonomy in its appointments than the universities, a second wave of losses occurred as scientists were drafted into the war. Lobbying from industrial scientists and industrialists, however, allowed scientists to be called back from the front into the laboratory. Vögler's and Prandtl's personal connections with Speer, Göring, and Milch guaranteed this. But the government's shift in policy toward science and scientists in 1942 was achieved through the justification that German science, especially physics, was on the decline vis-à-vis American science and therefore needed a boost in educational and research resources. For the National Socialist state, military power had taken precedence over ideology, but scientists were already looking toward the reconstruction of their fields for peacetime.

Because the various power centers in National Socialist Germany's polycratic state had conflicting and changing goals for science, the interface between National Socialism and science was more complex than the simplistic ideology and science dichotomy would suggest. For example, during the height of World War II scientists and administrators at the Society sought and won support for projects relating to plant breeding and agriculture. Many scientists opportunistically took advantage of the newfound financial support from Herbert Backe and the Ministry for Food and Agriculture to pursue their prewar goals. This in turn led to the flourishing of some areas of research. For the National Socialist state, however, support of agriculture and plant breeding was compatible with an ideological matrix of living space, blood and soil, autarky, and a New Order of German science in a conquered Europe. But the scientist often pursued the research independently of the justification for support. Ideology per se does not necessarily lead to the decline and destruction of science. During the war years, then, there was some complicity with the National Socialist state as the Kaiser Wilhelm Society slowly integrated itself more completely into the societal structure.

In other ways, too, the Society was thriving during the Third Reich. Its research budget increased from 5.5 million Reich marks in 1932 to 14.3 million Reich marks in 1944. This reflected the Society's alliance with the various power blocks—the ministerial bureaucracies, the army, the party, and industry—but World War II, apart from its destructive aspects, also had a stimulating effect on scientific research. Just as World War I had been a time of expansion and budget increases at the Society, so too did World War II offer large-scale support for scientific research. In other, nontotalitarian countries such as the United States, the military-industrial complex fueled scientific research during the war to a much greater degree; therefore, the historian must be careful to separate the influences of National Socialism from that of a war economy and society.

During the war, also, a great part of the nuclear power project in Germany took place at the institutes for physics (Berlin-Dahlem and Heidelberg) and chemistry. It was here that scientists, under the leadership of Werner Heisenberg, worked on a self-sustaining, energy-burning machine, and possibly a nuclear explosive. Many obstacles stood in the way of making quick progress, however—the deteriorating war context, the lack of resources, the attitude of the government, and the existing conflicts among the various groups. It seems, with the Kaiser Wilhelm institute scientists' emphasis on theory and pure research, practical steps were not taken to develop the research into a large engineering-style project.

The Society and its institutes emerged from World War II scattered throughout Germany as a result of the evacuation from Berlin to southwest Germany. Plans were under way by the occupying powers to dissolve the Society completely because it was seen to be part of Germany's war potential. The British, however, saw the Society in a more favorable light, and were the first to allow it to continue in the postwar years under its new name, the Max Planck Society. Far from being a phoenix-like new beginning for the Society, many of the traditions initiated and developed during its earliest years were to continue. Otto Hahn, who had been a scientific member of the Society since its founding, became one of those carriers of tradition and was elected president. Although it survived, the Society did not emerge unscathed from the debacle of the Third Reich, and as Hahn looked toward the future, postwar reconstruction of German science could begin.

Appendix

Emigres from the Kaiser Wilhelm Institutes

This Appendix was prepared using the List of Displaced Scholars published by the Notgemeinschaft der Deutschen Wissenschaft (1936), its supplement, and the more recent comprehensive biographical dictionary edited by Herbert Strauss and Werner Röder (1983). Names not listed in these sources were found in the files of the archive of the Max Planck Gesellschaft. Unfortunately, no list of emigrés exists at the Max Planck Gesellschaft Archive. I am grateful to Peter Kröner for providing me with a few additional names of biochemists who later became physicians. This data is far from complete, especially with regard to assistants who disappeared.

General List of Emigrés

Name	Position	Birthdate	Kaiser Wilhelm Institut	Dates	Field	Dismissal Dates	New Country/Position
Adler, Max	Assistant	1907	Strömungsforschung	1931–1933	Aerodynamics	1933	London
Auerbach, Charlotte	Doctoral Student	1899	Biologie	1931–1933	Biology. Mutation Genetics	1933	Great Britain
Baer, Erich E. F.	Assistant	1901	Physikalische Chemie	1927–1932	Physical Chemistry	1932	Switzerland, 1937=Canada
Beck, Paul	Researcher	1908	Metallforschung	1930–1932	Metallurgy	1933	Paris, since 35 Budapest
Beck, Walter	Privatdozent	1901	Physikalische Chemie	1925–1933	Physical Chemistry	1933	Warsaw
Bergmann, Max	Professor & Director	1886	Lederforschung	1933	Bioch. Org. Leather	1933	US: 34/35: Carnegie I. Tech. 36: Rock. I. Med.
Beutler, Hans	Privatdozent & Asst.	1896	Physikalische Chemie	1923–1933	Physical Chemistry	1934, emigr. 1936	US. 1936: U. Michigan, Ann Arbor
Bielschowsky, Max	Scientific Member	1896	Hirnforschung	1925–33, 36–39	Neurology	1933, 36	Netherlands, '33, Germany, '36, England '39
Bikermann, J. J.	Researcher	1898	Physikalische Chemie	1923/24	Physical Chemistry	1935	UK: 1935 Manchester U. Researcher, US, 45
Blaschko, Hermann	Assistant	1900	Medizinische Forschung, Heidelberg	1930–1933	Physiology	Not dismissed	UK: Cambridge U. Physiol. Dept.
Bodenstein, Dietrich	Assistant	1908	Biologie	1927–1933	Zoology	1933	US: Stanford, 34 or 35
Bredig, Max Albert	Assistant	1902	Physikalische Chemie	1928/29	Physical Chemistry	?	
Buchtal, Fritz	Assistant	1907	Faserstoffchemie	1929–1933	Muscle & Electro-physiology	1933	Copenhagen, 1933–35
Debye, Peter	Professor & Director	1884	Physik	1936–1940	Physics	1940(Emigr.)	US: Cornell, 1940
Delbrück, Max	Assistant	1906	Chemie	1932–37	Physics & Biology	1937(Emigr.)	US: Vanderbilt, 1937
Deutsch, Adam	Researcher	1907	Medizinische Forschung, Heidelberg	1930–1933	Organic Chemistry	1933	UK: Edinburgh Univ. since 1934
Duschinsky, F.	Assistant	1907	Physik	1933	Experimental Physics	?1933/34	Brussels University
Eisenschitz, Robert Karl	Researcher	1898	Chemie	1927–1933	Theoretical Physics	1933	UK: Royal Institution since 1934
Eisner, Hans	Researcher	n.d.	Physikalische Chemie	1930–1933	Colloidal Chemistry	1933?	Barcelona: since 1935
Ettisch, Georg	Privatdozent & Asst.	1890	Physikalische Chemie	1929–1930	Physico-chemical Biology	1933	Lisbon Univ. Cancer Institute
Farkas, Ladislaus	Assistant	1904	Physikalische Chemie	1928–1933	Physical Chemistry	1933	Cambridge, 1933/34; Jerusalem, 1935
Frank, Georg	Assistant	1899	Faserstoffchemie	1924–1933	Organic Chemistry	1933	Paris: Industrial activity, 1934
Freundlich, Herbert	o. Professor	1880	Physikalische Chemie	1923–1933	Physical Chemistry	1933	UK: University College, London, '33. US, '38
Friedlaender, Erich	Assistant	1901	Physikalische Chemie	1930–1933	Chemistry	1933	Paris: Perin's Laboratorie
Frommer, Leopold	Assistant	1894	Physikalische Chemie	1927–1933	Physical Chemistry	1933	UK: Industrial Activity, London, 1934
Fuchs, Walter Maximillan	Professor	1891	Kohlenforschung	1926–31 or 1927?	Chemistry	1933	UK: 1933 UK; 1934 US Rutgers, BRD 1949

Name	Position	Birth	Field (German)	Years	Field (English)	Emigr.	Destination
Gaffron, Hans	Assistant	1902	Biochemie/Biologie	1925–1937	Biochemistry	1937(Emigr.)	US: 1937, 1938/39, Rock. Fellow
Goldfinger, Paul	Assistant	1905	Physikalische Chemie	1929–33? or 27–29	Physical Chemistry	1933	Belgium: Asst. Univ. Liege
Goldschmidt, Richard	Professor	1878	Biologie	1914–1935	Genetics	1935	US; 1936 U. Cal. Berkeley
Gordon, Walter	Assistant	1893	Faserstoffchemie	1924–?	Physics	1933	Sweden, 1933–39 U. Stockholm
Gross, Fabius	Assistant	1906	Biologie	1930–1933	Zoology	1933	UK:1933/34, since '35 Marine Biol. Labs
Haber, Fritz	Director	1869	Physikalische Chemie	1911–33	Physical Chemistry	1933	UK
Heller, Wilfried	Assistant	1903	Physikalische Chemie	1931–1933	Chemistry	1933	France: Paris, Ast. Lab Rech. Physique. US, '38
Henke, Werner	Internist	1910	Medizinische Forschung	1934–1936	Virologist	1936	US: Univ. Pennsylvania Med school
Hertz, Mathilde	Privatdozent	1891	Biologie	1929?	Zoology	1935	UK: Cambridge, 1935, Dept. Zoology
Herz, William	Researcher	1908	Faserstoffchemie	Till 1933	Chemistry		1934/36 Industrial Act. Berlin
Herzog, Reginald Oliver	Professor, Director	1878	Faserstoffchemie	1919–1933	Fiber & textiles	1934	Turkey: 1934–35 Istanbul. Suicide 35
Hoffer, Max	Assistant	1906	Medizinische Forschung	1931–1933	Chemistry	1933	Switz.: Basel 1934, Hoffmann-La-Roche
Jacobsohn, Kurt	Researcher	n.d.	Physikalische Chemie	Till 1933	Chemistry	1933	Palestine, since 1935
Jollos, Viktor	Assistant/Prof.	n.d.	Biologie	1930–1934	Zoology	1934	US: Wisconsin, Zool. Dept. 1934
Kempner, Walter	Assistant	1903	Cell Physiology	1927–28, 33–34	Cellular physiology	1934	US: 1934, Duke Univ. Med. Cent.
Lasareff, Wladimir	Researcher	1904	Physikalische Chemie	1930–1933	Physical Chemistry	1933	Belgium: Liege, Lab. de Chimie Physique
Lederer, Edgar	Assistant	1908	Medizinische Forschung	1930–1933	Biochemistry	1933	France, Pasteur Inst., 33. USSR, 35. Fr. 1937
Laser, Hans	Privatdozent/Asst.	1899	Medizinische Forschung	1930–1934	Tissue Culture	1934	Molteno Institute Parasitology, 1934
Lehmann, Hermann	Assistant	1910	Medizinische Forschung	1934–1936	Biochemistry	1936	UK: 1936. 1936–42, at Cambridge.
Lowenbach, Hans	Researcher	1905	Himforschung (Neurophysiologie)	1933–1935	Psychiatry	1935	Norway, '35; US, '38
Marx, Walter	Research Fellow	1907	Medizinische Forschung	1933–34	Biochemistry	1934	US: Mt. Saini Hosp., 1934–37.
Meitner, Lise	Director, dept. Phys.	1878	Chemie	1912–1938	Theor. Physics, Radioactiv.	1938	Sweden, 1938, UK, 1960
Mesner, Gustav	Assistant	1905	Strömungsforschung	1931–1934	Aerodynamics, Hydro	1934	
Meyerhof, Otto	Professor/Director	1884	Medizinische Forschung	1924–1938	Biochemistry	1938	Paris till 1940, US: Univ. of Pennsylvania
Neuberg, Carl	Professor/Director	1877	Biochemie	1913–1936	Metabolism, Org. Chemie	1938	Palestine, 1938; US, 1940
Peterfi, Tibor	Professor/Research	1883	Biologie	1922–1935	Zoology	1934/35	Camb. Researcher Zool. Labs 1934/35. Copenh. 35, Turk, 39
Philip, Ursula	Researcher	1908	Biologie	1931–1934	Zoology	1934	UK: Univ. College, London
Plaut, Felix	Professor	1877	Deutsche Forsch. anst. f. Psych.	1918–1936	Psychiatry	1936	UK: 1930–40?

General List of Emigrés (*continued*)

Name	Position	Birthdate	Kaiser Wilhelm Institut	Dates	Field	Dismissal Dates	New Country/Position
Polanyi, Michael	Professor, Vice Direct	1891	Physikalische Chemie	1923–1933	Physical Chemistry	1933: Resigned	UK: 1933, Prof. Manchester Univ.
Rabel, Ernst	Director	1874	Ausländ. u. intern. Privatrecht	1926–1935	Law	1935	US: 1935 Ann Arbor Law School, Michigan
Rabinowitz, Bruno	Researcher	1903	Faserstoffchemie	1927–1934	Textile Tech. etc.	1934	Istanbul Univ. 1934, Dozent
Reis, Alfred	Professor	1882	Physikalische Chemie	1930–1933	Physical Chemistry	1933	Paris Univ. since 1933
Rheinstein, Max	Researcher	1899	Ausländ. u. intern. Privatrecht	1925–1933	Law	1933	US: 1933, Rockefeller at Columbia/Harvard, U. Chicago 35
Rosen, Boris	Researcher	1900	Physikalische Chemie	1928–1933	Spectroscopy etc.	1933	Belgium: Liege, Inst. Astr. 1934
Salzmann, Leo	Assistant	n.d.	Lederforschung	Till 1933	Org. & Synth. Chem. Dyes	1933	US: 1934 Industrial Activity
Seeligsberger, Ludwig	Assistant	1904	Lederforschung	Till 1933	Leather. Org. Chemistry	1933	Turkey, Ankara, Asst. Agricultural College
Simon, Ernst E.	Asst. later chief asst.	1902	Biochemie	1925–1933	Biochemistry	1933	France, 1933. Palestine 1935
Sollner, Karl	Privatdozent/Asst.	1903	Physikalische Chemie	1931–1933	Physical Chemistry	1933	UK; 1933–37 res. guest & cons. Un. College Lon. US 37
Stern, Curt	Privatd./Asst.	1902	Biologie	1928–1933	Zoology	1933	US: 1934 Asst. Prof. Rochester Univ.
Stern, Karl	Assistant	1906	Deutsche Forschans. f. Psych.	1932–1936	Neurology	1936	UK: since 1936, London, Hospital for Nervous Diseases
Tschachotins, Sergej	Assistant	1883	Medizinische Forschung	1930–1933	Physiology	1933	Copenhagen, 1933
Wassermann, Albert	Privatd. Asst.	1901	Chemie, Heidelberg	1931–1933	Biochemistry, Org. Chemie	1933	UK: London, Univ College 1933–35
Weiss, Joseph Joshua	Assistant	1905	Physikalische Chemie	1932–1933	Radiobiology	1933	UK: Cambridge, 1933, 34 w/Haber
Weissenberg, Karl	Professor	1893	Faserstoffchemie or Physik	1925–1933	Theor. Physics	1933	UK: Univ. College Southhampton
Weyl, Woldemar	Dept. Head	1901	Silikatforschung	1926–1936	Glass Technology	1936	US: Pennsylvania State Univ.

Directors and Replacements

Director	Institute	Date of Death	Departure Date	New Director	Arrival Date
Erwin Baur	Breeding Research	2-Dec-33		B. Husfeld (Temp.)	1933–36
				Wilhelm Rudorf	1-Apr-36
Max Bergmann	Leather Research		1933	Wolfgang Grassmann	1-Mar-34
Carl Correns	Biology	14-Feb-34		Fritz von Wettstein	1934
Peter Debye	Physics		1940	Werner Heisenberg	1942
Richard Goldschmidt	Biology		1936	Alfred Kühn	1-Apr-37
Fritz Haber	Physical Chemistry		1933	Gerhard Jander	
				Peter Adolf Thiessen	
K. W. Hausser	Physics	4-Jun-33			
Reginald Herzog	Fibre Chemistry		1934	Wilhelm Eitel (Temp.)	1934-35
Otto Meyerhof	Medical Research		1938	None	
Carl Neuberg	Biochemistry		1936	Adolf Butenandt	1-Nov-36
Oscar Vogt	Brain Research		1937	Hugo Spatz	1937

KWI for Physical Chemistry

Name	Position	Birthdate	Dates	Field	Dismissal	New Country/Position
Beck, Walter	Privatdozent	1901	1925–1933	Physical Chemistry	1933	Warsaw
Beutler, Hans	Privatdozent & Asst.	1896	1923–1933	Physical Chemistry	1934, emigr. 1936	US: 1936: U. Michigan, Ann Arbor
Bikermann, J. J.	Researcher	1898	1923/24	Physical Chemistry	1935	UK: 1935 Manchester U. Researcher
Goldfinger, Paul	Assistant	1905	1929–33 or 27–2	Physical Chemistry	1933	Belgium: Asst. Univ. Liege
Eisner, Hans	Researcher		1930–1933	Colloidal Chemistry	1933?	Barcelona: since 1935
Ettisch, Georg	Privatdozent & Asst.	1890	1929–1930	Physico-chemical Biology	1933	Lisbon Univ. Cancer Institute
Farkas, Ladsilaus	Assistant	1904	1928–1933	Physical Chemistry	1933	Cambridge, 1933/34; Jerusalem, 1935
Freundlich, Herbert	o. Professor	1880	1923–1933	Physical Chemistry	1933	UK: University College, London
Friedlaender, Erich	Assistant	1901	1930–1933	Chemistry	1933	Paris: Perin's Laboratoric
Frommer, Leopold	Assistant	1894	1927–1933	Physical Chemistry	1933	UK: Industrial Activity, London, 1934
Goldfinger, Paul	Assistant	1905	1929–33 or 27–2	Physical Chemistry	1933	Belgium: Asst. Univ. Liege
Heller, Wilfried	Assistant	1903	1931–1933	Chemistry	1933	France: Paris, Ast. Lab Rech. Phsique
Jacobsohn, Kurt	Researcher	n.d.	Till 1933	Chemistry	1933	Palestine, since 1935
Lasareff, Wladimir	Researcher	1904	1930–1933	Physical Chemistry	1933	Belgium: Liege, Lab. de CHimie Physique
Polanyi, Michael	Professor, Vice-Direc	1891	1923–1933	Physical Chemistry	1933: Resigned	UK: 1933, Prof. Manchester Univ.
Reis, Alfred	Professor	1882	1930–1933	Physical Chemistry	1933	Paris Univ. since 1933
Rosen, Boris	Researcher	1900	1928–1933	Spectroscopy etc.	1933	Belgium: Liege, Inst. Astr. 1934
Soellner, Karl	Privatdozent/Asst.	1903	1931–1933	Physical Chemistry	1933	UK; 1933–37 res. guest & cons. Un. College Lon. US 37
Weiss, Joseph Joshua	Assistant	1905	1932–1933	Radiobiology	1933	UK: Cambridge, 1933, 34 w/Haber

KWl for Biology

Name	Position	Birthdate	Dates	Field	Dismissal	New Country/Position
Auerbach, Charlotte	Doctoral Student	1899	1931–1933	Biology. Mutation Genetics	1933	Great Britian
Bodenstein, Dietrich	Assistant	1908	1927–1933	Zoology	1933	US: Stanford, 34 or 35
Gaffron, Hans	Assistant	1902	1925–1937	Biochemistry	1937 (Emigr.)	US: 1938/39, Rock. Fellow
Goldschmidt, Richard	Professor	1878	1914–1935	Genetics	1935	US; 1936 U. Cal. Berkeley
Gross, Fabius	Assistant	1906	1930–1933	Zoology	1933	UK: 1933/34, since '35 Marine Biol. Labs
Hertz, Mathilde	Privatdozent	1891	1929–?	Zoology	1935?	UK: Cambridge, 1935, Dept. Zoology
Jollos, Viktor	Assistant/Prof.	n.d.	1930–1934	Zoology	1934	US: Wisconsin, Zool. Dept. 1934
Peterfi, Tibor	Professor/Research	1883	1922–1935	Zoology	1934/35	Camb. Researcher Zool. Labs 1934/35. Copenh. 35
Philip, Ursula	Researcher	1908	1931–1934	Zoology	1934	UK:Univ. College, London
Stern, Curt	Privatd./Asst.	1902	1928–1933	Zoology	1933	US:1934 Asst. Prof. Rochester Univ.

KWl for Medical Research, Heidelberg

Name	Position	Birthdate	Dates	Field	Dismissal Date	New Country/Position
Blaschko, Hermann	Assistant	1900	1930–1933	Physiology	Not dismissed	UK: Cambridge U. Physiol. Dept.
Deutsch, Adam	Researcher	1907	1930–1933	Organic Chemistry	1933	UK: Edinburgh Univ. since 1934
Henle, Werner	Internist	1910	1934–1936	Virologist	1936	US: Univ. Pennsylvania Med school
Hoffer, Max	Assistant	1906	1931–1933	Chemistry	1933	Switz.: Basel 1924, Hoffmann-La-Roche
Lederer, Edgar	Assistant	1908	1930–1933	Biochemistry	1933	France, Pasteur Inst., 33. USSR, 35. Fr. 1937
Laser, Hans	Privatdozent/Asst.	1899	1930–1934	Tissue Culture	1934	Molteno Institute Parasitology, 1934
Lehmann, Hermann	Assistant	1910	1934–1936	Biochemistry	1936	UK: 1936. 1936–42, at Cambridge.
Marx, Walter	Research Fellow	1907	1933–34	Biochemistry	1934	US: Mt. Saini Hosp., 1934–37
Meyerhof, Otto	Professor/Director	1884	1924–1938	Biochemistry	1938	Paris till 1940, US: Univ. of Pennsylvania
Tschachotins, Sergej	Assistant	1883	1930–1933	Physiology	1933	Copenhagen, 1933

KWI for Fibre Chemistry

Name	Position	Birthdate	Dates	Field	Dismissal	New Country/Position
Buchtal, Fritz	Assistant	1907	1929–1933	Muscle & Electro-physiology	1933	Copenhagen, 1933–35
Frank, Georg	Assistant	1899	1924–1933	Organic Chemistry	1933	Paris: Industrial activity, 1934
Gordon, Walter	Assistant	1893	1924–?	Physics	1933	Sweden, 1933–39 U. Stockholm
Herz, William	Researcher	1908	Till 1933	Chemistry	?	1934/36 Industrial Act. Berlin
Herzog, Reginald Oliv	Professor, Director	1878	1919–1933	Fiber & textiles	1934	Turkey: 1934–35 Istanbul. Suicide 35
Rabinowitz, Bruno	Researcher	1903	1927–1934	Textile Tech. etc.	1934	Istanbul Univ. 1934, Dozent
Weissenberg, Karl	Professor	1893	1925–1933	Theor. Physics	1933	UK: Univ. College Southhampton

KWI for Leather Research

Name	Position	Birthdate	Dates	Field	Dismissal	New Country/Position
Bergmann, Max	Professor & Director	1886		Bioch. Org. Leather	1933	US: 34/35: Carnegie I. Tech. 36: Rock. I. Med.
Salzmann, Leo	Assistant	n.d.	Till 1933	Org. & Synth. Chem. Dyes	1933	US: 1934 Industrial Activity
Seeligsberger, Ludwig	Assistant	1904	Till 1933	Leather. Org. Chemistry	1933	Turkey, Ankara, Asst. Agricultural

Notes

Introduction

1. See Hüttenberger, 1976; Kershaw, 1985.

2. Merton, 1973, 267–78; Barber, 1978, quote on p. 9 (reprint of 1952 edition).

3. Merton, 1973, pp. 254–66 (reprint of "Science and the social Order" first published in 1938), and pp. 267–78 (reprint of "Science and Technology in a Democratic Order" first published under this title in 1942).

Chapter 1

1. This description is based on a photograph available at the archive of the Max Planck Gesellschaft (MPGA).

There are two books on the founding period of the Society—one by a West German social and economic historian, Burchardt (1975), and one by an East German scholar of society, Wendel (1975). Both pieced together the bureaucratic details involved in the negotiations to create the Society by the Prussian Cultural Ministry. My interpretation of this material differs in that I find it necessary to place these discussions in the context of the state of German science at the turn of the century as well as showing that an important part of the initiative came from the scientists themselves, who turned to the various ministers and bureaucrats with their suggestions. The purpose of this chapter is not to offer a detailed study of the creation of the Society, for which the reader can turn to Burchardt and Wendel, but rather to provide background on the origin and character of the Kaiser Wilhelm Society. After this chapter was written a book on the Kaiser's chemists was published; Johnson (1990) traces the transformation of the Chemical Reich Association into the chemistry institutes of the Society. This book is also a valuable contribution to the founding period of the Society. See also Beyerchen's (1988) stimulating account of science in the Wilhelmine period.

2. One thinks immediately of the prototypical example of the founding of the

Royal Society in seventeenth-century England, which was preceded by informal scientific meetings in London twenty years before, or of the time lag between plans
for the British Association for the Advancement of Science and its actual founding.

3. The "Preußische Kultusministerium" is referred to as the Prussian Ministry
of Education throughout this chapter. Its function was not restricted to culture in
a narrow sense but included science and education. The German literature uses the
phrase "Preußische Kultusministerium" to refer to the various Prussian ministries
as their names changed before and after World War I.

4. For biographical material see Sachse (1928) and the article by Franz Schnabel
in the *Neue Deutsche Biographie* (1953). For a more recent study on Althoff's "system" see Bernhard vom Brocke (1980).

5. Schmidt-Ott writes in his memorandum "Althoff's Pläne für Dahlem" that
Althoff left no summarized account of his plans for Dahlem. We are therefore
dependent on Schmidt-Ott's account and interpretation of Althoff's plans. Geheimes
Staatsarchiv (GStA), Berlin-Dahlem, Friedrich Schmidt-Ott Papers, Rep. 92, No.
13: "Anfänge der Kaiser Wilhelm Gesellschaft" and "Althoff's Pläne für Dahlem."
Partially reprinted in *Fünfzig Jahre Kaiser-Wilhelm-Gesellschaft und Max-Planck-
Gesellschaft zur Förderung der Wissenschaften*, 1911–1961 (1961). (Hereafter *50
Jahre*.) See also Schmidt-Ott's memoirs, *Erlebtes und Erstrebtes* (1952).

6. "Althoff's Pläne für Dahlem," p. 11.

7. Wendel (1975) and Burchardt (1975) seem to me to underestimate Emil
Fischer's role, perhaps because they did not use the Fischer Papers. His importance
in the founding of the Society is amply documented in the Emil Fischer Papers at
the Bancroft Library, University of California, Berkeley. See Fischer's letters to Althoff
and to the other Reich Chemical Association planners, Walther Nernst and Wilhelm
Ostwald.

Otto Jaeckel refers to Emil Fischer as Harnack's "mächtiger Hintermann" in a
letter to "Euere Excellenz" (Rudolf Valentini) of 29 August 1913. Zentrales
Staatsarchiv (ZStA) Merseburg, German Democratic Republic, 2.2.1/No. 21289/
Vol. II/Fol. 109–109d.

8. A copy of the 1909 memorandum is available in the Hugo A. Krüß Papers,
Staatsbibliothek Preußischer Kulturbesitz (StPKB) Biologie Institut, 1906–11:
"Denkschrift für die Errichtung Biontologische Institute in Dahlem."

9. Cited from Burchardt, 1975, p. 19.

10. StPKB, Krüß Papers, File 122, Kaiser Wilhelm Institut, Physik, December
1906.

11. For the founding and early history of the KWI for Physics see Macrakis
(1986, 1989a).

12. ZStA, Postdam, Reichsministerium des Innern (RMdI), No. 26782, Lenard
to the Minister, 1 September 1933.

13. See R. S. Turner, 1971.

14. E. Fischer and E. Beckmann, 1913, p. 8. See Cahan on the Physikalisch
Technische Reichsanstalt and Pfetsch (1974) (1989, pp. 103–27).

15. For material on the creation of the Chemische Reichsanstalt see ZStA,
Potsdam, RMdI, No. 5557: "Die Errichtung einer Chemischen Reichsanstalt," Fol.
1–10, 22 December 1908, Fischer, Nernst, and F. Oppenheim to "Seiner Excellenz
Dr. von Bethmann-Hollweg." For a detailed narrative history of the Chemische
Reichsanstalt see Johnson's (1980) dissertation, which puts the motive for the cre-
ation of the association in the context of "big science" in imperial Germany. His

book version (1990) looks at the Reich Chemical Association and its partial transformation into the Kaiser Wilhelm Society in the context of modernization. See also Wendel (1975) for a reproduction of the memorandum.

16. In the copy at the Merseburg archive the word "Stiftung" is crossed out and was later replaced by "Institut." See ZStA, Merseburg, 2.2.1/No. 21278/KWG Organisation und Vorbereitung, 1909–11. A final version is printed in *50 Jahre*, pps. 71–79.

17. "Denkschrift von Harnack an den Kaiser," 21 November 1909. Reproduced in *50 Jahre*, 1961, pp. 82, 89. This ringing nationalistic phrase is omitted from the second version of Harnack's memorandum "Gedanken über eine neue Art der Wissenschaftsförderung" (21 May 1910), MPGA.

18. Ibid.

19. ZStA, Merseburg, Rep. 76Vc, Sect. 1, Tit. XI, Pt. IX, No. 12, Vol. I, Fol. 72, *New York Staatszeitung*, 27 April 1910.

20. ZStA, Potsdam, Theodor Lewald Papers, 91, 6 February 1910, p. 2.

21. Valentini to Harnack, 10 December 1909, *50 Jahre*, p. 94.

22. Bethmann-Hollweg to the Kaiser, 7 April 1910, *50 Jahre*, p. 103; also Valentini to Königliche Staatsministerium, 13 April 1910, ZStA, Merseburg, Rep. 76Vc, Sect. 1, Tit. XI, Pt. IX, No. 12, Vol. I.

23. ZStA, Merseburg, Rep. 76Vc, Sect. 1, Tit. XI, Pt. IX, No. 12, Vol. I, 6 May 1910: "Aufzeichnung über eine Besprechung, betreffend die Durchführung der . . . Kaiserlichen Automobil-Club." Reprinted in *50 Jahre*, pp. 106–9.

24. Omitted from *50 Jahre*, but see ZStA, Potsdam, RMdI, No. 8970, Fol. 41–42.

25. ZStA, Merseburg, Rep. 76Vc, Sect. 1, Tit. XI, Pt. IX, No. 12, Vol. I, 6 May 1910.

26. Deutsche Staatsbibliothek, East Berlin, Adolf von Harnack Papers, Berlin, Emil Fischer to Adolf von Harnack, 14 October 1910.

27. ZStA, Potsdam, "Die Koppel-Stiftung," No. 1153, Fol. 21, and 3 October 1910, Fol. 156.

28. According to Weiss, the prize was designed to show that Darwinian biology did not pose a threat to the political status quo. Krupp left the execution of the contest to Ernst Haeckel and Krupp donoted 30,000 marks to be used to answer the question: "What can be learned from the theory of evolution about internal political developments and state legislation?" (Weiss, 1986, pp. 41–42). For biographical material on the Krupp family see Köhne-Lindenlaub, 1982.

29. Krupp Archiv, Essen, IV E 272, KWI for Biology, 1910–21. Krupp to Geheimes Civil-Cabinet, von Valentini, 2 July 1910, Fol. 333–34. More on Krupp and biology above in section on the creation of institutes.

30. See ZStA, Merseburg, Rep. 76Vc, Sect. 1, Tit. XI, No. 47, Vol. II, 1911–34.

31. See ZStA, Merseburg, Rep. 76Vc, Sect. 1, Tit. XI, Pt. IX, No. 12, Vol. I, Fol. 199–206.

32. ZStA, Merseburg, Rep. 76Vc, Sect. 1, Tit. XI; Pt. IX, No. 12, Vol. I, Versammlung, 11 January 1911.

33. Ibid.

34. Ibid. The minutes of this meeting are only partially reprinted in *50 Jahre*. For example, the discussion on the first bylaw and the institutes to found are omitted.

35. Ibid., Fol. 199, p.5.

36. The senate consisted of bankers and industrialists elected during the first meeting—Eduard Arnhold, Walther von Brüning, Ernst Giesecke, Max von Guilleaume, J. N. Heidtmann, Prince Henckel von Donnersmarck, Krupp von Bohlen und Halbach, Franz von Mendelssohn, and Wilhelm von Siemens—and members from the elite of industry named by the Kaiser—Böttinger, Count C. von Carmer, Willy von Dirksen, Leopold Koppel, Walther vom Rath, and Paul von Schwabach.

37. ZStA, Merseburg, Rep. 76Vc, Sect. 1, Pt. IX, No. 12, Vol. I, Fol.3/6.

38. Fischer, 1911, pp. 3–30.

39. ZStA, Merseburg, Rep. 92; Schmidt-Ott; B LXXVI 6 Vol. II; KWG; Biologie Fol. 75–87. Also available in the Krüß Papers.

40. For example, Driesch wrote to Harnack that he read in the newspapers that "his excellency" is in the process of forming scientific research institutes. Rather than advancing his own school of thought he takes up the cudgels for Wilhelm Roux's program of Entwicklungsmechanik and the "young science of exact zoology" because, at this late date, his interests have gravitated toward philosophy. Deutsche Staatsbibliothek [East] Berlin, Adolf von Harnack Papers. Hans Driesch to Adolf von Harnack, 24 October 1910.

41. At about 1900 what we consider "biology" was divided institutionally in Germany into botany and zoology, whereas in America there actually existed departments of biology which encompassed different subdisciplines. This division gave the appearance of a somewhat disunified discipline in Germany.

42. MPGA, Cohnheim, 26 January 1910, Merseburg, Rep. 76Vc, Sect. 1, Tit. 11, Pt. Vc, No. 47, Vol. I, Naturwissenschaftliche Forschungsinstitute, Fol. 26–34.

43. This meeting was printed as a report and published: *Zur Errichtung biologischer Forschungsinstitute durch die Kaiser-Wilhelm-Gesellschaft zur Förderung der Wissenschaften,* Stenographischer Bericht über die auf Einladung des Ministers der geistlichen und Unterrichtsangelegenheit am 3. Januar 1912 gepflogene Beratung. Also available at the MPGA, KWG, Generalverwaltung, KWI for Biology, 1222, the Krüß Papers, StPKB, and in the Merseburg files for the KWI for Biology. The individual "Gutachten" are also available at the MPGA, KWG, Generalverwaltung, Vorbereitung der Gründung biologischer und medizinischer Institut, 12–18 October 1911, the Krüß Papers, the Krupp Archiv, and the Merseburg files for the KWI for Biology.

44. See "Zur Errichtung . . . ," Krüß's overview of the suggestions in the Gutachten, pp. 10–17. See also Harnack's words: "It appears to be a general opinion that German science needs a research institute for heredity and developmental mechanics" (pp. 101–2).

45. For speculation on the social factors and conditions for the flourishing of genetics in America see Rosenberg, 1976, pp. 196–209.

46. Horder and Weindling argue that Theodor Boveri's research "continued on lines independent of Mendelism" (1985, p. 215).

47. No literature exists on the interesting question of why Mendelian genetics from 1900 on did not take hold in Germany. Harwood (1984) discusses the reception of Morgan's chromosome theory in Germany and the interwar debate over cytoplasmic inheritance, which points us in the right direction for the twenties and thirties.

48. T. W. Richards to Emil Fischer, 11 April 1913. Copy in Krüß Papers, KWI for Biology, Vol. 1. The opinions of Jacques Loeb and T. H. Morgan were also

sought; they both liked von Uexküll's approach, but Abraham Flexner thought of him as "wild and unsound" (ibid).

49. Goldschmidt, 1960, p. 78.

50. Ibid., p. 79.

51. See Chapter 2 for a fuller discussion of the industry-related institutes.

52. ZStA, Merseburg, Rep. 76c, Sect. 1, Tit. 11, Pt. IX, No. 12, KWG, Vol. III. Harnack in 3–5th Annual Report, April 1916.

53. Willstätter, 1949, p. 230.

54. ZStA, Merseburg, Rep. 76c, Sect. 1, Tit. 11, Pt. IX, No. 12, KWG, Vol. III, 1914–18. 12 August 1914 Meeting on Occasion of the War.

55. Johnson, 1990, p. 186; Rasch, 1987.

56. ZStA, Merseburg, Rep. 76Vc, Sect. 2, Tit. 23, Litt. A, No. 121. Forschungsinstitut für Gaskampf und Gasmittel. Haber to the Minister, 18 September 1917.

57. Haber, 1986, pp. 127–28, 139–41.

58. ZStA, Merseburg, Rep. 76Vc, Sect. 2, Tit. 23, Litt. A, No. 121. Forschungsinstitut für Gaskampf und Gasmittel.

59. ZStA, Merseburg, Rep. Vc, Sect. 1, Tit. 8, Stiftungs-Sachen, No. 17. Kaiser Wilhelm-Stiftung für Kriegstechnische Wissenschaft.

Chapter 2

1. Important studies on various aspects of science and science policy (primarily physics and the *Notgemeinschaft*) in the Weimar period by Forman (1974), Schroeder-Gudehus (1972), and, more recently, Feldman (1987) have been helpful in providing background insight and information for this chapter, although they might not be specifically cited.

2. ZStA, Merseburg, Rep. 76c, Sect. 1, Tit. 11, Pt. IX, No. 12, Vol. IV, 1918–22. Valentini to Harnack, 11 February 1919, Fol. 70–71.

3. Ibid. Minutes of senate meeting, 3 June 1919, Fol. 111–18.

4. MPGA, KWG, KWI for Biology, Hauptaken, 1917–22. Correns to Harnack, 24 December 1918.

5. ZStA, Merseburg, Rep. 76c, Sect.1, Tit. 11, Pt. IX, No. 12, Vol. IV, 1918–22. Executive Committee meeting, 17 February 1920, Fol. 184–86.

6. Ibid. Senate meeting, 11 May 1920, Fol. 226–37.

7. ZStA, Potsdam, RMdI, No. 8970/2, KWG, 1917–21. Memorandum, 20 May 1920, Fol. 44–58.

8. ZStA, Merseburg, Rep. 76c, Sect. 1, Tit. 11, Pt. IX, No. 12, Vol. IV, 1918–22. Koch, Minister for Science (Learning), Art, and National Culture, 13 July 1920, Fol. 250.

9. ZStA, Potsdam, RMdI, No. 8970/2, KWG, 1917–21. Minutes from the meeting on the financial position of the Society, 7 August 1920, at the Prussian Ministry for Science, Art and National Culture, Fol. 76–82.

10. Ibid. The German word used to describe the relationship is "Treuhänder," which literally means trustee.

11. ZStA, Merseburg, Rep. 76c, Sect. 1, Tit. 11, Pt. IX, No. 12, Vol. IV, 1918–22. 7 October 1920, Fol. 253, 281.

12. ZStA, Potsdam, RMdI, No. 8970/2, Becker to the Finance Minister, 20 December 1920.

13. ZStA, Merseburg, Rep. 76c, Sect. 1, Tit. 11, Pt. IX, No. 12, Vol. IV, 1918–22. Harnack to the Prussian Ministry for Science (Learning), Art and National Culture, 29 March 1921, Fol. 330. This question was also discussed in the senate meeting, 18 March 1921, Fol. 369–72.

14. Ibid. Minutes of senate meeting, 18 March 1921, Fol. 369–72.

15. Ibid.

16. Ibid. Statutes, Fol. 431, Prussian Diet, 18 March 1922, Fol. 469.

17. Ibid. Report on the seventh yearly meeting of the Kaiser Wilhelm Society, Fol. 373–74.

18. MPGA, KWG, 345, "Bericht über Finanzlage, 3. Dez. 1923."

19. The major works on the NGW are Zierold (1968) and Nipperdey and Schmugge (1970).

20. MPGA, KWG, Haber-Sammlung. Folder on Emergency Association of German Science. Haber announcement of the founding of the Emergency Association of German Science.

21. Forman, 1973, pp. 161–65. Section IV on "Science as *Machtersatz.*"

22. Adolf von Harnack Papers, Deutsche Staatsbibliothek [East] Berlin. Carl Heinrich Becker, "Recht und Staat im Neuen Deutschland." A reprint in the Harnack–Becker correspondence.

23. GStA, Becker Papers, Harnack to Becker, 20 March 1929.

24. MPGA, KWG, Protokolle des Verwaltungsausschuses, 88, Fritz Haber to Adolf von Harnack, 24 November 1925. Haber was also careful to point out that by electing a scientist to the council possible sources of financial support from industry or government would not be threatened.

25. MPGA, KWG, Wissenschaftlicher Rat, 178, Fritz Haber to Adolf von Harnack, 4 June 1928.

26. Ibid.

27. Ibid.

28. MPGA, KWG, 178, Ludwig Prandtl to Fritz Haber, 28 June 1928.

29. Ibid. Haber statement, 30 July 1928.

30. Ibid. Excerpts from the executive meeting, 3 November 1928.

31. Planck, ed. (1936). *25 Jahre Kaiser-Wilhelm-Gesellschaft zur Förderung der Wissenschaften*, pp. 147–51.

32. See Forman (1973) on internationalist ideology after World War I for the case of physics.

33. ZStA Potsdam, RMdI, No. 8970/10; from the KWG's application to the Reich Ministry of the Interior, Fol. 439–41: "Auslandsinstitute."

34. Harnack, 1928, pp. 20–21. The phrase is from a general sketch of the Society written by Friedrich Glum.

35. ZStA, Potsdam, RMdI, Fol. 439–41.

36. MPGA, KWG, 2531, Harnack-Haus, Liste der Veranstaltungen, 18 March 1930–March 1938 (includes 1929).

37. Ibid.

38. This institute is discussed in Chapter 6, in the section on eugenics at the Kaiser Wilhelm institutes.

39. "Zwischen Logarithmen und Experimenten ein Sprung in Kühles Wasser," *Berliner Zeitung*, 21 November 1937. Harnack House still exists in Berlin-Dahlem and is used by the American Military High Command.

40. Schreiber, 1951, p. 96.

41. ZStA, Potsdam, RMdI, No. 26783/1, KWG, 1922–29. See memo by the

Prussian Minister of the Interior on the change of name, 22 February 1929, Fol. 381–82. Also 14 March 1929, Fol. 388.

42. ZStA, Potsdam, RMdI, No. 26782/1. The vice president of the Kaiser Wilhelm Society (Krupp von Bohlen und Halbach) to Reich Minister Dr. Wirth, 2 July 1930. Copy also in MPGA, KWG, 195: "Namesänderung der KWG."

43. GStA, Berlin-Dahlem, C. H. Becker Papers, Rep. 92, K, No. 3715. Leipart to Krupp von Bohlen und Halbach, 14 July 1930. Also in MPGA, KWG, 195.

44. Ibid.

45. Schreiber, 1951, p. 119. From the Reichstag proceedings, Vol. 428 (176 Meeting 1930), p. 5486 B.

46. ZStA, Potsdam, RMdI, No. 26782/1, Ministry's note of the executive meeting, 28 October 1930.

47. ZStA, Merseburg, Rep. 76Vc, Sect. 1, Tit. 11, Pt. IX, No. 12a, III, KWG. Richter to Glum, 28 October 1929. Richter reports that he has heard from the Kaiser Wilhelm Society that the Ministry wants Harnack to resign so that Becker can take his place. He denies this. Some newspaper clippings from February 1930 also deny that Harnack is resigning. *Kreuzzeitung*, 6 February 1930; *Deutsche Zeitung*, 4 February 1930; *Berliner-Börsenzeitung*, 4 February 1930.

48. ZStA, Merseburg, Rep. 76c, Sect. 1, Tit. 11, Pt. IX, No. 12a, III. Saemisch to Krupp, 29 June 1930.

49. *Frankfurter Zeitung*, 10 July 1930; *Berliner Tageblatt*, 15 July 1930; *Berliner Lokalanzeiger* (n.d.).

50. ZStA, Merseburg, Rep. 76Vc, Sect. 1, Tit. 11, Pt. IX, No. 12a, III. Fol. 438, no title of newspaper. Fol. 440, *Berliner Lokalanzeiger*. Fol. 441, *Abendblatt der National-Zeitung*.

51. See Gay (1968) and Laqueur (1974) for "Weimar culture."

52. The institutes and founding dates have been collected from the *1928 Handbook of the Society* edited by Adolf von Harnack (1928).

53. See Reishaus-Etzold, 1973. One wonders how the phenomenon can be both "state monopolistic" and "chemistry monopolisitic."

54. See *1928 Handbook of the Society*, pp. 54–59, section on the Kaiser Wilhelm Institute for Coal Research in Mühlheim-Ruhr, esp. p. 55; from an excerpt of Fischer's lecture published in the journal *Steel and Iron*. For archival material relating to the institute see MPGA, KWG, 1319–49.

55. See *25 Jahre KWG*, 1936, pp. 87–90.

56. MPGA, KWG, 2059–2105; files on the Silesian coal institute in the Kaiser Wilhelm Society.

57. Rasch (1988) discusses these last two points in his article on the Silesian coal institute.

58. For information on the Kaiser Wilhelm Institute for Iron Research see *1928 Handbook*, pp. 64–70, the *25 Jahre KWG*, 1936, pp. 77–81, and *Jahrbuch der Max-Planck-Gesellschaft*, 1961, pp. 230–57. For archival material see MPGA, KWG, 1946–69.

59. See *1928 Handbook*, pp. 76, *25 Jahre KWG*, 1936, pp. 71–77, *Jahrbuch der MPG*, 1961, pp. 601–26. For archival material see MPGA, KWG, 1871–1945.

60. For information on the leather institute see *1928 Handbook*, pp. 81–85, *25 Jahre KWG*, 1936, pp. 90–93, and *Jahrbuch der MPG*, 1961, pp. 258–90. See also MPGA, KWG, 1790–1824.

61. See *1928 Handbook*, pp. 76–81; quote on pp. 77–78.

62. This information has been synthesized from the sections on the silicate

research institute from the *1928 Handbook*, pp. 85–89, *25 Jahre KWG*, 1936, pp. 81–84, and *Jahrbuch der MPG*, 1961, pp. 704–19, and from MPGA, KWG, 2276–2314.

63. For the case of the chemical industry and academic chemistry see Haber, 1971.

64. Chargaff, 1978, p. 50.

65. See the essays collected in Kleinkauf, von Döhren, and Joenicke (1988), Krebs (1979, 1981), and see Nachmansohn (1979). See Kohler (1982, pp. 38–39) for an American view of Warburg's lab.

66. Laqueur, 1974, p. 183.

67. See Döring, 1975. I would like to thank Michael Hubenstorf for bringing this book to my attention.

68. Biographical material on Otto Warburg has been pieced together from Hans Krebs's (1981) unsurpassed biography on Warburg and from Dean Burk's *Dictionary of Scientific Biography* article (Vol. 14, pp. 172–77). Krebs worked in Warburg's laboratory in Dahlem and knew him for much of his career. Burk, an American cell physiologist, was also closely associated with Warburg. For less than flattering remarks on Warburg's autocratic rule see Kohler (1982, pp. 38–39).

69. See Nachmansohn, 1979, pp. 268–75.

70. See Kleinkauf et al., 1988, p. 112.

71. From Krebs's description in Kleinkauf et al., 1988, p. 113.

72. Nachmansohn, 1979, pp. 311–27.

73. It is beyond the scope of this chapter to go into details of the very important work on genetics, development, and protozoology. Some recent work on German genetics between the wars has been written by Harwood (1984, 1985, 1987). Saha (1984) has written about Carl Correns and an alternative approach to genetics. Richmond (1986) has recently written on Richard Goldschmidt and sex determination. For Spemann see the biography by Mangold (1953).

74. See Goran, 1967, chapter on the Dahlem Kaiser Wilhelm institutes.

75. See Jaenicke (1935) and Goran (1967, chapter on the search for gold); Nachmansohn (1979, pp. 181–82) makes the parallel between wealth in the air and wealth in the water.

76. Coates 1939, p. 1664.

77. Chargaff, 1978, p. 51.

78. Planck, 1936, p. 5.

Chapter 3

1. MPGA, Otto Hahn Papers, Lise Meitner to Otto Hahn, 21 March 1933. Hahn was in America from the end of February to about May 1933 giving the George Fischer Baker lectures at Cornell University. This is an excerpt from just one of the remarkable letters Meitner wrote characterizing political and scientific developments in Germany at this time.

2. The most widely used English equivalents for the German term are "coordination," "alignment," and "synchronization"—words that fail to capture all the nuances of the German; therefore, in this study, the term *Gleichschaltung* will be used untranslated. Despite the importance of this term and concept few studies in English or German have defined its meaning, assuming readers interpret it as a general

rubric for the National Socialists' measures of coordination. Although it was a contemporaneous word and concept, the 1937 *Meyer's Lexicon* does not contain a separate entry; the "Gleichschaltung Laws," however, are referred to in the entry on the "Deutsches Reich" (Vol. 2, p. 1439). The standard reference work in Germany today, *Der grosse Brockhaus*, has a concise and accurate definition whereby "Gleichschaltung" is designated as a National Socialist slogan used to describe the "orientation of all state organs of the Reich and the federal states, the socio-political organizations and institutions to the National Socialist Reich government and its ideology. Simultaneously, the activity of academics, scientists and artists was regimented or suppressed" (Vol. 4, p. 562). Mehrtens (1985, p. 83) argues that the concept does not designate the mere process of integration into the National Socialist state but rather a more complex process in which the political and professional interests of those affected interacted with state and party organizations. See also Helmut Krausnick's "Stationen der Gleichschaltung" (1983).

3. The literature on the universities under National Socialism includes general studies such as Hartshorne's pioneering study written in 1937, and the 1966 lecture series at the University of Munich on universities in the Third Reich; studies on specific institutions such as Vezina (1982) on the University of Heidelberg, Adam (1977) on the University of Tübingen, Becker, Dahms, and Wegeler (1987) on the University of Göttingen; and studies on university professors such as Kelly's (1973) dissertation on the efforts of the NSDAP to create a National Socialist professoriate. Most of the literature on scholars and scientists focuses on the universities while neglecting research institutions such as the KWG.

4. Hartshorne, 1937, p. 112. This statement is not in Planck's one-paragraph recollection of his visit to Hitler. Hartshorne reported on a rumor about the Planck–Hitler meeting. It could be that Hitler made this or a similar statement to Carl Bosch, who also lobbied Hitler on behalf of Jewish scientists.

5. Hahn, 1966, p. 112.

6. *Reichsgesetzblatt*, Pt. I, No. 34, 7 April 1933.

7. MPGA, KWG, General Administration Files, 531: "Gesetz zur Wiederherstellung des Berufsbeamtentums, Schriftverkehr, Statistik, Erlasse, 25 March 1933–28 September 1933." Hereafter MPGA, KWG, 531. Aktennotiz, 7 April 1933, by Ernst Telschow.

8. Ibid. See Cranach letter to Planck, 10 April 1933, and Planck's letter to Cranach and Telschow, 12 and 14 April 1933.

9. Frank, 1949, p. 381.

10. Archive for the History of Quantum Physics, Bohr Scientific Correspondence (22,2), H. Kopfermann to Bohr, 23 May 1933. Archive located at the Office of the History of Science and Technology, Berkeley.

11. MPGA, KWG, 531. Aktennotiz, 21 April 1933, by Cranach.

12. Glum, 1964, p. 440.

13. MPGA, KWG, 531. Aktennotiz, 21 April 1933, by Cranach.

14. MPGA, KWG, 541, Gesetz . . . KWI for Physical Chemistry, Haber to Schmidt-Ott, 22 April 1933.

15. Fritz Haber to Minister for Science, Art and Folk Culture, 30 April 1933. Many copies are available in various archives. See MPGA, Haber-Sammlung, 881. Also reproduced in *50 Jahre*, 1961, p. 190.

16. ZStA, Merseburg, Rep. 76Vc, Sect. 2, Litt. A., No. 108. Planck to Vahlen, 11 August 1933.

17. MPGA, KWG, 534, Gesetz . . . KWI for Biology, Richard Goldschmidt to Friedrich Glum, 9 May 1933. Goldschmidt to the Kaiser Wilhelm Society, Arndt, 19 September 1933, where he reports that he implemented the ordered notices.

18. Ibid. Otto Meyerhof to Friedrich Glum, 5 August 1933. In this letter he was also specifically referring to a Jewish secretary in his institute who had served the Society for many years.

19. MPGA, KWG, 531, Präsident (Glum in Vertretung) to the Directors of the Kaiser Wilhelm Institute, 27 April 1933.

20. MPGA, KWG, 531: "Aufzeichnung über eine Sitzung der Direktoren der Berliner Kaiser Wilhelm Institute am 5. Mai 1933." This translation is faithful to the German, which uses a lot of passive voice. The passive voice adds anonymity to the processes, as if no one is responsible.

21. This is not apparent in the minutes of the meeting recorded at the MPG archives, but Warburg reported it to Rockefeller Foundation representatives. Rockefeller Archives (RF), Tarrytown, New York, H. M. Miller Diaries, pp. 19–20.

22. MPGA, KWG, 531: "Aufzeichnung. . . ."

23. Bundesarchiv (BA), R 18/5328, Fol. 103, Eitel; "Denkschrift über eine Neuorientierung der Kaiser Wilhelm Gesellschaft." After World War II, Wilhelm Eitel became a "Project Paperclip" scientist. Project Paperclip was an American postwar recruitment program for German scientists, which ignored many scientists' National Socialist background. See Lasby (1971) and Bower (1987) on Project Paperclip. In order to qualify, Eitel underwent a thorough political check. The results of this investigation are in his file at the National Archives. Although American officials found that he did indeed join the party, many colleagues testified on his behalf stating he was susceptible to social movements. Otto Hahn, for example, said Eitel had joined the Nazi movement early, probably "because of his enthusiasm for new movements in general." American officials apparently heard a rumor that Eitel had been actively engaged in dismissing Jewish scientists. But even Hartmut Kallmann, a Jewish scientist forced to leave Haber's institute, showed that the dismissal of scientists was the result of a governmental order.

American officials were also searching for a missing Frick–Eitel correspondence. Frick was the Minister of the Interior. The material I have presented here amply documents the Eitel–Frick contact. I found the Eitel memorandum in the Reich Ministry of Interior's Frick file for the Kaiser Wilhelm Society.

24. National Archives (NA), Record Group (RG) 330, Box 37. Eitel's statement on his affiliation with the National Socialist party.

25. For the fate of universities see works cited in note 3. See Grau, Schlicker, and Zeil (1979) for a study of the Berlin Academy of Sciences during the "fascist dictatorship." On the Notgemeinschaft/Forschungsgemeinschaft in "three epochs" (Weimar, Third Reich, and the Federal Republic) see Zierold (1968).

26. None of the earlier accounts of this meeting have established the exact date it occurred except for a guess of the spring. (Macrakis [1986, p. 359] first established the date of the meeting.) O'Flaherty's thin article specifically on "Max Planck and Adolf Hitler" says "Planck, who is the main source of information about the Hitler affair, does not tell us the exact date of the visit" (1956, p. 438). O'Flaherty correctly adds it probably took place shortly after Haber's resignation. Planck's (1947) account printed shortly after the war in *Physikalische Blätter* is one paragraph. The introductory paragraph by the magazine editors refers to a spring 1933 meeting. Other secondary sources about this meeting (Beyerchen, 1977, pp. 42–43; Heilbron, 1986, p. 153) are based primarily on Planck's account. The exact

date can be established in Hans Heinrich Lammers to Friedrich Glum, 9 May 1933, MPGA, KWG, Financial Files, 361. See also BA, R 43 II, 1227a, Max Planck to Adolf Hitler, 2 May 1933.

27. BA, R 43 II, 1227a, Max Planck to Adolf Hitler, 2 May 1933.

28. Planck, 1947, p. 143.

29. BA, R 43 II, 1227a. Telegram, Planck to Hitler, 23 May 1933. Also quoted in the printed minutes of the meeting, MPGA, KWG, 126, 22; Hauptversammlung am 23 May 1933.

30. This is quoted from *The New York Times* story headlined "German Scientists Rally behind Hitler," 24 May 1933. The phrase "rifle at rest" is not quoted in the report on the meeting; it is, however, in Planck's talk deposited in MPGA, KWG, 127, 22, Hauptversammlung am 23 May 1933, Vol. II: Rede des Herrn Präsidenten. "Gewehr bei Fuß zu stehen."

31. BA, R 18/5328, Fol. 109–10.

32. Ibid. Mendelssohn and Schottländer had belonged to the Society since it was founded during the Kaiserreich. Merton, who was in his late fifties, represented the metal industry, which maintained its own research institute within the KWG.

33. ZStA, Merseburg, Rep. 76c, Sect. 1, Tit. 11, Pt. IX, No. 12, Vol. VIII; MPGA, KWG, 535, Gesetz zur Wiederherstellung des Berufsbeamtentums, KWI for Textile Chemistry. Ewald Rech, "Die Kaiser Wilhelm-Institute in Dahlem. Eine Bruttstätte jüdische Ausbeuter, Bedrücker und Marxisten!," 21 May 1933.

34. MPGA, KWG, 531, Planck to the Reich Minister of the Interior, 19 June 1933.

35. MPGA, KWG, 545, Planck to the Prussian Minister of Science, Art, and Education, 13 June 1933.

36. MPGA, KWG, Gesetz, 543, Planck to Erwin Baur, 21 July 1933. MPGA, KWG, Gesetz, 534, Planck to Richard Goldschmidt, 21 July 1933. MPGA, KWG, 539, Planck to Richard Kuhn, 21 July 1933.

37. MPGA, KWG, 531, 18 September 1933.

38. See MPGA, KWG, 531, Aktennotiz, 2 October 1933—a two-page report on the meeting by the KWG. See BA 21 (29 September 1933) for a longer report by the government and for a list of the intended personnel changes. See also documents relating to this action at ZStA, Potsdam, RMdI, KWG, 26782/4. Glum wrote to the Reich Ministry of the Interior discussing the NSBO meeting. Hecker apparently had received an order from the Reich Ministry to check if the second through fourth paragraphs of the dismissal law had been properly applied. Glum to the Reich Minister, 30 September 1933.

39. Ibid.

40. Hecker also uses this analogy for his activities: they (*the Obleute*) are the "eyes" and the findings go on the "head" of the organization. BA, R 21, Fol. 193, p. 5.

41. BA, R 21, Fol. 181, 29 September 1933.

42. The German is "Elephant im Porzellanladen." For detailed documentation of this whole action see ZStA, Merseburg, Rep. 76Vc; Sect. 2, Tit. XXIII, Litt. A, No. 123a; KWI for Biochemistry, 1933–35. This includes many letters to and from Neuberg and the president and director of the KWG and letters with Delatrée-Wegner's story. Even institute members quoted what Neuberg allegedly said. Copies of these files are also available at the Academy Archives and the MPG archive.

43. Academy Archive of the German Democratic Republic, East Berlin, KWG, 63, NSDAP. See Aktennotiz by Cranach, 7 April 1934, for example. See also ZStA,

Potsdam, RMdI, No. 26782/4 where letters to Planck from Glum (17 October 1933) and Cranach (11 October 1933) document their political activity and reliability. By 18 May 1934, Glum was still writing statements denying an alleged "democratic/pacifist attitude before the National Socialist revolution." Glum was also accused of writing a subversive book called *Das geheime Deutschland*.

44. As we can see from the chart, however, a vague designation "other institutes" is used, thus not making it clear whether this includes solely industry-supported institutes or others. There is also a discrepancy in the number of personnel, which later became 1,061.

45. BA, R 18/5328, "Vermerk" by Pfundtner on Vögler visit, 8 November 1933.

46. MPGA, KWG, Gesetz zur Wiederherstellung des Berufsbeamtentums, Direktoren, die Gleichzeitig Staatsbeamte sind, 13 June 1933.

47. MPGA, KWG, 538, Gesetz, KWI for Leather Research, Planck to Reich Minister of the Interior, 26 May 1933. Bergmann to Planck, 3 July 1933.

48. MPGA, KWG, 534, Gesetz zur Wiederherstellung des Berufsbeamtentums, and ZStA, Potsdam, RMdI, KWG, 26782/3, Planck to Reich Minister of the Interior, 21 July 1933.

49. ZStA, Potsdam, RMdI, KWG, 26782/3, copy of Hertz's filled-out questionnaire for the law for the restoration of the civil service, signed 11 September 1933, expert report filled out by a Dr. Groth from the "Expert for Race Research at the Reich Ministry of the Interior," 17 October 1933, and attached genealogical table.

50. Ibid. Planck to the Reich Minister of the Interior, 11 November 1933.

51. MPGA, KWG, Gesetz, KWI for Breeding Research, 543, Erwin Baur to Glum, 22 May 1933. Buttmann to the President of the KWG, 21 March 1934. Fanny Du Bois-Reymond to Glum, 30 March 1934. Du Bois-Reymond's questionnaire for the law for the restoration of the civil service, her genealogical table, and her expert report are also in the files of the Reich Minister of the Interior in Potsdam.

52. Nachmansohn, 1979, p. 254. See also Krebs, 1981, p. 59.

53. For the story of the building of the Cell Physiology Institute by the Rockefeller Foundation see Macrakis (1986, 1989). Glum wrote to Warburg on 20 May 1933 that the law cannot be applied at his institute because of the "form of financing." MPGA, KWG, 543.

54. Ibid.

55. Siemens Archive, Munich, Memorandum Re: Notice for Professor Warburg, Dahlem, 14 June 1941. I have found only two documents pertaining to Warburg's case; one is a memo written on 14 June 1941 that I have seen only in the Siemens Archive. Siemens was a senator, industrialist, and, at one point in the 1940s, vice president of the Society. The other document quoted extensively below is Warburg's affidavit at the Nuremberg trials.

56. Institut für Zeitgeschichte (IFZ), Munich, Nuremberg Trial Documents. Brack Document No. 13; see also Warburg's affidavit. I have quoted from a document originally in English. Warburg was apparently dismissed when there was no president active at the Society.

57. Siemens Archive, Notice for Professor Warburg, p. 3.

58. RF, 1.1/717/10/57, Rüdin to Felix Plaut, 25 October 1935.

59. Nachmansohn, 1979, p. 283.

60. American Philosophical Society (APS), Carl Neuberg Papers, Neuberg to Butenandt, 7 March 1947. I would like to thank Lily Kay for sending me this folder.

61. ZStA, Merseburg, Rep. 76Vc, Sect. 2, Tit. XXIII, Litt. A, No. 123a, Max Planck to Minister Rust, 24 July 1934. A most remarkable five-page letter trying to persuade the Minister to keep Neuberg in the interests of the Society. Neuberg had received Rockefeller support.

62. Interview, Ernst Telschow and Adolf Butenandt with Kristie Macrakis, Tutzing bei München, June 1985. Transcript available at the American Institute of Physics.

63. MPGA, KWG, 536, Gesetz zur Wiederherstellung des Berufsbeamtentums, KWI for Brain Research. Oscar Vogt to the KWG, 21 March 1933. Also in ZStA, Merseburg.

64. Ibid. Draft of letter "in the name of the president" of the Kaiser Wilhelm Society, July 1933.

65. Ibid. Minutes of a meeting about the Kaiser Wilhelm Institute for Brain Research, 22 September 1933.

66. MPGA, KWG, 547, Gesetz, Leaves and Dismissal because of Communist Party Membership, 1934–39. Oscar Vogt to Max Planck, 13 March 1934.

67. Ibid. Ludwig Prandtl to Glum, 13 March 1934.

68. See the Notgemeinschaft der deutschen Wissenschaft (1936) listing of scientists. The emigré table is based on this source as well as on the newer and valuable multivolume work edited by Strauss and Röder (1983). Despite this tool, it is still difficult to arrive at a complete and accurate count.

69. APS, Neuberg to Butenandt, 7 March 1947, where he tells Butenandt of his life after leaving Germany.

70. Hahn, 1966, p. 109.

71. Max von Laue, "Fritz Haber," *Die Naturwissenschaften*, 1934, Vol. 22, p. 1. Bodenstein also wrote an obituary in the proceedings of the Prussian Academy of Science.

72. ZStA, Merseburg, Rep. 76Vc, Sect. 2, Tit. 23, Litt. F.XVI, 1933–34. NSDAP, Deputy to the Führer to Bernhard Rust, 1 March 1934 to Deputy of the Führer, Rudolf Heß, 24 March 1934.

73. Hahn 1957, p. 244, and Max-Planck-Gesellschaft Administration, Personnel Files, Munich: "Otto Hahn."

74. Krupp Archive, Essen, IV E 251, KWG, Allgemeines, Vol. 8: "Persönliche Erlebnisse bei der Vorbereitung zu Gedächtnisfeier für Fritz Haber am 29 Januar 1935," Planck, 6 February 1935. This personal report is marked "strictly confidential" and has remained buried in the archives until its first appearance here.

75. This is Planck's description and reaction to the Minister's circular in his "Persönliche Erlebnisse. . . ," 6 February 1935.

76. 15 January 1935, Kunisch (In Vertretung) an die Herren Rektoren der Universitäten, Abschrift. Copies available at MPGA, Max von Laue Papers, Siemens Archive, SAA, LG, 880, Krupp Archive, IV E 251, KWG, Allgemeines, Vol. 8.

77. Krupp Archive, IV E 251, Allgemeines, Vol. 8, 17 January 1935, Planck to Gustav Krupp von Bohlen und Halbach.

78. Max Planck to Bernhard Rust, 18 January 1935, Krupp Archive, MPGA, and Siemens Archive.

79. Ibid. Planck's personal remembrance, Krupp Archive.

80. Ibid. 24 January 1935, Bernhard Rust to Max Planck.

81. Planck's personal remembrance, Krupp Archive.

82. Ibid.

83. Ibid.

84. Hahn, 1960, p. 13.

85. "Nazis Gag Haber Services," *The New York Times*, 26 January 1935, p. 10; "Haber Memorial Held in Berlin," *The New York Times*, 30 January 1935, p. 6.

86. See Hoffmann's monumental work on the history of German resistance, for starters (1977, p. x).

Chapter 4

1. See files at the Bundesarchiv (BA), R 43 II, 1229. Ernst Rüdin to the Führer und Reichskanzler, where Rüdin's requests for increased funding for race hygiene studies are approved and the institute receives increased support from the new regime. Rüdin wrote directly to the Reich Chancellor Hitler asking for a grant of RM 20,000 on 22 November 1935. He wrote asking for funding to "fulfill the race hygiene advances of the state." Hitler's State Secretary and head of the Reich Chancellery warmly supported Rüdin and offered him financial support. BA, R 2/ 12019: "Sitzungsbericht betreffend das Kaiser Wilhelm Institut für Physikalische Chemie und Elektrochemie am 5. Dezember. 6 December 1933"; MPGA, KWG, KWI for Physical and Electrical Chemistry: "Einseztung Janders."

2. Hartshorne, 1937, pp. 54–56.

3. Ibid.; Maier, 1966, p. 88.

4. Maier, 1966, pp. 102–5.

5. Rust and Krieck, 1936.

6. Ibid.

7. See Maier, 1966; Krieck, 1936; Baeumler, 1934; and Heidegger, 1934.

8. BA, R 73/15179: "Wissenschaft und Vierjahresplan." 18 January 1937. From Bachér's lecture, pp. 17–31.

9. Ibid.

10. Das Preußische Ministerium für Wissenschaft, Erziehung und Volksbildung; also known as "Das Preußische Kultusministerium," the Prussian Cultural Ministry. The German name of the Reich Ministry was either Das Reichsinnenministerium or Reichsministerium des Innern.

11. MPGA, KWG, 169: "Verhältnis Kaiser-Wilhelm-Gesellschaft zur Preußischen Unterrichtsverwaltung und zum Reich," 1 July 1930–23 October 1940. Aktenvermerk.

12. ZStA, Merseburg, Rep. 76Vc, Sect. 1, Tit. 11, Pt. IX, No. 12a, Vol. III, KWG. Richter to Glum, 28 October 1929. Richter reported that he heard from the Kaiser Wilhelm Society that the Ministry wants Hamack to resign so that Becker can take his place. He denies this. Some newspaper clippings from February 1930 also deny that Harnack is resigning: *Kreuzzeitung*, 6 February 1930; *Deutsche Zeitung*, 4 February 1930; *Berliner-Börsenzeitung*, 4 February 1930.

13. See *Handbuch über den Preußischen Staat*, Herausgegeben vom Preussischen Staatsministerium für das Jahr 1935, Vol. 139 (Berlin: R.V. Deckers Verlag). This handbook lists the new ministry as "Reichs- und Preußisches Ministerium für Wissenschaft, Erziehung and Volksbildung." There was a decree on 1 May 1934 unifying the Prussian Ministry with the Reich Ministry. See also ZStA, Potsdam, the introduction to the finding aid book for the Reichserziehungsministerium (REM) documents in Potsdam by Hans-Stephan Brather, 25 April 1960.

14. ZStA, Potsdam, Ministerium für Wissenschaft, Kunst und Volksbildung:

Hauptbüro. Betrifft: Entstehung bezw. Entwicklung des Ministeriums seit der Machtergreifung, January 1939–42. REM, No. 2. This quote comes from an unpublished book by REM which chronicles the creation and development of the Ministry and its three sections, including science, since the seizure of power.

15. See the *Handbuch über den Preußischen Staat* for a description of the office for science. See MPGA, KWG, 606, Circular, 12 May 1939, for the official statement on Mentzel's appointment as head.

16. See Siegmund-Schultze (1984, p. 28) for quote from academy yearbook and general biographical information. Kater (1974, p. 136) refers to Vahlen as "Papa." *Degeners Wer ist's?* 10th edition, Berlin: Verlag Hermann Degener (1935), p. 1639; Kürschners-Deutscher Gelehrten-Kalender (1941), p. 969. Berlin Document Center (BDC), file on Theodor Vahlen. Archive of the Humboldt University (AHU) Berlin, personal file on Vahlen.

17. BDC, file on Otto Wacker. Otto Wacker to the Reich Minister (Rust), 5 April 1939.

18. Goudsmit, 1947, pp. 142–45.

19. AHU, personnel file on Erich Schumann; BDC, Schumann file; Glum, 1964, pp. 451–52.

20. For biographical material on Mentzel see Zierold, 1968, p. 190, and Fischer, 1984, pp. 125–28. See also archival material in BA, Militärarchiv, Freiburg, RL 3156, Milch Files, for stinging attacks on Mentzel's scientific abilities. For documentation of his membership in the NSDAP, SA, and SS see material in BDC. There is a copy of the Habilitation committee's report on Mentzel of 12 November 1933 in his BDC file.

21. Glum, 1964, p. 450.

22. See Konrad Meyer's BDC file and Heinrich Becker's article on agricultural institutes at the University of Göttingen in Becker et al., 1987, pp. 416, 420–21.

23. MPGA, KWG, 128, Hauptversammlung, Vol. I, 4 June 1934. Buttmann to Planck, 7 May 1934.

24. BA, R 18/5328. To the president of the Physikalisch-Technische Reichsanstalt, Johannes Stark, n.d. The letter has no signature but is probably from Wilhelm Frick. It is very likely, however, that Stark himself drafted the letter.

25. Ibid.

26. Ibid., p. 8.

27. Ibid. "Vorschläge für die Organisation der wissenschaftlichen Forschung durch das Reichsinnenministerium."

28. Ibid. "Forschungsgemeinschaft und Forschungsdienst " For minutes on the first meeting on the subject of the unification of German science see "Note," 17 October 1933.

29. Ibid. Albert Vögler to Reich Minister Frick, 19 October 1933. Enclosure 2 with Vögler to Frick letter: "Richtlinien für die Arbeit der Kaiser Wilhelm Institute."

30. Ibid. Note on Vögler visit.

31. Ibid. "Deutsche Forschung." Fol. 335–39.

32. MPGA, KWG, 202, "Reichsakademie der Forschung (Deutsche Forschungsakademie) Reichsforschungsrat," 12 October 1934–31 December 1935. Planck and president of the NGW (no name or signature) to Reichsminister, 12 October 1934. It is beyond the scope of this chapter to offer a full-scale discussion and analysis of the Reich Academy. For more detailed accounts see Zierold, 1968, pp. 194–206. For Stark's account of Rust's attempts at creating an academy and Stark's opposi-

tion in defense of "freedom of research" see Stark, 1987, pp. 123–31. See also Heiber, 1966, pp. 809ff. See also BA, R 21/ 205: "Denkschrift zur Gründung der Reichsakademie der Forschung." R 21/10998: "Organisation der Reichsakademie der Forschung."

33. BA, R 21/ 10998: "Begründung," p. 3. Bylaws cited in full in Zierold, 1968, pp. 194–97. Quote on p. 196.

34. Hartshorne, 1937, pp. 25–26.

35. James Franck Papers, University of Chicago, Fritz Haber to James Franck, 3 June 1933.

36. RF 717.13.110, Haber to L. W. Jones, 8 October 1933. This is not my translation. Original German not in file.

37. Ibid.

38. Ibid. L. W. Jones to Warren Weaver, 14 October 1933.

39. Ibid. L. W. Jones to Fritz Haber, 14 October 1933.

40. MPGA, Otto Hahn Papers, Otto Hahn to Max Planck, 16 October 1933.

41. MPGA, KWG, 92, Einladung und Protokolle des Verwaltungsausschusses, 18 October 1933. I am quoting from the unedited minutes of the meeting. The final version deleted the sentence on Jander.

42. MPGA, KWG, 1169, KWI for Physical Chemistry and Electrochemistry, 1169: "Einsetzung Professor Jander als kommissarischer Direktor, 1933." Telschow to Glum, 4 August 1933.

43. ZStA, Merseburg, Rep. 76Vc, Sect. 2, Tit. XXIII, Litt. 4, KWI for Physical Chemistry and Electrochemistry 1933–34. Planck to Vahlen, 11 August 1933.

44. Ibid. Pfundtner to Prussian Minister, 12 August 1933.

45. Ibid. Planck to the Minister for Science, Art and People's Culture. The angry tone of this statement is further highlighted because there is no salutation such as "Dear Minister——."

46. Ibid. Gerhard Jander to Vahlen, 14 April 1933.

47. Ibid. Becker (Reichswehrministerium, Heereswaffenamt) to Vahlen, 10 April 1933.

48. BA, R 2/12019: "Sitzungsbericht betreffend das Kaiser Wilhelm-Institut für physikalische Chemie und Elektrochemie am 5. Dezember," 6 December 1933.

49. Ibid.

50. Krüß Papers, STPKB, KWI, Notebook 27, Planck to Bernhard Rust, 11 April 1935.

51. Ibid.

52. Ibid.

53. BDC, File on Peter Adolf Thiessen.

54. MPGA, KWG, 1178, KWI for Physical Chemistry Minutes of Meeting 19 June 1935. The word obviously (*selbstverständlich*) was added in the final edited version.

55. *Die Naturwissenschaften*, 11 June 1937, Vol. 24/25, p. 371.

56. MPGA, KWG, 1175, KWI for Physical Chemistry, Thiessen to Telschow, 4 May 1940, where Thiessen informs Telschow of the honor and encloses an invitation to celebrate on Wednesday, 22 May 1940.

57. MPGA, KWG, 188, Beziehungen zum Reichswehrministerium, 1933–42. Summary of relation of KWG to the Reichswehrministerium. Planck to von Blomberg, 15 December 1933.

58. BA, R 26 III, l: "Bildung eines Forschungsrats."

59. Ibid.

60. Zierold, 1968, p. 217.
61. Ibid.
62. BA, R 26 III, 1: "Bildung eines Forschungsrats."
63. BA, R 43 II/1232b, Rusts speech, 25 May 1937. See also *Völkischer Beobachter*, 26 May 1937, No. 146: "Eröffnung des Reichsforschungsrates in Anwesenheit des Führers."
64. MPGA, KWG, 203, Reichsforschungsrat, Führers Erlass, 9 June 1942.
65. See Boelcke, 1969, p. 121.
66. Bundesmilitärarchiv, Freiburg, RL 3156, Milch Papers: "Stenographischer Bericht über die Besprechung über den Reichsforschungsrat," 6 July 1942.
67. Ibid., pp. 26–27.
68. Ibid., p. 45.
69. Ibid, p. 50. The Society has Vögler to thank for his "personal attempts" in securing the UK-Stellung of KWG scientists. See minutes of the KWG senate meeting of 1942.
70. Ibid. See list at end of minutes of meeting.
71. MPGA, KWG, 203, Reichsforschungsrat Schriftverkehr, 16 March 1937–12 January 1945. Göring, der Reichsmarschall des Großdeutschen Reiches, to Albert Vögler, 24 July 1942.
72. For a complete list see Zierold, 1968, p. 244. In 1943 there were eleven heads, by 1944 there were twenty (see pp. 250–51).
73. Ibid.
74. Zierold discusses the formation of two card index files (1968, pp. 246–47). The first one had a research index with the names of researchers and their area of research, an institute index with a listing of all research institutes including those of the Wehrmacht and industry, and a subject index of research areas. Work for this index was done at the library of the Technische Hochschule in Berlin under the direction of the head librarian Predeek, who was appointed by Mentzel on 17 May 1943. By November, however, the index had been destroyed by an air raid on Berlin. Because most of the material was destroyed a new index was begun in Rossla. It must be this index that has survived in the Bundesarchiv (R 26 III, Vol. 8) and on microfilm at the National Archives (T-84).
75. Ibid., p. 248.
76. Ibid., pp. 248–49. For more details on the background to the decision and on Osenberg see Ludwig, 1974, pp. 237ff, 243 ff, and Zierold, 1968, pp. 248ff.
77. Zierold, 1968, pp. 248–49.
78. Ibid., p. 250.
79. MPGA, KWG, Reichsforschungsrat, Schriftverkehr, 16 March 1937–12 January 1945. Telschow to Vögler, 6 May 1943. Telschow wrote to Vögler explaining that the RFR has no head at the moment. Mentzel would soon be talking to Reichsmarschall Göring about the final steps. Vögler never did become president, and I have found no other documents referring to his candidacy.
80. Dr. Erxleben to Bechtold, 9 September 1942, concerning Heisenberg's appointment at the Kaiser Wilhelm Institute for Physics. Institute for Contemporary History, Munich, MA-116/5/ Rosenberg Files.
81. Ludwig Prandtl Papers, Ramsauer Memorandum to Rust, 20 January 1942. See also Beyerchen, 1977, pp. 184–90.
82. See Hölsken, 1984.
83. ZStA, Potsdam, REM, No. 932, Forschungsinstitute, 1938–42, Fol. 49. Note, 23 January 1939, by Mentzel.

Chapter 5

1. MPGA, KWG, 95, Sammlung der Berichte über die Hauptversammlungen. Bericht über die 25. Hauptversammlung der Kaiser Wilhelm Gesellschaft zur Förderung der Wissenschaften, 10/11 January 1936, p. 3.

2. Ibid., p. 5.

3. Ibid., p. 6

4. This is quoted from *The New York Times*, 12 January 1936, account of the celebration: "Reich Scientists Uphold Freedom."

5. "Förderung der Wissenschaft von gestern, vorgestern und heute," *Völkischer Beobachter*, 11 January 1936.

6. "The Last Stand," *The New York Times*, 13 January 1936. The subheading of this chapter is borrowed from *The New York Times* article.

7. "Blick nach innen: ein beschränkter Kreis," *Das Schwarze Korps*, 9 January 1936.

8. Archives du Centre de Documentation Juive Contemporaine, CXLV-625, Philipp Lenard to Herr Minister (Rosenberg), 18 January 1936. Ibid., CXLV-594, Lenard to Rosenberg, 9 January 1936.

9. BA, R 43 II/ 1227. Reichsminister Bernhard Rust to Herr Reichskanzler! Mein Führer [Hitler]! 3 February 1936.

10. Ibid. See also answer, 8 February 1936. Copy of Krupp von Bohlen und Halbach letter from 30 January 1936 enclosed where he mentions a meeting on 9 January 1936 about the KWG.

11. The claim that Stark wanted to become president of the KWG is based on a letter from Bernhard Rust to Adolf Hitler where Rust states that Stark, who is overburdened with work at the NGW and PTR, has offered his services for the KWG presidency. Rust thought that a Stark candidacy would be rejected by many influential people. The claim is perpetuated by Beyerchen, 1977, p. 144, Zierold, 1968, p. 208, and Hermann, 1973, p. 91.

12. It seems that Planck's term officially ended in March 1936 but was extended until June 1937. I have found no written documents explaining the extension of his term by a little over a year. The search for a successor seemed to have dragged on about a year. Kleinert reprinted excerpts from the correspondence between Lenard and Stark as it relates to the presidency of the KWG (1980, p. 35).

13. Ibid., Lenard to Stark, 8 May 1933 (p. 36), and 6 April 1933 (p. 37).

14. Ibid., Stark to Lenard, 3 February 1933 (p. 35).

15. Ibid., Lenard to Ministerialdirektor, 6 April 1936 (p. 37).

16. Ibid., Stark to Lenard, 6 April 1936 (p. 37).

17. Most of the information for this section is pieced together from MPGA, KWG, 46; "Schriftverkehr zur Satzung und Satzungsänderung, 1934–1944; Schriftverkehr zum Wechsel im Präsidentenamt 1936/1937."

18. See Planck's letter of 5 March 1937 to Albert Vögler, Carl Bosch, Gustav Krupp von Bohlen und Halbach, Hugo Andreas Krüß, Friedrich Saemisch, Schmidt-Ott, Stauss, Otto, Fritz Thyssen, Hjalmar Schacht, Kurt Schröder, Carl Eduard Herzog von Coburg, Peter Debye, Eugen Fischer, Fritz von Wettstein, Max Hartmann, in which a meeting between 26 and 29 April is announced.

19. Planck refers to Bosch's meetings at the Ministry in a letter of 2 March 1937, Planck to Bosch, MPGA, KWG, 46.

20. BA, R 2/12543.

21. See MPGA, KWG, 46, for drafts of the changes in the statutes. Emphasis added.

22. See MPGA, KWG, 41, for the final printed version of the statute of 22 June 1937.

23. MPGA, KWG, 56: "Auszug aus den Niederschriften über die Sitzung des Senats . . . am 29. Mai 1937." Of course, during the Third Reich one was very careful about what was committed to paper in an official document that could easily fall into the hands of the wrong people. The representatives of the REM who sat on the boards also received copies of the minutes.

24. Interview, Ernst Telschow and Adolf Butenandt with Kristie Macrakis, Tutzing bei Munich June, 1985.

25. Glum, 1964, p. 487.

26. BA, R 2, 12543, Presseausschnitt, 11 September 1937. No title.

27. General information on the Four Year Plan is based on reading in Petzina (1968), the sole book devoted exclusively to the Four Year Plan; Carr (1972) places the developments in the context of foreign policy; see Milward's (1965) incisive analysis of the German war economy.

28. Quoted from Ludwig (1974, p. 217), who is quoting from Eichholtz (1969, p. 141).

29. Petzina, 1968, p. 123.

30. Hayes, 1987, p. 183. Hayes believes it is "one of the legends of the Third Reich" that the "Four Year Plan began as or became 'in practice an IG Farben plan.'"

31. MPGA, KWG, 2891: "Ministerpräsident Generaloberst Göring Rohstoff- und Devisenstab." Telschow to Köster, director, KWI for Metal Research, 14 July 1936, and Telschow to Körber, director, KWI for Steel Research, 15 July 1936. These letters are almost identical except for the one paragraph in which Telschow coerces Körber to go along with the project.

32. Ibid. Telschow to Körber, 15 July 1936.

33. Ibid. Löb to Körber, 22 July 1936.

34. Ibid. See letter from July 1936.

35. Ibid. Thiessen to Göring, 15 July 1936.

36. BA, R 73, 15179: "Wissenschaft und Vierjahresplan." Reden anläßlich der Kundgebung des NSD-Dozentenbundes, 18 January 1937. Summary of Thiessen's lecture, pp. 4–16.

37. MPGA, KWG, 1799, KWI für Lederforschung als "Vierjahresplan-Institut" (Institut der Reichsstelle für Wirtschaftsausbau), 8 February 1939–15 October 1944. See listing of a budget for twelve Four Year Plan institutes.

38. See MPGA, KWG, 230, Reichsstelle für Wirtschaftsausbau, Verträge, 15 April 1940–24 March 1944. Contracts between the German Reich and Dr. Isolde Hausser, a research contract from April 1940 to March 1941, the German Reich and Professor Rudorf, director of the KWI for Breeding Research, Aktennotiz about a conference between the RWA and the KWI for Leather Research on 11 April 1940.

39. See Beyerchen, 1977, p. 72.

40. Academy Archive of the German Democratic Republic, East Berlin, KWG, No. 6. Planck to directors of the Kaiser Wilhelm institutes, 27 June 1936.

41. Ibid. Thienemann to the KWG, 16 July 1936.

42. Ibid. Rudorf to the KWG, 29 July 1936.

43. Ibid. The Reich and Prussian Minister for Science, Education and People's Education, 19 February 1937. This letter is signed by Zschintzsch, a state secretary.

44. Ibid.

45. Ibid. The Reich and Prussian Minister for Science, Education and People's Education to the KWI for Leather Research, 15 April 1937.

46. Ibid. Mentzel to the KWG, 30 November 1939.

47. Ibid.

48. Ibid.

49. See Wendel, 1985.

50. Academy Archives KWG. No. 6 Graßman to the KWG, 13 December 1939.

51. Ibid. Fritz von Wettstein to the KWG, 16 December 1939.

52. Ibid. Walther Bothe to KWG, 12 December 1939.

53. Ibid. Erlaß, 14 November 1940, Reich Ministry for Science, Education and People's Education.

54. Ibid. 18 June 1942, Reich Ministry for Science, Education and People's Education.

55. Archive of the Academy of Sciences of the German Democratic Republic, East Berlin. Files of the Kaiser Wilhelm Society, 29, Deutsch-Englische Beziehungen, Gründung eines Kaiser Wilhelm Institut in England. Aktennotiz, 25 July 1938. See Aktennotiz, 1 August 1938, conference with Minister Wacker.

56. Ibid. Aktennotiz, 1 October 1938. See also Krüß's description of his meeting with Bragg and Edward Andrade in England. StPKB, Krüß Papers, 8 October 1938.

57. StBK, Krüß Papers, Bosch to Bragg, 14 October 1938; Telschow to Krüß, 9 February 1938; list of twenty-nine people for a dinner at Harnack House for the English exchange professors, 24 February 1939.

58. Ibid. F. G. Donnan to Krüß, 5 March 1939.

59. The exchange of visits was reported in *Nature*, 17 June 1939, where Verschuer's and Kuhn's talks in England are described in detail. See Anon., 1939.

60. MPGA, KWG, 1086: "Ausländische Wissenschaftler am Kaiser Wilhelm Institut für Biologie (Mr. Wigglesworth, Mr. White)." Wettstein to Telschow, 25 October 1938.

61. Ibid. Telschow to Wigglesworth, 7 November 1938.

62. Ibid. Wettstein to the President of the KWG, 16 March 1939.

Chapter 6

1. Watson, 1968, p. 68.

2. In Chapter 7 we will examine Wettstein's activities as an organizer in the later years of the Third Reich.

3. See Jahn et al., 1985, Vol. 2, p. 525.

4. See the obituary by Alfred Kühn (1947). I would like to thank Georg Melchers, a student of Wettstein at the Kaiser Wilhelm Institute for Biology, for giving me these reprints as well as more than a dozen others on biologists at the institute and their work. Wettstein edited and wrote an introduction for Carl Correns's collected works on heredity published in 1924.

5. Interview with Karl Zimmer (with the author) where he refers to Wettstein's "Austrian diplomacy" in 1943 to keep Zimmer from the draft as one of the "cor-

nerstones of armament." Finally, see Wettstein to Kühn, 1 June 1944, Alfred Kühn Papers.

6. See Hartmann's (1956) collected works. See Chapter 2 for more on Hartmann, who had joined the department of protozoology at the Kaiser Wilhelm Institute for Biology in 1914.

7. Querner, 1974, p. 516.

8. Georg Melchers, an assistant to Wettstein at the Kaiser Wilhelm Institute for Biology during the thirties, had studied in Göttingen and refers to this "general biology" in Melchers (1968) and a short unpublished article he gave me which was presented in a radio broadcast on 21 April 1965. Melchers is now head of the Max Planck Institute for Biology in Tübingen.

9. Alfred Kühn Papers, Fritz von Wettstein to Herr Geheimrat [Planck], 15 September 1936, a seven-page letter written in longhand.

10. This is based on Macrakis (1993).

11. RF, 1.1/717/13/123. W. E. Tisdale to Warren Weaver, 10 August 1934. This was probably also part of the Rockefeller Foundation's emphasis on cooperative research.

12. Nachmansohn, 1979, pp. 233–34. See also Krebs, 1981.

13. Max-Planck-Gesellschaft Administration, Personnel Files, Munich: "Fritz von Wettstein." Planck to Eugen Fischer, chairman of the biomedical section, 10 March 1933.

14. Ibid. Fischer to Planck, 30 March 1933. The last sentence was left out in the version given to the scientific council in order not to offend Renner.

15. Ibid. Wettstein to Glum, 25 October 1933.

16. Ibid. Wettstein to Planck, 16 December 1933.

17. Ibid. Glum to Wettstein, 9 February 1934. Verwaltungsausschuss, 6 March 1933. Last quote from Aktennotiz, 16 March 1934.

18. Ibid. Planck to Wettstein, 13 April 1934.

19. Wettstein's BDC file contains no evidence of party membership or affiliation with any National Socialist organization.

20. BDC. Blume to Kreispersonalamtsleiter, Göttingen, 16 October 1936.

21. See GStA, Dahlem, Rep. 90, 978, for a "Qualification Report" by Rudolf Mentzel where he states that the scientist is "one of our most talented and industrious scientists." There is no proof, he writes, that the scientist will not behave loyally to the National Socialist state. If he is not found a suitable position in Germany, Mentzel writes that he might emigrate to the United States. The scientist had actually been given an attractive offer at Harvard University in 1935. (Last point not reported by Mentzel.)

22. BDC file on scientist 1.

23. BDC file on scientist 2. NSDAP to Kreispersonalamt, 10 May 1935, and Kreispersonalamtleiter to the Landestelle Südhannover-Braunschweig des Reichsministerium für Volksaufklärung und Propaganda, 29 May 1935.

24. Ibid. Blume (NSDB Hochschulgruppe Göttingen) to the Personalamt der Kreisleitung Göttingen.

25. See Kay's (1986) excellent article on Stanley's crystallization of tobacco mosaic virus.

26. Butenandt, 1977, pp. 3–5.

27. Ibid.

28. Ibid., pp. 7–10, for details on the construction and functioning of an air-driven centrifuge.

29. MPGA, KWG, 2906: "Vorschlag zur Errichtung einer Zweigstelle für Virusforschung der Kaiser Wilhelm-Institute für Biochemie und Biologie," 17 July 1939.

30. MPGA, KWG, 2906, Telschow to General Director Bötzkes, Deutsche Industrie Bank, 15 November 1940.

31. James Watson, for example. Quote from Waterson and Wilkinson, 1978, p. 124.

32. Butenandt (1977) describes the three stages that the institute for virus research was supposed to undergo.

33. Schramm, 1943.

34. See the biographical novel by Granin (1988).

35. Max Delbrück Papers, Pasadena, CA, interview with Max Delbrück by Caroline Harding, p. 49. See Zimmer's contribution on the target theory in Cairns, Stent, and Watson (1966, pp. 33–42).

36. See Carlson, 1966, p. 158–65. Others may disagree. For a concise history of "genetics in the atomic age" see Auerbach (1965).

37. BA, R 73/12475. Minutes of the Notgemeinschaft's meeting on cooperative work in the area of hereditary damage by radiation.

38. For a fictionalized account of the protection of Peter Welt at the genetics department of the KWI for Brain Research see Welt (1986). See also Granin for a list of others protected during the Third Reich (1988, pp. 191–92).

39. BA, R 73/15215. Report to DFG by N. Timoféeff-Ressovsky, 23 July 1943 and 28 April 1944. These notes of thanks are repeated in several other reports.

40. BA, R 73/15057 and 15058. Hans Stubbe's applications and reports. German Research Council figure culled from card at BDC.

41. BDC, file on Hans Stubbe.

42. Ibid. The head of the Security Police and SD to the Reich Minister for Science and Education, 30 November 1943.

43. Lang, 1987.

44. BA, R 73 (DFG project files)/11065.

45. BA, R 73/13128. Reichsforschungsrat Fachgliederung Landbauwissenschaft und allgemeine Biologie. II. Biologie. 8 February 1938.

46. Ibid.

47. BA, R 73, 11227. See also DFG file at the MPGA.

48. Baader and Schultz (1980) sparked a lively research program in 1980 at the Berlin Gesundheitstag. Other important studies in German include Mann (1973) and Lilienthal (1979, 1985). For a comprehensive work synthesizing much recent literature see Weingart, Kroll, and Bayertz (1988). There have also been many medical dissertations written in German dealing with many different aspects of eugenics in Germany. For recent work in English see Weiss (1986, 1987a, 1987b) and Proctor (1988).

49. Müller-Hill found that documents such as correspondence with Dr. Joseph Mengele, expert reports, and memoranda were destroyed before or after Verschuer informed the general administration that the contents of the institute had been transported from Berlin to the west (1984, pp. 24–25; 1988, p. 20).

50. Weindling (1985) has shown this nicely in his article on the founding of the institute in Weimar Germany.

51. See MPGA, KWG, 2413.

52. See Verschuer's (1964) article on the scientific activity of the institute from 1927 to 1945.

53. MPGA, KWG, 2404, KWI for Anthropology, Niederschrift über die Sitzung des Kuratoriums, 5 July 1933.

54. MPGA, KWG, 2401, KWI for Anthropology, Tätigkeitsbericht, July 1933–1 April 1935.

55. MPGA, KWG, 808: "Vorträge in Berlin." List of Winter Lecture Series 1932–33. Press notice and summary of Fischer Lecture. Eugen Fischer, "Rassenkreuzung und geistige Leistung," *Internationales Ärtzliches Bulletin*, March/April 1936, p. 35.

56. MPGA, KWG, Hauptversammlung, 126. KWG to Rüdin, 10 April 1933, thanking him for agreeing to lecture on such short notice. See also Aktennotiz, 21 December 1932, about preparations for Warburg's lecture at the 1933 yearly meeting. KWG, 127, excerpts from Rüdin's lecture at the twenty-second yearly meeting.

57. MPGA, KWG, 127, excerpts from Rüdin's lecture on 23 May 1933.

58. MPGA, KWG, 2401, Tätigkeitsbericht.

59. ZStA, Postdam, Reichserziehungsministerium (REM), No. 965, Rassenpolitisches Amt der NSDAP, 9 July 1934, circular, No. 17.

60. MPGA, KWG, 2401, Tätigkeitsbericht, July 1933–1 April 1935.

61. Ibid.

62. Ibid.

63. ZStA, Potsdam, REM, No. 965, Fischer to general administration of the KWG, 5 July 1939. Zum Erlass des Herrn Reichserziehungsministers Vaterschaftsgutachten.

64. MPGA, KWG, 2401, Tätigkeitsbericht.

65. Gütt, Rüdin, and Ruttke (1934); see also Proctor's discussion of the Sterilization Law (1988, Chapter 4).

66. See Nyiszli, 1960, p. 63; Langbein, 1972, p. 383.

67. BA, R 73, 15345. Verschuer to Breuer of the DFG, 20 March 1944. Benno Müller-Hill was the first to find this document, buried with many other papers in Verschuer's DFG file.

68. Müller-Hill, 1984, 1988, pp. 66–67; see also Aly, 1985, pp. 64–71, on the Hallervorden collection.

69. BDC. Files on Fischer, Rüdin, Lenz, and Verschuer. Letter from Himmler to the "Stab des Stellvertreters des Führers," 17 August 1938, from Fischer file.

Chapter 7

1. MPGA, KWG, 56: "Wahl des Präsidenten, Vizepräsidenten, des Schatzmeisters, der Schriftführer, sowie der Senatoren, 1.1.1935–27.1.1944." Telschow to Carl Friedrich von Siemens, 6 May 1940; Telschow also wrote to Planck on 5 May 1940 reiterating this suggestion.

2. Ibid. "Stellungnahme zur Präsidenten-Kanditatur der KWG." Statements from Krauch, Mentzel, Vögler, Krüß, Bruns, Siemens, Schmidt-Ott, Saemisch, and Winkler.

3. Ibid. Planck to Telschow, 8 May 1940. Carl Friedrich von Siemens assumed the role of first vice president after the death of Otto Wacker in 1940.

4. For biographical material see Robert Wistrich, 1983, pp. 327–28; for relations with politics and his role as an industrialist and supporter of Papen see Henry Turner, 1985, pp. 210, 212, 293f, 311, 331–33.

5. See *50 Jahre*, 1961, pp. 37–38. See also Klass, 1957, pp. 300–302.

6. According to Turner, Vögler was reported by Hans Schäffer, a Jewish state secretary, to have "dressed down" Hitler and Göring (1985, p. 252). For Göring reference see MPGA, 1953, Glum to Körber, 29 July 1933.

7. MPGA, KWG, Reichsforschungsrat, 16 March 1937–12 January 1945. Telschow to Vögler, 6 May 1943.

8. MPGA, KWG, 56. Telschow to Saemisch, 16 May 1940; Memorandum, 23 May 1940; Memorandum on presidential election, 3 June 1940; Siemens to Reich Minister Rust, 17 December 1940; Memorandum, 15 November 1940.

9. Ibid. Telschow to Saemisch, 16 May 1940; Memorandum, 23 May 1940; Memorandum on presidential election, 3 June 1940; Siemens to Reich Minister Rust, 17 December 1940; Memorandum, 15 November 1940.

10. Ibid. Memorandum, 29 May 1940; Memorandum, 30 August 1940.

11. Ibid. Siemens to Rust, 17 December 1940; draft of letter to Rust, undated, but 19 December written in pencil.

12. Vögler to Telschow, 14 January 1941; Krüß Papers, StPKB, KWG, 1928–43. Vögler to Mentzel, 13 May 1941.

13. MPGA, KWG, 56, Rust to Telschow, 5 June 1941. Copies also in the Siemens Archive and the Krüß Papers.

14. Siemens Archive, SAA, Lg 880, Telschow to von Siemens, 9 June 1941; MPGA, KWG, 56, 16 June 1941. Ammer's statement from 11 June 1941.

15. MPGA, KWG, 56. Notes on discussion with Siemens, 17 June 1941; notes on discussion with Saemisch, 19 June 1941; Memorandum, 16 June 1941. From von Wettstein's statement on the Rust letter.

16. Ibid. Note about the meeting of the advisory council on 20 June 1941, 21 June 1941; Memorandum, 27 June 1941; Telschow to Saemisch, 12 July 1941; Vögler to von Siemens, 3 July 1941, Siemens Archive; Brack to Parteigenosse [Party Member] Dr. Telschow, 29 July 1941. Göring ordered Brack, who was from the Chancellery of the Führer, to convey the message.

17. MPGA, KWG, 56. Minutes from the senate meeting of 31 July 1941.

18. Düwell presents some useful typologies in his book on Germany's foreign *Kulturpolitik*, 1918–32, (1976, p. 36).

19. ZStA, Potsdam, REM, No. 3191, Minutes of Meeting on International Organizations on 12 November 1940, 11 December 1940, p. 9.

20. Ibid., p. 11.

21. Ibid. Statement by Zschintzsch (from the Reich Ministry of the Interior) marked "confidential," 10 October 1939.

22. Ibid. Note on meeting of 17 January 1941.

23. Ibid. Foreign Office to REM and Reich Ministry of the Interior, 17 September 1940. See Siegmund-Schultze (1986) for the example of mathematics in schemes for a new order of European science.

24. ZStA, Potsdam, REM, No. 3191, Minutes of 12 November 1940 Meeting, 11 December 1940, p. 40.

25. Ibid., pp. 21–23.

26. Ibid., p. 24.

27. Archive of the Academy of Sciences of the German Democratic Republic, East Berlin, KWG, 7, NSDAP, Reichsleitung, signed Dr. Bader, to director, KWI for Law and International Law, 18 February 1942. Although referred to as "Amt Rosenberg," the office is also known as Rosenberg Ministry.

28. Ibid. Aktennotiz, 9 March 1942, by Telschow.

29. See Adams, 1981, pp. 506, 511.

30. Archive of the Academy of Sciences of the GDR, East Berlin, KWG, 7, Aktennotiz, 10 February 1942, by Telschow.

31. Ibid. Wettstein to Telschow, 9 March 1942.

32. BA, R 26 III, No. 175. Sievers to Konrad Meyer, 30 September 1943. For biographical material on Vavilov see Joravsky, 1970, pp. 30–32, 107.

33. *Jahrbuch 1941 der Kaiser-Wilhelm-Gesellschaft zur Förderung der Wissenschaften*, p. 83.

34. For the example of Werner Heisenberg as a goodwill ambassador see also Walker, 1989, pp. 105–18, 222–28.

35. A very large Kaiser Wilhelm Institute for Animal Breeding was founded in Rostock in northeastern Germany in 1939, but it is not considered in detail here for reasons of conceptual unity and space, and because it related less to the ideology of *Lebensraum*.

36. MPGA, KWG, 138, Hauptversammlung 26, Der Oberbürgermeister der Hauptstadt Breslau to Planck, 24 May 1937. The Mayor of Breslau had already written to Planck inviting the Society to hold its yearly meeting in Breslau, which it eventually did in 1939.

37. MPGA, KWG, 2912: "Institut für landwirtschaftliche Arbeitswissenschaft in der KWG, 4 April 1940–6 December 1940." Aktennotiz, 4 April 1940, by Telschow; BDC: "Otto Fitzner."

38. MPGA, KWG, 2912: "Grundgedanken für ein Institut für landwirtschaftliche Arbeitswissenschaft." Probably by Preuschen, the future director, 7 April 1940.

39. Ibid. Aktennotiz, 5 September 1940, by Telschow.

40. Ibid. Aktenvermerk, 20 September 1940.

41. Ibid. Aktenvermerk, 26 September 1940. Re: call of Preuschen about visit with Backe.

42. Ibid. Mentzel, from the office of the "Reichsminister für Wissenschaft, Erziehung und Volksbildung," to the KWG, 11 October 1940.

43. Ibid. Telschow's speech at the founding meeting in Breslau, 6 December 1940.

44. Ibid. Aktennotiz, 4 April 1940, by Ernst Telschow.

45. BDC, NSDAP party card Gerhardt Preuschen.

46. I would like to thank Monika Renneberg for helping me make this point more explicit.

47. MPGA, KWG, 2912: "Institut für landwirtschaftliche Arbeitswissenschaft in der KWG, 4 April 1940–6 December 1940 [Tasks and work methods of the Institute for the science of agriculture]." Lecture by Dr. G. Preuschen at the institute opening, 6 December 1940.

48. Ibid. "Stichworte für die Rede von Prof. Dr. Mentzel."

49. Ibid. "Stichworte für die Rede von Staatssekretär Backe."

50. Ibid. See also newspaper clippings: "Brücke zum europäischen Südosten," *Oberschlesischer Kurier*, 8 December 1940.

51. MPGA, KWG, 2913, Institut für landwirtschaftliche Arbeitswissenschaft, 11 December 1940–23 January 1945. Note by Telschow, 22 February 1941.

52. Rich, 1974, p. 258.

53. Hoppe, 1979.

54. MPGA, KWG, 2924: "Deutsch-Bulgarisches Institut für landwirtschaftliche Forschung." Telschow to the Reich Ministry for Nutrition and Agriculture, 1 April 1941.

55. Ibid.

56. Ibid. "The Tasks of the German-Bulgarian Institute for Agricultural Research."

57. Ibid. Program für die Grundsteinlegung des Bulgarisch-Deutschen Instituts für Landwirtschaftliche Forschung in Sofia . . . vom 11. bis zum 15. September 1942.

58. Ibid. 12 September 1942, Pressenotiz.

59. Ibid. From an unattributed speech by a Bulgarian.

60. Ibid. Aktennotiz, 6 September 1942, by Telschow.

61. Ibid. Telschow to Mentzel, 14 January 1943. Emphasis added.

62. BDC: "Arnold Scheibe."

63. MPGA, KWG, 2927: "Deutsch-Bulgarisches Institut für landwirtschaftliche Forschung." Mentzel, President of the RFR, to Scheibe, 20 January 1944. See also the thirteen DFG cards with a listing of contracts, BDC.

64. MPGA, KWG, 2931, Deutsch-Bulgarisches Institut für landwirtschaftliche Forschung, Kuratorium.

65. MPGA, KWG, 2924. Telschow to Mentzel, 14 January 1943.

66. MPGA, KWG, 2949, Deutsch-Griechisches Forschungsinstitut für Biologie. Three documents refer to "Dr. Tzonis' plan": "Gutachten über die Gründung eines Griechisch-Deutschen Forschungsinstitutes für Biologie," by Max Hartmann, 15 January 1938; Roth, Foreign Ministry, to the head of the KWG, c. 24 August 1940; Hartmann to Telschow, 26 August 1940.

67. Ibid. "Gutachten über die Gründung eines Griechisch-Deutschen Forschungsinstitutes für Biologie," by Max Hartmann, 15 January 1938.

68. Ibid. "Zweck und Richtungen des Deutschgriechischen Biologischen Instituts."

69. Ibid. "Gründungsstatut des Deutsch-Griechischen Instituts für Biologie."

70. MPGA, Rep. 14, Deutsch-Griechisches Institut für Biologie, Fritz von Wettstein to Ernst Telschow, 4 January 1941.

71. MPGA, KWG, 2949, Hartmann to Telschow, 26 August 1940.

72. Ibid. Telschow to Roth at the Foreign Office, 30 August 1940.

73. Ibid. "Bericht über die Verhandlung von Prof. M. Hartmann über das deutsch-griechische Institut für Biologie in Athen vom 3. bis 17 Dezember 1941."

74. MPGA, KWG, 2950; "Bericht von Professor Dr. M. Hartmann über seine Tätigkeit in Athen vom 9.Juni bis 10. Juli 1942 für das Deutsch-Griechische Institut für Biologie in Piräus."

75. MPGA, KWG, 2946: "Plan eines Deutsch-Ungarischen Instituts für landwirtschaftliche Forschung, 2.9.1941–15.6.1943." Wilmowsky to Vögler, 2 September 1941.

76. Ibid. Note on a meeting at the Foreign Office on 13 October 1941 by Ernst Telschow.

77. Ibid. Rudolf Mentzel to the KWG, 21 October 1941; Albert Vögler to Mentzel, 6 November 1941; Mentzel to the president of the KWG, 26 February 1942.

78. MPGA, KWG, 2963, KWI for Cultivated Plant Research, 13 October 1941, Wettstein to the president of the KWG.

79. Ibid. Report on biological research trip to the Peloponnisos and Crete, 1942.

80. MPGA, KWG, 2603–6, KWI for Plant Breeding.

81. Robert Edwin Herzstein, 1982, p. 110.

82. Alfons Fischer, 1939. For the economic relationship between Greater Germany and southeastern Europe see Robert W. Krugmann, 1939.

83. ZStA, Potsdam, REM, No. 690, quoted by Rössler, 1990, p. 90. See also Christoph Kleßmann, "Osteuropaforschung und Lebensraumpolitik," in ed. Peter Lundgreen 1985, pp. 364–67.

84. See Rudi Goguel, 1964, pp. 132–75, Kleßmann, 1985, pp. 364–67; Rössler, 1990, pp. 84–102, for information on the German East Institute. See Goguel, pp. 90–131; Kleßmann, pp. 367–69; Rössler, pp. 103–11, for the Reich University in Poland. Rössler's discussion focuses primarily on geography at the two institutions. See also Michael Burleigh, 1988.

85. *Die Naturwissenschaften*, 5 November 1943, Vol. 31, p. 513.

86. MPGA, KWG, KWI for Biology, Telschow to Hartmann, 16 March 1941. Telschow asks Hartmann to give a lecture and mentions who receives the yearbook in which it will appear.

87. *Jahrbuch 1940 der Kaiser-Wilhelm-Gesellschaft zur Förderung der Wissenschaften*, preface (no page number). Signed Dr. Telschow, August 1940.

88. StbPK, Krüß Papers, Niederschriften über die Sitzung des Senats der Kaiser Wilhelm Gesellschaft, 31 July 1941.

89. Ibid. Niederschriften über die Sitzung des Senats, 24 April 1942.

90. MPGA, KWG, 94, Einladungen und Protokolle des Verwaltungsausschusses, 12 December 1939. For the case of the University of Göttingen see Becker et al., 1987, p. 42.

91. StPKB, Krüß Papers, Niederschriften über die Sitzung des Senats der Kaiser Wilhelm Gesellschaft, 31 July 1941.

92. *Die Naturwissenschaften*, 18 July 1941, Vol. 29, p. 425. "Die Weltgeltung deutscher Wissenschaft: zum 30jährigen Bestehen der Kaiser-Wilhelm-Gesellschaft," *Völkische Beobachter*, 11 January 1941.

93. *Die Naturwissenschaften*, 9 October 1942, Vol. 30, p. 609.

94. *Jahrbuch 1942 der Kaiser-Wilhelm-Gesellschaft zur Förderung der Wissenschaften*, p. 5. This yearbook covered the period 1 April 1941–31 March 1942.

95. *Die Naturwissenschaften*, 5 November 1943, Vol. 31, p. 514.

96. MPGA, KWG, 858, meetings of directors and staff of the KWG, 14 January 1928–31 January 1944. For actual minutes of the meeting see Alsos 461 document in the Bundesarchiv, minutes of directors' meeting, 9 November 1943.

97. Simon, 1947, p. 63.

98. Kevles, 1979, p. 320. Kevles provides a figure of 1,700 physicists who contributed to the war effort.

99. Prandtl Papers. This information comes from a secret report written by Prandtl for Telschow in lieu of attending the directors' meeting on November 1943. Enclosure from Prandtl to Telschow, 5 November 1943.

100. MPGA, KWG, 94, program for the meeting of the advisory council, 12 December 1939.

101. MPGA, KWG, 1956, KWI for Iron Research, report on institute activities 1939.

102. Ibid. 20 January 1941, Reich Minister for Aviation: war contract. 15 October 1941, service Deferments.

103. BA, No. 592-1 Kleine Erwerbungen. "Kriegswichtige Arbeiten des Kaiser-Wilhelm-Instituts für Eisenforschung in Düsseldorf," 16 September 1942. This report on work important for the war is marked "secret." For more examples of the kind

of war research pursued by this institute see this three-and-a-half–page listing. This document was apparently captured by the Alsos Mission. A copy of the original is in the Bundesarchiv. See also the Library of Congress microfilm collection of the German captured material, reel 131 (ALSOS RFR 461).

104. These figures are based on the financial files of the Society, MPGA, KWG, 360–80, and the announcements in the senate meetings.

105. StPKB, Krüß Papers, Niederschriften, Sitzung des Senats, 31 July 1941.

106. Krüß Papers and Archive of the Academy of Science, GDR, Sitzung des Senats, Niederschriften, 24 April 1942.

107. MPGA, KWG, Niederschriften, Sitzung des Senats, 11 November 1943.

108. MPGA, KWG, 385. Förderergemeinschaft der deutschen Industrie, 26 February 1943–14 April 1945. See Graßmann letter to Telschow, 2 December 1944; Förderergemeinschaft letter to Telschow about electron microscope, 20 January 1945; Vögler letter to Siemens, 8 January 1945.

109. For the founding of the Förderergemeinschaft in 1942 and the general relation between science and industry see Pohl, 1985.

110. *Jahrbuch 1942 der Kaiser-Wilhelm-Gesellschaft zur Förderung der Wissenschaften*, pp. 89–91.

111. MPGA, KWG, 2530, Harnack-House, Veranstaltungen, Korrespondenz, 28 November 1939–27 November 1944. This information is from the listing of meetings for each month from 1939 to 1945.

112. MPGA, KWG, 82, Niederschrift über die Sitzung des Senats der Kaiser-Wilhelm-Gesellschaft, 11 November 1943. Minutes also available in the Archive of the Academy of Sciences, GDR. The institutes partially transferred by November 1943 were anthropology, physiology of work, biochemistry, biology, biophysics, chemistry, brain research, metal research, physics, physical chemistry and electro-chemistry, silicate research, and international law.

113. BA, Kleine Erwerbungen, No. 592-1, Körber to Telschow, 24 June 1943.

114. This description of the bombing and fire is based on a report in MPGA, KWG, 1145, KWI for Chemistry: "Bericht über den Angriff vom 15.2.44." Max von Laue's observations are from a letter to his son, Theodore, 26 May 1945, Von Laue Papers, reprinted in Beyerchen, 1977, p. 194.

115. MPGA, KWG, 1145, KWI for Chemistry: "Bericht über die Fliegerschäden in Dahlem nach dem Angriff am 15. Februar 1944."

116. Ibid. "Bericht über den Angriff in der Nacht vom 24. März 1944." For details of the work to fight the fire see this report, which praises Professor Butenandt from the KWI for Biochemistry for his help.

117. See Bollmann, Baier, Forstmann, and Reinold, 1956, pp. 9–10.

118. Ibid.

Chapter 8

1. Other Kaiser Wilhelm institutes worked indirectly on problems associated with nuclear research. For example, the genetics department of the KWI for Brain Research and the KWI for Biophysics (Boris Rajewsky, director) worked on the genetic effects of radiation.

2. Lise Meitner Papers, Churchill College, Cambridge University. Otto Hahn to Lise Meitner, 19 December 1938.

3. It is beyond the scope of this chapter to examine the prehistory of the discovery of fission. For an analysis of the Rome work see Amaldi (1984). See also the collection of essays in Shea (1983), particularly Weart's essay, "The Discovery of Fission and a Nuclear Physics Paradigm," and Krafft's, "Internal and External Conditions for the Discovery of Fission by the Berlin Team."

4. See Krafft, 1983 pp. 145–150, "The Production of 'Transuranic elements.'"

5. O. Hahn and F. Straßmann, 1939.

6. L. Meitner, and O. R. Frisch, 1939.

7. For a good review of this work see Turner, 1940.

8. See Stuewer, 1985.

9. David Irving Microfilm Collection (IM) 29, Abraham Esau to General Becker, 13 November 1939. See also Irving, 1967, p. 35.

10. MPGA, Bothe Papers, [10], 2-1-3, 1934–39. Dames, Reichs-Ministerium für Wissenschaft, Erziehung und Volksbildung, to Professor Dr. Bothe, 24 April 1939. Copies of this letter were sent to eight other people including Schumann and Peter Debye.

11. Walker, 1987, p. 30; 1989, p. 17.

12. IM 29. Harteck and Groth to the Heereswaffenamt, 24 April 1939. This paragraph translated in a letter from Major R. R. Furman to S. A. Goudsmit, 25 May 1945.

13. Siegfried Flügge, 1939a.

14. IM, 29, Esau to General Becker, 13 November 1939.

15. Walker, 1989, p. 19.

16. Bagge, Diebner, and Jay, 1957, p. 22; Irving, 1967, p. 43.

17. Irving, 1967, p. 45.

18. "Operation Epsilon." Report from 6–7 August 1945. NA, Military Branch.

19. Irving, 1967, p. 45.

20. For the story of the decision to fund the KWI for Physics in the Third Reich see Macrakis, 1986, 1989.

21. Sources for the history of quantum physics, American Institute of Physics, New York, and Office for the History of Science and Technology, University of California, Berkeley, transcript of interview with Peter Debye.

22. Deutsches Museum, Munich, Sommerfeld Papers, 1977–28 (A, 61) 18. Peter Debye to Arnold Sommerfeld, 30 December 1939.

23. MPGA, KWG, KWI for Physics, 1652, Aktennotiz, 17 October 1939. Oberkommando des Heeres to the KWG, 25 January 1940.

24. IM 29, Werner Heisenberg, 6 December 1939: "Die Möglichkeit der technischen Energiegewinnung aus der Uranspaltung" (G-39); 29 February 1940: "Bericht über die Möglichkeit technischer Energiegewinnung aus der Uranspaltung (II)" (G-40).

25. For a detailed analysis of Harteck's work see Walker, 1987, esp. Chapter 16; 1989, pp. 137–49; see also Irving, 1967, pp. 47–50, 59–65, 85–91, 112–14, 127–29, 172–74, 237–39, 264–66.

26. Irving notes that it was called Virus House to keep unwanted visitors away (1967, p. 56).

27. IM 29. Werner Heisenberg, 1941: "Bericht über Versuche mit Schichtenordnungen von Praparat(sic) 38 und Paraffin am Kaiser Wilhelm-Institut f. Physik in Bln-Dahlem" (G-93). Heisenberg's description from part b, "Das Außenlabor."

28. IM 29, Schumann, Chef der Forschungsabteilung, to Harteck, 5 December 1941.

29. "Energiegewinnung aus Uran," February 1942. I would like to thank Mark Walker for sending me a copy of this 134-page report.

30. MPGA, KWG, KWI for Physics, 1652, Aktennotiz, 22 January 1942, by Telschow.

31. MPGA, KWG, RFR, 203, Aktennotiz, 26 January 1942, by Telschow.

32. IM 29, Rust to Lorenz, 12 February 1942.

33. IM 29, list of papers for the second scientific conference of the research group "Atomic Physics" on 26 February 1942. Also reprinted in Irving, 1967, p. 109.

34. IM, Werner Heisenberg, 26 February 1942: "Die theoretischen Grundlagen für die Energiegewinnung aus der Uranspaltung." After the war Heisenberg wrote to Goudsmit that the talk was "adapted to the intelligence level of a Reich Minister of that time." Heisenberg to Goudsmit, 5 January 1948, American Institute of Physics (AIP), Samuel Goudsmit Papers.

35. For the program of the scientific conference held at the Kaiser Wilhelm Institute for Physics see National Archives, Captured German Documents T-175, Reel No. 125 (also available at the Institut für Zeitgeschichte): "Arbeitstagung im Kaiser-Wilhelm-Institut für Physik, Berlin-Dahlem, vom 26. bis 28.2.1942." See, for example, IM 30, Walther Bothe: "Die Vermehrung schneller Neutronen in Uran und einige andere Arbeiten aus dem K.W.I.Heidelberg" (G-131). Carl-Friedrich von Weizsäcker; "Verbesserte Theorie der Resonanzabsorption in der Maschine" (G-197), March 1942. O. Hahn and F. Strassmann: "Zur Frage nach der Entstehung des 2,3 Tage-Isotops des Elements 93 aus Uran" (G-151). F. Bopp, E. Fischer, W. Heisenberg, C. F. v. Weizsäcker, and K. Wirtz: "Untersuchungen mit neuen Schichtenordnungen aus U-Metall und Paraffin" (G-127).

36. MPGA, KWG, 203, Reichsforschungsrat: "Physik und Landesverteidigung," 27 February 1942 (newspaper clipping [newspaper illegible]).

37. Ibid. Reichsforschungsrat, Albert Vögler to General Leeb, 27 February 1942.

38. MPGA, KWG, 1652, Leeb to Generaldirektor, 4 March 1942; Vögler to Leeb, 6 March 1942.

39. Ibid. Auszüge aus der Niederschriften des Senats, 24 April 1942.

40. Ludwig Prandtl Papers, series of letters between Prandtl and Heisenberg in 1937–38. Werner Heisenberg Papers, Heisenberg to Himmler, 4 February 1943.

41. The Heisenberg–Irving version of the meeting, for which there is no other evidence, and which is doubted by some scholars, is this: Heisenberg dealt with the military applications of nuclear fission and apparently explained how a bomb could be made. Two sorts of nuclear explosives existed, reported Heisenberg, those created by U-235 and element 94. The word "bomb" appeared to be a surprise even to the general director of the KWG, Ernst Telschow, who had, up until that point, thought in terms of a uranium burner or furnace. See IM 32 (from Irving's correspondence with the scientists in preparation for his book), Telschow to David Irving, 13 July 1966. After Heisenberg's speech E. Milch asked how large a nuclear bomb needed to be in order to destroy a large city, to which Heisenberg replied, as big as a pineapple. (See Irving, 1967, p. 120.) But in his letter to David Irving, Heisenberg writes that Telschow says he remembers it was as big as a "football." IM 32, Heisenberg to Irving, 10 June 1966.

42. Irving, 1967, pp. 226–28.

43. Ibid., p. 225. For the reorganization of the Reich Research Council see Chapter 4.

44. Bundes militärarchiv, Freiburg, RL 3156, Milch Papers: "Stenographischer Bericht über die Besprechung über den Reichsforschungsrat," 6 July 1942. See also Chapter 4 for a detailed account of the meeting.

45. Esau officially received the title on 8 December 1942. See Aktennotiz, 8 February 1943, by Telschow. Copies in MPGA, KWG, 203, Heisenberg Papers, and IM 29 (from Reichsforschungsrat Papers). See also Schumann's letter to Heisenberg, 18 January 1943, where he writes that Göring has named Esau "plenipotentiary for all questions of atomic physic" and ordered that the Research Group for atomic physics be administratively under the Reich Research Council (Heisenberg Papers).

46. MPGA, KWG, 1653, Telschow to Vögler, 24 July 1942.

47. Ibid.

48. IM 29, Esau to Mentzel, 24 November 1942.

49. IM 29, Mentzel to Görnnert, the Reich Marshalls's Office.

50. Heisenberg Papers, Aktennotiz, 8 February 1943, by Telschow on 4 February meeting.

51. IM 29, Telschow to Mentzel, 1 March 1943.

52. See IM 30, F. Bopp, E. Fischer, W. Heisenberg, C. F v. Weizsäcker, and K. Wirtz: "Vorläufiger Bericht über Ergebnisse an einer Schichten-Kugel aus 38-Metall und Paraffin" (G-126), 6 January 1942. Same authors: "Untersuchungen mit neuer Schichtenanordnung aus Metall und Paraffin" (G-127), 6 January 1942. W. Heisenberg: "Bemerkungen zu dem geplanten halbtechnischen Versuch mit 1,5t D_2O und 3t 38-Metall" (G-161), 31 July 1942. W. Heisenberg, F. Bopp, E. Fischer, C. F von Weizsäcker, and K. Wirtz: "Messungen an Schichtenanordnungen aus 38-Metall und Paraffin" (G-162), 30 October 1942.

53. IM 31, Carl Ramsauer: Reports of the German Academy of Aeronautical Research. Address given on 2 April 1943. W. Süss also gave a report at the Rector's conference in Salzburg on 26 August 1943, "The Present Position of German Science and German Universities," where he also referred to the rise of American science and the decline of German science.

54. IM 31. Werner Heisenberg: "Die Energiegewinnung aus der Atomkernspaltung" (G-217), from the conclusion.

55. Cf. Walker, 1987, pp. 149–50.

56. IM. Mentzel to Görnnert, 12 November 1943.

57. Werner Heisenberg and Karl Wirtz, "Großversuche zur Vorbereitung der Konstruktion eines Uranbrenners," in Walther Bothe and Siegfried Flügge [eds.] (1948), pp. 143–65; esp. p. 157.

58. See Bagge, Diebner, and Jay, 1957, p. 40.

59. From Gerlach's foreword to a planned printed report from the scientists. The four main conclusions are quoted in Irving, 1967, p. 265.

60. IM 31. Irving's notes on fragmentary interview with Karl Wirtz, 8 December 1965.

61. Irving, 1967, p. 263.

62. See Irving, 1967, p. 263; Fischer, 1987, p. 66.

63. Compare also Groves's statement that after the scientists' capture Diebner seemed hostile toward Heisenberg, who in turn considered Diebner an inferior scientist (1962, p. 244). Goudsmit states that Heisenberg's clique limited their conversation with Diebner to monosyllables (1947, p. 121).

64. Heisenberg and Wirtz, 1948, p. 153.

65. See Walker, 1987, pp. 235–36.

66. MPGA, KWG, KWI for Physics, 1653, Vögler to Heisenberg, 31 October 1944.

67. IM 29, F. Bopp, W. Bothe, E. Fischer, E. Fünfer, Heisenberg, Ritter, and K. Wirtz: "Bericht über einen Versuch mit 1,5 to D$_2$O und U und 40cm Kohlerück-streumantel. (B 7)" (G-300), 1 March 1945.

68. Ibid.

69. This passage is based on Irving's penultimate chapter: "To the Brink of Criticality" (1967, pp. 266–69). I have also used Paul Rosbaud's statement made before the dropping of the atomic bomb on Hiroshima (IM 29, 5 August 1945).

70. Irving. Ibid.

71. Heisenberg and Wirtz, 1948, pp. 158–59.

72. Irving, 1967 pp. 271–72. For a reprint of Hitler's technical emergency decree see Goudsmit, 1947, p. 194.

73. NA, Record Group 165, Intelligence Division, Alsos Mission File, 1944–45, Reports; here Alsos Mission Report 4 March 1944. Goudsmit, 1947, pp. 14–15; Groves, 1962, p. 230. It is beyond the scope of this chapter to discuss the goals and history of the Alsos Mission. For detailed studies see reprint (1983) of Goudsmit (1947) with an introduction by R. V. Jones, where Goudsmit relates his activities as scientific head of the mission while using "Nazi Germany" as an example of what can happen to science in a totalitarian regime. To Goudsmit science can flourish only in a democracy. See also Leo Mahoney's (1981) dissertation on the War Department's scientific intelligence mission (Alsos), 1943–45. The documents seized by the mission are available, in part, at the National Archives in the G-2 files, Record Group 319, Army Staff. For the administrative organization and operation of the mission see G-2 Intelligence, Record Group 165, Alsos Mission.

74. Goudsmit, 1947, pp. 77–81. Walther Bothe was the director of the physics department and Richard Kuhn was the director of the organic chemistry division.

75. Ibid., pp. 77–80.

76. Ibid., p. 96.

77. IM 29, Fritz Bopp to the KWG, 3 June 1945. Goudsmit, 1947, pp. 110–11.

78. See R. V. Jones's introduction to the reprint edition of Goudsmit's *Alsos* (1983, p. xiv). In his book on Paul Rosbaud, Kramish acknowledges Jones's statement about being responsible for the bugging but notes that this had been done many years before (1986, p. 243).

79. Operation Epsilon. NA, Military Records Branch.

80. Ibid. Report for week of 18–31 July 1945. Diebner quote, p. 10.

81. Ibid. Report for week of 6 August 1945, and Groves, 1962, p. 334. The Gerlach description is from a letter Max von Laue wrote to Paul Rosbaud, 4 April 1959, quoted in its entirety in Kramish (1986, pp. 245–47), and matches the Operation Epsilon transcript.

82. Goudsmit Papers, Max von Laue to Theodore von Laue, 7 August 1945.

83. Operation Epsilon, report on 6–7 August 1945.

84. Ibid. p. 9. Weizsäcker in countless interviews, including with the author, January 1986, Starnbergersee.

85. Ibid.

86. Ibid.

87. Ibid.

88. See Bernstein's discussion in the *New York Review of Books*, 13 August 1992, pp. 47–53.

89. Ibid.

90. Operation Epsilon, report on 6–7 August 1945.

91. Ibid.

92. Max von Laue to Paul Rosbaud, 4 April 1959, quoted in Kramish, 1986, pp. 245–47. Emphasis in original.

93. It is beyond the scope of this chapter to address many of the questions raised by the German nuclear power project. Rose (1984) addresses the question of whether the Germans could have built the bomb and answers it polemically that Heisenberg did not know how to build the bomb, but he would have if he could have, with no moral scruples.

Epilogue

1. For general background on the occupation and division of Germany see Berghahn, 1987, Chapters 5 and 6, esp. pp. 176–77.

2. Morgenthau, 1945, p. 73.

3. "Directive of the United States Joint Chiefs of Staff to the Commander-in-Chief of the United States Forces of Occupation Regarding the Military Government of Germany (JCS 1067)," April 1945. Ruhm von Oppen, 1955, p. 24 (Doc. No. 31). RG 227 National Archives Memorandum Dinner Meeting on 23 February 1945 at the Cosmos Club, 24 February 1945.

4. Hermann, 1973, p. 116.

5. There are no references to when Planck officially became president in the papers for the year 1945. In 1945 Planck is referred to as "honorary senator" and "earlier president."

6. *Dokumente zur Gründung*, 1981, p. 78. Max Planck to Otto Hahn, 25 July 1945.

7. Ibid. Otto Hahn to Max Planck, no date.

8. Havemann, 1991, pp. 64–65.

9. *Dokumente zur Gründung*, 1981, p. 86. Berlin scientists, including Hans Nachtsheim, to the administration of the KWG, attention Dr. [Herbert] Müller, 7 July 1945. See Havemann's (1978) autobiography.

10. *Deutsche Volkszeitung*.

11. ZStA, Potsdam, R-2, 1428. Zustand und Tätigkeit der Kaiser Wilhelm Gesellschaft, 1945–48. Robert Havemann report, 27 August 1945.

12. See letter reprinted in Bollman et al., 1956, p. 38. Planck to institute directors, 15 September 1945.

13. Stamm, 1981, p. 87.

14. MPGA, MPG, A 2/1.6. Planck to the Allied Scientific Commission, 25 June 1945.

15. Ibid., A 2/1. Directive to institute directors, signed Telschow. No date, but probably summer 1945.

16. MPGA, MPG, A 2/4. Remarks on research, by Telschow, 8 January 1946. Copy given to Bertie Blount.

17. MPGA, MPG, A 2/1. Respondek on the KWG, 12 November 1970.

18. *Dokumente zur Gründung*, 1981, pp. 86–87.

19. MPGA, MPG, A 2/4. Memorandum by Otto Hahn, no date.

20. Quoted from excerpt in MGPA, MPG, A2/1. Aus dem Tagebuch des amerikanischen Botschafters in Berlin. See also Dodd, 1941, p. 431.

21. See Macrakis (1986, 1989) for the details of the decision to fund the Kaiser Wilhelm Institute for Physics during the Third Reich.

22. MPGA, MPG, A2/4. Aktennotiz, 11 July 1946.

23. MPGA, MPG, A2/1. Blount Erinnerungen.

24. MPGA, MPG, A2/4. Otto Hahn to Sir Henry Dale, 12 July 1946. Written in English. Translated by Dr. Kauenhoven.

25. MPGA, MPG, A2/1. Blount Erinnerungen.

26. ZStA, Potsdam, R-2, 1428. Zustand und Tätigkeit der Kaiser Wilhelm Gesellschaft, 1945–48. Archive of the Academy of Sciences, GDR, Kaiser Wilhelm Gesellschaft, 10.

27. See Heinemann, 1990, pp. 438–54, for details of the shift from a single-zone to a trizonal Society.

28. Alfred Kühn Papers, Kühn to Richard Goldschmidt, 25 October 1949.

29. Berghahn, 1987, pp. 185–87.

30. NA.RG 227, OSRD, Box 4a. Report on the activities of Roger Adams. No date. For an informative and revealing account of the postwar program and the shift from intellgence missions to exploitation programs, see Gimbel 1990.

31. NA, Investigative Records Repository, XE 019019.

32. Berghahn, 1987.

33. Data based on material from the Berlin Document Center.

34. MPGA, KWG, 683-1: "Alte Kämpfer." Prussian Ministry circular on taking care of old fighters of the National Socialist movement, 19 April 1934. KWG to twenty-one Kaiser Wilhelm institutes, 30 April 1934, asking how many old fighters are at each institute and how many were employed because of the circular.

35. NA, Suitland. RG 466 Hicog files, Military Security Board. Hahn/Heisenberg to McCloy 13 November 1950. McCloy to Chancellor Adenauer 5 May 1951. Nordstrom to Hahn, 8 October 1952.

36. See Bower, 1987; Lasby, 1971; and Hunt, 1985.

Sources

Archival Material

Germany

Archiv der Akademie der Wissenschaften der deutschen Demokratischen Republik, Berlin, GDR

Archiv zur Geschichte der Max-Planck-Gesellschaft (MPGA), Berlin

Archive of the Humboldt University (AHU), Berlin, GDR

BASF Archiv, Ludwigshafen, FRG

Berlin Document Center (BDC), West Berlin

Bundesarchiv (BA), Koblenz (FRG)

Bundesmilitärarchiv, Freiburg

Deutsches Museum, Manuscript Collection, Munich FRG

Geheimes Staatsarchiv (GStA), Berlin (Carl-Heinrich Becker Papers, Friedrich Schmidt-Ott Papers, Staatsministerium)

Institut für Zeitgeschichte (IfZ), Munich, FRG

Krupp Archiv, Essen, FRG

Landesarchiv, Berlin

Max-Planck-Gesellschaft Adminstration, Personnel Files, Munich, FRG

Politisches Archiv des Auswärtigen Amtes, Bonn, FRG

Siemens Archiv, Munich, FRG

Staatsbibliothek Preußischer Kulturbesitz (StPKB), Manuscript Collection, Berlin

Zentrales Staatsarchiv (ZStA), Merseburg and Postdam (GDR)

Werner Heisenberg Papers, Max-Planck-Institut für Physik, Munich, FRG

Alfred Kühn Papers, University of Heidelberg, FRG

Ludwig Prandtl Papers, Max-Planck-Institut für Strömungsforschung, Göttingen, FRG

Ernst Rüdin Papers, Edith Zerbin-Rüdin, Munich, FRG

Otmar von Verschuer Papers, University of Münster, FRG

United States

Max Delbrück Papers, California Institute of Technology, Pasadena
Emil Fischer and Richard Goldschmidt Papers, Bancroft Library, University of California, Berkeley
Samuel Goudsmit Papers, American Institute of Physics (AIP), New York City
History of Quantum Physics Archive, Office for History of Science and Technology, Berkeley, California
Library of Congress (LC), Manuscript Collections, German Captured Material, Washington, D.C.
National Archives (NA), Washington, D.C.
Carl Neuberg Papers, American Philosophical Society (APS), Philadelphia, Pennsylvania
Rockefeller Archives (RF), Tarrytown, New York

England

David Irving Microfilm Collection on Nuclear Research in the Third Reich (IM)
Hans Krebs Papers, Contemporary Science Archives, Oxford
Lise Meitner Papers, Churchill College, Cambridge University, Cambridge

France

Archives du Centre de Documentation Juive Contemporaine, Paris

Interviews

Hermann Blaschko
Erika Bollman
Gerhard Borrman
Adolf Butenandt
Georg Melchers
Georg Menzer
Dietrich Schmidt-Ott
Ernst Telschow
Carl-Friedrich von Weizsäcker
Karl Wirtz
Karl Zimmer

Books and Articles

Adam, Uwe Dietrich (1977). *Hochschule und Nationalsozialismus: die Universität Tübingen im Dritten Reich*. Tübingen: Mohr.
———— (1979). *Judenpolitik im Dritten Reich*. Düsseldorf: Droste.
Adams, Mark (1981). "Nikolay Ivanovich Vavilov." *Dictionary of scientific biography*, Supplement, 15. New York: Charles Scribner's Sons.
———— (1980). "Science, ideology, and structure: The Kol'tsov Institute, 1900–1970." In *The social context of soviet science*, ed. Linda L. Lubrano and Susan Gross Solomon, 173–204. Boulder Colo.: Westview Press.

Albrecht, Richard (1987). "'. . . daß Sie Ihre Tätigkeit einstellen müssen': Die Entlassung Sergej Tschachotins aus dem Heidelberger Kaiser-Wilhelm-Institut 1933." *Berichte zur Wissenschaftsgeschichte*, *10*, 105–112.

Aly, Götz (1985). "Der saubere und der schmutzige Fortschritt." In *Reform und Gewissen: "Euthanasie" im Dienst des Fortschritts*, ed. Götz Aly, Karl Friedrich Masuhr, Maria Lehmann, Karl Heinz Roth, and Ulrich Schultz, 9–78. Berlin: Rotbuch Verlag.

Amaldi, Edoardo (1984). "Neutron work in Rome in 1934–36 and the discovery of uranium fission." *Riv. Stor. Sci.*, *1*, 1–24.

Anon. (1930). "Auslandsbeziehungen der Kaiser-Wilhelm-Gesellschaft zur Förderung der Wissenschaften." *Forschungen und Fortschritte*, *6*, 15–16.

Anon. (1939). "The Royal Society and the Kaiser Wilhelm Gesellschaft: exchange of visits." *Nature*, *143*, 1035–36.

Auerbach, Charlotte (1965). *Genetics in the atomic age*, 2d ed. New York: Oxford University Press.

Azmanov, Iskren (1989). "Development, functioning and research programme of the Bulgarian-German research institute for agriculture in the period 1940–1944." Unpublished manuscript.

Baader, Gerhard, and Ulrich Schultz, eds. (1980). *Medizin und Nationalsozialismus: Tabuisierte Vergangenheit—Ungebrochene Tradition?* Berlin: Verlagsgesellschaft Gesundheit.

Baeumler, Alfred (1934). *Männerbund und Wissenschaft*. Berlin: Junker und Dünnhaupt.

Bagge, Erich, Kurt Diebner, and Kenneth Jay (1957). *Von der Uranspaltung bis Calder Hall*. Hamburg: Rowohlt.

Barber, Bernard (1978). *Science and the Social Order*. Reprint of 1952 edition. Westport: Greenwood Press.

Baur, Erwin, Eugen Fischer, and Fritz Lenz (1936). *Menschliche Erblehre*, 4th ed., rev. Munich: J. F. Lehmanns Verlag.

Becker, Carl Heinrich (1919). *Kulturpolitische Aufgabe des Reiches*. Leipzig: Verlag von Quelle & Meyer.

Becker, Heinrich, Hans-Joachim Dahms, and Cornelia Wegeler (1987). *Die Universität Göttingen unter dem Nationalsozialismus: das verdrängte Kapitel ihrer 250 jährigen Geschichte*. Munich, London, New York, Oxford, Paris: K. G. Saur.

Ben-David, Joseph (1971). *The scientist's role in society: a comparative study*. Englewood Cliffs, N.J.: Prentice-Hall.

Berghahn, V. R. (1987). *Modern Germany: Society, economy and politics in the twentieth century*. 2d ed. Cambridge: Cambridge University Press.

Bergmann, Anna, Gabriele Czarnowski, and Annegret Ehmann (1989). "Menschen als Objekte humangenetischer Forschung und Politik im 20. Jahrhundert." In *Der Wert des Menschen: Medizin in Deutschland, 1918–1945*, ed. Christian Pross and Götz Aly, 121–142. Berlin: Edition Hentrich.

Berninger, Ernst H. (1974). *Otto Hahn in Selbstzeugnissen und Bilddokumenten*. Hamburg: Reinbek.

Beyerchen, Alan D. (1977). *Scientists under Hitler: politics and the physics community in the Third Reich*. New Haven: Yale University Press.

——— (1988). "On the stimulation of excellence in Wilhelmian science." In *Another Germany: a reconsideration of the Imperial era*, eds. Jack R. Dikes and Joachim Remak, 139–68, Boulder, Colo.: Westview Press.

Bleker, Johanna and Norbert Jachertz (1989). *Medizin im Dritten Reich*. Cologne: Deutscher-Ärtzte-Verlag.

Boelcke, Willi A., ed. (1969). *Deutschlands Rüstung im zweiten Weltkrieg: Hitlers Konferenzen mit Albert Speer, 1942–1945*. Athenaion: Akademische Verlagsgesellschaft.

Bollmann, Erika, Eva Baier, Walther Forstmann, and Marianne Reinold (1956). *Erinnerungen und Tatsachen: die Kaiser-Wilhelm-Gesellschaft zur Förderung der Wissenschaften, Göttingen-Berlin, 1945/1946*. Stuttgart: Georg Thieme Verlag.

Borkin, Joseph (1978). *The crime and punishment of I. G. Farben*. London, New York: Free Press.

Born, Max (1948). "Max Karl Ernst Ludwig Planck, 1858–1947." *Royal Society of London, Obituary Notices*, 6, 161–88.

Bothe, Walther, and Flügge, Siegfried, eds. (1948). *Nuclear physics and cosmic rays*. Fiat review of German science, 1939–1946. Wiesbaden: Dieterich'sche Verlagsbuchhandlung.

Bower, Tom (1987). *The paperclip conspiracy: the hunt for the Nazi scientists*. Boston: Little, Brown and Company.

Bracher, Karl Dietrich (1969). *Die deutsche Diktatur: Entstehung, Struktur, Folgen des Nationalsozialismus*. Frankfurt: Ullstein.

Bracher, Karl Dietrich, Wolfgang Saur, and Gerhard Schulz (1960). *Die nationalsozialistische Machtergreifung: Studien zur Errichtung des totalitären Herrschaftssystem in Deutschland 1933/34*. Frankfurt: Ullstein.

Brämer, Rainer, ed. (1984). *Naturwissenschaften im NS-Staat*. Marburg: Soznat.

Brauer, Ludolph, Albrecht Mendelssohn-Bartholdy, and Adolf Meyer, eds. (1930). *Forschungsinstitute, Ihre Geschichte, Organisation und Ziele*. Hamburg: Paul Hartung Verlag.

Brocke, Bernhard vom (1980). "Hochschul- und Wissenschaftspolitik in Preußen und im Deutschen Kaiserreich 1882–1907: das 'System Althoff'." In *Bildungspolitik in Preußen zur Zeit des Kaiserreichs*, ed. Peter Baumgart, 9–118. Stuttgart.

Broszat, Martin (1969). *Der Staat Hitlers*. Munich: Deutscher Taschenbuch Verlag.

Broszat, Martin, and Elke Fröhlich, eds. (1979). *Bayern in der NS-Zeit*, 6 vols. Munich, Vienna: Oldenbourg.

Burchardt, Lothar (1975). *Wissenschaftspolitik im Wilhelminischen Deutschland: Vorgeschichte, Gründung und Aufbau der Kaiser-Wilhelm-Gesellschaft zur Förderung der Wissenschaften*. Göttingen: Vandenhoeck & Ruprecht.

Burleigh, Michael (1988). *Germany turns Eastward: a study of Ostforschung in the Third Reich*. Cambridge: Cambridge University Press.

Busch, Alexander (1959). *Die Geschichte des Privatdozenten: eine soziologische Studie zur großbetrieblichen Entwicklung der deutschen Universitäten*. Stuttgart: Ferdinand Enke Verlag.

Butenandt, Adolf (1977). "The historical development of modern virus research in Germany, especially in the Kaiser-Wilhelm-/Max-Planck-Society, 1936–1954." *Medical Microbiology and Immunology*, 164, 3–14.

——— (1981). *Das Werk eines Lebens*, 4 vols. Göttingen: Verlag Vandenhoeck & Ruprecht.

Cahan, David (1989). *An institute for an empire*. Cambridge: Cambridge University Press.

Cairns, John, Gunther Stent, and James D. Watson (1966). *Phage and the origin of molecular biology*. New York: Cold Spring Harbor Laboratory of Quantitative Biology.

Caplan, Janet (1977). "The politics of administration: the Reich Interior Ministry and the German Civil Service, 1933–1943." *Historical Journal, 20*, 707–36.

Carlson, E. A. (1966). *The gene: a critical history.* Philadelphia: Saunders.

Carmon, A. (1979). "The diverse and changing fortunes of the University of Heidelberg under National Socialism." *Minerva, 16*, 516–44.

Carr, William (1972). *Arms, autarky and aggression: a study in German foreign policy, 1933–1939.* London: Edward Arnold.

Chargaff, Erwin (1978). *Heraclitean fire: sketches from a life before nature.* New York: Rockefeller University Press.

Coates, J. E. (1939). "The Haber Memorial Lecture." *Journal of the Chemical Society*, November, pp. 1642–72.

Cocks, Geoffrey (1985). *Psychotherapy in the Third Reich: the Göring Institute.* New York: Oxford University Press.

Cocks, Geoffrey, and Konrad H. Jarausch (1990). *German professions, 1800–1950.* New York: Oxford University Press.

Die deutsche Universität im Dritten Reich: eine Vortragsreihe der Universität München. (1966). Munich: Piper Verlag.

Dodd, William E. (1941). *Ambassador Dodd's diary, 1933–1938.* Edited by William E. Dodd, Jr., and Martha Dodd; with an introduction by Charles A. Beard. New York: Harcourt, Brace and Company.

Dokumente zur Gründung der Kaiser-Wilhelm-Gesellschaft und der Max-Planck-Gesellschaft zur Förderung der Wissenschaften (1981). Exhibition, Staatsbibliothek Preußischer Kulturbesitz, Berlin, 21 May–19 June 1981. Organized by the Max-Planck-Gesellschaft zur Förderung der Wissenschaften. Munich: Max-Planck-Gesellschaft.

Donnevert, Richard, ed. (1939). *Wehrmacht und Partei,* 2d. ed., enlarged. Leipzig: Verlag von Johann Ambrosius Barth.

Döring, Herbert (1975). *Der Weimarer Kreis: Studien zum politischen Bewußtsein verfassungstreuer Hochschullehrer in der Weimarer Republik.* Meisenheim am Glan: Verlag Anton Hain.

Douglas, Mary (1986). *How institutions think.* New York: Syracuse University Press.

DuBois, Josiah E., Jr. (1952). *The devil's chemists: 24 conspirators of the international Farben cartel who manufacture wars.* Boston: Beacon Press.

Düwell, Kurt (1971). "Staat und Wissenschaft in der Weimarer Epoche: zur Kulturpolitik des Ministers C. H. Becker." *Historische Zeitschrift, 1*, 31–65.

——— (1976). *Deutschlands auswärtige Kulturpolitik, 1918–1932: Grundlinien und Dokumente.* Cologne, Vienna: Böhlau Verlag.

———, and Werner Link, eds. (1981). *Deutsche auswärtige Kulturpolitik seit 1871.* Cologne, Vienna: Böhlau Verlag.

Eckert, Michael (1985). Die "Deutsche Physik" und das Deutsche Museum." *Physikalische Blätter, 41*, No. 4, 87–92.

Eichholtz, Dietrich (1969). *Geschichte der deutschen Kriegswirtschaft, 1939–1945.* Berlin: Akademie-Verlag.

Ein Ehrentag der deutschen Wissenschaft: die Eröffnung des Reichsforschungsrat am 25. Mai 1937 (1937). [Berlin]: Pressestelle des Reichsministeriums für Wissenschaft, Erziehung und Volksbildung.

Engel, Michael (1984). *Geschichte Dahlems.* Berlin: Berlin-Verlag Spitz.

Ericksen, Robert P. (1984). "The Göttingen University theological faculty: a test case in *Gleichschaltung* and denazification." *Central European History, 17*, No. 4, 355–83.

Farias, Victor (1989). *Heidegger und der Nationalsozialismus. Aus dem Spanischen und Französischen übersetzt von Klaus Laermann.* Frankfurt: Fischer.

Farquharson, J. E. (1976). *The plough and the swastika: the NSDAP and agriculture in Germany, 1928–45.* London, Beverly Hills: Sage Publications.

Feldman, Gerald D. (1973). "A German scientist between illusion and reality: Emil Fischer, 1909–1919." In *Deutschland in der Weltpolitik des 19. und 20. Jahrhunderts,* ed. Immanuel Geiss and Bernd Jürgen Wendt, 341–62. Düsseldorf: Bertelsmann Universitätsverlag.

———— (1987). "The politics of *Wissenschaftspolitik* in Weimar Germany: a prelude to the dilemmas of twentieth-century science policy." In *Changing boundaries of the political,* ed. Charles S. Maier, 255–85. Cambridge: Cambridge University Press.

Festschrift der Kaiser Wilhelm Gesellschaft zur Förderung der Wissenschaften zu ihrem zehnjährigen Jubiläum (1921). Berlin: Verlag von Julius Springer.

Fiat Review of German Science, 1939–1946. Vol. V: *Biology.* Wiesbaden: Klemm. Published by the Office of Military Government for Germany, Field Information Agencies, Technical.

Fischer, Alfons (1939). "Die Bedeutung der südosteuropäischen Länder für die Versorgung Deutschlands mit pflanzlichen Ölrohstoffen," *Leipziger Vierteljahresschrift für Südosteuropa,* vol. 3, 177–183.

Fischer, Emil (1911). "Neuere Erfolge und Probleme der Chemie." *Internationale Wochenzeitschrift für Wissenschaft, Kunst und Technik,* 5, cols. 1–20.

Fischer, Emil, and Ernst Beckmann (1913). *Das Kaiser-Wilhelm-Institut für Chemie, Berlin-Dahlem.* Braunschweig: Verlag von Friedr. Vieweg & Sohn.

Fischer, Helmut J. (1982). "Der totale Staat und das totale Durcheinander: Wissenschaftsförderung und Überwachung im Dritten Reich." *Frankfurter Allgemeine Zeitung,* No. 121, 27 May.

———— (1984). *Erinnerungen. Part I: Von der Wissenschaft zum Sicherheitsdienst,* Vol. 3. Ingolstadt: Quellenstudien der Zeitgeschichtlichen Forschungsstelle.

———— (1985). *Erinnerungen. Part II: Feuerwehr für die Forschung,* vol. 6. Ingolstadt: Quellenstudien der Zeitgeschichtlichen Forschungsstelle.

———— (1987). *Hitler und die Atombombe: Bericht eines Zeitzeugen.* Edited by the Research Institute for Contemporary History. Ingolstadt. Asendorf: Mut-Verlag.

Fischer, Peter (1985). *Licht und Leben: Ein Bericht über Max Delbrück, den Wegbereiter der Molekularbiologie.* Constance: Universitätsverlag.

Flügge, Siegfried (1939a) "Die Ausnutzung der Atomenergie." *Deutsche Allgemeine Zeitung.*

———— (1939b). "Kann der Energieinhalt der Atomkerne technisch nutzbar gemacht werden?" *Die Naturwissenschaften,* 27, 402–10.

Forman, Paul (1967). *The environment and practice of atomic physics in Weimar Germany: a study in the history of science.* Ph.D. Dissertation. University of California, Berkeley.

———— (1971). "Weimar culture, causality, and quantum theory, 1918–1927: adaptation by German physicists and mathematicians to a hostile intellectual environment." *Historical Studies in the Physical Sciences,* 3, 1–115.

———— (1973). "Scientific internationalism and the Weimar physicists: the ideology and its manipulation in Germany after World War I." *Isis,* 64, 151–80.

———— (1974). "The financial support and political alignment of physicists in Weimar Germany." *Minerva,* 12, 39–66.

Forman, Paul, John L. Heilbron, and Spencer Weart (1975). "Physics circa 1900: personnel, funding, and productivity of the academic establishments." *Historical Studies in the Physical Sciences*, 5, 3–185.

Frank, Philipp (1949). *Einstein: Sein Leben und seine Zeit*. Munich, Leipzig, Freiburg.: Paul List.

Friedrich-Freska, Hans (1961). "Genetik und biochemische Genetik in den Instituten der Kaiser-Wilhelm-Gesellschaft und der Max-Planck-Gesellschaft." *Die Naturwissenschaften*, 48, 10–22.

Fünftausend Köpfe (1967). *Wer war was im Dritten Reich*. Stockhorst: Blick + bild Verlag.

Fünfzig Jahre Kaiser-Wilhelm-Gesellschaft und Max-Planck-Gesellschaft zur Förderung der Wissenschaften, 1911–1961. (1961). Göttingen: Generalverwaltung der Max-Planck-Gesellschaft zur Förderung der Wissenschaften e.V.

Gallin, Alice (1986). *Midwives to Nazism: university professors in Weimar Germany, 1925–1933*. Macon, Ga.: Mercer University Press.

Gay, Peter (1968). *Weimar culture: the outsider as insider*. New York: Harper & Row.

Gerlach, Walther (1984). *Otto Hahn: ein Forscherleben unserer Zeit*. Edited by Dieter Hahn. Stuttgart: Wissenschaftliche Verlagsgesellschaft.

Geuter, Ulfried (1984). *Die Professionalisierung der deutschen Psychologie im Nationalsozialismus*. Frankfurt: Suhrkamp.

Giles, Geoffrey J. (1985). *Students and National Socialism in Germany*. Princeton: Princeton University Press.

Gimbel, John (1968). *The American occupation of Germany*. Stanford: Stanford University Press.

Gimbel, John (1990). *Science, technology and reparations: exploitation and plunder in Postwar Germany*. Stanford: Stanford University Press.

———— (1986). "U.S. policy and German scientists: the early cold war." *Political Science Quarterly*, 101, 433–51.

Glass, Bentley (1981). "A hidden chapter of German eugenics between the two world wars." *Proceedings of the American Philosophical Society*, 125, No. 5, 357–67.

Glum, Friedrich (1931). "Die Auslandsbeziehungen der Kaiser Wilhelm Gesellschaft zur Förderung der Wissenschaften." *Forschungen und Fortschritte*, 7, 315–16.

———— (1964). *Zwischen Wissenschaft, Wirtschaft und Politik: Erlebtes und Erdachtes in vier Reichen*. Bonn: H. Bouvier Verlag.

Goguel, Rudi (1964). "Über die Mitwirkung deutscher Wissenschaftler am Okkupationsregime in Polen im Zweiten Weltkrieg, untersucht an drei Institutionen der deutschen Ostforschung," Dissertation, Humboldt-Universität, Berlin (East).

Goldberg, Stanley (1992). "Inventing a climate of opinion: Vannevar Bush and the decision to build a bomb." *Isis*, 83, 429–52.

Goldschmidt, Richard (1956). *The golden age of zoology: portraits from memory*. Seattle and London: University of Washington Press.

———— (1960). *In and out of the ivory tower: the autobiography of Richard B. Goldschmidt*. Seattle: University of Washington Press.

Goran, Morris (1967). *The story of Fritz Haber*. Norman: University of Oklahoma Press.

Goudsmit, Samuel (1947). *Alsos*. New York: Schuman.

———— (1983). *Alsos*. Introduction by R. V. Jones. Los Angeles, San Francisco: Tomash Publishers.

Granin, Daniil (1988). *Der Genetiker: Das Leben des Nikolai Timofejew-Ressowski, genannt Ur.* Translated by Erich Ahrndt. Cologne: Pahl-Rugenstein.

Grau, Conrad, Wolfgang Schlicker, and Liane Zeil (1979). *Die Berliner Akademie der Wissenschaften in der Zeit des Imperialismus.* Part III: *Die Jahre der faschistischen Diktatur.* Berlin: Akademie-Verlag.

Graumann, C. F., ed. (1985). *Psychologie im Nationalsozialismus.* Berlin, Heidelberg, New York, Tokyo: Springer-Verlag.

Grothusen, Klaus-Detlev, ed. (1987). *Der Scurla Bericht: Die Tätigkeit deutscher Hochschullehrer in der Türkei, 1933–1939.* Frankfurt: Dagyeli.

Groves, Leslie R. (1962). *Now it can be told.* New York: Harper & Brothers.

Gütt, Arthur, Ernst Rüdin, and Falk Ruttke (1934). *Gesetz zur Verhütung erbkranken Nachwuchses vom 14. Juli 1933.* Munich: Lehmanns Verlag.

Haber, L. F. (1971). *The chemical industry, 1900–1930: international growth and technological change.* Oxford: Clarendon Press.

——— (1986). *The poisonous cloud: chemical warfare in the First World War.* Oxford: Clarendon Press.

Haberer, Joseph (1969). *Politics and the community of science.* New York: Van Nostrand.

Hahn, O. and F. Straßmann (1939). "Über den Nachweis und das Verhalten der bei der Bestrahlung des Urans mittles Neutronen entstandenen Erdalkalimetale." *Die Naturwissenschaften*, vol. 27, 11–15.

Hahn, Otto (1957). "Einige persönliche Erinnerungen an Max Planck." *Mitteilungen aus der Max-Planck-Gesellschaft zur Förderung der Wissenschaften*, No. 5, 243–46.

——— (1960). "Zur Erinnerung an die Haber-Gedächtnisfeier vor 25 Jahren, am 29. Januar 1935, im Harnack-Haus in Berlin-Dahlem." *Mitteilungen aus der Max-Planck-Gesellschaft zur Förderung der Wissenschaften*, No. 1, 3–13.

——— (1966). *Otto Hahn: a scientific autobiography.* Translated and edited by Willy Ley. New York: Charles Scribner's Sons.

——— (1986). *Mein Leben*, rev. ed., enlarged. Munich, Zurich: Piper Verlag.

Harnack, Adolf von, ed. (1928). *Handbuch der Kaiser Wilhelm-Gesellschaft zur Förderung der Wissenschaften.* Berlin: Verlag von Reimar Hobbing.

Hartmann, Hans (1953). *Max Planck als Mensch und Denker*, 4th ed. Basel, Thun, und Düsseldorf: Ott.

Hartmann, Max (1925). *Biologie und Philosophie.* Berlin: Verlag von Julius Springer.

——— (1956). *Gesammelte Vorträge und Aufsätze*, 2 vols. Stuttgart: G. Fischer.

Hartshorne, Edward Y. (1937). *The German universities and National Socialism.* Cambridge, Mass.: Harvard University Press.

Harwood, Jonathan (1984). "The reception of Morgan's chromosome theory in Germany: Inter-war debate over cytoplasmic inheritance." *Medizinhistorisches Journal*, 19, 3–32.

——— (1985). "Geneticists and the evolutionary synthesis in interwar Germany." *Annals of Science*, 42, 279–301.

——— (1987). "National styles in science: genetics in Germany and the United States between the World Wars." *Isis*, 78, 390–414.

Havemann, Robert (1978). *Robert Havemann: Ein deutscher Kommunist.* Reinbek: Rowohlt.

——— (1991). *Dokumente eines Lebens.* Berlin: Ch. Links Verlag.

Hayes, Peter (1987). *Industry and ideology: I. G. Farben in the Nazi era.* Cambridge: Cambridge University Press.

Heiber, Helmut (1966). *Walter Frank und sein Reichsinstitut für Geschichte des neuen Deutschlands*. Stuttgart: Deutsche Verlagsgesellschaft.

Heidegger, Martin (1934). *Die Selbstbehauptung der deutschen Universität*. Second Edition. Breslau.

Heilbron, John L. (1986). *The dilemmas of an upright man: Max Planck as spokesman for German science*. Berkeley: University of California Press.

Heinemann, Manfred (1990). "Der Wiederaufbau der Kaiser-Wilhelm-Gesellschaft und die Neugründungen der Max-Planck-Gesellschaft (1945–1949)." In *Forschung im Spannungsfeld von Politik und Gesellschaft: Geschichte und Struktur der Kaiser-Wilhelm-Max-Planck-Gesellschaft*, ed. Rudolf Vierhaus and Bernhard vom Brocke, 407–70. Stuttgart: Deutsche Verlags-Anstalt.

Heisenberg, Elizabeth (1984). *Inner exile: recollections of a life with Werner Heisenberg*. Translated by S. Cappellan and C. Horns; introduction by Viktor Weisskopf. Boston, Basel, Stuttgart: Birkhäuser.

Herbig, Jost (1976). *Kettenreaktion: das Drama der Atomphysiker*. Munich: Carl Hanser.

Herf, Jeffrey (1984). *Reactionary modernism: technology, culture, and politics in Weimar and the Third Reich*. Cambridge: Cambridge University Press.

Hermann, Armin (1973). *Max Planck: in Selbstzeugnissen und Bilddokumenten*. Hamburg: Rowohlt.

Herzstein, Robert Edwin (1982). *When Nazi dreams come true*. London: Abacus.

Hildebrand, K. (1984). *The Third Reich*. London: George Allen & Unwin.

Hirschfeld, Gerhard, and Lothar Kettenacker (1981). *Der "Führerstaat": Mythos und Realität*. Stuttgart: Klett-Cotta.

Holdermann, Karl (1953). *Im Banne der Chemie: Carl Bosch, Leben und Werk*. Düsseldorf: Econ-Verlag.

Hölsken, H. D. (1984). *Die V-Waffen. Enstehung—Propaganda—Kreigseinsatz*. Stuttgart.

Hoffmann, Peter (1977). *The history of the German resitance, 1933–1945*. Cambridge, Mass.: MIT Press.

Hoppe, Hans-Joachim (1979). *Bulgarien—Hitlers eigenwilliger Verbündeter: Eine Fallstudie zur nationalsozialistischen Südosteuropapolitik*. Stuttgart: Deutsche Verlags-Anstalt.

Horder, T. J., and P. J. Weindling (1985). "Hans Spemann and the organizer." In *A history of embryology*, ed. T. Horder, J. Witkowski, and C. C. Wylie, 182–242. Cambridge: Cambridge University Press.

Hunt, Linda (1985). "U.S. coverup of Nazi scientists." *Bulletin of the Atomic Scientists*, April, pp. 17–24.

Hüttenberger, Peter (1976). "Nationalsozialistische Polykratie." *Geschichte und Gesellschaft*, 2, 417–42.

IM Frieden der Menschheit, im Krieg dem Vaterlande . . .": 75 Jahre Fritz-Haber-Institut der Max-Planck-Gesellschaft (1986). Berlin.

Irving, David (1967). *The German atomic bomb: the history of nuclear research in Nazi Germany*. New York: Da Capo Press.

Jaenicke, J. (1935). "Haber's research on the gold content of sea water." *Die Naturwissenschaften*, 23, 57.

Jahn, Ilse, Rolf Löther, and Konrud Senglaub (1985). *Geschichte der Biologie: Theorien, Methoden, Institutionen, Kurzbiographien*. Jena: Gustav Fischer Verlag.

Jahrbuch 1951 der Max-Planck-Gesellschaft zur Förderung der Wissenschaften e.V. 40

Jahre Kaiser-Wilhelm-Gesellschaft zur Förderung der Wissenschaften, 1911–1951. Göttingen: Hubert & Co.

Jahrbuch der Kaiser-Wilhelm-Gesellschaft zur Förderung der Wissenschaften (1939–1942). Leipzig: Haag-Drugulin.

Jahrbuch der Max-Planck-Gesellschaft zur Förderung der Wissenschaften e.V. 1961. Part II (1962). Göttingen: Hubert & Co.

Johnson, Jeffrey (1980). *The chemical Reichsanstalt association: big science in Imperial Germany.* Ph.D. dissertation, Princeton University.

———— (1985). "Academic chemistry in Imperial Germany." *Isis*, 76, 500–24.

———— (1990). *The Kaiser's chemists: science and modernization in Imperial Germany.* Chapel Hill: University of North Carolina Press.

Jungk, Robert (1958). *Brighter than a thousand suns: a personal history of the atomic scientists.* Translated by James Cleugh. New York: Harcourt Brace Jovanovitch.

Kamensky, Ihor (1961). *Secret Nazi plans for Eastern Europe: A study of Lebensraum policies.* New York: Bookman Associates.

Karlson, Peter (1990). *Adolf Butenandt: Biochemiker, Hormonforscher, Wissenschaftspolitiker.* Stuttgart: Wissenschaftliche Verlagsgesellschaft.

Kater, Michael (1974). *Das "Ahnenerbe" der SS, 1935–1945.* Stuttgart: Deutsche Verlags-Anstalt.

———— (1983). *The Nazi party: a social profile of members and leaders, 1919–1945.* Oxford: Basil Blackwell.

Kaupen-Haas, Heidrun, ed. (1986). *Der Griff nach der Bevölkerung, Aktualität und Kontinuität nazistischer Bevölkerungspolitik.* Nordlingen: Franz Greno.

Kay, Lily E. (1986). "W. M. Stanley's crystallization of the tobacco mosaic virus, 1930–1940." *Isis*, 77, 1–34.

Kelly, Reece Conn (1973). *National Socialism and German university teachers: the NSDAP's efforts to create a National Socialist professoriate and scholarship.* Ph.D. dissertation, University of Washington.

Kershaw, Ian (1985). *The Nazi dictatorship: problems and perspectives of interpretation.* London: Edward Arnold.

———— (1987). *The "Hitler myth": image and reality in the Third Reich.* Oxford: Oxford University Press.

Klass, Gert von (1957). *Albert Vögler, einer der Grossen des Ruhrreviers.* Tübingen: Rainer Wunderlich Verlag.

Klee, Ernst (1983). *"Euthanesie" im NS-Staat: Die "Vernichtung lebensunwerten Lebens."* Frankfurt: Fischer Verlag.

Kleinert, Andreas (1980). "Lenard, Stark und die Kaiser-Wilhelm-Gesellschaft." *Physikalische Blätter*, 36, 35–43.

Kleinberger, Aharon F. (1980). "Gab es eine nationalsozialistische Hochschulpolitik?" In *Erziehung und Schulung im Dritten Reich.* Part 2: *Hochschule, Erwachsenbildung*, ed. Manfred Heinemann, 9–30. Stuttgart: Klett-Cotta.

Kleinkauf, Horst, Hans von Döhren, and Lothar Jaenicke, eds. (1988). *The roots of modern biochemistry: Fritz Lipmann's squiggle and its consequences.* Berlin, New York: Walter de Gruyter.

Kohler, Robert (1982). *From medical chemistry to biochemistry: the making of a biomedical discipline.* Cambridge: Cambridge University Press.

Kohlstedt, Sally Gregory (1983). "Institutional history." *Osiris*, 1, 17–36.

Köhne-Lindenlaub, Renate (1982). "Krupp." *Neue Deutsche Biographie*, 13, 128–145. Berlin: Duncker & Humblot.

Krafft, Fritz (1983). "Internal and external conditions for the discovery of nuclear fission by the Berlin team." In *Otto Hahn and the rise of nuclear physics*, ed. William R. Shea, 135–65. Dordrecht: Reidel.

Kramish, Arnold (1986). *The griffin: the greatest untold espionage story of World War II*. Boston: Houghton Mifflin.

Krause, Eckart, Ludwig Huber, and Holger Fischer, eds. (1991). *Hochschulalltag im "Dritten Reich": Die Hamburger Universität, 1933–1945*, 3 vols. Berlin, Hamburg: Dietrich Reimer Verlag.

Krausnick, Helmut (1983). "Stationen der Gleichschaltung." In *Der Weg ins Dritten Reich, 1918–1933*, 156–76. München: Piper Verlag.

Krebs, Hans (1979). *Otto Warburg: Zellphysiologe, Biochemiker, Mediziner: 1883–1970*. With contributions by Roswitha Schmid. Stuttgart: Wissenschaftliche Verlagsgesellschaft.

——— (1981). *Otto Warburg: cellphysiologist, biochemist, and eccentric*. Oxford: Clarendon Press.

Krebs, Hans, and Fritz Lipmann (1988). "Dahlem in the late nineteen twenties." In *The roots of modern biochemistry: Fritz Lipmann's squiggle and its consequences*, ed. Horst Kleinkauf, Hans von Döhren, and Lothar Jaenicke, 111–24. Berlin, New York: Walter de Gruyter.

Krieck, Ernst (1936). *Nationalpolitische Erziehung*. Leipzig: Armanen Verlag.

Kröner, Peter (1983). *Vor fünfzig Jahren: die Emigration deutschsprachigerwissenschaftler, 1933–1939*. Münster: Gesellschaft für Wissenschaftsgeschichte.

Krugmann, Robert W. (1939). *Südosteuropa und Großdeutschland: Entwicklung und Zukunftsmöglichkeiten der Wirtschaftsbeziehungen*. Breslau: Verlags- und Druckerei.

Kuczynski, Jürgen (1975). "Das Rätsel der Kaiser Wilhelm-Gesellschaft." In *Wissenschaftsstrategie. Studien zu einer Geschichte der Gesellschaftswissenschaft*, Vol. 2, pp. 170–208. Berlin: Akademie Verlag.

Kühn, Alfred (1947). "Fritz von Wettstein zum Gedächtnis." *Jahrbuch der Akademie der Wissenschaften in Göttingen*. Reprint with no volume number, pp. 1–6.

Künzel, Friedrich (1984). *Max Plancks Wirken an der Berliner Akademie der Wissenschaften als Ordentliches Mitglied und Sekretär zwischen 1894 und 1947*. Dissertation, Humboldt-Universität Berlin.

Lang, Anton (1980). "Some recollections and reflections." *Annual Review of Plant Physiology, 31*, 1–28.

——— (1987). "Elisabeth Schiemann: life and career of a woman scientist in Berlin." *Englera, 7*, 17–28.

Langbein, Hermann (1972). *Menschen in Auschwitz*. Vienna: Europa Verlag.

Laqueur, Walter (1974). *Weimar: a cultural history, 1918–1933*. New York: G. P. Putnam.

Lasby, Clarence (1971). *Project paperclip*. New York: Atheneum.

Leitko, Hubert, et al. [Autorenkollektiv] (1987). *Wissenschaft in Berlin: Von den Anfängen bis zum Neubeginn nach 1945*. Berlin: Dietz Verlag.

Lifton, Robert Jay (1986). *The Nazi doctors*. New York: Basic Books.

Lilienthal, Georg (1979). "Rassenhygiene im Dritten Reich." *Medizinhistorisches Journal, 14*, 114–37.

——— (1985). *Der "Lebensborn e. V.," ein Instrument nationalsozialistischer Rassenpolitik*. Stuttgart: Gustav Fischer.

Lösch, Niels (1990). *Das Kaiser-Wilhelm-Institut für Anthropologics, menschliche Erblehre und Eugenik*. Masters thesis, Freie Universität, Berlin.

Lubrano, Linda L., and Susan Gross Solomon, eds. (1980). *The social context of Soviet science.* Boulder, Colo.: Westview Press.

Ludwig, Karl-Heinz (1979). *Technik und Ingenieure im Dritten Reich.* Düsseldorf: Droste Verlag.

Lundgreen, Peter, ed. (1985). *Wissenschaft im Dritten Reich.* Frankfurt: Suhrkamp.

Macrakis, Kristie (1986). "Wissenschaftsförderung durch die Rockefeller-Stiftung im Dritten Reich: die Entscheidung, das Kaiser-Wilhelm-Institut für Physik finanziell zu unterstützen." *Geschichte und Gesellschaft, 12,* 348–79.

——— (1989a). "The Rockefeller Foundation and German physics under National Socialism." *Minerva, 27,* No.1, 33–57.

——— (1989b). *Scientific research in National Socialist Germany: the survival of the Kaiser Wilhelm Gesellschaft.* Ph.D. dissertation, Harvard University.

——— (1993). "Adolf Butenandt." *Biographical dictionary of the Nobel Prize laureates in chemistry.* Washington: American Chemical Society.

Mahoney, Leo J. (1981). *A history of the war department scientific intelligence mission (ALSOS), 1943–1945.* Ph.D. dissertation, Kent State University.

Maier, Charles S. (1988). *The unmasterable past: history, holocaust, and German national identity.* Cambridge, Mass.: Harvard University Press.

———, ed. (1987). *Changing boundaries of the political: essays on the evolving balance between the state and society, public and private, in Europe.* Cambridge: Cambridge University Press.

Maier, Hans (1966). "Nationalsozialistische Hochschulpolitik." In *Die deutsche Universität im Dritten Reich: eine Vortragsreihe der Universität München,* 73–102, Munich: Piper Verlag.

Mangold, Otto (1953). *Hans Spemann: ein Meister der Entwicklungsphysiologie. Sein Leben und sein Werk.* Stuttgart: Wissenschaftliche Verlagsgesellschaft.

Mann, Günter (1973). "Rassenhygiene—Sozialdarwinismus." In *Biologismus im 19. Jahrhundert,* ed. Günter Mann, 73–93. Stuttgart: Ferdinand Enke.

Mehrtens, Herbert (1985). "Die 'Gleichschaltung' der mathematischen Gesellschaften im nationalsozialistischen Deutschland." *Jahrbuch Überblicke Mathematik,* 83–103.

——— (1986). "Angewandte Mathematik und Anwendungen der Mathematik im nationalsozialistischen Deutschland." *Geschichte und Gesellschaft, 12,* 317–47.

——— (1987). "The social system of mathematics and National Socialism: a survey." *Sociological Inquiry, 57,* 159–82.

Mehrtens, Herbert, and Steffen Richter, eds. (1980). *Naturwissenschaften, Technik und NS-Ideologie: Beiträge zur Wissenschaftsgeschichte des Dritten Reiches.* Frankfurt: Suhrkamp.

Meitner, L., and O. R. Frisch (1939). "Disintegration of uranium by neutrons: a new type of nuclear reaction," *Nature, 143,* 237.

Merton, Robert K. (1938). "Science and the social order." *Philosophy of Science, 5,* 321–37.

——— (1973). *The sociology of science: theoretical and empirical investigations.* Chicago and London: University of Chicago Press.

Milward, Alan (1965). *The German economy at war.* London: University of London Athlone Press.

Morgenthau, Henry (1945). *Germany is our problem.* New York and London: Harper & Brothers.

Morsbach, Adolf (1930). "Deutsche Wissenschaft und Ausland: Auslandsarbeit der Kaiser-Wilhelm-Gesellschaft." *Hochschule und Ausland, 4,* 3–7.

Müller-Hill, Benno (1984). *Tödliche Wissenschaft: Die Aussonderung von Juden, Zigeunern und Geisteskranken 1933–1945.* Hamburg: Reinbek.
—— (1987). "Genetics after Auschwitz." *Holocaust and Genocide Studies,* 2, No. 1, 3–20.
—— (1988). *Murderous science: elimination by scientific selection of Jews, Gypsies, and others, Germany, 1933–45.* New York: Oxford University Press.
Nachmansohn, David (1979). *German-Jewish pioneers in science, 1900–1933.* New York: Springer-Verlag.
Niethammer, Lutz (1972). *Entnazifierung in Bayern: Säuberung und Rehabilitierung unter amerikanischer Besatzung.* Frankfurt: Fischer.
Nipperdey, Thomas, and Ludwig Schmugge (1970). *50 Jahre Forschungsförderung in Deutschland: Ein Abriss der Geschichte der Deutschen Forschungsgemeinschaft 1920–1970.* Bad Godesberg: privately printed in the Deutsche Forschungsgemeinschaft.
Nye, Mary Jo (1984). "Scientific decline: is quantitative evaluation enough?" *Isis,* 75, 697–708.
Nyiszli, Miklos (1960). *Auschwitz: a doctor's eyewitness account.* New York: Frederick Fell.
O'Flaherty, James C. (1956). "Max Planck and Adolf Hitler." *American Association of University Professors Bulletin,* 42, 437–44.
Olby, Robert (1974). *The path to the double helix.* Foreword by Francis Crick. New York: Macmillan.
Orlow, Dietrich (1968). *The Nazis in the Balkans: a case study of totalitarian politics.* Pittsburgh: University of Pittsburgh Press.
Osietzki, Maria (1984). *Wissenschaftsorganisation und Restauration: der Aufbau außeruniversitärer Forschungseinrichtungen und die Gründung des westdeutschen Staates, 1945–1952.* Cologne, Vienna: Böhlau Verlag.
Pachaly, Erhard (1964). *Adolf von Harnack als Politiker und Wissenschaftsorganisator des deutschen Imperialismus in der Zeit von 1914 bis 1920.* Humboldt Universität, Berlin (GDR). Dissertation.
Petzina, Dietmar (1968). *Autarkiepolitik im Dritten Reich.* Stuttgart: Deutsche Verlagsanstalt.
Pfetsch, Frank (1970). Scientific organisation and science policy in Imperial Germany, 1871–1914: the foundation of the Imperial Institute of Physics and Technology. *Minerva,* 8, 557–80.
—— (1974). *Zur Entwicklung der Wissenschaftspolitik in Deutschland, 1750–1914.* Berlin: Duncker & Humblot.
Planck, Max (1936), editor. *25 Jahre Kaiser-Wilhelm-Gesellschaft zur Förderung der Wissenschaften.* Three volumes. Berlin: Springer-Verlag.
—— (1947). "Mein Besuch bei Adolf Hitler." *Physikalische Blätter,* 3, 143.
Pohl, Hans (1985). "Zur Zusammenarbeit von Wirtschaft und Wissenschaft im 'Dritten Reich': die Förderergemeinschaft der Deutschen Industrie." *Vierteljahrschrift für Sozial- und Wirtschaftsgeschichte,* 72, No. 4, 508–35.
Proctor, Robert N. (1988). *Racial hygiene: medicine under the Nazis.* Cambridge, Mass.: Harvard University Press.
Pross, Christian, and Götz Aly, eds. (1989). *Der Wert des Menschen: Medizin in Deutschland, 1918–1945.* Berlin: Edition Hentrich.
Querner, Hans (1974). "Alfred Kühn." *Dictionary of Scientific Biography,* 516–17. New York: Charles Scribner's Sons.

Rasch, Manfred (1987). *Vorgeschichte und Gründung des Kaiser-Wilhelm-Instituts für Kohlenforschung in Mülheim a.d. Ruhr.* Hagen: v.d. Linnepe Verlag.

———— (1988). "Die Montanindustrie und ihre Beziehungen zum Schlesischen Kohlenforschungsinstitut der Kaiser-Wilhelm-Gesellschaft. Ein Beitrag zu Wissenschaft und Wirtschaft in der Zwischenkriegszeit." *Technikgeschichte, 55,* 7–24.

Read, Anthony, and David Fisher (1988). *The deadly embrace: Hitler, Stalin, and the Nazi–Soviet pact, 1939–1941.* New York, London: W. W. Norton.

Reishaus-Etzold, Heike (1973). "Die Einflussnahme der Chemiemonopole auf die 'Kaiser-Wilhelm-Gesellschaft zur Förderung der Wissenschaften e.V.' während der Weimarer Republik." *Jahrbuch für Wirtschaftsgeschichte, 1,* 37–60.

Reitlinger, Gerald (1960). *The house built on sand: the conflicts of German policy in Russia, 1939–1945.* New York: Weidenfeld & Nicolson.

Rich, Norman (1973). *Hitler's war aims. Vol. 1: Ideology, the Nazi state, and the course of expansion.* New York: W. W. Norton.

———— (1974). *Hitler's war aims. Vol. 2: The establishment of the new order.* New York: W. W. Norton.

Richmond, Marsha (1986). *Richard Goldschmidt and sex determination: the growth of German genetics, 1900–1935.* Ph.D. dissertation, Indiana University.

Richter, D., ed. (1974). *Lipmann symposium: energy, regulation and biosynthesis in molecular biology.* New York, Berlin: de Gruyter.

Richter, Jochen (1976a). "Oskar Vogt, der Begründer des Moskauer Staatsinstituts für Hirnforschung." *Psychiatrie, Neurologie und medizinische Psychologie. Zeitschrift für die gesamte Nervenheilkunde und Psychotherapie, 28,* No. 7, 385–95.

———— (1976b). "Oskar Vogt und die Gründung des Berliner Kaiser-Wilhelm-Instituts für Hirnforschung unter den Bedingungen imperialistischer Wissenschaftspolitik." *Psychiatrie, Neurologie und medizinische Psychologie. Zeitschrift für die gesamte Nervenheilkunde und Psychotherapie, 28,* No. 8, 449–57.

Richter, Steffen (1979). "Wirtschaft und Forschung: Ein historischer Überblick über die Förderung durch die Wirtschaft in Deutschland." *Technikgeschichte, 46,* 20–44.

Ringer, Fritz (1969). *The decline of the German mandarins: the German academic community, 1890–1933.* Cambridge, Mass.: Harvard University Press.

Rössler, Mechtild (1990). *"Wissenschaft und Lebensraum: "Geographische Ostforschung im Nationalsozialismus: Ein Beitrag zur Disziplingeschichte der Geographie.* Berlin: Reimer.

Rose, Paul (1984). "Heisenberg, German morality and the atomic bomb, 1939–1945." Unpublished manuscript.

Rosenberg, Charles (1976). *No other Gods: on science and American social thought.* Baltimore: John Hopkins University Press.

Roth, Karl Heinz (1986). "Schöner neuer Mensch: Der Paradigmenwechsel der klassischen Genetik und sein Auswirkung auf die Bevölkerungsbiologie des 'Dritten Reich'." In *Der Griff nach der Bevölkerung, Aktualität und Kontinuität nazistischer Bevölkerungspolitik,* ed. Heidrun Kaupen-Haas, 11–63. Nordlingen: Franz Greno.

Rüdin, Ernst (1934). *Rassenhygiene im völkischen Staat: Tatsachen und Richtlinien.* Munich: J. F. Lehmanns Verlag.

Ruhm von Oppen, Beate, ed. (1955). *Documents on Germany under occupation, 1945–1954.* London, New York, Toronto: Oxford University Press.

Rust, Bernhard, and E. Krieck (1936). *Das nationalsozialistische Deutschland und die Wissenschaft.* Hamburg: Hanseatische Verlagsanstalt.

Sachse, Arnold (1928). *Friedrich Althoff und sein Werk*. Berlin: E. S. Mittler & Sohn.

Saha, Margaret Somosi (1984). *Carl Correns and an alternative approach to genetics: the study of heredity in Germany between 1880 and 1930*. Ph.D dissertation, Michigan State University.

Schmidt-Ott, Friedrich (1952). *Erlebtes und Erstrebtes, 1860–1950*. Wiesbaden: Franz Steiner.

Schnabel, Franz (1952). "Friedrich Althoff." *Neue Deutsche Biographie*, Vol., 1, pp. 222–24. Berlin: Duncker & Humblot.

Scholder, Klaus, ed. (1982). *Die Mittwochs-Gesellschaft. Protokolle aus dem geistigen Deutschland 1932 bis 1944*. Berlin: Severin and Siedler.

Schramm, Gerhard (1943). "Über die Spaltung des Tabakmosaikvirus in niedermolekulare Proteine und die Rückbildung hochmolekularen Proteins aus den Spaltstücken." *Die Naturwissenschaften*, 31, 94–96.

Schreiber, George (1923). *Die Not der deutschen Wissenschaft und der geistigen Arbeiter. Geschehnisse und Gedanken zur Kulturpolitik des Deutschen Reiches*. Leipzig: Quelle & Meyer.

——— (1951). "Die Kaiser-Wilhelm-Gesellschaft im Reichsetat und Reichsgeschehen." In *Jahrbuch 1951 der Max-Planck-Gesellschaft zur Förderung der Wissenschaften e.V. 40 Jahre Kaiser-Wilhelm-Gesellschaft zur Förderung der Wissenschaften, 1911–1951*, 60–107. Göttingen: Hubert & Co.

——— (1954). *Deutsche Wissenschaftspolitik von Bismarck bis zum Atomwissenschaftler Otto Hahn*. Cologne, Opladen: Westdeutscher Verlag.

Schroeder-Gudehus, Brigitte (1963). *Deutsche Wissenschaft und internationale Zusammenarbeit, 1914–28*. Geneva: Dumaret & Golay.

——— (1972). "The argument for the self-government and public support of science in Weimar Germany." *Minerva*, 10, 537–70.

Schumann, Erich (1939). "Wehrmacht und Forschung." In *Wehrmacht und Partei*, 2d. ed., enlarged, ed. Richard Donnevert, 133–51. Leipzig: Verlag von Johann Ambrosius Barth.

Seier, Hellmut (1964). "Der Rektor als Führer. Zur Hochschulpolitik des Reichserziehungsministeriums, 1934–45." *Vierteljahreshefte für Zeitgeschichte*, 12, 105-146.

——— (1984). "Universität und Hochschulpolitik im nationalsozialistischen Staat." In *Der Nationalsozialismus an der Macht*, ed. Klaus Malettke, Göttingen: Vandenhoeck & Ruprecht, 143–65.

——— (1988). "Die Hochschullehrschaft im Dritten Reich." In *Deutsche Hochschullehrer als Elite, 1815–1945*, ed. Klaus Schwabe, 247–95. Boppard.

Shea, William R., ed. (1983). *Otto Hahn and the rise of nuclear physics*. Dordrecht, Boston, Lancaster: Reidel.

Siegmund-Schultze, Reinhard (1984). "Theodor Vahlen—zum Schuldanteil eines deutschen Mathematikers am faschistischen Mißbrauch der Wissenschaft." *Zeitschrift für Geschichte der Naturwissenschaft, Technik und Medizin*, 21, 17–32.

——— (1986). "Faschistische Pläne zur 'Neuordnung' der europäischen Wissenschaft. Das Beispiel Mathematik." *Zeitschrift für Geschichte der Naturwissenschaft, Technik und Medizin*, 23, No. 2, 1–17.

Simon, Leslie (1947). *German research in World War II: an analysis of the conduct of research*. New York: John Wiley.

Smith, Woodruff D. (1985). *The ideological origins of Nazi imperialism*. New York: Oxford University Press.

Speer, Albert (1970). *Inside the Third Reich: memoirs*. Translated by Richard and Clara Winston. New York: Macmillan.

Stamm, Thomas (1981). *Zwischen Staat und Selbstverwaltung: die deutsche Forschung im Wiederaufbau, 1945–1965.* Cologne: Verlag Wissenschaft und Politik.

Stanley, W. M. (1935). "Isolation of a crystalline protein possessing the properties of tobacco-mosaic virus." *Science, 81,* 644–45.

Stern, Fritz (1961). *The politics of cultural despair.* Berkeley, Los Angeles: University of California Press.

———— (1987). *Dreams and delusions: the drama of German history.* New York: Alfred A. Knopf.

Strauss, Herbert A., Tilmann Buddensieg, and Kurt Düwell, eds. (1987). *Emigration: Deutsche Wissenschaftler nach 1933, Entlassung und Vertreibung.* Berlin: Technische Universität Berlin.

Strauss, Herbert A., and Werner Röder, eds. (1983). *International biographical dictionary of central European emigres, 1933–1945,* 2 vols. Munich, New York, London, Paris: K. G. Saur.

Stuewer, Roger H. (1985). "Bringing the news of fission to America." *Physics Today,* October, pp. 2–10.

Timoféeff-Ressovsky, N. W. (1937). *Experimentelle Mutationsforschung in der Vererbungslehre.* Dresden, Leipzig: Verlag von Theodor Steinkopff.

Timoféeff-Ressovsky, N. W., K. G. Zimmer, and M. Delbrück (1935). "Über die Natur der Genmutation and der Genstruktur." *Nachtrichten der Gesellschaft der Wissenschaften zu Göttingen, Math.-Phys. Kl.* 6, 189–245.

Tollmien, Cordula (1987). "Das Kaiser-Wilhelm-Institut für Strömungsforschung verbunden mit der Aerodynamischen Versuchsanstalt." In *Die Universität Göttingen unter dem Nationalsozialismus: das verdrängte Kapitel ihrer 250 jährigen Geschichte,* ed. Heinrich Becker, Hans-Joachim Dahms, and Cornelia Wegeler, 464–88. Munich, London, New York, Oxford, Paris: K. G. Saur.

Tröger, Jörg, ed. (1984). *Hochschule und Wissenschaft im Dritten Reich.* Frankfurt, New York: Campus Verlag.

Turner, Henry (1985). *German big business and the rise of Hitler.* New York: Oxford University Press.

Turner, Louis (1940). "Nuclear fission." *Reviews of Modern Physics, 12,* 1–29.

Turner, R. Steven (1971). "The growth of professorial research in Prussia, 1818 to 1848—causes and contexts." *Historical Studies in the Physical Sciences, 3,* 137–82.

Verschuer, Otmar von (1964). "Das ehemalige Kaiser-Wilhelm-Institut für Anthropologie, menschliche Erblehre und Eugenik." *Zeitschrift für morphologische Anthropologie, 55,* 127–74.

Vezina, Birgit (1982). *"Die Gleichschaltung" der Universität Heidelberg im Zuge der nationalsozialistischen Machtergreifung.* Heidelberg: Universitätsverlag.

Vierhaus, Rudolf, and Bernhard vom Brocke, eds. (1990). *Forschung im Spannungsfeld von Politik und Gesellschaft: Geschichte und Struktur der Kaiser-Wilhelm-/Max-Planck-Gesellschaft.* Stuttgart: Deutsche Verlags-Anstalt.

Viga, Friedrich (1960). *Die Rolltreppe.* Munich: Günter Olzog Verlag.

———— (1962). *Im Schatten des Dämons: Romanhaftes Zeitbild Deutschlands aus den Jahren 1933–1945.* Munich: Günter Olzog Verlag.

Wacker, Otto (1939). *Wissenschaft und Nachwuchs.* Lecture held at the Greater Germany rectors conference on 3 March 1939. Gräfenhainichen: Heine.

Walker, Mark (1987). *Uranium machines, nuclear explosives, and National Socialism: the German quest for nuclear power, 1939–1949.* Ph.D. dissertation, Princeton University.

———— (1989). *German National Socialism and the quest for nuclear power, 1939–1949.* Cambridge: Cambridge University Press.

Waterson, A. P., and Lise Wilkinson (1978). *An introduction to the history of virology.* Cambridge: Cambridge University Press.

Watson, James (1968). *The double helix.* New York: Atheneum.

Weart, Spencer R. (1983). "The discovery of fission and a nuclear physics paradigm." In *Otto Hahn and the rise of nuclear physics,* ed. William Shea, 91–133. Dordrecht, Boston, Lancaster: Reidel.

Weindling, Paul (1985). "Weimar eugenics: the Kaiser Wilhelm Institute for Anthropology, Human Heredity and Eugenics in social context." *Annals of Science,* 42, 303–18.

Weingart, Peter, Jürgen Kroll, and Kurt Bayertz (1988). *Rasse, Blut und Gene: Geschichte der Eugenik und Rassenhygiene in Deutschland.* Frankfurt: Suhrkamp.

Weinreich, Max (1946). *Hitler's professors: the part of scholarship in Germany's crimes against the people.* New York: Yiddish Scientific Institute.

Weiss, Sheila (1986). "Wilhelm Schallmeyer and the logic of German eugenics." *Isis,* 77, 33–46.

———— (1987a). "The race hygiene movement in Germany." *Osiris,* 3, 193–236.

———— (1987b). *Race hygiene and national efficiency: the eugenics of Wilhelm Schallmayer.* Berkeley: University of California Press.

Welt, Elly (1986). *Berlin Wild.* New York: Viking.

Wende, Erich (1959). *C. H. Becker, Mensch und Politiker. Ein biographischer Beitrag zur Kulturgeschichte der Weimarer Republik.* Stuttgart: Deutsche Verlagsanstalt.

Wendel, Günter (1975). *Die Kaiser-Wilhelm-Gesellschaft, 1911–1914: Zur Anatomie einer imperialistischen Forschungsgesellschaft.* Berlin: Akademie-Verlag.

———— (1984). Die Berliner Institute der Kaiser Wilhelm Gesellschaft und ihr Platz im System der Wissenschaftspolitik des imperialistischen Deutschland in der Zeit bis 1933. *Kolloquienreihe des Instituts für Theorie, Geschichte und Organisation der Wissenschaft der Akademie der Wissenschaften der DDR.* Berlin, No. 39, pp. 27–69.

———— (1985). *Studien zur Geschichte der Wissenschaftsorganisation und Politik in Deutschland im 19. und 20 Jahrhundert.* Dissertation (B), Humboldt-Universität, Berlin.

Willstätter, Richard (1949). *Aus meinem Leben, von Arbeit, Muße und Freunden.* Weinheim: Verlag Chemie.

———— (1965). *From my life.* Translated by Lilli S. Hornig. New York, Amsterdam: W.A. Benjamin.

Wistrich, Robert (1983). *Wer war wer im Dritten Reich.* Munich: Harnack.

Zahn-Harnack, Agnes (1951). *Adolf von Harnack,* 2d ed. Berlin: De Gruyter.

Zierold, Kurt (1968). *Forschungsförderung in drei Epochen: Forschungsgemeinschaft. Geschichte, Arbeitsweise, Kommentar.* Wiesbaden: Franz Steiner.

Index